FROM MEDIEVAL TO MODERN WALES

Kenneth O. Morgan and Ralph A. Griffiths

From Medieval to Modern Wales

HISTORICAL ESSAYS IN HONOUR OF KENNETH O. MORGAN AND RALPH A. GRIFFITHS

edited by
R. R. Davies
and
Geraint H. Jenkins

*Published on behalf of the History and Law Committee
of the Board of Celtic Studies*

UNIVERSITY OF WALES PRESS
CARDIFF
2004

British Library Cataloguing in Publication Data
A catalogue record for this book is available from the British Library.

ISBN 0-7083-1881-9

Typeset at the University of Wales Press
Printed in Great Britain by MPG Books Limited, Bodmin, Cornwall

Contents

Contents

Figures

Foreword

This volume of essays is a collective tribute, on behalf of the whole community of the historians of Wales, to Kenneth O. Morgan and Ralph A. Griffiths for their remarkable double act as editors of *The Welsh History Review / Cylchgrawn Hanes Cymru* for around forty years. The *WHR* first appeared in 1960, and it is hugely gratifying to all of us that Glanmor Williams, the founding father of the journal and the *doyen* of the historians of Wales, has, with Ieuan Gwynedd Jones, written the introductory chapter to this volume. Kenneth O. Morgan joined the editorial team in 1961 and took over the editorship in 1965 with Ralph A. Griffiths as his assistant and, in effect, joint editor. Since then seventy-six individual numbers of the journal have appeared under their editorial imprimatur, always with exemplary punctuality and to the highest standards of editing and presentation. This must be very close to a record in the annals of British academic journals.

Under their editorship of the *WHR* the academic study of the history of Wales can be said to have come of age. Of course pioneering and sterling work on the history of Wales had been published before 1960 and national and local publications had provided a further outlet for articles and editions. But it is through the annual accumulation of a body of scholarly work of high quality that the credentials of a subject, especially a minority subject in comparative terms as is the history of Wales, are firmly established. That is precisely the service that the *WHR*, alongside other publications, has performed. It has played a crucial role in the transformation of the history of Wales as an academic subject during the last two generations.

The number of historians of Wales is never likely to be large. It has, therefore, been of critical importance that during these formative years in the shaping of Welsh historiography, two of the premier historians of medieval and modern Britain – whose writings, status and reputation extend far beyond Wales – should have been so willing to give of their time, expertise and guidance as editors of the *WHR*. This volume is a modest token of our deep sense of appreciation and gratitude to both of them.

There is hardly a historian of Wales in the last forty years who has not been touched, directly or indirectly, by the work of Kenneth and Ralph, both in general and as editors of the *WHR*. It was, therefore, an invidious task to choose a team of contributors for the current volume; we could easily have selected a very different and equally distinguished team. In the end we invited a team whose interests reflected the chronological range of the *WHR* itself and the current enriching diversity of approaches to the study of the past of Wales. We imposed no format or theme on the contributors; rather were we anxious to reflect the ecumenical eclecticism which has been one of the features of the *WHR*. The editors wish to thank the contributors for their exemplary promptness and ready co-operation throughout the process of assembling this volume.

Appropriately, this volume is published with the financial assistance of the University of Wales Board of Celtic Studies, whom we thank most warmly. We also owe a large debt of thanks to Mrs Nia Davies of the University of Wales Centre for Advanced Welsh and Celtic Studies for processing the material with admirable thoroughness and efficiency, and to Ms Ceinwen Jones of the University of Wales Press for her encouragement and advice.

December 2003

R. R. Davies
Geraint H. Jenkins

The Contributors

Professor Emeritus A. D. Carr, Department of History and Welsh History, University of Wales, Bangor

Professor R. R. Davies, Chichele Professor of Medieval History, All Souls College, University of Oxford

Mr Neil Evans, Honorary Research Fellow, School of History and Archaeology, Cardiff University

Professor R. J. W. Evans, Regius Professor of Modern History, Modern History Faculty, University of Oxford

Professor Geraint H. Jenkins, Director, University of Wales Centre for Advanced Welsh and Celtic Studies

Professor Angela V. John, School of Humanities, University of Greenwich

Professor Aled Jones, Sir John Williams Professor, Department of History and Welsh History, University of Wales, Aberystwyth

Professor Emeritus Ieuan Gwynedd Jones, Department of History and Welsh History, University of Wales, Aberystwyth

Professor J. Gwynfor Jones, School of History and Archaeology, Cardiff University

Professor Emeritus Prys Morgan, Department of History, University of Wales, Swansea

Dr Paul O'Leary, Senior Lecturer, Department of History and Welsh History, University of Wales, Aberystwyth

Dr Huw Pryce, Reader, Department of History and Welsh History, University of Wales, Bangor

Dr Llinos Beverley Smith, Former Senior Lecturer, Department of History and Welsh History, University of Wales, Aberystwyth

The Contributors

Mr Richard Suggett, Investigator, Royal Commission on the Ancient and Historical Monuments of Wales

Dr Steven Thompson, Lecturer, Department of History and Welsh History, University of Wales, Aberystwyth

Dr Eryn M. White, Lecturer, Department of History and Welsh History, University of Wales, Aberystwyth

Professor Emeritus Glanmor Williams, Department of History, University of Wales Swansea

Abbreviations

AC	*Archaeologia Cambrensis*
BBCS	*Bulletin of the Board of Celtic Studies*
CA	*The Carmarthen[shire] Antiquary*
DNB	*Dictionary of National Biography*
DWB	*The Dictionary of Welsh Biography down to 1940* (London, 1959)
EHR	*English Historical Review*
JHSCW	*Journal of the Historical Society of the Church in Wales*
JMHRS	*Journal of the Merioneth Historical and Record Society*
JWRH	*Journal of Welsh Religious History*
LlC	*Llên Cymru*
NLW	National Library of Wales
NLWJ	*National Library of Wales Journal*
PBA	*Proceedings of the British Academy*
PP	*Past and Present*
PRO	Public Record Office
TCHS	*Transactions of the Caernarvonshire Historical Society*
TDHS	*Transactions of the Denbighshire Historical Society*
THSC	*Transactions of the Honourable Society of Cymmrodorion*
TRHS	*Transactions of the Royal Historical Society*
TRS	*Transactions of the Radnorshire Society*
WHR	*Welsh History Review*

1

The Castor and Pollux of Welsh History

IEUAN GWYNEDD JONES AND GLANMOR WILLIAMS

It must surely be the greatest rarity for a learned journal to be edited by one person for an unbroken spell of forty-two years, and still more exceptional for that same individual to have enjoyed the constant collaboration of a single assistant editor for thirty-eight years. Yet such has been the singular good fortune of the *Welsh History Review* (henceforward *WHR*). Professor Kenneth O. Morgan (now Lord Morgan) became its assistant editor in 1961, was appointed editor in 1965, and has served in that capacity ever since. Professor Ralph A. Griffiths was invited to become assistant editor in 1965 and has remained as such since then. The first number under their joint auspices appeared in June 1966. The pair might, with justice, be hailed as the 'Castor and Pollux' of Welsh history, in the firmament of which they have shone as luminously and inextinguishably as those 'Heavenly Twins' of Greek legend.

The idea of founding a journal intended primarily to meet the needs of students of Welsh history was first mooted in the 1950s at the History and Law Committee of the Board of Celtic Studies of the University of Wales. At that time, the chairman of the Committee was Glyn Roberts, Professor of Welsh History at the University College of North Wales, Bangor, and it was he who first conceived the project. The special debt which *WHR* owed to Professor Roberts was recognized by its first editor,[1] Glanmor Williams, now the sole surviving member of the History and Law Committee as it existed in the 1950s. He wrote in the 1963 number of *WHR* that he had lost 'the wisest of counsellors' and the 'dearest of friends', 'whose advice and encouragement were of enormous benefit'.[2] Not only had Glyn Roberts first conceived of the idea, but it was he also who had been largely responsible for piloting the proposal through the History and Law

[1]   Glanmor Williams, *WHR*, 1, special number (1963), editorial; Glanmor Williams, *A Life* (Cardiff, 2002), p. 120.
[2]   *WHR*, 1, special number (1963), editorial.

Committee. The path ahead was not easy – founding a new journal can never be without its hazards! Some members of the committee, although they could not be said to be hostile to the initiative, had their doubts and misgivings, and were not reluctant to air them. Serious questions were raised. Was there any real need for a new journal when the Board of Celtic Studies itself had already been publishing for more than thirty years its own *Bulletin*,[3] for a third of which the History and Law Committee was responsible? Were there not enough journals already in being which catered very largely for the needs of Welsh historians? Among those publications mentioned were the *Transactions of the Honourable Society of Cymmrodorion*, *Archaeologia Cambrensis*, and the *National Library of Wales Journal*, the serried ranks of county historical journals, the wide range of religious and denominational annals, and other similar periodicals. Furthermore, did not such distinguished and long-established publications as the *English Historical Review*, the *Transactions of the Royal Historical Society* and *History* offer the hospitality of their pages to those Welsh historians who had something worthwhile putting in print? Would there be a viable supply of materials of good quality to sustain a new journal? Was there a potential readership numerous and interested enough to buy and read it? These and other similar hesitations were not without foundation; yet, for all that, it remained undeniable that there was not one outlet which was devoted entirely to the publication of articles on Welsh history and certainly none which carried within its pages a full review section in which all those books and journals which might conceivably interest Welsh historians could be commented upon. So, after much earnest discussion, the History and Law Committee persevered with its plan and decided to launch the new publication in 1960. It was to be called the *Welsh History Review* (the name was suggested by Professor David Williams) and, initially, it was intended that it should appear once a year.

Since *WHR* first appeared, all those original hesitations and uncertainties have triumphantly been dispelled, and the thanks for that are almost wholly due to Kenneth O. Morgan and Ralph A. Griffiths. As a pair, they were uncommonly well suited to work in double harness. Fortunately, they had been close colleagues and friends in the department of history at the University College of Swansea before they began their collaboration on *WHR*. They had even shared a flat together for a time. Moreover, they were thoroughly acquainted with each other's temperament and outlook. Intellectually, they were well matched, and both were exceptionally energetic, conscientious, industrious and plainspoken. Each was deeply interested in the theoretical and practical problems of the study of history

---

[3] *Bulletin of the Board of Celtic Studies* (University of Wales Press, 1922–).

and how the fruits thereof could most effectively be published. While the one (Griffiths) was a dedicated medievalist, the other (Morgan) was chiefly interested in modern history. Although they were young, each had already had important studies to his credit appear in print, and had further commitments on the stocks. Both had a serious, deep-rooted commitment to history, but neither was, in any sense, a 'narrow' Welsh historian and they both had wider interests in British, European and world history. They were sufficiently alike in their outlook on history in general to make each of them *simpatico* to the other, but they were also different enough to complement one another.

Having jointly assumed responsibility for producing *WHR*, Morgan and Griffiths soon became proverbial for the ease and smoothness with which they worked in harmony. There never seemed to be any suggestion of strife or discord, and any minor disagreements there may have been were kept entirely private and confidential to themselves. How else could they have cooperated so felicitously for so long? They became just as widely acknowledged for the courtesy and promptness with which they dealt with contributors, the punctuality with which they assembled the materials for each number, and the regularity with which they presented them to the University Press and the printers, always returning proofs on time, immaculately corrected. It is a remarkable fact that, year in and year out, both numbers of *WHR* have always appeared unfailingly when due, and this despite the fact that over almost the whole period of their editorship the editors have been based at a considerable distance apart from one another. For an exceptionally long period, both the men responsible for the journal have shown a phenomenal sense of devotion to duty. Kenneth O. Morgan once described how he regarded editing it as a 'central commitment', which involved him in 'much hard work, but also an intense intellectual and personal pleasure'.[4] The same could just as truly be said of Ralph A. Griffiths; and, indeed, Morgan observed that without his colleague's 'unique dedication, reliability and scholarly judgement', *WHR* 'could never have appeared as it has done'.[5] Both have fulfilled their onerous tasks on an entirely voluntary basis without any expectation of financial reward. It is all the more to their credit that neither has allowed his responsibility to *WHR* to diminish the steady and copious stream of admirable books, papers and reviews which has flowed from his pen in the course of the years. Nor has the time-consuming task of editing *WHR* prevented them from shouldering the considerable additional burden of being two out of the three editors charged with seeing through the press on

[4]   *WHR*, 10, no. 3 (1981), 282.
[5]   Ibid.

behalf of the History and Law Committee a series of volumes entitled 'Studies in Welsh History', each a book of some 80,000 words, twenty of which appeared between 1977 and 2000. This represented yet another major contribution to the field of Welsh historical study which offered a further opportunity to successful postgraduate students to present their work to the public in printed form. The editors of *WHR* had, therefore, amply fulfilled the bright hopes which the History and Law Committee had entertained for the new journal when it was launched. It is testament to the quality of their editorial methods and criteria that they have made *WHR* a widely known and highly respected journal. As a result, they have attracted a wide spectrum of gifted scholars, ranging from celebrated veteran historians to hopeful young recruits, to publish within its pages.

The editors themselves would readily acknowledge the long-term support and cooperation they have been accorded at the hands of the University of Wales Board of Celtic Studies, the University of Wales Press, and their printers. For over forty years the Board and the University Registry have stood staunchly by *WHR* and rendered it all necessary academic, financial and moral support. Even during the 1970s and 1980s, when British universities as a whole suffered severe cuts in their finances, there was never any suggestion of reducing the financial resources allocated to *WHR* by the Board of Celtic Studies. Successive directors of the University of Wales Press and members of their staff have found it a pleasure to cooperate with the editors and have been happy to work in concert with them. A successful journal also needs printers who are both good craftsmen and reliable ones. Here, again, fortune has smiled on *WHR*. Production of it was first entrusted to the experienced Cardiff firm of William Lewis Ltd, and they were succeeded in their business, including the printing of *WHR*, by another excellent Cardiff company, Qualitex Ltd. In due course, in 1994, Qualitex was followed by another accomplished Welsh firm, Dinefwr Press,[6] which still acts as *WHR*'s printers. Until 1992 Gareth Wyn Evans, assistant secretary at the University of Wales Registry, admirably performed the demanding task of overseeing the typesetting and printing of *WHR*, a task which has since been undertaken by the University of Wales Press itself.

Over a long period of years it was not found necessary to establish an editorial board. Doubtless, the editors must, on occasion, have been able to refer some contributions to well-informed friends for their expert opinion, but not until 1996 were they invited by the Board to set up an editorial board, whom they could consult whenever it seemed necessary or prudent to do so. With characteristically sound judgement, they chose an

---

[6]   *WHR*, 17, no. 1 (1994), back cover.

editorial board of four, two of whom were drawn from outside Wales: Professor R. R. Davies, FBA, and Professor R. J. W. Evans, FBA, both from Oxford; and Professor Aled Jones of Aberystwyth and Dr Huw Pryce of Bangor. Two of the four were medievalists, and two were primarily interested in the period after 1700. All four were scholars of ripe judgement, long experience and comprehensive knowledge of historical publishing.

During the half-century or so that *WHR* has been in existence it is hardly too much to say that there has been spectacular progress in the study of the history of Wales. To this *WHR* has lavishly contributed. Although it would not be too much to claim that all periods have been more intensively brought under scrutiny, there has been a particularly pronounced surge of interest in the history of the past two hundred years. More courses in Welsh history have been taught in schools and in higher institutions of education, and there has been a palpable increase of interest in the subject among the lay public and the media. Nor has the growth of interest been confined either to historians of Welsh origin, or to those resident in Wales, but it has manifested itself also in several countries outside the United Kingdom. Another striking feature has been the increased interest in the Welsh past shown by scholars based in other academic disciplines. Those concerned with the study of the Welsh language and its literature would naturally be expected freely to cross the border into Welsh history, as the late Professor Thomas Jones so memorably did in the very first number of *WHR*.[7] Legal historians, too, especially those immersed in the distinctive characteristics of laws associated with the name of Hywel Dda (d. 950), have been frequent visitors. So, too, have economic and social historians, attracted especially by the major contributions made by Wales to the rise of modern industry since about 1750. Historical geography has usually loomed large on the horizons of Welsh geographers, and they have always had major contributions to make to the study of Welsh history, not only of the past two hundred years but of earlier periods as well. Nor is it always easy to tell when human geography ends and sociology begins, so we need not wonder that many sociologists have extended their studies to the Welsh past. Nor can it be said at what point archaeology stops and history starts, if indeed it ever makes sense to try to draw sharp distinctions between the two disciplines. Consequently, a number of archaeologists have turned to *WHR* and found it a congenial haven in which to publish their findings. *WHR*'s editors, far from viewing all those 'migrants' with suspicion, have warmly encouraged them and welcomed their offerings. Thereby, they have provided their readers not only with an incontestably historical journal but also one with

7   *WHR*, 1, no. 1 (1960), 1–18.

a strong and exciting inter-disciplinary flavour. This has added to the piquancy of its contents, but has also drawn wider attention in Wales itself, and well beyond its borders, to all the innovatory and fascinating developments emerging on the Welsh history scene.

Looking back over the published volumes of the journal, one of the trends which is likely to strike the reader is the way in which those who might be described as the 'Young Turks' of the earlier numbers evolved over the years into the 'elder statesmen' of the subject. Such a development would, no doubt, have taken place in any event, whether or not *WHR* had come into being, but it does seem clear all the same that the journal's very existence served to give some of these promising young historians both the opportunity and the confidence to publish sooner, and possibly more extensively, than they might otherwise have done. Among the earliest contributors were Kenneth O. Morgan himself, who published his first article in the first number – an essay on 'Gladstone and Wales',[8] and Ralph A. Griffiths, who gave his views on 'Gruffydd ap Nicholas and the fall of the House of Lancaster' a few years later.[9] Other notable contributors at an early stage were Gwyn A. Williams,[10] Ieuan Gwynedd Jones,[11] Peter D. G. Thomas,[12] J. Beverley Smith,[13] and David J. V. Jones.[14] Representative of a somewhat later generation who, nevertheless, emerged early in *WHR* and are now well-known figures were Geraint H. Jenkins,[15] Martin J. Daunton,[16] Llinos Beverley Smith[17] and Huw Pryce.[18]

The obituaries published in *WHR* are the reverse side of the coin and record the passing from the scene of a whole generation of early giants of Welsh history, who had made such an enormous contribution to the growth of the subject in the twentieth century. In their midst were such influential figures as Glyn Roberts (1904–62), the 'only begetter' of *WHR* itself, in the words of A. H. Dodd (1891–1978), himself for a generation the heir to the peerless John Edward Lloyd at Bangor. Or their colleagues there – R. T. Jenkins (1881–1969) and Thomas Richards (1878–1962), the 'David and Jonathan' of an earlier race of Welsh historians. Then there was John Goronwy Edwards (1891–1976), so long a 'mover and shaker' at

---

[8]   Ibid., 65–82.
[9]   *WHR*, 2, no. 3 (1965), 213–32.
[10] *WHR*, 1, no. 2 (1961), 161–92.
[11] Ibid., 193–224.
[12] *WHR*, 1, no. 3 (1963), 279–300.
[13] *WHR*, 3, no. 2 (1976), 139–71.
[14] Ibid., 173–205.
[15] *WHR*, 7, no. 4 (1975), 403–26.
[16] *WHR*, 6, no. 1 (1972), 16–48.
[17] *WHR*, 10, no. 2 (1980), 127–53.
[18] *WHR*, 13, no. 3 (1987), 265–81.

Oxford, before going on to the Institute of Historical Research as its director from 1948 to 1960. Or those two very different, but towering, figures who worked together at Cardiff, William Rees (1887–1978), on medieval history, and David Williams (1900–77), expert on modern Wales, until the latter moved to Aberystwyth, where he was joined by another fine medievalist, T. Jones Pierce (1905–64). All these great shapers of Welsh history and others besides were duly remembered, and their achievements sensitively and appreciatively recorded by judiciously chosen obituarists. Sad to relate, however, as well as these veterans of what might be saluted as the 'Praetorian Guard', the untimely passing of a younger generation such as Keith Williams-Jones (1926–79), David J. V. Jones (1941–94) or Gwyn Alfred Williams (1925–95) had to be remembered as well.

One of the most praiseworthy characteristics of *WHR* is that it has never been excessively inward-looking or parochial in attitude. Its pages have always been thrown open to any authors who had an interest in the Welsh past or any cognate subject. Immigrants to Wales, like S. B. Chrimes, who succeeded William Rees as professor at Cardiff, or Charles L. Mowat, who followed A. H. Dodd at Bangor, or Muriel Chamberlain, who spent virtually the whole of her teaching career at Swansea, although not one of them was primarily associated with Welsh history, nevertheless showed a genuine interest in the land of their adoption. Thus, S. B. Chrimes, biographer of Henry VII, contributed valuable essays on his connections with Wales,[19] and Muriel Chamberlain, an expert on Canadian history, wrote on the fortunes of the Welsh in Canada,[20] while Charles Mowat was a regular reviewer on many topics. Probably the most notable example of the enlistment of non-Welsh scholars to a single number, however, was that assembled to honour David Williams on his retirement in 1967.[21] They included Hilary Marquand, Bridget and Christopher Hill, and Richard Cobb, all of them former colleagues of David Williams. In addition, of course, it should be pointed out that a large proportion of those who have contributed articles or reviewed books have been drawn from a variety of universities and countries, and this has served to intensify the journal's distinctly international tone and flavour. It has created a cosmopolitan image of a publication sustained by a widespread body of contributors, which has, in turn, served to raise the hopes and expectations of younger historians submitting their own work to it for the first time.

Because most of those who have written for *WHR* and read it have not been Welsh-speaking, inevitably most of its contents have been submitted

---

[19]   *WHR*, 10, no. 3 (1981), 320–33.
[20]   *WHR*, 19, no. 2 (1998), 265–88.
[21]   *WHR*, 3, no. 4 (1967), 335–481: 'Essays Presented to David Williams'.

in English. From the outset, however, it was made plain that the editors welcomed contributions written in either English or Welsh. There have, indeed, been occasional articles written in Welsh. There is, for example, a characteristically telling one by R. R. Davies on 'Buchedd a Moes y Cymry' (The Manners and Morals of the Welsh)[22] and another by Philip S. Edwards on Anglesey politics in the sixteenth century.[23] Since potential contributors have always been warmly encouraged to submit Welsh-language articles, complete with English synopses, one cannot but suspect that the editors may well feel understandably a little disappointed to find that more have not been forthcoming. All the more so in view of the significant place they have always accorded to the Welsh language in the review sections. It has been the usual practice for all the relevant books published in Welsh to be reviewed in Welsh, accompanied by a brief English synopsis so that readers who do not understand Welsh may never-theless be aware in general of the scope and quality of the book being reviewed. The reviewers themselves have been encouraged to take their responsibilities conscientiously, with the result that Welsh-language reviews have been of notably high quality; like, for example, those by R. Geraint Gruffydd,[24] Prys Morgan[25] or E. D. Evans.[26] Reading these reviews and many other similar Welsh ones, it becomes abundantly evident that there is no lack of Welsh historians who are able to write reviews in their native language with fluency and authority. In spite of the paucity of articles in Welsh, however, the editors can console themselves to some extent by recalling that over the past fifteen years there has annually been produced a first-rate Welsh-language historical publication, *Cof Cenedl* (A Nation's Memory). Its editor, Geraint H. Jenkins, is a regular contributor to *WHR* and is someone who has obviously learnt much from his association with it.

The articles published in *WHR* have covered the whole span of Welsh history from the end of the Roman Empire down to the present day. Although the journal has been the product of two men, for which both should take equal credit, it would seem that there has been – and un-surprisingly so – a division of labour between them, with Griffiths having been responsible for the period down to the end of the seventeenth century, and Morgan for the remainder. This seems borne out by the rubric included from volume 17 onwards,[27] which requests would-be contributors

---

22   *WHR*, 12, no. 2 (1984), 155–79.
23   *WHR*, 10, no. 1 (1980), 43–68.
24   *WHR*, 5, no. 2 (1970), 186–7.
25   *WHR*, 7, no. 1 (1974), 115–16.
26   *WHR*, 10, no. 1 (1980), 115–16.
27   *WHR*, 17, no. 4 (1995), back cover.

writing on the period before 1700 to send their material to Griffiths and those concerned with later periods to forward their contributions to Morgan. One of the more noticeable developments of the past twenty years or so has been a tendency for rather greater concentration on Welsh history of the past two centuries. This would be a trend in historical studies no less observable in universities, colleges and schools in general, not only because of a perceptible shift in student taste and interest, but also because it has become more difficult to find students possessing the linguistic equipment (especially the knowledge of Latin) to study medieval or early modern history in depth. It may also be that 'birds of passage' from other disciplines such as geography, political science or economics, tend to be more absorbed with modern history. Geographers, like for example Harold Carter,[28] or W. T. R. Pryce,[29] have offered stimulating essays bearing on the problems of modern Wales. Yet, on the other hand, their fellow geographers, G. R. J. Jones[30] or Colin Thomas,[31] have made equally enlightening forays into the world of medieval Wales.

The truth is that all aspects of Welsh life within the framework of the timescale earlier mentioned have received their reasonable share of attention: the economy, politics, government, law, administration, social relationships, religion, language(s), literature(s), education and any pertinent topic. On occasion, a whole number has been devoted to a study in depth of a single subject, like the memorable survey of the Welsh laws,[32] or the one on Welsh labour history.[33] The former number was particularly notable for the magisterial study of the subject since 1928 undertaken by Sir Goronwy Edwards, in which he seized the opportunity of making a number of pregnant suggestions for the future investigation of the problems arising, as did Sir Idris Foster in his contribution. Two equally appealing special numbers were the one devoted to Welsh labour history and the other to celebrate the twenty-first anniversary of the founding of *WHR*.[34] The former emanated from a major colloquium held at Swansea and published six articles on such major issues of nineteenth- and twentieth-century history as Chartism (D. J. V. Jones), the agricultural labourer (David W. Howell), Liberalism and Labour, 1885–1929 (Kenneth O. Morgan), Gwynedd politics (Cyril Parry), working-class leadership, 1900–20 (Peter Stead) and trade unionism, 1926–39 (David Smith). Two other papers, by

28 *WHR*, 9, no. 1 (1978), 32–56. This article was written with Sandra Wheatley.
29 *WHR*, 7, no. 3 (1975), 307–40.
30 *WHR*, 2, no. 1 (1964), 19–36.
31 *WHR*, 6, no. 2 (1972), 143–60.
32 *WHR*, 1, special number (1963), 'The Welsh Laws'.
33 *WHR*, 6, no. 3 (1973), 'Welsh Labour History Number'.
34 *WHR*, 10, no. 3 (1981), 'Twenty-First Anniversary Number'.

John Saville and Ieuan Gwynedd Jones, were included in the colloquium but were published elsewhere in accordance with their authors' wishes. The twenty-first anniversary number also contained six articles on a wide variety of topics in medieval and modern Welsh history, including one on Wales and England in the tenth century, another on Wales and Scotland in the Middle Ages, and one on peace movements in Wales, 1899–1945. Not only did this number bring together some of the brightest of the younger school of Welsh historians, like Gwyn A. Williams, but it also featured three distinguished 'guests' in the persons of Henry Loyn, G. W. S. Barrow and S. B. Chrimes, all of whom had already reviewed extensively for the journal and would continue to do so.

One of the crowning glories of *WHR* has been its superb review sections. The prominent place which it has chosen to allot to reviews of books has been possibly what has marked it off more clearly than anything else from the other periodicals (in Welsh or English) which, in their own way, carry a good deal of material relating to Welsh history. It has produced an abundant flow of reviews discussing all periods and subjects concerned with the history of Wales, including those written by non-Welsh authors from as far away as the United States and Australia, no less than those stemming from the pens of Welsh men and women, of course. It has also included within its remit reviews of historical works written by authors born in Wales but not necessarily written on Welsh subjects, for example, those by Keith Thomas or Henry Loyn; or again, books by authors resident in Wales and well-known there, though not of Welsh birth, like Peter Smith or Ivan Roots. It has further extended its boundaries to survey those works which explore topics having connections with Wales or possibly being of interest to Welsh historians. They include the biographies of a number of leading English monarchs, whose activities had a close bearing on the destinies of Wales, or McFarlane's study of the major aristocratic families of the later Middle Ages, or the lives of prominent political figures such as Asquith, Keir Hardie, or leading Americans emigrating from Wales, or politico-social movements such as Chartism or trade unionism. As might be expected, too, the history of neighbouring Celtic countries – Ireland, Scotland or Brittany – come under close scrutiny, especially those themes and developments which have relevance to comparable events in Wales, such as Scottish or Irish nationalism.

From time to time, as occasion warranted, there have appeared 'review articles', which took note of a number of works all celebrating the same event or institution. The editors themselves provided excellent examples of the genre. Ralph A. Griffiths examined the 'year of the castle' (1983),[35]

---

[35]   *WHR*, 12, no. 2 (1984), 249–53.

which looked back particularly to the Edwardian castles of 1283 and provided an admirable survey of several publications produced seven hundred years later. Kenneth O. Morgan, then vice-chancellor of the University College of Wales, Aberystwyth, took as his theme, 'A people's university?'[36] and gave an incisive conspectus of a group of works which had been published in previous years to commemorate the founding of individual colleges of the University of Wales, as well as the university itself in 1893. A number of such memorable review articles have appeared over the years, for example, those by R. F. Walker, Malcolm Jones, John Guy and Neil Evans.[37]

Of no less interest to readers are those lists which have been included of relevant items culled from the pages of other periodical literature. From the outset,[38] two lists have appeared at regular yearly intervals drawn from an extensive circle of journals, the majority of them published in Wales. The one list contains a note of articles relating to the period before 1660, the other to the years after 1660. Some of the contributors responsible for these lists have been remarkably diligent in compiling them over a long period of time. Both Morgan and Griffiths are to be complimented for having set a conspicuous early example, drawing up careful lists over a number of years (1960–6). Other notable contributors over a long period were Prys Morgan, Geraint H. Jenkins, Huw Pryce and J. Gwynfor Jones. It is interesting to observe that several of the items to be found in these lists should have been garnered from what might, at first sight, have seemed to be out-of-the-way publications, which readers of *WHR*, left to themselves, might not have thought of consulting, for example, *Province*, *Taliesin*, *Ysgrifau Beirniadol* or the *Transactions of the Shropshire Archaeological Society*!

Equally commendable have been those eight lists of university post-graduate theses successfully submitted to a number of widely dispersed university institutions in Britain and North America. These are the outcome of the devoted labours of David Lewis Jones of the House of Lords Library, which he has published at regular intervals over a term of thirty years from 1971 to 2001.[39] They have furnished a most valuable overview of research work on the history of Wales that has been in progress at several places in the United Kingdom and elsewhere. Those submitted in Welsh university institutions are not unexpectedly given a prominent place. These lists are all the more useful and the more conveniently

---

[36]   *WHR*, 17, no. 2 (1994), 255–8.
[37]   *WHR*, 7, no. 3 (1975), 357–65; 8, no. 4 (1977), 475–8; 13, no. 4 (1987), 477–80; 17, no. 1 (1994), 115–19.
[38]   *WHR*, 1, no. 1 (1960).
[39]   *WHR*, 5, no. 3 (1971), 261–304ff.

consulted for having their contents systematically arranged in chronological order and by subject headings. So, for instance, there are two broad
sections on the recent history of Wales: the one from 1789–1918 and the
other from 1919 onwards. The years from 1789 to 1918 are further sub-
divided under political history, religious history, social and economic
history, educational and cultural history. A much more recent but
potentially very valuable feature has been the inclusion of lists of accessions of archives. This is the 'Select digest of the accessions to repositories
relating to the history of Wales', drawn up by Mary Ellis of the Historical
Manuscripts Commission.[40] It includes a number of national, university
and county archives, among them the National Library of Wales and the
National Museum of Wales.

Relatively inexperienced authors – and possibly even those who have
long been at the game – will have found clear and succinct 'notes for
contributors' of articles and reviews to be of considerable help.[41] One only
hopes that hopeful authors will have taken note of them before submitting
their typescripts for publication! The editors are further to be complimented for having taken great care to supply meticulous indexes to each
volume of their publication. They have made certain that not only are the
titles of articles and their authors included, but also that the same care has
been taken to insert the titles of books reviewed, together with details of
their authors, prices and dates of publication. Always ready to move with
the times and appeal to new readers, in 1996 they abandoned the grey
cover which had adorned the journal since its inception in favour of bolder
colours, including red, blue and purple.

The University of Wales Press has to its credit a splendid array of
periodical publications which have created a favourable impression world-
wide. One of the most admired of them is *WHR*, for the quality of which
Morgan and Griffiths have been almost wholly responsible. For some
forty years they have undeniably conveyed an image of enthusiasm,
encouragement, open-mindedness, creativity, regularity, dependability and
devotion to the best interests of Welsh history. Generations of younger
historians have grown up in a world in which *WHR* has always existed;
they find it difficult to conceive of surroundings in which that bright and
steadily burning lamp of scholarship has not been shining. Like all the rest
of us in the field, they are acutely aware of being profoundly indebted to
WHR and invigoratingly stimulated by it. In recent years, much has
been said and written in praise of what is frequently described as the

---

[40]   Mary Ellis, 'Select Digest of Manuscript Accessions to Repositories 1996 relating
to the History of Wales', *WHR*, 19, no. 1 (1998), 130–9.
[41]   *WHR*, 18, no. 2 (1996).

'renaissance' or 'revival' of Welsh history in the second half of the twentieth century. The history of that phenomenon has yet to be written, and the role of those who participated in it still to be assessed. But of one thing we can all be certain: among the sturdiest and most distinguished of its pillars has been *WHR*. Without it, much of that renaissance might perhaps have been stillborn and would, surely, long ago have languished sadly. That it has been so flourishing, like a giant refreshed, owes an immeasurable debt of honour to the lustre and leadership conferred upon it by the indefatigable exertions of those two 'heavenly twins' of twentieth-century Welsh history, Kenneth Owen Morgan and Ralph Allan Griffiths. Long may their fame endure!

2

Modern Nationality and the Medieval Past: The Wales of John Edward Lloyd*

HUW PRYCE

On Tuesday, 14 December 1909 a delighted John Edward Lloyd wrote to his parents in Liverpool that he had received a letter that morning from Longmans & Co., 'a first rate firm', accepting his *History of Wales* for publication.[1] The work, which appeared in January 1911, represented the culmination of a quarter of a century's engagement with the early Welsh past.[2] Lloyd had first traversed much of the same ground in his early twenties while an undergraduate at Oxford, when he won the prize for an essay in a competition for a 'History of Wales for use in Day Schools' at the 1884 National Eisteddfod.[3] In the following decade, after his appointment in 1892 as registrar and lecturer in Welsh history at the University College of North Wales, Bangor, he began collecting materials for a more ambitious study, the first fruits of which were presented in three bilingual textbooks covering Welsh history from the Stone Age to 1282.[4] It was only after the last of these volumes was published that he embarked, in January 1901, on writing the large-scale *History* for which he is most

* Ralph A. Griffiths has contributed significantly to advancing our understanding of important aspects of medieval Welsh history largely unexplored by Lloyd, while Kenneth O. Morgan has done much to illuminate the cultural and political context to which Lloyd belonged: it is a pleasure to offer this essay to them both. In preparing it, I have been greatly indebted to Neil Evans for valuable discussion and comment; my thanks go also to the staff of the Department of Archives and Manuscripts at Bangor, to Robert Johnston for guidance on the history of archaeology, and to several other colleagues for helpful suggestions.

[1] University of Wales Bangor Archives, The Papers of Sir John Edward Lloyd (hereafter UWBA, Lloyd Papers), 353.

[2] John Edward Lloyd, *A History of Wales from the Earliest Times to the Edwardian Conquest* (2 vols, London, 1911).

[3] Idem, 'History of Wales', *Transactions of the Royal National Eisteddfod of Wales, Liverpool, 1884* (Liverpool, 1885), pp. 341–408.

[4] Idem, *Llyfr Cyntaf Hanes* (Caernarfon, 1893); idem, *Ail Lyfr Hanes* (Caernarfon, 1896); idem, *Trydydd Llyfr Hanes* (Caernarfon, 1900); the English text of all three volumes was reprinted as idem, *Outlines of the History of Wales for the Use of Schools and Colleges* (Carnarvon, 1906).

famous.[5] The importance of the resulting two volumes in the development of modern Welsh historiography has long been recognized. Lloyd not only set new standards of rigorous, painstaking scholarship but also sought to make the ancient and medieval origins of Wales coherent and comprehensible through exercising his formidable powers of synthesis.[6] Moreover, though inevitably dated in important respects, Lloyd's *History* remains an essential port of call for historians of medieval Wales – no mean achievement for a historical work approaching its centenary.

The aim of this chapter is to explore some of the influences which led Lloyd to write the kind of history he did, and in particular the extent to which his nationalist convictions helped to shape his interpretation of the past. What follows will therefore largely take us back from 1911 to Lloyd's intellectual formation in the late Victorian era rather than forward to the impact of his work on subsequent historiography. It is, of course, well known that Lloyd was strongly committed to the revival of national feeling in Wales expressed, for example, by the establishment of the university colleges and also of the Cymru Fydd or Young Wales movement within the Liberal Party.[7] Sir Goronwy Edwards argued that this commitment touched Lloyd's heart but never went to his head: 'What it did for him as a student of Welsh history was to sustain his studies, not to determine his conclusions.'[8] This assessment is true up to a point – the *History of Wales* is, after all, notable for its critical approach to historical evidence – yet the antithesis it implies between nationalist sentiment on the one hand and 'scientific' historical methodology on the other is perhaps too sharply drawn. Indeed, one contention of the present discussion is that his nationalism explains not only *why*, but also *how*, Lloyd sought to recover the Welsh past.

His family background and especially his higher education provided fertile ground for the growth of nationalist convictions. Born in Liverpool in 1861, Lloyd belonged to a Welsh-speaking middle class, strongly Non-conformist in religion and Liberal in politics. Yet his upbringing also gave him first-hand experience of rural Wales, for holidays were spent with

---

[5] UWBA, Lloyd Papers 212 (notes by Lloyd recording dates at which each chapter and subsection of the *History of Wales* were completed).

[6] For perceptive appreciations of Lloyd's achievement as a historian see J. Goronwy Edwards, 'Sir John Edward Lloyd, 1861–1947', *PBA*, 41 (1955), 319–27; R. T. Jenkins, 'Syr John Edward Lloyd', *Y Llenor*, 26 (1947), 77–87; and Glanmor Williams, 'Preface', in Sir J. E. Lloyd, *A History of Wales*, I (facsimile repr. of 3rd edn, London, 1939; Carmarthen, 1988), pp. ix–xviii (I owe this reference to my student Margaret Bradbury).

[7] Kenneth O. Morgan, *Wales in British Politics 1868–1922* (paperback edn, Cardiff, 1991), pp. 51, 69–70; idem, *Rebirth of a Nation: Wales 1880–1980* (Oxford and Cardiff, 1980), chap. 4.

[8] Edwards, 'Sir John Edward Lloyd', 320.

relatives at Penygarnedd in the Tanat valley in north-east Montgomery-shire, an area for which he retained a lifelong affection and whose influence was reflected in his speaking the Powysian dialect of Welsh.[9] Crucially, at the age of 16 he was sent to the University College of Wales, Aberystwyth (founded in 1872), where he remained from October 1877 until April 1881. Here, Lloyd's nationalist views were developed in the company of fellow students of a similar persuasion – as Edward Anwyl noted in a review of the *History of Wales*, its author

> belongs, as one of the old students of Aberystwyth College, to a circle of patriots, such as the late Mr T. E. Ellis, and a number of famous persons who are still living, who have left a deep mark on the history of Wales, and who were able to combine, in a remarkable way, patriotism and success.[10]

Like Ellis and many other members of the circle to which Anwyl referred, Lloyd completed his higher education at Oxford. Following in the footsteps of his mentor, Aberystwyth's principal Thomas Charles Edwards, Lloyd was admitted to Lincoln College in October 1881 and took a first in classical Moderations in 1883, followed by a first in modern history two years later.[11] While at Oxford Lloyd's nationalism remained unabated. Through his membership of various societies, including the Aberystwyth College Club (the 'A.C.C.'), composed of former Aberystwyth students, and other time spent with friends such as Owen M. Edwards, T. E. (Tom) Ellis, John Puleston Jones and J. Arthur Price (a Tory with very different political views from his), he had ample opportunities to discuss current affairs and to articulate his support for Welsh causes.[12] Though he is mainly remembered now as a historian of the Middle Ages, Lloyd shared the lively concern of his compatriots at Oxford with the present and future of Wales, a concern reflected in papers he read at this time on topics such as the condition of contemporary Welsh literature and the necessity of developing a Welsh tradition in the visual arts (a subject also close to Tom Ellis's heart); the latter paper was marked by a Romantic sensibility influenced by the medievalism of John Ruskin – whose lectures Lloyd attended at Oxford in 1883 and 1884 – in its criticism of the puritanical tendencies of the Nonconformist tradition. Political issues, including

---

[9] UWBA, Lloyd Papers 17; Edwards, 'Sir John Edward Lloyd', 319.

[10] *Y Brython* (13 April 1911), 3. Cf. J. E. Lloyd, 'A Retrospect (1877–1881)', in Iwan Morgan (ed.), *The College by the Sea* (Aberystwyth, 1928), pp. 70–2.

[11] Edwards, 'Sir John Edward Lloyd', 319; *DWB*, p. 197.

[12] UWBA, Lloyd Papers 251 (1884 diary: 15 April, 15 and 24 October); 252 (1885 diary: 19–20 January, 4 March, 21–2 and 28 April).

Welsh disestablishment, also engaged his attention.[13] Indeed, in a letter congratulating Lloyd on his recent first in history, J. Arthur Price was moved to declare that 'After your brilliant University career I shall expect to hear of your advocating National claims in the Imperial Parliament.'[14]

There is no evidence that Lloyd himself seriously contemplated a political career (his participation in Liberal meetings in Montgomeryshire and Merionethshire during the 1886 general election notwithstanding).[15] Nor did he fulfil his youthful intention, which had caused his parents much consternation, of becoming a Congregational minister.[16] Though he remained a lay preacher, it was in history rather than the ministry that Lloyd found his vocation.[17] That his inclination lay in this direction had been shown not only by his decision in 1883 to switch to modern history rather than complete the classics course by proceeding to Greats, but also by the composition of his essay on Welsh history for the Liverpool Eisteddfod in 1884. Thomas Charles Edwards gave Lloyd the opportunity to continue his historical studies by appointing him a lecturer in Welsh and history at Aberystwyth, a post he took up in September 1885. His reputation as a historian was sufficient by May 1888 for a correspondent from the college to write 'that we hope Mr J. E. Lloyd will adopt the suggestion recently made by one of the Cardiff papers lately [*sic*], and bring out a History of Wales'.[18] Indeed, W. Warde Fowler, Lloyd's former classics tutor at Lincoln College, was under the impression that such a work was already under way by then.[19]

Dedication to Welsh scholarship, especially history, did not mark a retreat from the wider project of national renewal. For one thing, Lloyd shared the commitment of many of his contemporaries to improving Welsh education. When drafting his unsuccessful application for the post of principal of the University College of Wales at Aberystwyth in 1891 he claimed that 'It has been my endeavour to acquaint myself with every educational movement in Wales, whether academic or popular, and in some of these movements I have been privileged to take a considerable share.'[20] In addition to his duties at Aberystwyth, he was a member of the

---

[13] UWBA, Lloyd Papers 23 (letter from Thomas Hughes, 1883), 78–80, 251 (1884 diary: 18 October); cf. *Speeches and Addresses by the late Thomas E. Ellis, M.P.* (Wrexham, 1912), pp. 29–63.

[14] UWBA, Lloyd Papers 22 (8 July 1885); cf. Edwards, 'Sir John Edward Lloyd', 319–20.

[15] UWBA, Lloyd Papers 253 (1886 diary: 6–10, 12–13 July).

[16] UWBA, Lloyd Papers 19, 25.

[17] Edwards, 'Sir John Edward Lloyd', 319: 'the study of Welsh history was his calling in more than a merely professional sense'.

[18] *Cymru Fydd*, [1] (1888), 309.

[19] UWBA, Lloyd Papers 314, no. 171 (letter to Lloyd, 3 June 1888).

[20] UWBA, Lloyd Papers 232.

Council of the Society for Utilizing the Welsh Language (Cymdeithas yr Iaith Gymraeg, later called in English the Welsh Language Society), which successfully persuaded the Education Commission of 1886–8 to ensure that Welsh was recognized as a grant-earning subject in elementary schools; and as registrar at Bangor he played an important role in developing another of the colleges of the University of Wales founded in 1893.[21] As already mentioned, it was in the 1890s, too, that he wrote textbooks on Welsh history which appeared in the Young Wales Schools Series and followed the Welsh orthography advocated by Cymdeithas yr Iaith Gymraeg – an orthography which had its origins in proposals by John Morris-Jones to Cymdeithas Dafydd ap Gwilym at Oxford.[22] This endeavour no doubt met the approval of his friend Tom Ellis, who, writing from Luxor to O. M. Edwards in February 1890, urged that Oxford Welshmen should produce books in Welsh and English for the new intermediate schools.[23] Indeed, like Edwards, Lloyd is a prime example of the role played in this period by an Oxford-educated intellectual elite in fostering Welsh education.

For this elite, and for Welsh Liberals of a nationalist persuasion more generally, the study of the Welsh past had a vital part to play in the creation of a brighter Welsh future. In 1894 Lloyd argued that an understanding of agriculture in medieval Wales could help resolve current controversies over land reform:

For the present has its roots in the past, and apart from the past cannot be rightly measured and understood, a truth which the government have recognised in the case of our own country by appointing Professor Rhys and Mr Seebohm members of the Welsh Land Commission.[24]

(The historical sections of the Commission's Report, completed in August 1896, were in turn expanded by John Rhŷs and David Brynmor-Jones into their volume *The Welsh People*.[25]) On the whole, however, Lloyd avoided drawing explicit parallels between Welsh history and specific political or

---

[21] Morgan, *Wales in British Politics*, pp. 98–104; John Edward Lloyd, 'Cymdeithas yr Iaith Gymraeg: Trem ar Hanes y Mudiad', *Y Llenor*, 10 (1931), 208–9; J. Gwynn Williams, *The University College of North Wales: Foundations 1884–1927* (Cardiff, 1985), pp. 133–4.

[22] Cf. Lloyd, 'Cymdeithas yr Iaith Gymraeg', 210–11; J. E. Caerwyn Williams, 'Cymdeithas Dafydd ap Gwilym, Mai 1886–Mehefin 1888', in Thomas Jones (ed.), *Astudiaethau Amrywiol a gyflwynir i Syr Thomas Parry-Williams* (Caerdydd, 1968), pp. 173–6. In accordance with the aims of Cymdeithas yr Iaith Gymraeg, Lloyd hoped that the bilingual format of these texts would help Welsh-speakers to learn English.

[23] [T. E. Ellis], 'Llythyr o'r Aipht', *Cymru Fydd*, 3 (1890), 192.

[24] J. E. Lloyd, *Early Welsh Agriculture* (Bangor, 1894), p. 14.

[25] (London, 1900), pp. vii–ix.

social issues in his own day. Instead, knowledge of the past had contemporary significance for him – and even more so, of course, for the indefatigable popularizer O. M. Edwards – primarily as a tool in the task of nation building.[26]

Lloyd's most explicit statements to this effect occur in a lecture on 'The Future of Welsh Literary and Historical Research', delivered at the end of the First World War, in which he offered an invaluable insight into his understanding of the relationship between nationalism and history. The Welsh, he argued, were right

> to treasure the memories of the past and to keep a firm hold of the threads of our national history. Only thus can we keep alive a genuine national spirit, fed by the noblest traditions and inspired by the highest ideals. And here, let me emphasise one important point, which may not be quite obvious. I do not believe that in the long run any traditions can nourish a healthy national life unless they are true. . . . wherever national feeling is strong, there is the tendency to idealize the past until it is made unreal, to assert that national greatness and honour are to be preferred to the claims of historical science and that history must be content to be the humble instrument of national propaganda.[27]

That these were long-held convictions is suggested by a report of the establishment of the Celtic Society at Aberystwyth in 1889, with Lloyd, '[o]ur patriotic Welsh lecturer', as president: 'It will tend to permeate the Welsh students with patriotism of the most enlightened description. There is such a thing as blind patriotic zeal which all true Welshmen would do well to discourage and banish from our midst.' To this end, the society 'has, as its objects, the furtherance of the study of Celtic antiquity in general, with a special reference to the antiquities, literature, art, &c., of Wales'.[28]

Of course, Lloyd's belief that the cultivation of 'national history' was essential to the fostering of 'a genuine national spirit' has many parallels elsewhere in nineteenth-century Europe, and his work is but one of numerous examples of the privileged position accorded to the nation in the historiography of the period – not least because, as his Oxford history

---

[26] Cf. Hazel Davies, *O. M. Edwards* (Cardiff, 1988), pp. 4, 75–8.

[27] UWBA, Lloyd Papers 93 (8 November 1918). Cf. J. E. Lloyd, 'The Organization of Welsh Historical and Archaeological Research', *THSC* (1910–11), 117–18.

[28] W. Jenkyn Jones, 'University College of Wales, Aberystwyth. Easter Term', *Cymru Fydd*, [2] (1889), 391. Likewise J. Gwenogvryn Evans called for 'a disciplined, enlightened national feeling': 'Welsh Colleges and Professors of Welsh', *Cymru Fydd*, 3 (1890), 750.

tutor, Richard Lodge, concluded apropos of Tudor England, 'A nation's character is the product of its history.'[29] Yet, while Lloyd would probably have concurred with this generalization, his approach to constructing a national history for the Welsh contrasted with some prevailing assumptions. One such assumption was that attention should be focused on those nations that had achieved statehood or, in Ranke's words, 'on nations that have played a pre-eminent active role in history'.[30] Of nowhere was this truer than Oxford, where the emergence of history as an academic discipline was inextricably bound up, thanks to William Stubbs (1825–1901), J. R. Green (1837–83) and E. A. Freeman (1823–92), with a concept of the continuity of the English nation and of the political institutions which had secured its liberty. Although each of these historians had his own distinctive emphases – contrast, for example, Stubbs's *Constitutional History of England* (1874–8) with Green's *Short History of the English People* (1874), a work dealing as much with society and culture as with political developments – all started from the premise that England was a long-established and powerful nation state.[31] Since nineteenth-century Wales lacked political sovereignty, its historians were deprived of the option of presenting its past primarily in terms of political and institutional continuity. This point is emphasized in Lloyd's eisteddfod essay:

> although Wales has no political history apart from the rest of Britain before the beginning of the seventh century, the same races appear in the main to have inhabited it all through the historic period; and the thread of continuous interest which we lose in the political story, we find in the social, the religious, the intellectual development of the people; instead of the history of a state we get the history of a nation. At no time, indeed, does the history of Wales present features of strong political interest . . . the one noble and striking feature of the narrative is the unquenchable vigour of the national resistance, the bravery and resolution of the national leaders. On the other hand, the general history of the nation is fraught with interest . . .[32]

[29] Above, n. 27; Reba N. Soffer, *Discipline and Power: The University, History, and the Making of an English Elite, 1870–1930* (Stanford, CA, 1994) (quotation at pp. 141–2).
[30] Quoted in Rees Davies, *The Matter of Britain and the Matter of England* (Oxford, 1996), p. 18.
[31] Cf. John Kenyon, *The History Men: The Historical Profession in England since the Renaissance* (2nd edn, London, 1993), pp. 156–76; J. W. Burrow, *A Liberal Descent: Victorian Historians and the English Past* (Cambridge, 1981), chaps 5–8; James Campbell, 'Stubbs and the English State', in idem, *The Anglo-Saxon State* (London, 2000), pp. 247–68.
[32] Lloyd, 'History of Wales', pp. 341–2.

Shortly afterwards Isambard Owen took a similar line in an address at the National Eisteddfod in 1886: 'If history be taken, in the modern sense, as the story of a people and not that of its rulers, the history of the Welsh is devoid neither of interest nor of instruction.'[33]

True, the contrast Lloyd drew between state and nation was somewhat overdrawn. It could be held that in practice, especially in his later *History of Wales*, he deferred to the equation of the two by concentrating on the period at which Wales came nearest to achieving statehood.[34] Moreover, as for nationalists in, say, Ireland or Bohemia, history was arguably used by Lloyd to sustain aspirations to statehood by celebrating the independence achieved in the Middle Ages and also, crucially, by maintaining that the sense of nationality created then had not been extinguished by subsequent conquest and could therefore form the basis for political autonomy in the present.[35] At the very least, his was a national history in which politics played a central role: witness the great effort expended in trying to unravel the complexities of Welsh political history before the Edwardian conquest. Ultimately, though, the state-building efforts of medieval rulers were considered significant because they helped to forge a nation rather than a state. In advancing this interpretation Lloyd, of course, subscribed to the widely held conviction that the personal qualities of leaders could do much to shape the course of history. For instance, he asserted of Gruffudd ap Llywelyn (d. 1063)

> that his vigorous personality and independent attitude did much to infuse into his fellow countrymen a greater confidence in themselves, and so helped them after his death to offer a united resistance to the invader. His successes fired them, as the Elizabethans were fired by the triumphs of Drake and the sea-dogs.[36]

Of Llywelyn ab Iorwerth (d. 1240), whose virtues he had already extolled in lectures admired by Tom Ellis, Lloyd wrote in his *History* that 'no man ever made better or more judicious use of the native force of the Welsh people for adequate national ends', while the same work famously concluded with the following verdict on Llywelyn ap Gruffudd (d. 1282): 'It was for a far distant generation to see that the last Prince had not lived in

[33] Isambard Owen, 'Race and Nationality', *Y Cymmrodor*, 8 (1887), 2.

[34] Cf. Williams, 'Preface', pp. xii–xiii.

[35] Cf. G. P. Gooch, *History and Historians in the Nineteenth Century* (2nd edn, London, 1952), pp. 397–400; R. F. Foster, 'History and the Irish Question', *TRHS*, 5th ser., 33 (1983), 169–92; UWBA, Lloyd Papers 93, pp. 3–4.

[36] J. E. Lloyd, 'Wales and the Coming of the Normans (1039–1093)', *THSC* (1899–1900), 123. Cf. idem, 'History of Wales', p. 387.

vain, but by his life-work had helped to build solidly the enduring fabric of Welsh nationality.'[37] The latter conclusion had already been foreshadowed in the eisteddfod essay, which attributed to Edward I's conquest 'the ruin of Welsh independence, but not of Welsh nationality'.[38]

Yet Lloyd's patriotic interpretation of Welsh history added up to much more than the celebration of heroic princes. It also informed his commitment to the methods and findings of modern 'scientific' scholarship, a commitment that, as we shall see, in turn helped him to present a more complex picture of the historical origins of Welsh nationality than that presented hitherto. As the 1918 lecture cited above makes clear, he believed that the debunking of legends and traditions and the construction of a new narrative of the Welsh past based on 'the most authentic sources' would serve to strengthen a sense of Welsh nationality by placing it on firmer foundations than before.[39] Of course, Lloyd was not the first Welsh scholar to advocate a critical approach to evidence. He was familiar with Thomas Stephens's *Literature of the Kymry* (1849) and praised Gweirydd ap Rhys's *Hanes y Brytaniaid a'r Cymry* (1872–4) for 'its strongly critical spirit'. Significantly, though, he found the latter work wanting on account of its failure to offer a constructive alternative.[40] Lloyd was not content merely to expose myths or to confine his attention to particular problems: he sought to present a fresh account of early Welsh history as a whole. This commitment to broad synthesis based on 'scientific' research methods probably owed much to his experiences at Oxford.[41] Students in the modern history school were required to master periods, including English history down to 1847, conveniently packaged by authorities such as Macaulay, Ranke, Froude, Stubbs and Freeman.[42] Lloyd clearly rose to the challenge, for, according to one of his examiners, the notable Balliol history tutor A. L. Smith, he showed 'a striking power of getting up a period or subject of History'.[43] Moreover, he shared the assumption of the Oxford history tutors that the past could, indeed should, be digested by historians in order to create a body of knowledge that was both reliable

[37] Lloyd, *History of Wales*, II, pp. 693, 764. Cf. T. E. Ellis, 'The Memory of the Kymric Dead' [1892], in idem, *Speeches and Addresses*, p. 11; UWBA, Lloyd Papers 314, nos 118–19. For the second quotation, see J. Goronwy Edwards, 'Hanesyddiaeth Gymreig yn yr Ugeinfed Ganrif', *THSC* (1953), 26; idem, 'Sir John Edward Lloyd', 324.

[38] Lloyd, 'History of Wales', p. 408. Cf. idem, *Outlines of the History*, p. 148.

[39] Cf. idem, *Outlines of the History*, p. 16.

[40] UWBA, Lloyd Papers 41A, no. 8.

[41] Cf. John Rhŷs and David Brynmor-Jones, *The Welsh People* (London, 1900), p. 129.

[42] Reba N. Soffer, 'Modern History', in M. G. Brock and M. C. Curthoys (eds), *The History of the University of Oxford*, VII, *Nineteenth-Century Oxford*, part 2 (Oxford, 2000), pp. 361–84. UWBA, Lloyd Papers 251 (1884 diary, p. 33) provides a revealing list of historical works.

[43] UWBA, Lloyd Papers 232 (testimonial, 26 June 1891).

and usable for teaching. In a lecture to a Welsh Language Society summer school at Aberystwyth in 1903, Lloyd observed that Welsh history was difficult to teach primarily because it had not 'been properly worked up by historical students', whereas, as he put it in another lecture two years later, historians of England such as Hume, Green and Stubbs had 'furnished [a] general outline in which [the] story is told continuously with due regard to proportion'.[44]

The necessity for history to be based on original sources, critically interpreted, was likewise a commonplace in late Victorian Oxford. When Lloyd began his studies in the modern history school, established just over a decade earlier in 1872, the Regius chair was still held by Stubbs, whose numerous editions of medieval chronicles and other texts exemplified the critical approach to sources that characterized the 'scientific' history originating in Germany. How far Lloyd was influenced in his treatment of evidence by the example of Stubbs or other Oxford historians is, admittedly, uncertain. After all, he neither devoted himself to the editing of manuscripts nor was he drawn, in contrast to Stubbs's pupil T. F. Tout, to the archival riches of the Public Record Office, whose potential for the historian of Wales was demonstrated more or less contemporaneously by J. E. Morris and E. A. Lewis.[45] Yet, though his synthesizing ambitions (as well as, from 1892, his administrative responsibilities at Bangor) made extensive use of unpublished materials impracticable, his identification with 'scientific' history cannot be dismissed as mere rhetoric.[46] Of the importance of such materials he had no doubt: thus the deficiencies of Ab Ithel's edition of the *Annales Cambriae* prompted him to publish his own transcription of the text for 1035–93 from the two extant manuscripts.[47] He also knew full well that serious study of the period after 1282 would require extensive recourse to archival sources, and he once told Thomas Richards that the *History* ended where it did 'because he felt that the apparatus had become unmanageable'.[48] This is a telling comment. Lloyd was fortunate that a great deal of the sources for Welsh history down to 1282 were available in print by the time he wrote his *History*: he was therefore able to concentrate on mastering the available body of evidence and subjecting it to detailed scrutiny. That he possessed the requisite critical faculties is suggested by the observation of his history tutor at

---

[44] Ibid., 41A, nos 1, 8.

[45] John E. Morris, *The Welsh Wars of Edward I* (Oxford, 1901); Edward Arthur Lewis, *The Mediaeval Boroughs of Snowdonia* (London, 1912).

[46] Cf. Williams, 'Preface', p. xv.

[47] Lloyd, 'Wales and the Coming of the Normans', 165–79.

[48] UWBA, Lloyd Papers 41A, no. 1; Thomas Richards, 'Sir John Lloyd', *TCHS*, 8 (1947), 2.

Oxford that Lloyd 'showed a very independent mind: refusing to accept second-hand conclusions, he was always anxious to work things out for himself'.[49]

One striking aspect of the evidence Lloyd used is its breadth and diversity. He brought to his task a conviction that the historian of early Wales needed to draw upon advances in other disciplines, notably archaeology, philology and literature. It was quite possibly in these respects that he was most directly influenced by his years in Oxford, where his contact with John Rhŷs, professor of Celtic at Jesus College, and J. Gwenogvryn Evans, then living at Clarendon Terrace on the Banbury Road, exposed him to cutting-edge scholarship on early Welsh history and medieval Welsh texts.[50] Significantly it was Rhŷs who headed the select list – which also comprised Egerton Phillimore, Alfred Neobald Palmer and Hugh Williams – of those to whom Lloyd acknowledged a 'general indebtedness . . . for the pioneer work which has so greatly facilitated the scientific study of Welsh history. I owe to them what cannot be expressed in the debt of citation and reference, namely, outlook and method and inspiration.'[51]

His openness to archaeology explains why Lloyd, not only in his eisteddfod essay but also in his textbooks for schools and in the *History*, placed the origins of Welsh history in the Stone Age. The sixteenth-century historians Humphrey Llwyd and David Powel had followed the lead of their principal source, *Brut y Tywysogyon* (in turn conceived as a continuation of *Brut y Brenhinedd*, as the Welsh versions of Geoffrey of Monmouth's *Historia Regum Britanniae* were known), and commenced their account of Welsh history with the flight of Cadwaladr the Blessed to Brittany, where he reputedly died in AD 689. True, this horizon had been pushed back somewhat by some of their successors: for example, in 1697 William Wynne began his revised version of Powel's *Historie of Cambria* with the end of Roman Britain, while Jane Williams (Ysgafell), whose *History of Wales* (1869) Lloyd explicitly claimed to supersede in the preface to his own *History*, opened her narrative with speculations about 'The Cymry of Ancient Britain' and proceeded to cover the whole period of Roman rule in Britain. However, this was as nothing by comparison with the starting point chosen by Lloyd. Though less well known than the final sentence on the fall of Llywelyn ap Gruffudd, the first sentence of his

[49] UWBA, Lloyd Papers 232 (testimonial by Richard Lodge, 28 June 1891).

[50] Cf. Brynley F. Roberts, 'Scholarly Publishing 1820–1922', in Philip Henry Jones and Eiluned Rees (eds), *A Nation and its Books: A History of the Book in Wales* (Aberystwyth, 1998), pp. 229–30; UWBA, Lloyd Papers 251 (1884 diary, p. 32).

[51] Lloyd, *History of Wales*, I, p. viii. For an earlier acknowledgement of Rhŷs's influence, see idem, *Llyfr Cyntaf Hanes*, p. 3.

History is no less revealing of its author's purpose: 'The region now known as Wales was inhabited by man in the earliest period during which science has clearly shown him to have dwelt in the British Isles.'[52] Lloyd had learned the lessons of the new discipline of prehistoric archaeology by his early twenties. Not only did he take for granted the three-age scheme of dating – referring to the successive ages of stone, bronze and iron – devised by Danish archaeologists, notably Christian Jürgensen Thomasen (1788–1865), but he also seized upon the more recent discovery, made by English and French archaeologists in the 1860s, of the Palaeolithic or Old Stone Age, a discovery that provided compelling evidence for human life in Britain extending back tens of thousands of years, a vastly longer time span than had previously been imagined.[53]

Lloyd thus restored – and indeed hugely extended – the chronological depth of Welsh history by resting it on far sounder foundations than the myth-making of Geoffrey of Monmouth. Although the latter's account of Trojan origins extending back to 1115 BC had been discredited in scholarly circles, it still cast a long shadow over popular perceptions of the Welsh past, especially thanks to the continuing popularity in the nineteenth century of Theophilus Evans's ardently pro-Galfridian *Drych y Prif Oesoedd* (A Mirror of the First Ages), originally published in 1716.[54] Moreover, whereas the legendary history propagated by Geoffrey had offered consolation to the Welsh by reminding them of their glorious British – and ultimately Trojan – origins and holding out the prospect of recovering their rightful status in the future, Lloyd presented a picture that chimed comfortably with the progressive, evolutionary assumptions of the later nineteenth century by depicting the Welsh of the present as a marked improvement on their ancestors. Nowhere are such assumptions more explicit than in the conclusion to the first of his school textbooks, which covered the period from the Palaeolithic to the end of Roman Britain:

---

[52] Idem, *History of Wales*, I, p. 1. Cf. idem, 'History of Wales', p. 353: 'we must now leave prehistoric Britain, as built for us by scientific observation up to the very verge of the Christian era'.

[53] Lloyd, 'History of Wales', pp. 342–3. Cf. Bruce G. Trigger, *A History of Archaeological Thought* (Cambridge, 1989), pp. 73–102; Glyn Daniel, *A Hundred and Fifty Years of Archaeology* (London, 1975), pp. 40–54, 85–6.

[54] Cf. Brynley F. Roberts (ed.), *Brut y Brenhinedd: Llanstephan MS. 1 Version* (Dublin, 1971), pp. 62–74; Geraint H. Jenkins, 'Historical Writing in the Eighteenth Century', in Branwen Jarvis (ed.), *A Guide to Welsh Literature c.1700–1800* (Cardiff, 2000), pp. 27–9.

We began with ancestors singularly unlike the enlightened, religious Welshmen of the present age, and have traced their history until we have seen them approach us more closely. Yet they are still far enough off; many centuries have yet their work to do ere they appear in their present guise.[55]

As this passage shows, the forward march of civilization had already begun in prehistory. True, Lloyd did not claim that the Welsh were descended from the cave dwellers of the Palaeolithic; rather, he followed the geologist and archaeologist William Boyd Dawkins (1837–1929) in identifying the earliest ancestors of the Welsh as 'the small dark people' of the Neolithic.[56] However, he held that this people had been conquered towards the beginning of the Bronze Age by taller, round-headed Celts from the continent, namely Goidelic-speakers who were ancestors of the Irish, and that towards the end of that epoch these in turn were driven out of lowland Britain into the mountainous west and north (including Wales) by the arrival in Britain of another Celtic people, namely the Brythons, who, thanks to their longer stay on the continent, 'stood higher in civilisation', resembling the Gauls described by classical writers.[57] Later, in the fifth century AD, this 'Brythonic race secured a lasting supremacy throughout Wales', and the language they imposed developed into Welsh.[58] This interpretation was heavily indebted to Rhŷs's philological arguments concerning the ethnic origins of Britain and thus, more generally, to the assumption, widely shared in the late nineteenth century thanks to Dawkins and other archaeologists and anthropologists, that civilization had advanced in prehistory through a series of racial invasions.[59] Finally, the Welsh emerged as a distinct nation, 'isolated and self-contained, dependent henceforth upon its own resources for its development', after the defeat of the Brythons or Kymry by the Northumbrian king Oswiu at the battle of the Winwaed in 655.[60]

---

[55] Lloyd, *Llyfr Cyntaf Hanes*, p. 127. Such progressionist views are expressed even more strongly in Rhŷs and Brynmor-Jones, *Welsh People*, pp. xxiv, 259–60, and Owen M. Edwards, *Wales* (London, 1901), p. 9. For the wider intellectual context, see George W. Stocking, Jr, *Victorian Anthropology* (New York, 1987), esp. chaps 5–6; Peter J. Bowler, *The Invention of Progress: The Victorians and the Past* (Oxford, 1989).

[56] W. Boyd Dawkins, 'The Ancient Ethnology of Wales', *Y Cymmrodor*, 5 (1882), 209–23.

[57] Lloyd, 'History of Wales', pp. 342–53; idem, *Llyfr Cyntaf Hanes*, pp. 21–31 (quotation at p. 29); idem, *History of Wales*, I, pp. 2–20, 30.

[58] Idem, *History of Wales*, I, p. 111.

[59] Cf. J. Rhŷs, *Celtic Britain* (London, 1882), pp. 2–4, 257–8, 270–2; Rhŷs and Brynmor-Jones, *Welsh People*, pp. 13, 32–5; Bowler, *Invention of Progress*, pp. 109–17.

[60] Lloyd, *History of Wales*, I, p. 191. 655 had already been accorded the same significance in idem, 'History of Wales', pp. 365, 381–2.

Like Rhŷs and Dawkins, Lloyd further believed that, in Wales, early conquests had resulted in racial amalgamation rather than the elimination of earlier races through ethnic cleansing. In contrast to the claims of Stubbs and Freeman for the predominantly Germanic origins of the English, the racial composition of the Welsh was depicted as being emphatically mongrel.[61] This was because Lloyd and like-minded Welsh scholars adopted the anthropological views of T. H. Huxley and other Victorian scientists by defining race essentially in terms of physical features, as revealed for past populations by skeletal remains. Thus it was that distant racial origins could be invoked to celebrate physical characteristics of the Welsh in the present – as Dawkins put it, 'That small dark race then, whose flashing eyes and raven tresses some of us admire so very much in the ladies, is to be looked upon as the most ancient element in the Welsh population.'[62] Although they never inspired Lloyd to such gallantry, these racial assumptions certainly informed his understanding of Welsh history: by accepting that the Welsh were a people of mixed race, he endowed them with an ancestry far more ancient than that of the English, who traced their origins to the forests of Germany.

One consequence of this view was that there could be no simple correlation between race and Welsh nationality. Something more was needed to explain the distinctiveness of the Welsh people. O. M. Edwards took refuge in geographical determinism: it was the need to adapt to their mountainous environment which had given the various races that had settled in Wales their common character.[63] Lloyd, too, expressed similar views, but his analysis was far more subtle, stressing less the geographical factors themselves than the consequences of adaptation – in short, pastoralism. He summed up his approach in notes probably written in the 1890s:

> Agricultural community at mercy of superior military force: pastoral not. Hence Welsh able to maintain independence. Same causes favoured tribal isolation: no opportunity for conquest which creates strong monarchy. Pastoral habits further make tie of association personal and not local –

---

[61] Lloyd, 'History of Wales', p. 351, n. 1; idem, *History of Wales*, I, p. 30; UWBA, Lloyd Papers 80, p. 5. Cf. Rhŷs and Brynmor-Jones, *Welsh People*, pp. 13, 34–5; Edwards, *Wales*, pp. 8–17; William Stubbs, *The Constitutional History of England* (3rd edn, 3 vols, Oxford, 1880), I, pp. 2, 6, 10–11; Burrow, *Liberal Descent*, pp. 109–18, 128, 189–92, 214–15; Rosemary Jann, *The Art and Science of Victorian History* (Columbus, OH, 1985), pp. 178–9.

[62] Dawkins, 'Ancient Ethnology of Wales', 221. Cf. Rhŷs and Brynmor-Jones, *Welsh People*, pp. 13, 23, 32–5; Edwards, *Wales*, pp. 11–12.

[63] Edwards, *Wales*, chap. 1.

hence strength of family and clan feeling. Pastoral way of life means much leisure – hence cultivation of poetry, music, tale telling, and oratory.[64]

According to Lloyd, this way of life connected the medieval Welsh to their Iron Age ancestors: the pastoralism Caesar had attributed to the tribes of the mountainous interior of Britain was essentially the same as that depicted by Gerald of Wales over a millennium later.[65] Indeed, aspects of it had continued into the nineteenth century.[66] It did not follow, of course, that Welsh nationality was synonymous with pastoralism. The implication may be, rather, that the preservation well into the Middle Ages of a distinctive form of society had established the necessary continuity over time to allow the creation of a sense of national identity sufficiently durable to weather the loss of political independence in 1282. Lloyd certainly suggests that the main significance of Welsh pastoralism lay in its remarkable longevity 'under the shadow of the sternest, most rigid feudalism'.[67] Moreover, barbarous and backward though it was, this pastoral, tribal society was geared above all to the defence of liberty. In other words, the ultimately vain struggle for independence to which Lloyd explicitly ascribed the survival of a distinctive Welsh identity was intrinsic to medieval Welsh society: its basis was popular, not merely princely.[68] (A further implication of this view might be that the origins of British liberty were not exclusively Teutonic.)

In attempting to trace the emergence of a Welsh nation Lloyd thus stressed both evolutionary progression and conservative continuity: on the one hand, the Welsh were depicted as the heirs of an increasingly civilized series of races; yet, on the other, their distinctiveness as a people derived from a pastoral way of life that was essentially primitive. Nevertheless, exactly what national self-consciousness consisted of and how it had survived for six centuries after 1282 are never adequately explained. Welsh nationality is often invoked as if it were a timeless spirit existing throughout – perhaps even beyond – history, albeit one requiring leaders to kindle its full potential: for example, during the ninety years after Hywel Dda's death in 950 'the man had not yet arisen who could gather the whole nation around his banner and breathe life and force into the national

---

[64] UWBA, Lloyd Papers 35, facing p. 2; cf. ibid. 41A, no. 9; Lloyd, *Llyfr Cyntaf Hanes*, pp. 104, 131; idem, *History of Wales*, II, pp. 604–11; idem, 'Wales: the Land and its People', *Wales*, 2 (1912), 359–68.

[65] Lloyd, 'History of Wales', pp. 365, 383–5; idem, *Early Welsh Agriculture*, p. 3.

[66] Idem, 'Wales: the Land and its People', 362.

[67] Idem, 'History of Wales', p. 365. Lloyd reiterated this point in *History of Wales*, I, p. 291; II, p. 605.

[68] Idem, *Outlines of the History*, p. 148; above, nn. 36–8.

aspirations'.[69] The philosophical basis of such statements would merit further investigation; suffice it to say that they echo 'the informing spirit embodied in a people' posited by J. G. Herder (1744–1803) and also have parallels in the work of other nineteenth-century historians.[70] Lloyd was no less vague when, in 1903, he implied that the reincarnation of medieval nationality in the modern era was due above all to the alchemy of memory: though political unity had rarely been achieved, 'Welsh nationality [is] nevertheless real, because it is the expression of attachment to [the] past, favoured by all physical and social surroundings'.[71]

If the full import of this assertion remains elusive, the importance Lloyd attached to the past as a source of inspiration for a revived sense of national identity in the present cannot be doubted. In this respect, his attitude was fairly commonplace among nationalist intellectuals both in Wales and elsewhere in Europe. Nor was he alone in conceiving of nationality as a continuous thread whose character in the past could be extrapolated from contemporary patriotic sentiments. Yet if his nationalist convictions fed some anachronistic assumptions they also helped to sharpen his critical faculties: precisely because the past was so important, it was imperative to try and delineate its contours accurately. The 'scientific' approach adopted to this end served not only to legitimize the historical roots of Welsh nationality but also to underline how far the Welsh had advanced by the late Victorian and Edwardian eras; the methods deployed by Lloyd to recover the ancient and medieval past were therefore emblematic of the modern, enlightened Wales which he hoped his work as a historian would help to create.

---

[69] Idem, *History of Wales*, I, p. 343.
[70] Cf. J. W. Burrow, *The Crisis of Reason: European Thought, 1848–1914* (New Haven, CT, 2000), pp. 88, 134–6; idem, *Liberal Descent*, pp. 147, 252–3.
[71] UWBA, Lloyd Papers 41A, no. 8.

3

Inside the Tent Looking Out: The Medieval Welsh World-View

A. D. CARR

The lands on the periphery of medieval Europe were often regarded by contemporaries as inward-looking, unsophisticated and indeed barbarous. Celts, Scandinavians, Slavs and Magyars were all viewed in this way by contemporary commentators who had little understanding of them or of how they themselves appeared to those whom they sought to describe.[1] Even Gerald of Wales, born and bred at Manorbier in Pembroke-shire, looked at the land of his birth from the point of view of an outsider. There is no lack of contemporary comment on the Welsh from the twelfth century onwards, but no Welsh writer set out to describe the English or the French, although *Brut y Tywysogyon* tells us that the fugitive Madog ap Rhirid of the Powys dynasty returned from Ireland in 1110 'unable to suffer the evil ways and evil customs of the Irish' and later in the twelfth century Gerald of Wales wrote the *Topography of Ireland.*[2] There has always been a tendency, especially from the vantage point of the south-east of England, to dismiss the Welsh as a parochial and narrow-minded people with little awareness of, or interest in, a wider world. This reflects invincible ignorance in our own day; when applied to the Middle Ages it is equally misleading. Travel in medieval Europe may not have been as easy as it is now, but people were constantly on the move.[3] They were aware of other countries and were open to new ideas and influences. Wales, like Ireland, was an integral part of western Christendom and the countries around the Irish Sea were not its remotest and furthest-flung branches. The Welsh dioceses were closer to mainland Europe than were those of Hólar or Skálholt in Iceland and, like them, were never out of contact with Rome. A small and

---

[1] Robert Bartlett, *Gerald of Wales 1146–1223* (Oxford, 1982), pp. 158–77.
[2] Thomas Jones (ed. and trans.), *Brut y Tywysogyon, or The Chronicle of the Princes, Peniarth MS 20 Version* (Cardiff, 1952), p. 35; Gerald of Wales, *The History and Topography of Ireland,* trans. J. J. O'Meara (Harmondsworth, 1982).
[3] For a general discussion of travel in the Middle Ages, see Norbert Ohler, *The Medieval Traveller* (Woodbridge, 1989).

mountainous country with a limited amount of fertile soil was one from which young men, in particular, had to leave and seek their fortunes; this was as true of medieval Wales as it was of Norway or Switzerland. Those who returned were as familiar with faraway places as were their nineteenth-century seafaring descendants in Cardiganshire or Llŷn.

A study of medieval Welsh awareness of the outside world needs to draw on both historical and literary evidence. Medieval poetry, especially the court poetry of the twelfth and thirteenth centuries, illustrates the cultural fund on which the poets could draw.[4] Historically, they could not but be aware of the Matter of Britain. Indeed, medieval Welsh self-awareness was encapsulated in Geoffrey of Monmouth's *Historia Regum Britanniae* of *c.*1138 which put them on a par with the Romans by describing their Trojan descent and made them feel part of a wider world.[5] Given that the *Historia* was sometimes seen as a continuation of Dares Phrygius's *De Excidio Troiae,* comparisons of royal and princely patrons with such heroes as Hector and Achilles are understandable: Prydydd y Moch, for example, compared both Gruffydd ap Cynan ab Owain Gwynedd and his son Hywel to the latter.[6] The poets show some familiarity with the Matter of Rome, while in a Christian society one would expect a knowledge of the heroes of the Old Testament alongside the great names of classical antiquity: thus, in a poem in praise of Rhodri ab Owain Gwynedd, Prydydd y Moch mentioned Cain, Abel, Absalom, Samson, Jason, Hercules, Hector and Alexander as well as Marcolf, Cato and Solomon.[7] In the *Canu Mawr*, the Prydydd's great *awdl* in praise of Llywelyn ab Iorwerth, the prince's uncle Dafydd ab Owain Gwynedd was compared to Julius Caesar, as was the prince himself by Dafydd Benfras.[8] Nor was the Matter of France forgotten: in the *Canu Mawr* Prydydd y Moch compared himself to an elephant, sounding forth the praises of Llywelyn; the reference is, of course, to Roland's horn in the Charlemagne cycle, made from an elephant's tusk.[9]

---

[4] This theme is discussed by D. Myrddin Lloyd, *Agweddau ar Hanes Dysg y Gogynfeirdd* (Caerdydd, 1977).

[5] Brynley F. Roberts, 'Testunau Hanes Cymraeg Canol', in Geraint Bowen (ed.), *Y Traddodiad Rhyddiaith yn yr Oesau Canol* (Llandysul, 1974), pp. 280–8; idem, 'Sieffre o Fynwy a Myth Hanes Cenedl y Cymry', in Geraint H. Jenkins (ed.), *Cof Cenedl VI: Ysgrifau ar Hanes Cymru* (Llandysul, 1991), pp. 3–32.

[6] Elin M. Jones (ed.), *Gwaith Llywarch ap Llywelyn 'Prydydd y Moch'* (Caerdydd, 1991), p. 111, l. 19; p. 132, l. 24.

[7] Ibid., p. 42, ll. 4–14.

[8] Ibid., p. 213, l. 21; N. G. Costigan (Bosco), R. Geraint Gruffydd, Nerys Ann Jones, Peredur I. Lynch, Catherine McKenna, Morfydd E. Owen and Gruffydd Aled Williams (eds), *Gwaith Dafydd Benfras ac Eraill o Feirdd Hanner Cyntaf y Drydedd Ganrif ar Ddeg* (Caerdydd, 1995), p. 416, l. 25.

[9] Jones (ed.), *Gwaith Llywarch ap Llywelyn*, p. 219, l. 202.

Gruffydd ap Llywelyn ab Iorwerth was likewise compared to Charlemagne himself by Einion Wan.[10]

The question which is prompted by this material is one of provenance: how did the poets acquire this knowledge? Prydydd y Moch referred to Roland's horn, but the Charlemagne cycle contained in the Red Book of Hergest and edited by Stephen J. Williams was not translated into Welsh until the thirteenth and fourteenth centuries.[11] The same is true of other sources. The first surviving translation of Geoffrey of Monmouth's *Historia Regum Britanniae*, for example, dates from the early thirteenth century and, as Rachel Bromwich has pointed out, poetry does not reflect a knowledge of Geoffrey's work as such until a translation was available.[12] Many of these poetic references come from the triads, which were perhaps originally material learned by apprentice poets summarizing Welsh tradition and the historic memory. Thus Marcolf, Cato and Solomon, for example, were the subject of one triad, the Three Men who received the Wisdom of Adam, while Hercules, Hector and Samson were the Three Men who received the Might of Adam.[13] This poses a further question: where had the original composers of the triads heard of these heroes of the ancient world?

Medieval prose texts are in many ways more interesting to the historian. Many of these texts were translations of Latin or French originals. This must be significant since what was translated would often have reflected the interests of the patrons for whom they were made. Some were devotional works, reflecting an interest in the world to come rather than the world in which they lived: the Franciscan friar Gruffydd Bola, for example, translated the Athanasian Creed for a member of the Deheubarth dynasty in the early thirteenth century.[14] But a great deal of other functional prose was translated: there are treatises on hunting, farming (a translation of Walter of Henley) and milling and there is at least one alchemical text.[15] Medical texts, particularly those associated with the physicians of Myddfai, reflect contemporary European medical knowledge, based on the works of Hippocrates and Galen, while other medical topics include anaesthesia and uroscopy.[16] Personal names indicate that there were many medical

[10] Costigan *et al.* (eds), *Gwaith Dafydd Benfras*, p. 38, l. 14.

[11] Stephen J. Williams (ed.), *Ystoria de Carolo Magno: O Lyfr Coch Hergest* (Caerdydd, 1930); Brynley F. Roberts, 'Tales and Romances', in A. O. H. Jarman and G. R. Hughes (eds), *A Guide to Welsh Literature I* (Swansea, 1976), pp. 236–8.

[12] Rachel Bromwich, *Trioedd Ynys Prydein* (Cardiff, 1961), pp. lxxx–lxxxi.

[13] Ibid., pp. 122, 128.

[14] Glanmor Williams, *The Welsh Church from Conquest to Reformation* (Cardiff, 1962), pp. 85–6.

[15] Morfydd E. Owen, 'Functional Prose: Religion, Science, Grammar, Law', in Jarman and Hughes (eds), *Guide to Welsh Literature, I*, pp. 248–75.

[16] Ibid., pp. 264–6; Nesta Lloyd and Morfydd E. Owen (eds), *Drych yr Oesoedd Canol* (Caerdydd, 1986), pp. 134–52.

practitioners in medieval Wales: the protest by the former burgesses of Llan-faes in Anglesey against their removal to Newborough at the end of the thirteenth century was led by a physician, Master Einion.[17] The existence of medical treatises shows that some of them were educated professional physicians rather than village herbalists and *gwŷr hysbys* (cunning men).

Every translation introduced some Welsh men and women to a world beyond Wales. Some of them acquired their views of this world from translations of works of geography and travel. Three of these merit particular mention.[18] The earliest of these was *Delw y Byd*, a translation of part of *Imago Mundi,* a geographical and cosmological encyclopaedia compiled in the early twelfth century by Honorius Augustodonensis.[19] There are three separate translations of it into Welsh, the earliest dating from the mid-thirteenth century at the latest, and, although none is of the entire work, the very existence of these translations reflects a curiosity about a world beyond the confines of Britain. The twelfth-century poet Cynddelw Brydydd Mawr knew of *Imago Mundi* before the existence of any of these surviving translations. This fact, like Prydydd y Moch's knowledge of the story of Roland, raises interesting questions about the broader cultural context of contemporary court poetry; it indicates that there was some knowledge of geography in Wales, drawn from earlier Latin texts, even before the appearance of *Delw y Byd*.[20] Some Welshmen would also probably have been familiar with the *Mappa Mundi,* which is believed to have reached its home at Hereford cathedral not long after the Edwardian conquest and which shows the castles of Conwy and Caernarfon.[21]

The second translation is that of *Epistola Presbyteri Johannis*, the famous account of the kingdom, somewhere in the east, of the mythical Christian priest-king Prester John.[22] A letter purporting to be from John first appeared in western Europe in the middle of the twelfth century. Although it was a fabrication, it had a wide currency and was translated into most European languages as well as into Hebrew. The letter, which described

[17] A. D. Carr, *Medieval Anglesey* (Llangefni, 1982), p. 235.

[18] Medieval awareness of a world beyond Europe is discussed by J. R. S. Phillips, *The Medieval Expansion of Europe* (Oxford, 1988).

[19] Henry Lewis and P. Diverres (eds), *Delw y Byd* (Caerdydd, 1928); Lloyd and Owen (eds), *Drych yr Oesoedd Canol*, pp. 106–14, 116–18, 123–7.

[20] Lloyd and Owen (eds), *Drych yr Oesoedd Canol*, pp. 117–18.

[21] Valerie I. J. Flint, 'The Hereford Map: its Author(s), Two Scenes and a Border', *TRHS*, 6th series, 8 (1998), 23, 43.

[22] Gwilym Lloyd Edwards (ed.), *Ystoria Gwlat Ieuan Vendigeit* (Caerdydd, 1999); the Prester John legend is discussed in the introduction, pp. lx–lxxxvii; Lloyd and Owen (eds), *Drych yr Oesoedd Canol*, pp. 118–21.

the utopian polity which was John's kingdom, had been rendered into Welsh by the mid-fourteenth century. It was included in the Book of the Anchorite of Llanddewi-brefi, compiled for the Carmarthenshire squire Gruffydd ap Llywelyn ap Philip ap Trahaearn. The idea of a powerful Christian ruler in the east acted as a kind of comfort blanket for a western Christendom which, from the late twelfth century, was becoming increasingly aware of the resurgence of Islamic power in the Middle East, especially after the fall of Jerusalem in 1187 and the failure of successive crusades. This idea led to a belief that if only contact could be made with Prester John there could then be a massive Christian campaign advancing from both east and west to recover the Holy Land. However, for Gruffydd ap Llywelyn ap Philip and others who might read or hear this account, the attraction was probably the exotic detail – the elephants, dromedaries, camels, hippopotami and crocodiles, as well as all kinds of mythical creatures, both human and animal, along with the fantastic riches, with which John's realm abounded – rather than the revival of the crusading ideal. Some of these animals might already have been familiar from bestiaries, but it would be interesting to know the identity of the first Welshman who actually saw an elephant or a hippopotamus. Some Welsh visitors to the thirteenth-century Tower of London might have seen the elephant presented to Henry III by the king of France in the royal menagerie there.

The third of these works is *Ffordd y Brawd Odrig*, a translation of an account of the journey of an Italian Franciscan friar, Odoricus of Pordenone, to the Far East in the 1320s, a generation after Marco Polo, in quest of Prester John.[23] Odoricus travelled from Constantinople to Trebizond and then through Armenia and Iran and down the Persian Gulf to India, where he recovered the remains of some of his fellow friars recently martyred there. He then went on to Ceylon (Sri Lanka), Sumatra, Java and Borneo and to China. He spent three years in Peking (Beijing) and returned overland by way of Tibet, arriving back in Italy in 1330 and dying the following year. He was accompanied by James, an Irish friar. The account of his travels was translated into several languages. It appears to have been translated into Welsh by 'Sir' Dafydd Fychan from Glamorgan at the request of Rhys ap Thomas ab Einion of Ynystawe, the brother of Hopcyn ap Thomas, one of the leading cultural patrons of his day. It is strange to think that a Welsh squire of the fifteenth century may have been familiar with a description of Lhasa, the capital of Tibet, which was, until the second half of the twentieth century, a remote and mysterious place.

---

[23] Stephen J. Williams (ed.), *Ffordd y Brawd Odrig* (Caerdydd, 1929); Lloyd and Owen (eds), *Drych yr Oesoedd Canol,* pp. 121–3.

Odoricus described Tibet as it had been under its kings before the establishment of the Buddhist theocracy of the Dalai Lama towards the end of the fourteenth century. That such a work was translated is a clear indication of Welsh interest in the outside world. Indeed, the existence of such texts (and who knows what has not survived) indicates that the leaders of native Welsh society, for whom such translations were made, shared the general European view of, and curiosity about, the world.

Later medieval poetry reveals a similar awareness. Although the most imaginative of all medieval works of travel, the 'Travels of Sir John Mandeville', was not translated until the late sixteenth century, earlier poets, among them Lewys Glyn Cothi and Lewys Môn, had heard of it.[24] Likewise, Prester John or Preutur Siôn is mentioned by several poets. As Gwilym Lloyd Edwards has pointed out, to compare a patron to Prester John was the greatest compliment possible since the very name implied so many virtues.[25] Among those so compared were William Griffith I of Penrhyn and William Herbert of Raglan, both by Guto'r Glyn.[26] Translation was not always necessary to introduce members of the Welsh squire-archy to new worlds, for there were many in medieval Wales who could read Latin and French for themselves. Llywelyn Bren, the leader of the 1315 revolt in Glamorgan, owned three Welsh books and five others, one of which was that medieval predecessor of the modern coffee table book, the *Roman de la Rose*.[27] Another possible example of cultural influence from across the English Channel was the eisteddfod held by the Lord Rhys at Cardigan in 1176; it has been suggested that this competitive gathering of poets and musicians may have been held in imitation of those assemblies in south-west France which were held under the patronage of Henry II's queen, Eleanor of Aquitaine.[28]

Knowledge of the world could come from contemporary literature, but access to such literature was not available to all. Even for those who were literate or who had access to the written word, awareness would more often have been the fruit of personal experience. There were three main reasons for travelling in the Middle Ages: war, business and religion or occasionally a combination of such reasons. Welshmen served in English royal armies before the Edwardian conquest. Owain ap Cadwgan of Powys went to Normandy with Henry I in 1114 and, if the *Brut* is to be believed,

[24] Dafydd Johnston (ed.), *Gwaith Lewys Glyn Cothi* (Caerdydd, 1995), p. 238, l. 38; Eurys I. Rowlands (ed.), *Gwaith Lewys Môn* (Caerdydd, 1975), p. 331, l. 52.
[25] Edwards (ed.), *Ystoria Gwlat Ieuan Vendigeit*, p. lii.
[26] Ifor Williams and J. Llywelyn Williams (eds), *Gwaith Guto'r Glyn* (2nd edn, Caerdydd, 1961), p. 54, l. 62; p. 161, l. 26.
[27] J. H. Matthews (ed.), *Cardiff Records* (6 vols, Cardiff, 1898–1911), I, p. 58.
[28] J. E. Caerwyn Williams, 'Yr Arglwydd Rhys ac "Eisteddfod" Aberteifi 1176', in Nerys Ann Jones and Huw Pryce (eds), *Yr Arglwydd Rhys* (Caerdydd, 1996), pp. 94–128.

was knighted there, the first Welshman to receive this accolade.[29] In 1174 the Lord Rhys sent a contingent of a thousand men from Deheubarth to assist Henry II in France, and six years earlier Henry had used Welsh mercenaries in the siege of Chaumont-sur-Epte in Normandy.[30] Welsh troops served with Henry in France again in 1188 and Richard I recruited men in Wales during the next decade. When Archbishop Baldwin of Canterbury came to Wales in 1188 to preach the Third Crusade, Gerald of Wales claimed that about 3000 people took the cross, although we do not know how many of those swayed by the oratory of the archbishop (or, more accurately, his interpreter) actually made their way to the Middle East.[31] Quite apart from those who volunteered for the Third Crusade, some Welshmen must have found their way to the Holy Land. Soldiering, after all, offered a living and an opportunity to see the world, whatever the motive.

Military service in continental Europe was therefore familiar enough in Wales before 1282. It was not long before Edward I was raising troops from his new Welsh lands for campaigns in Scotland and France; indeed, the levying of men to go to France may have helped to precipitate the Welsh revolt of 1294–5, and an eye-witness account by the Ghent chronicler Lodewyk van Velthem of the Welsh recruited by Edward for his 1297 expedition to Flanders in their camp near the city is well known.[32] Six hundred men from Wales were sent to Brittany in 1342 in support of John de Montfort and 7000 were recruited for the campaign of 1346, led by Edward III himself, which culminated in the English victory at Crécy. These included the Merioneth poet Llywelyn Goch ap Meurig Hen, sent home in disgrace to face a charge of murder (towards the end of his life Llywelyn admitted to having broken all of the Ten Commandments).[33] Artevelde, the leader of the Flemish insurgents, had a Welsh bodyguard in 1345, and Welshmen served with the Black Prince at Poitiers in 1356 (although there is no mention of them on the alleged site of the battle) and in Castile in 1367. Some of these Welsh fighting men, such as the knights Sir Hywel ap Gruffydd (known as Syr Hywel y Fwyall or Sir Hywel of the Axe because of his feats with his battleaxe at Poitiers) from Eifionydd or Sir Gregory Sais from Flintshire, distinguished themselves. Sir Gregory

---

[29] Jones (ed.), *Brut y Tywysogyon . . . Peniarth MS 20 Version*, p. 38.

[30] A. D. Carr, 'Dulliau Rhyfel yr Arglwydd Rhys', in Jones and Pryce (eds), *Yr Arglwydd Rhys*, p. 88.

[31] Gerald of Wales, *The Journey through Wales; and, The Description of Wales*, ed. Lewis Thorpe (Harmondsworth, 1978), p. 204.

[32] A. D. Carr, 'Welshmen and the Hundred Years War', *WHR*, 4, no. 1 (1968), 22–3.

[33] Ibid., 24; idem, 'The Coroner in Fourteenth-Century Merioneth', *JMHRS*, 11, part 3 (1992), 250–1; Dafydd Johnston (ed.), *Gwaith Llywelyn Goch ap Meurig Hen* (Aberystwyth, 1998), p. 40.

married an heiress from Poitou, while Sir Hywel became constable of Cricieth castle.[34] Others followed the last heir of the Gwynedd dynasty, Owain ap Thomas ap Rhodri or Owain Lawgoch, into French service, probably from a mixture of motives. Some of them may have shared in his defeat by the Swiss at Fraubrunnen in 1375, while others remained in France after Owain's assassination in 1378. One of them, Ieuan Wyn, once captain of John of Gaunt's castle of Beaufort and Owain's lieutenant who subsequently inherited his company, was possibly of the lineage of Ednyfed Fychan, his father having been a sheriff of Flintshire notorious for his oppressive behaviour. Another, Petit Griffon, settled in Touraine, having married a local girl, Marguerite Gillebert. Other Welsh names appear on French muster rolls both before and after Owain's death and some were still serving there in the 1390s.[35]

The renewal of Anglo-French hostilities under Henry V meant the involvement of more Welshmen in campaigns in France.[36] Many did not go unrewarded: some obtaining grants of denizenship exempting them from the provisions of the penal statutes passed at the start of the Glyndŵr revolt and others were awarded lands in Normandy. At least two Welshmen were among the first students admitted to the new University of Caen. But despite Henry's initial success, the French recovery saw lands and lordships revert to their original owners, and when the Welsh captain Matthew Gough surrendered Bayeux in 1450 the Norman interests of his compatriots were finally extinguished.[37]

Poets were well informed about English campaigns in France and about the part played by their patrons. Guto'r Glyn, who addressed several Welsh participants in his odes, among them Matthew Gough and Sir Richard Gethin, may actually have served in France himself; in the previous century Llywelyn Goch ap Meurig Hen had praised the exploits of Goronwy ap Tudur of Penmynydd there.[38] In a *cywydd* to Sir Hywel y Fwyall, Iolo Goch referred to his conduct at Poitiers and in one to Owain Glyndŵr he mentioned Owain's service at Berwick under Sir Gregory Sais. Gruffydd Llwyd also mentioned Sir Hywel and Sir Gregory when bemoaning the fact that Owain had not been knighted.[39]

---

[34] Carr, 'Welshmen and the Hundred Years War', 28–30; idem, 'A Welsh Knight in the Hundred Years War: Sir Gregory Sais', *THSC* (1977), 40–53.

[35] Idem, *Owen of Wales: The End of the House of Gwynedd* (Cardiff, 1991), pp. 19–67.

[36] Idem, 'Welshmen and the Hundred Years War', 35–41.

[37] C. T. Allmand, *Lancastrian Normandy 1415–1450* (Oxford, 1983), p. 104.

[38] Williams and Williams (eds), *Gwaith Guto'r Glyn,* pp. 1–10; Saunders Lewis, 'Gyrfa filwrol Guto'r Glyn', in J. E. Caerwyn Williams (ed.), *Ysgrifau Beirniadol IX* (Dinbych, 1976), pp. 80–100; Johnston (ed.), *Gwaith Llywelyn Goch ap Meurig Hen*, p. 32.

[39] D. R. Johnston (ed.), *Gwaith Iolo Goch* (Caerdydd, 1988), p. 7; Rhiannon Ifans (ed.), *Gwaith Gruffudd Llwyd a'r Llygliwiaid Eraill* (Aberystwyth, 2000), p. 147.

For every *uchelwr* who was drawn to the colours there would have been many more archers and men-at-arms. Recruited from every part of Wales, both royal lands and the March, their service abroad meant that they returned home, often after years of campaigning, with an awareness of a world beyond the limits of their own neighbourhoods and very different from theirs. They must also have returned as very different people; country boys from Cantref Mawr or Eifionydd had come home as tough and hard-bitten soldiers who had fought and plundered their way across France. There would have been problems, for such men must have found it hard to settle down to their former lives and veterans might have contributed substantially to the decline in standards of law and order in the last quarter of the fourteenth century. Many would have found their way into the *pleidiau* or retinues of local squires, bodies of kinsmen and dependants who might be used to help leaders of local communities to enforce that leadership. Such a pool of military experience no doubt contributed to Owain Glyndŵr's forces after 1400.

In the fifteenth century the methods of recruitment were different and units tended to be smaller and more professional than they had been at the beginning of the Hundred Years War. Some men remained in the service of the Crown or of a magnate after returning from France: Matthew Gough met his death defending London Bridge against Jack Cade and his rebels in 1450, while Guto'r Glyn's friend, Siôn Dafi from Cyfeiliog in Powys, another veteran of the French wars, became a member of Edward IV's guard (as Guto himself might also have been) and had his hand cut off for striking someone within the precincts of the court.[40] More intriguing, perhaps, than these was Maurice de Says, 'originally from Wales', who was one of the butlers of Louis XI of France in 1474.[41] War, then, gave many medieval Welshmen the opportunity to travel and must have widened the horizons of those who came home. Some must have gone further afield than France and returned to regale their neighbours with stories of the wonders they had seen. If an English exile could have found his way into the service of Genghis Khan in the thirteenth century, then Welshmen might well have penetrated some of the remoter parts of their contemporary world and returned home to tell the tale.[42] And traffic travelled both ways: in the late fourteenth century a squire from Llanfairfechan in Caernarfonshire brought home a French prisoner of war, known locally as Bertram le French, while in the Carmarthenshire

[40] Carr, 'Welshmen and the Hundred Years War', 39–41; Lewis, 'Gyrfa filwrol Guto'r Glyn', 90–5; Williams and Williams (eds), *Gwaith Guto'r Glyn*, pp. 104–5.

[41] Archives Nationales, Paris, K169, no. 60. I am grateful to Mlle Claudine Billot of CNRS, Paris, for this reference.

[42] This is discussed by Gabriel Ronay, *The Tartar Khan's Englishman* (London, 1978).

commote of Maenordeilo in 1386–7 there is a reference to a Jew, notwithstanding that Jews had been formally expelled from the king's realms in 1290.[43]

The fifteenth century certainly witnessed Welshmen moving on to a wider stage. At the beginning of the century Henry Don or Dwnn of Kidwelly was a ruthless local landowner who was one of Owain Glyndŵr's key supporters.[44] His grandson Gruffydd also took part in the revolt and received a pardon in 1413. Two years later he fought at Agincourt and in 1421 he was granted denizenship. This was followed by a long period of service in Normandy: he was captain of several towns and was instrumental in the capture of Harfleur in 1440. He was granted lands in Normandy by way of reward and held office back home in the lordship of Kidwelly as constable and deputy steward.[45] Gruffydd's three sons also served in France: the career of one of them, Sir John Dwnn, illustrates the upward mobility of some gentry families in the fifteenth century.[46] Like his father, he backed the Yorkist party; he was deputy chamberlain of south Wales in 1474–5, having been knighted after Edward IV's victory at Tewkesbury in 1471. His wife was a daughter of Lord Hastings and was one of the queen's ladies-in-waiting. By 1477 he was a member of the council and was sent on several diplomatic missions to France and Burgundy. He built up a substantial estate in England in the counties of Essex, Buckinghamshire and Lincolnshire. After Bosworth he made his peace with Henry VII and went on further diplomatic missions. He commissioned a painting, now in the National Gallery in London, from the Flemish painter Hans Memling. He died in 1503 and was buried at Windsor. But the greatest example of upward mobility was the great-grandson of the Newborough burgess Maredudd ap Tudur who, in 1485, became king of England.

Business, trade and the desire to make a fortune led many Welshmen to England long before 1485. There were Welsh communities in border towns like Hereford, Tewkesbury and Bristol. It has been suggested, not altogether convincingly, that a citizen of Bristol of Welsh extraction, Richard ap Meurig, who was involved in the financing of John Cabot's expedition in 1497, gave his name to America. This story should probably

---

[43] PRO Wales 20/1, m. 10b; William Rees, *South Wales and the March 1284–1415* (Oxford, 1924), p. 222n.

[44] R. R. Davies, *The Revolt of Owain Glyn Dŵr* (Oxford, 1995), pp. 200–1.

[45] Carr, 'Welshmen and the Hundred Years War', 37; Ralph A. Griffiths, *The Principality of Wales in the Later Middle Ages: The Structure and Personnel of Government, I, South Wales, 1277–1536* (Cardiff, 1972), pp. 201–2. For a more recent discussion, see idem, 'After Glyn Dŵr: an Age of Reconciliation', *PBA*, 117 (2002), 139–64, esp. 159–62.

[46] Griffiths, *Principality of Wales*, pp. 187–8.

be taken in the same spirit as the claim current in south Wales during the Second World War that the Soviet marshal Timoshenko was actually called Thomas Jenkins and was of Welsh descent.[47] The most important Welsh expatriate community has always been in London and this was probably already the case in the later Middle Ages. One example of a London Welshman was Lewis John from Carmarthenshire, a merchant and a friend of Henry V, who became master of the mint, a member of parliament and a member of the king's council.[48] He was knighted, married the daughters of two earls in succession, and acquired a large estate in Essex where he was the ancestor of a county family.

There is no doubt that trade brought Wales into contact with a wider world. Most ports had their own ships: in a return of 1325 Chepstow had four, Tenby three, Carmarthen two, and Cardiff, Haverfordwest and Beaumaris one each.[49] The Welsh seafaring tradition was already well established, although the lack of much direct evidence regarding Welsh shipping is frustrating. Beaumaris, Carmarthen and Tenby certainly had an extensive foreign trade: two Tenby ships laden with salt were seized by Spaniards at the Isle of Oléron in 1352 and in 1405 six Tenby merchants received nearly £1000 in compensation for their three ships seized in Spain.[50] Wool was exported; merchants from Italy often bought the wool clip from the Cistercian abbeys, and much wine was imported from France and Spain. Contemporary poetry also provides indirect evidence of trading links as well as reflecting access to imported luxuries: the presence on the tables of the poets' patrons of wines and exotic delicacies like oranges, ginger, sugar and cinnamon all bear witness to contact with a world far beyond Offa's Dyke.

Religion could also widen horizons. Some Welsh clerks were educated at universities abroad: Gerald of Wales, at least in his own opinion, was one of the ornaments of the University of Paris in the twelfth century and others also looked beyond Oxford or Cambridge. Some, shut out from preferment at home after the middle of the fourteenth century, had to

---

[47] Ralph A. Griffiths, *The Reign of King Henry VI* (London, 1981), p. 567; idem, 'Medieval Severnside: the Welsh Connection', in R. R. Davies, Ralph A. Griffiths, Ieuan Gwynedd Jones and Kenneth O. Morgan (eds), *Welsh Society and Nationhood: Historical Essays Presented to Glanmor Williams* (Cardiff, 1984), pp. 86–9; A. E. Hudd, 'Richard Ameryk and the Name America', in H. P. R. Finberg (ed.), *Gloucestershire Studies* (Leicester, 1957), pp. 120–9; John Davies, *Hanes Cymru* (London, 1990), p. 586.

[48] A. D. Carr, 'Sir Lewis John: A Medieval London Welshman', *BBCS*, 23, part 3 (1967), 260–70.

[49] J. Goronwy Edwards (ed.), *Calendar of Ancient Correspondence Concerning Wales* (Cardiff, 1935), pp. 218–19.

[50] Carr, *Medieval Anglesey*, pp. 112–14, 242; Ralph A. Griffiths, 'Carmarthen', in idem (ed.), *Boroughs of Medieval Wales* (Cardiff, 1978), pp. 152–3; R. F. Walker, 'Tenby', ibid., p. 315.

make their careers elsewhere: one of the best examples was the canonist and chronicler Adam of Usk, who spent much of his life in England and France and at Rome.[51] Many Welsh students studied at Oxford and some at Cambridge; they were frequently involved in brawls and in 1402 several of them were accused of plotting on behalf of Owain Glyndŵr.[52] Most of these were clerics like Master Dafydd Lygadbrith, who was presented to the rectory of Llanddyfnan in Anglesey in 1399 and indicted at Oxford for seditious activity in 1402, but it was not unknown for laymen to spend some time at the schools.[53] The Cardiganshire poet Ieuan ap Rhydderch had had some university education and boasted of the breadth of his learning in one of his poems.[54]

However, the prime reason for religious travel throughout Europe was undoubtedly pilgrimage, an activity as much social as religious. Wales had no lack of shrines of its own; pilgrims regularly visited St David's, Bardsey, Llanddwyn and Pen-rhys among other places. But they also went further afield, to Canterbury and Walsingham and to Rome, Santiago de Compostela and even Jerusalem.[55] The Welsh, as members of the western church, were never unaware of Rome; according to the *Brutiau*, Cadwaladr ap Cadwallon went there to die in 682 and Cyngen, king of Powys, did the same in 856, as did Joseph, bishop in Morgannwg, in 1045. Hywel Dda's visit there in 928 is well known.[56] The Anglesey poet Robin Ddu composed a *cywydd* to the ship on which he travelled to Rome for the Holy Year of 1450 and in 1506 a Welsh pilgrim called Maurice London arrived at the English College in Rome. Because he was ill and could only speak Welsh, an interpreter had to be employed. This is an interesting reference since it indicates the presence of Welsh-speakers in Rome in the early sixteenth century.[57] In 1431 the bishop of Bangor, John Cliderow, went on pilgrimage to Jerusalem. In 1361 the Welsh captain Sir Gregory Sais petitioned the pope for leave to visit the Holy Sepulchre with a retinue of fifty,

---

[51] Williams, *The Welsh Church*, p. 224; C. Given-Wilson (ed. and trans.), *The Chronicle of Adam Usk 1377–1421* (Oxford, 1997), pp. xiii–xxxviii.

[52] Rhŷs W. Hays, 'Welsh Students at Oxford and Cambridge Universities in the Middle Ages', *WHR*, 4, no. 4 (1969), 325–61; Ralph A. Griffiths, 'Some Partisans of Owain Glyndŵr at Oxford', *BBCS*, 22, part 3 (1963), 282–92.

[53] Carr, *Medieval Anglesey*, p. 283; Griffiths, 'Some Partisans', 289.

[54] Henry Lewis, Thomas Roberts and Ifor Williams (eds), *Cywyddau Iolo Goch ac Eraill* (Caerdydd, 1937), pp. 228–32.

[55] G. Hartwell Jones, *Celtic Britain and the Pilgrim Movement* (London, 1912); Terry John and Nona Rees, *Pilgrimage: A Welsh Perspective* (Llandysul, 2002); Davies, *Revolt of Owain Glyn Dŵr*, pp. 24–5. For the cult of an English saint in Wales, see Keith Williams-Jones, 'Thomas Becket and Wales', *WHR*, 5, no. 4 (1971), 350–65.

[56] Jones (ed.), *Brut y Tywysogyon . . . Peniarth MS 20 Version*, pp. 1, 4, 14; J. Williams ab Ithel (ed.), *Annales Cambriae* (London, 1860), p. 17.

[57] Jones, *Celtic Britain*, pp. 223–6, 239.

although one cannot avoid the cynical thought that this might have been intended as cover for a company of mercenaries travelling around France after the Treaty of Brétigny.[58] There are other references to the Jerusalem pilgrimage: in 1128 Morgan ap Cadwgan of the royal house of Powys went there to do penance for the killing of his brother Maredudd and died in Cyprus on the way home, while in 1235 no less a person than Ednyfed Fychan, seneschal of Llywelyn ab Iorwerth, was granted a safe conduct by Henry III for his journey through England on the way to the Holy Land, although history does not relate whether he actually went.[59] Rome and Jerusalem offered the greatest spiritual benefits, but the most popular overseas pilgrimage seems to have been to Santiago de Compostela. The traditional route, or Chemin de Saint-Jacques, lay through western France (where, in the church at Aulnay, medieval pilgrims could have seen representations of elephants) and across the Pyrenees, but most travellers from Wales probably went by sea to La Coruña.[60] Lewys Glyn Cothi wished Gruffydd ap Rhys of Branas in Edeirnion a safe journey to Santiago and did the same for Elliw, daughter of Henry ap Hywel from Dyffryn Aeron, and there is another reference to the pilgrimage from the lordship of Powys. On 9 July 1382 an inquisition was held at Welshpool to ascertain whether John de Charlton, the heir to the lordship, was of full age. Three men swore that on 31 May 1361 they had been in Welshpool church to take leave of their neighbours before setting out together for Santiago when they saw John being christened.[61]

In a world dominated by oral culture many people in medieval Wales would have been at least bilingual and a second language could often be a conduit for new influences and ideas.[62] There is no firm evidence of the linguistic skills of the native princes, but Gruffydd ap Cynan must have spoken Norse and possibly Irish as well as Welsh, while later rulers, members of an European aristocratic milieu in which French was the *lingua franca* of polite society, would probably have had some knowledge of that language. Llywelyn ab Iorwerth and Llywelyn ap Gruffudd both had Anglo-Norman wives and were probably reasonably fluent in the language. The same may have been true of men such as Ednyfed Fychan and other leading figures around the princes. Bilingualism is likely to have

[58] Ibid., p. 568; Carr, 'A Welsh Knight', 41.

[59] Jones (ed.), *Brut y Tywysogyon . . . Peniarth MS 20 Version*, p. 50; David Stephenson, *The Governance of Gwynedd* (Cardiff, 1984), p. 208.

[60] Jones, *Celtic Britain*, pp. 244–74.

[61] Johnston (ed.), *Gwaith Lewys Glyn Cothi*, pp. 188–90, 500–1; *Calendar of Inquisitions Post Mortem* XV (London, 1970), no. 659.

[62] The best discussion of language in medieval Wales is Llinos Beverley Smith, 'The Welsh Language before 1536', in Geraint H. Jenkins (ed.), *The Welsh Language before the Industrial Revolution* (Cardiff, 1997), pp. 15–44.

prevailed on both sides of the border, especially in the towns where the two peoples met and traded; many, both Welsh and English, would have spoken both languages at least to some degree. At the end of the fifteenth century Sir John Wynn of Gwydir's great-grandfather Maredudd ab Ieuan was sent to school at Caernarfon to learn English and Latin.[63] Indeed, some Welshmen, especially those holding any sort of office, may even have been trilingual to some degree in Welsh, English and Latin by the later Middle Ages. Many had occasion to travel to England: according to Siôn Cent, travel to England was among the pleasures of the leaders of the native community and Guto'r Glyn described a disastrous droving expedition on behalf of his patron, the parson of Corwen, which took him to Warwick, Coventry, Lichfield and Stafford.[64] Other poets could also speak English: Tudur Penllyn composed a bilingual *cywydd* as a conversation in questionable taste between the poet and an English girl, while Ieuan ap Hywel Swrdwal composed an *awdl* in English in honour of the Virgin Mary, using Welsh metres.[65] Another example of both knowledge of English and literacy is a memorandum in English in the hand of Gwilym Fychan (William Griffith I) of Penrhyn in Caernarfonshire (d. 1483), although it must be conceded that his mother was English.[66] It was not only in the English border counties that Welsh was spoken outside Wales: when Alexander Dalby, the dean of Chester, was nominated by the Black Prince to the vacant see of Bangor in 1366, the pope wrote to the archbishop of Bordeaux, in whose diocese there were many Welsh-speakers, instructing him to discover whether Dalby was capable of preaching a Welsh sermon.[67] Dalby was not appointed, but he may have been a member of a Ruthin burgess family; if this were the case, he may well have been able to speak Welsh.[68]

There are many questions yet to be asked about *mentalités* in medieval Wales, even if answers are not always likely to be forthcoming. What is certain is that the horizons and world-view of the Welsh were not bounded by their own localities or even by the British Isles. For some, this awareness came through poets or storytellers or through a wide range of works translated from French or Latin. For others, it was the result of direct

---

[63] John Wynn, *History of the Gwydir Family, and Memoirs*, ed. J. Gwynfor Jones (Llandysul, 1990), p. 49.

[64] Lewis, Roberts and Williams (eds), *Cywyddau Iolo Goch ac Eraill*, p. 290; Williams and Williams (eds), *Gwaith Guto'r Glyn*, pp. 84–6.

[65] Thomas Roberts (ed.), *Gwaith Tudur Penllyn ac Ieuan ap Tudur Penllyn* (Caerdydd, 1958), pp. 53–4; Dylan Foster Evans (ed.), *Gwaith Hywel Swrdwal a'i Deulu* (Aberystwyth, 2000), pp. 124–6.

[66] University of Wales Bangor Archives, Penrhyn Further Additional, 20 June 1431.

[67] *Calendar of Papal Registers 1362–1404* (London, 1902), p. 25.

[68] Denbighshire Record Office, DD/WY 81.

personal experience through travel, in pursuit of military service, employment or religious devotion. The eyes of others were opened by their acquisition of another language and the awareness of another culture which came with it. Literary influences were probably more pronounced among the leaders of native society who were the main source of cultural patronage. On the other hand, travellers came from every level of society. For every Hywel y Fwyall, Gregory Sais or Matthew Gough there were scores of common soldiers; likewise pilgrimage was not solely a form of upper-class devotion and some from humble backgrounds even found their way to Jerusalem. Medieval Wales may have been seen by some contemporaries as remote, but it was very far from being a hermit nation.

4

The Identity of 'Wales' in the Thirteenth Century

R. R. DAVIES

There is a beguiling simplicity about the names of countries, lands and peoples. We tend to regard them as 'hard', objectified, non-contentious pieces on the chessboard of human history. They are, of course, nothing of the sort. They are the creations of time, circumstances and power. As with all human institutions, and the labels that are attached to them, they are often the focus of deep loyalties and affection. Men and women have fought, and fight, in their name and for their names. Yet viewed on a long, and sometimes not so long, timescale, countries and nations, lands and peoples are subject to change and challenge, redefinition and even extinction. Wales was, and is, no exception. 'When was Wales?' was the typically startling question which the late Gwyn Alfred Williams was fond of asking. He provided his own pithy answer: 'If we want Wales, we will have to make Wales.'[1] If there was any century in which men and women set out heroically, and hopelessly, to 'make' Wales it was assuredly the thirteenth century, the age of the two Llywelyns. One of the features of their enterprise was the way they sought to appropriate the term 'Wales' (Wallia, Cymru) for their own ends and to make it a watchword of their political programme and political dreams. Such is the theme of this essay, offered with affection and gratitude to two of the 'makers' of the historiography of Wales in the second half of the twentieth century.

'Wales', we might observe at the outset, is a foreign, English word, and so is 'Welsh'. Both are derived from the Old English *Walh* or *Wealh*. To those, such as Gerald of Wales, who were ultra-sensitive to the etymology of words, 'Wales' was a term to be avoided because of its pejorative

---

[1] Gwyn A. Williams, *When was Wales?* (London, 1979); idem, The *Welsh in their History* (London, 1982), p. 201.

45

connotations with the concept of 'alien'.[2] Yet such sensitivities were misplaced. The names of countries and peoples are often bestowed upon them by outsiders, notably by neighbours who thereby demarcate their own identity by inventing labels for countries and peoples who do not partake of that identity. So it was with the English identification of Wales and the Welsh. Secondly, we might observe that 'Wales' in its various forms – *Wallia, Walis, Gualis* and *Walonia* among them – and 'the Welsh' – likewise in variant guises such as *Guali, Gualenses, Walenses* – were well-established, commonplace terms in English and Anglo-Norman sources from at least the later eleventh century, notably and frequently in Domesday Book.[3] Whether the two terms were quite as novel as the documentation suggests may be open to question; what is beyond doubt is that the late tenth and eleventh centuries were crucial in shaping the nomenclature of the countries of Britain. It was then that the names 'England' and 'Scotland' are first recorded in their recognizably modern vernacular forms. 'Wales' can also be added to the roster. Thirdly, we may observe that 'Wales' was for contemporaries a clearly recognized and fairly definitively demarcated geographical unit. This was already the case in Asser's day, though the word 'Wales' as such was not then in currency.[4] By the early twelfth century we have ample evidence that Wales was clearly identified as a distinct country or region, and now under its own name, in the minds and charters of Anglo-Norman kings and barons.[5] It was self-evidently not part of, and was distinct from, England. Indeed England's early definition of its own identity may well have served to bring the separate, non-English identity of Wales into clearer focus.[6]

Did the Welsh themselves partake of this view of the identity of the country? The broad answer would seem to be 'yes'. Three reasons may be

---

[2] *Descriptio Kambrie*, I. 7 in J. S. Brewer *et al.* (eds), *Giraldi Cambrensis Opera* (8 vols, London, 1861–91), VI, p. 179, trans. Lewis Thorpe (Harmondsworth, 1978), p. 232; Giraldus Cambrensis, 'De Invectionibus', ed. W. S. Davies, *Y Cymmrodor, 30* (1920), 93–4.

[3] For full documentation on the terminology, see Huw Pryce, 'British or Welsh? National Identity in Twelfth-Century Wales', *EHR*, 116, no. 468 (2001), 775–801, esp. 792–3.

[4] Simon Keynes and Michael Lapidge (eds and trans), *Alfred the Great: Asser's Life of King Alfred and Other Contemporary Sources* (Harmondsworth, 1983), p. 71. The term that Asser uses is *Britannia*.

[5] Among scores of examples one might cite Charles Johnson and H. A. Cronne (eds), *Regesta Regum Anglo-Normannorum 1066–1154*, II, *Regesta Henrici Primi 1100–1135* (Oxford, 1956), nos 846, 1014, 1043, 1490, etc.; Robert B. Patterson (ed.), *Earldom of Gloucester Charters* (Oxford, 1973), nos 31, 32, 104, 110 etc.; R. W. Banks (ed.), 'Cartularium Prioratus S. Johannis Evangeliste de Brecon', *AC*, 4th series, 14 (1883), 137–68 at 144.

[6] For this theme, see R. R. Davies, *The First English Empire: Power and Identities in the British Isles 1093–1343* (Oxford, 2000), pp. 191–203.

cited – over and above the usual sparseness of direct and directly datable evidence – for giving a less than categoric answer. First, sources written in Latin in Wales fairly consistently refer to Wales as *Britannia* and to the Welsh as *Britones* until *c*.1130, as Huw Pryce has recently shown in a masterly article.[7] So long as the shadow of an earlier and glorious terminology lay so heavily on their vocabulary, the image of Wales would be slow to come clearly into view. Secondly, the vernacular word *Cymry* – whose earliest usage may even date to the seventh century – had the double disadvantage of being both geographically imprecise (it could refer to all west Britons including those of Cumbria, Cornwall and even Brittany) and of not distinguishing between people (modern *Cymry*) and country (modern *Cymru*). Thirdly, as was to be expected in a deeply fragmented country, the focus of much of the vernacular annalistic and poetic sources of medieval Wales was regional and dynastic. Wales, and even its major divisions, were conceived of as an assemblage of countries (W. *gwladoedd*);[8] it was perhaps not easy in such a world for the image of a single country to acquire prominence.

Yet that is but half the story. Literary and legal sources in particular indicate that alongside the memory of the Island of Britain as a single entity there existed a sense of Wales and its boundaries. *Clawdd Offa*, Offa's Dyke, demarcated the land boundary of Wales in the native law texts, as it had once done for Asser in Alfred's day.[9] Literary lore as preserved in the Triads of the Island of Britain (possibly composed in the mid-twelfth century) was even more precise, identifying by name the four corners of Wales. It was such a Wales that Gruffydd ap Cynan (d. 1137) of Gwynedd no doubt had in mind when, in a letter to the archbishop of Canterbury, he referred to 'the clergy and people of all Wales'. Likewise when Gwenwynwyn of Powys launched a major offensive against the English in 1198 his declared ambition was to restore 'the ancient bounds and limits' of the Welsh. Defending those boundaries – *ffin Cymru* – was the duty of the good prince: that is precisely what Llywelyn ab Iorwerth (d. 1240) had done with his army and that is why he deserved the poet's plaudits.[10]

---

[7] Pryce, 'British or Welsh?', 775–801.

[8] R. R. Davies, *Conquest, Coexistence and Change: Wales 1063–1415* (Oxford, 1987), reissued as *The Age of Conquest: Wales 1063–1415* (Oxford, 1991, 2000), pp. 12–13.

[9] Keynes and Lapidge (eds), *Alfred the Great*, p. 71; Dafydd Jenkins (ed.), *Llyfr Colan* (Cardiff, 1963), § 634; Walter Map, *De Nugis Curialium: Courtiers' Trifles*, ed. M. R. James, C. N. L. Brooke and R. A. B. Mynors (Oxford, 1983), pp. 166–9.

[10] Rachel Bromwich (ed.), *Trioedd Ynys Prydein: The Welsh Triads* (2nd edn, Cardiff, 1978), pp. 228–37; M. Rule (ed.), *Eadmeri Historia Novorum in Anglia* (London, 1884), pp. 259–60; Thomas Jones (ed.), '"Cronica de Wallia" and Other Documents from Exeter Cathedral Library MS. 3514', *BBCS*, 12 (1948), 27–44 *sub anno* 1198; Elin M. Jones (ed.), *Gwaith Llywarch ap Llywelyn 'Prydydd y Moch'* (Caerdydd, 1991), no. 25, l. 8.

It is indeed from the remarkable corpus of vernacular court poetry that we gain the impression of Wales not only as a well-defined land but also as a much-loved and well-known country. An imaginary jaunt around Wales, *cylch Cymru*, was a poetic conceit which allowed the poet to display his knowledge of the country and its component parts. The earliest poem in the canon of Welsh court poetry is in fact a late eleventh-century ode which mentions more than thirty of the districts of Wales individually; it is paralleled by a later poem in honour of the military exploits of Llywelyn ap Gruffudd (d. 1282), which enumerates almost every corner of Wales in its recitation of the range of his campaigns.[11] There may be an element of bravura showiness in these lists, but they also surely show that the Wales of the court poets was an intimate and well-defined country. Nor is this surprising. The poets indeed encompassed the whole of Wales in their search for patronage, and the vernacular prose tales of the period (the *Mabinogi*) likewise bring the whole of Wales effortlessly into the geographical frame of reference of their narratives. Wales, to borrow the striking phrase of James Campbell about contemporary England,[12] was a compassable country in the imagination of its literary and learned classes. It was also personified and treated as the object of pity or affection – a sad or bereft Wales, a blessed Wales (*Cymru wen*).[13] Wales, according to these texts, was most assuredly a country and regarded as such by natives and outsiders alike. But – and this is crucial – it was *not*, nor was it regarded as, a political, governmental or jurisdictional unit. It lacked what Susan Reynolds has very serviceably termed 'regnal solidarity'.[14] That is an issue to which we will need to return.

Wales, then, was a country; equally, the Welsh were a people, a separate people. The English and the Anglo-Norman rulers of England had no hesitation on that score. From the folios of Domesday Book in 1086 (to start no earlier) through their writs and charters and in the passages of their narrative histories, they consistently identified, and greeted, the Welsh as a distinct people, *Walenses*. They could even distinguish, as they did occasionally, between the Welsh, the English, the French and the

---

[11] Kathleen Anne Bramley, Nerys Ann Jones, Morfydd E. Owen, Catherine McKenna, Gruffydd Aled Williams and J. E. Caerwyn Williams (eds), *Gwaith Llywelyn Fardd I ac Eraill o Feirdd y Ddeuddegfed Ganrif* (Caerdydd, 1994), no. 15 (Englynion cylchu Cymru); J. E. Caerwyn Williams (ed.), *Gwaith Meilyr Brydydd a'i Ddisgynyddion* (Caerdydd, 1994), no. 1 (anonymous); N. G. Costigan (Bosco) *et al.* (eds), *Gwaith Dafydd Benfras ac Eraill o Feirdd Hanner Cyntaf y Drydedd Ganrif ar Ddeg* (Caerdydd, 1995), no. 25.

[12] James Campbell, *Essays in Anglo-Saxon History* (London, 1986), p. 220.

[13] Williams (ed.), *Gwaith Meilyr Brydydd*, no. 7, ll. 63, 85; no. 10, l. 15 (Gwalchmai ap Meilyr); Costigan *et al.* (eds), *Gwaith Dafydd Benfras*, no. 27, l. 10 ('Mawr ben Cymru wen a'i chymhenrwydd', Dafydd Benfras).

[14] Susan Reynolds, *Kingdoms and Communities in Western Europe, 900–1300* (Oxford, 1984), p. 261.

Flemings within Wales itself.[15] That was a recognition that there was, or could be, a distinction between ethnic identity and geographical identity; it was a distinction which was pregnant for the future. If pressed to identify the distinctive features of Welsh identity – or indeed of ethnic identity generally – our medieval forebears would readily have drawn up a list – laws, customs, lifestyles, dress, language, *mores*, economic practice would figure on it. In certain respects, indeed, the separate identity of the Welsh from their neighbours the English was brought into sharper focus as the twelfth and thirteenth centuries progressed – with the formalizing and institutionalizing of the legal and administrative distinctions between them within Wales itself, and with the periodic rhetorical hyping of the distinction, by both parties, for their own political purposes.[16] Thus, to cite two well-known instances, when the papal legate in 1267 declared it his intention to bring 'the war and discord . . . between the English and the Welsh' to an end, or when the burgesses of Llan-faes complained in 1295–6 that they were treated as English in Wales and Welsh in England, we capture the reality and importance of ethnic distinctions in Britain.[17]

The Welsh for their part were equally convinced, and indeed protective, of their identity as a people. They may have exulted in their British ancestry and in their claim to be the true proprietors of Britain, but from at least the tenth century – as the poem *Armes Prydein* makes abundantly clear[18] – they had been comfortable with the vernacular collective term, *Cymry*. Their law texts drew a distinction between the *Cymro* and the alien (*alltud*) and spoke of the privileged position of the freeman born to Welsh parents (*Cymro famtad*).[19] Local, regional, dynastic and kindred loyalties certainly figured prominently in medieval Wales; but not to the exclusion of the emblems of a common Welsh identity – law, customs, language, mythology and borders. Indeed these emblems were arguably cultivated and exploited more vigorously than ever before in the thirteenth century.

---

[15] Thomas Philips (ed.), *Cartularium S. Johannis Baptistae de Carmarthen* (Cheltenham, 1865), p. 33; and, for a late example (1223), William Dugdale (ed.), *Monasticon Anglicanum* (6 vols, revised edn, London, 1817–30), V, p. 267.

[16] R. R. Davies, 'The Peoples of Britain and Ireland, 1100–1400: I. Identities', *TRHS*, 6th series, 4 (1994), 1–20; idem, *Domination and Conquest: The Experience of Ireland, Scotland and Wales 1100–1300* (Cambridge, 1990), pp. 116–18.

[17] J. Goronwy Edwards (ed.), *Littere Wallie* (henceforth *LW*) (Cardiff, 1935), p. 1; William Rees (ed.), *Calendar of Ancient Petitions Relating to Wales* (Cardiff, 1975), p. 82. Many other examples could be quoted, for example *Close Rolls* (henceforward *CR*), *1242–7*, pp. 423, 519 (*guerra inter regem et Wallenses; guerra contra Wallenses*).

[18] Pryce, 'British or Welsh', 779, n. 20. See also David N. Dumville, 'Brittany and "Armes Prydein Vawr"', *Études Celtiques*, 20 (1983), 145–59.

[19] Jenkins (ed.), *Llyfr Colan*, § 530; Aled Rhys Wiliam (ed.), *Llyfr Iorwerth* (Cardiff, 1960), § 89; Stephen J. Williams and J. Enoch Powell (eds), *Cyfreithiau Hywel Dda yn ôl Llyfr Blegywryd* (Caerdydd, 1942), p. 58.

That, for example, was the significance of the claim advanced by Llywelyn ap Gruffudd – and echoed by others – that 'the Welsh should enjoy their . . . laws and customs as did other nations' (*naciones*).[20] By this definition a people was not simply an aggregation of individuals; it was a corporate community with its own rights, liberties and identity. There was explosive potential here. 'A nation', commented Max Weber, 'is a community of sentiment.' Susan Reynolds echoes his view: 'The nation itself is the product of its members' belief that it exists.'[21] By those definitions the Welsh by the thirteenth century were not only an identifiable people; they also seemed to be on the way to making themselves into a nation. That was the challenge which the English faced.

From this cursory review we can conclude that the terms Wales and Welsh (in both their various vernacular and Latin forms) were securely established and uncontentious terms in the vocabulary and world-views of both the English or Anglo-Normans and the Welsh by the twelfth century. Why, therefore, did they become in a measure contested terms thereafter, and particularly from *c.*1200?

We might begin by reasserting that words and labels – including the names of countries and peoples – are not value-free terms; they are a way of constructing and categorizing the world. As such, their connotations and usage are subject to change, as perceptions alter and power relationships are modified. One of those changes has recently been admirably analysed and documented by Huw Pryce. He has shown how in Cambro-Latin writings – that is, works written in Latin in Wales – the terms 'Britannia' and 'Britones' were steadily replaced by the terms 'Wallia' and 'Walenses' from *c.*1130, quite probably (so he argues) in response to the impact of Anglo-Norman terminology.[22] The Welsh certainly did not abandon their grand British memories and dreams, but they had adjusted their terminology to the world in which they lived and to the language of their neighbours.

Ultimately more important and more challenging was what happened within Wales itself. From the late eleventh century the Anglo-Norman lords began to bring parts of southern and eastern Wales in particular under their sway, colonized them with English and Flemish settlers, and

[20] For all this, and for supporting evidence, see R. R. Davies, 'Law and National Identity in Thirteenth-Century Wales', in idem, Ralph A. Griffiths, Ieuan Gwynedd Jones and Kenneth O. Morgan (eds), *Welsh Society and Nationhood: Historical Essays Presented to Glanmor Williams* (Cardiff, 1984), pp. 51–69.

[21] John Hutchinson and Anthony D. Smith (eds), *Nationalism* (Oxford, 1994), p. 25; Reynolds, *Kingdoms and Communities*, p. 253.

[22] Pryce, 'British or Welsh?', 775–801.

established castles, boroughs, monasteries and manors throughout them. The heroic age of this act of conquest, colonization and settlement was the century or so after 1070. It arguably altered the pattern of power and the ethnic configuration of Wales more profoundly than any sequence of events in the history of the country until the industrialization of the country. It was bound, sooner or later, to pose a challenge to the adequacy of the terminology for describing the country and its peoples. The challenge was originally met in two rather limited ways. As far as the country was concerned, no effort was at first made to invent a single word to describe the areas brought under Anglo-Norman control. Rather were the *conquistadores* either content to adopt (and often to mangle) the existing Welsh regional and local names (for example, Glamorgan, Brecon) or to create a new lordship, honorial and manorial terminology. As far as the settlers were concerned they clearly had to be distinguished from the ethnic Welsh (*Walenses*). This was readily done – as the evidence amply shows – by addressing them as 'the French, the English' and, where necessary, 'the Flemings in Wales' (*in Wallia*). That was at least an acknowledgement that Wales was now a land of multiple peoples.[23]

The next stage in the process seems to have happened in the second half of the twelfth century. Two major reasons seem to have inaugurated it. The one, and the less important, was the abandonment in England (and more or less simultaneously, as it happens, in Scotland) of multiple address clauses, that is, the habit of greeting the French (Norman) and English as separate groups. This was a recognition of the regnal solidarity of both of these countries; men (and women) could in effect be greeted simply as citizens or subjects without reference to their ethnic background.[24] This was not a solution which could be adopted in Wales (or for that matter in Ireland). The country clearly lacked 'regnal solidarity'; it was profoundly divided ethnically. The distinction between the Welsh and the English *in Wales* remained dominant; indeed, as has been suggested above, it was more deeply entrenched and institutionalized in the thirteenth century.[25] Wales was to remain a land of two peoples. That meant that the word 'Welsh' was henceforward contentious. In a fashion it has remained so ever since.

The second reason which helped to inaugurate a shift in terminology came with the growing awareness that the division, fluid as it was, of Wales into areas respectively under native Welsh and Anglo-Norman control was

---

[23] This comment is based on a review of the charter evidence (ecclesiastical and secular) for the period.

[24] For England, see R. C. van Caenegem, *The Birth of the English Common Law* (Cambridge, 1973), p. 139, n. 34; for Scotland, see G. W. S. Barrow (ed.), *Regesta Regum Scottorum*, II, *The Acts of William I* (Edinburgh, 1971), p. 77.

[25] See, for example, *LW*, p. 28 (1259: 'the English and Welsh of the king').

to remain a permanent, or semi-permanent, feature of the landscape of power and loyalty in the country. By c.1170 at the latest it must have been increasingly clear that Wales was not likely to be readily conquered as a whole (as had earlier been confidently asserted). By then the good and worthwhile lands which could be seized had been seized; the momentum of the colonizing movement was in decline; the king of England preferred *détente* to further confrontation with the Welsh; and the Welsh for their part had showed – notably under Owain Gwynedd (d. 1170) and the Lord Rhys (d. 1197) – that on their own terrain they could be formidable military opponents. In short, an uneasy equilibrium of power had been attained between native rule and foreign settlement in Wales.

That ultimately required a new terminology to be created. And so it was. It was from about the late 1160s or so that the terms 'the March' or 'the March of Wales' begin to appear with growing regularity, especially in the royal documentation. It was a convenient blanket term to describe the plurality of lordships which composed the districts of Wales under English control.[26] Terminology often follows where power had already led; it did so on this occasion. By the early thirteenth century the term had been fully accepted (though it had not been, nor ever was to be, defined). Nothing could make that clearer than the fact that it was constitutionally canonized, as it were, by being mentioned in clause 56 of Magna Carta in 1215 and by the fact that royal letters could refer to the barons of the March (*barones de Marchia*) as if they were a well-known and identifiable body.[27]

The new terminology was an indication that a new landscape of power had emerged in Wales. The consequences were spelled out very soon. Magna Carta c.56 made it clear that the law of the March (of Wales) was to be distinguished from the law of Wales as well as from that of England. It remained to work out the political implications of the distinction between 'Wales' and 'the March of Wales'. Many of the early references to the term 'March' (or 'Marches') are simply locational: 'to the March', 'in the March', etc.[28] But when Henry III's advisers articulated a contrast between the tenants of 'the earls and barons of England in the parts of

---

[26] See, most recently, Kevin Mann, 'The March of Wales: a Question of Terminology', *WHR*, 18, no. 1 (1996), 1–13; Brock W. Holden, 'The Making of the Middle March of Wales, 1066–1250', *WHR*, 20, no. 2 (2001), 207–26. An alternative to 'the March' was to refer to the area as 'our Englishry' (*de Angelcheria nostra*), *CR 1254–68*, p. 497.

[27] Magna Carta, *c.*56; *Rotulus Litterarum Clausarum* (Record Commission, 1833), I, p. 12 (1204); *Rotuli Litterarum Patentium 1201–16* (Record Commission, 1835), pp. 88, 100, 109 etc.; *Patent Rolls* (henceforward *PR*) *1216–25*, p. 109 (1217); *CR 1231–4*, p. 312 (1233).

[28] *PR 1225–32*, p. 81; *CR 1231–4*, pp. 131, 341, 343, 360 etc.

Wales', elsewhere termed 'our magnates of the March', on the one hand, and 'the magnates of Wales' (by whom he meant the leaders of native Welsh society), on the other, he was making it clear that there were now *two* power units in the geographical 'Wales', and that he was ultimate lord of both groups.[29] It was the sweeping English victories from 1240 which allowed the king to exploit the terminological opportunities to the full. In particular, the critical Treaty of Woodstock (30 April 1247), which was concluded at the high-water mark of English domination of Wales in Henry III's reign, institutionalized the distinction between Wales (*Wallia*) and the March of Wales (*Marchia Wallie*) in its clauses.[30]

There would be no going back on this division. Wales might survive as a geographical expression, but as a term of political art and power it had been replaced by the twin concepts of 'Wales' (in a restricted sense) and 'the March of Wales'. Even Llywelyn ap Gruffudd in the years of his remarkable success 1256–76 accepted the distinction as the working premise for the reordering of the balance of power in the country.[31] Thus, in a desperate last-minute set of proposals he made to Edward I in early 1277, Llywelyn distinguished between 'the barons of Wales' to be judged by 'their peers in Wales' (*Wallia*) on the one hand and 'the English barons in the March' who were to be judged by 'the customs of the March' (*consuetudines Marchie*) on the other.[32] Later that year the overwhelming success of the English campaign of 1277 allowed Edward I to impose the most demeaning terms on Llywelyn at the Treaty of Aberconwy in November 1277. What proved to be much the most contentious clause in that treaty was the one which provided that disputes should be settled 'according to the laws of the March for cases arising in the March and according to the laws of Wales for disputes arising in Wales'.[33] The March/Wales duality had again been formally and jurisdictionally confirmed.

The emergence and acceptance of the duality was no more than a recognition that Wales was, and had been for a long time, a divided, half-conquered country. The word 'March' helped to cope with the power realities and the terminological awkwardness prompted by that situation. But it did not resolve it, even terminologically. It did *not* make it clear what

---

[29] *CR 1237–42*, pp. 124–5; but it is also to be observed that in this sequence of important letters the king also referred to 'the magnates of North Wales and Powys'.

[30] *LW*, pp. 9–10 (1241), pp. 7–8 (1247).

[31] Thomas Rymer (ed.), *Foedera, Conventiones, Litterae* etc. (revised edn, 4 vols, London, 1816–69), I, p. 404. For discussion, see J. Beverley Smith, *Llywelyn ap Gruffudd: Prince of Wales* (Cardiff, 1998), pp. 129–32; but note that the quotation at n. 157 is incomplete and thereby does not identify the mutuality of the obligation – on both parties.

[32] J. Beverley Smith, 'Offra Principis Wallie Domino Regi', *BBCS*, 21, Part 4 (1966), 362–7, and for discussion Smith, *Llywelyn ap Gruffudd*, pp. 409–11.

[33] *LW*, p. 120.

exactly was 'the March' and thereby what was 'Wales'. It was on the rock of that ambiguity (arguably a deliberate ambiguity) that the peace settlement of 1277 eventually foundered.[34] Furthermore the adoption of the word 'March' had obvious implications for the meaning – or perhaps more correctly meanings – of the word Wales. Directly or otherwise it raised the questions 'What was Wales?' and 'Whose Wales was it?' It is to those issues which we now turn.

Wales, as we have seen, was a well-accepted term of geography and even of sentiment among English and Welsh alike. But it was not as yet a term or concept of political discourse or power. In so far as political leaders in Wales gave themselves designations, they were overwhelmingly patrilineal or regional titles. Occasionally they might be referred to as king or head of Wales, but in a metaphorical and adulatory context, rather than as a specific political claim, least of all *vis-à-vis* other princes or dynasties in Wales.[35] Significantly the only major recorded occasion on which the term *Wallia* was used in the royal style – as *rex Wallie* – in the twelfth century was in Owain Gwynedd's correspondence with Louis VII in the 1160s.[36] The context in which the term was deployed on this occasion – in negotiations with a foreign king – of itself indicates the measure of challenge and pretension, the shaping of new political claims, that might inhere in the word. It was in the thirteenth century, and in the service of the house of Gwynedd and its policies, that this potential was realized.

Even when we have made due allowance for the sharp increase in the amount of surviving documentary evidence, it is striking how frequently and, as it were, casually the princes of Gwynedd now appropriated the term 'Wales' for their own purposes. A brief selection of examples will make the point. Llywelyn ab Iorwerth might (notwithstanding the style he normally used) be called 'lord of Wales' (*dominus Wallie*); his wife could be saluted as lady of Wales on her death; he could promise not to receive the

---

[34] For the Arwystli dispute, see J. Conway Davies (ed.), *The Welsh Assize Roll 1277–84* (Cardiff, 1940), esp. pp. 38–81; Smith, *Llywelyn ap Gruffudd*, pp. 470–93; idem, 'England and Wales: the Conflict of Laws', in Michael Prestwich, R. H. Britnell and Robin Frame (eds), *Thirteenth Century England*, VII (Woodbridge, 1999), pp. 189–205; R. R. Davies, *The King of England and the Prince of Wales 1277–84: Law, Politics and Power* (Cambridge, 2003).

[35] Thus the *Brut* could refer to Gruffudd ap Cynan as 'tywysog Gwynedd a phen a brenin . . . Cymru oll' or to the Lord Rhys as 'tywysog Deheubarth ac anorchfygedig ben holl Cymru', Thomas Jones (ed. and trans.), *Brut y Tywysogyon: or The Chronicle of the Princes: Peniarth MS. 20 Version* (henceforth *BT P20*) (Cardiff, 1952), *sub annis*.

[36] Huw Pryce, 'Owain Gwynedd and Louis VII: the Franco-Welsh Diplomacy of the First Prince of Wales', *WHR*, 19, no. 1 (1998), 265–81. See also J. Beverley Smith, 'Owain Gwynedd', *TCHS*, 32 (1971), 8–17.

king's enemies 'in Wales'; his grandson, Llywelyn ap Gruffudd, could refer to his chief officer as the steward or the justiciar 'of Wales' and talk of his 'bailiffs of Wales' and the 'merchants of Wales'; likewise he could announce that the treachery of Gruffudd of Powys was notorious and public 'throughout Wales'; he could even grandly refer to the rights (*jura*) of himself and his ancestors 'in Wales'.[37] If the princes themselves could use the word so freely, it was little wonder that their poets showed no restraint in praising the all-Wales claims of their princely patrons: 'true king of Wales', 'great head of Wales', 'the man who was for Wales' were the kinds of tributes which came readily to their pens.[38] If we make due allowance for the poetic licence involved in such hyperbolic phrases, we will find that they are not far removed from the comments made in the contemporary narrative sources. It was not without a measure of justification, for example, that the native Latin chronicler remarked of Llywelyn ab Iorwerth in 1215 that he held 'the monarchy and principality of almost the whole of Wales' and called him 'prince of the whole of Wales' (*totius Wallie*) four years later. By 1264 his grandson had achieved the same status as 'prince over all Wales'.[39]

The princes of Gwynedd seemed to have appropriated 'Wales' for their own lexicon and purposes. Even the English government seemed to have conceded as much: when it now referred to 'Wallia' or 'the (Welsh) barons of Wales' it was not the whole of geographical Wales which it had in mind, but the area controlled by native rulers and that, in effect, meant by the prince of Gwynedd and his native dependants. 'Wales' had, as it were,

---

[37] David Stephenson, *Thirteenth-Century Welsh Law Courts* (Aberystwyth, 1980), p. 12 (*dominus Wallie*): *BT, P20 s.a.* 1237 'arglwyddes Cymru'; *Cal. Patent Rolls 1232–47*, p. 130; H. R. Luard (ed.), *Annales Monastici* (5 vols, London, 1864–9), I, p. 101 (*domina Wallie*); Rymer (ed.), *Foedera*, I, p. 150 (*in Wallia*, 1218); *LW*, pp. 26, 85 (justiciar of Wales): J. Goronwy Edwards (ed.), *Calendar of Ancient Correspondence Concerning Wales* (henceforth *CACW*) (Cardiff, 1935), p. 69 (bailiffs of Wales); *LW*, p. 185 (merchants of Wales); ibid., pp. 45, 138, 169, 174 (all documents issued by Llywelyn ap Gruffudd); W. W. Shirley (ed.), *Royal . . . Letters . . . of the Reign of Henry III* (2 vols, London, 1862–6), p. 314 (*jura nostra in Wallia*). Note also the charter of Gruffudd Maelor (d. 1269) of northern Powys referring to 'the lord of Wales', presumably Llywelyn ap Gruffudd: Frederic Seebohm, *The Tribal System in Wales* (London, 1895), appendix D, pp. 103–4. Huw Pryce has recently argued that by adopting the title 'prince of Aberffraw and lord of Snowdon' *c.*1230 Llywelyn ab Iorwerth was 'effectively proclaiming himself prince of Wales': 'Negotiating Anglo-Welsh Relations: Llywelyn the Great and Henry III', in Björn K. U. Weiler and Ifor W. Rowlands (eds), *England and Europe in the Reign of Henry III (1216–72)* (Aldershot, 2002), pp. 13–29, at p. 20.

[38] For examples, see Costigan *et al.* (eds), *Gwaith Dafydd Benfras*, no. 5, l. 8 (Einion Wan); nos 26, l. 46; 27, l. 60; 30, ll. 77–8 (Dafydd Benfras).

[39] Jones (ed.), 'Cronica de Wallia', *s.a.* 1216; J. Williams ab Ithel (ed.), *Annales Cambrie* (London, 1860), *s.a.* 1219; *BT, P20, s.a.* 1264.

contracted into what was occasionally known as *pura Wallia*;[40] it was, negatively, that part of geographical Wales which could not be categorized as 'the March of Wales'.

There was more to this reiteration of the word Wales than mere verbal usage. Terms are part of 'the things we do with words', as the title of J. L. Austin's famous book put it. Wales was just such a term. Its bland simplicity concealed the fact that it was part of the programme to construct the ideology and justify the structures of a new political unit, the principality of Wales. This is not the place to lay out the arguments and evidence for such a claim. Much of it has in any case already been persuasively and expertly advanced, in particular by J. Goronwy Edwards and J. Beverley Smith.[41] We will content ourselves instead with explaining briefly the role of the concept and term 'Wales' in the attempt to create the new polity.

If a new, unitary polity was to be shaped in native Wales, it required features which proclaimed its distinctiveness and demarcated its individuality. One feature was already to hand, native law. No one could deny that the Welsh had their own law, but the role it could play in helping to promote the forging of a Welsh political unit remained to be exploited. The men of the thirteenth century set to the task with a will. The prologues of the law texts – none of which in their present form predates the thirteenth century – announced that the laws had been revised by Hywel Dda 'as prince of the whole of Wales', at an assembly of men 'from every cantref in Wales' and the curse of 'the whole of Wales' was to be visited on those who failed to observe them in Wales. Thirteenth-century inquiries served to underline the national status of Welsh law: it was, so it was claimed, 'the common law' of Wales; it ran 'throughout Wales and the Marches as far as the power of the Welsh extends'; it was even claimed that Edward I had acknowledged that Welsh law should be enjoyed by all Welshmen. It is little wonder that defence of the law of Wales became the rallying call for Welshmen in the last desperate years of native Welsh independence. It remained the emblem of their common ethnicity, if not their nationality, at the very time when the vision of a quasi-independent polity was evaporating before their eyes.[42]

Polities need their own laws and jurisdiction as manifestations of their individuality: they also need, as political scientists observe, a common

---

[40] A particularly revealing usage of the word 'Wallia' in this restricted 'Welsh' sense is the letter of July 1262 which asserted that Llywelyn was not 'verus heres Wallie': *CR 1261–4*, p. 143. Usages of the phrase *pura Wallia* are rare; but see, for example, C. T. Martin (ed.), *Registrum . . . Johannis Peckham* (3 vols, London, 1882–5), II, p. 440.

[41] *LW*, esp. pp. xxxvi–l; Smith, *Llywelyn ap Gruffudd*, chap. 6.

[42] See Davies, 'Law and National Identity', in idem *et al.* (eds), *Welsh Society and Nationhood*, n. 20; also Huw Pryce, 'The Prologues to the Welsh Lawbooks', *BBCS*, 33 (1986), 151–87.

ideology and mythology. The Welsh already enjoyed a rich and resonant common literary and pseudo-historical heritage, concentrating in particular on the glorious past (and prophetic future) of the sovereignty of the Island of Britain and the historically umbilical link with the men of the Old North. What such a heritage lacked was a specifically Wales – as opposed to Britain – focus on the one hand and a realistic and contemporary political agenda on the other. It was in the thirteenth century, and to meet the needs of an embryonic principality of Wales, that these needs began to be met. Mythologically, the descent of the Welsh from Brutus and particularly from his son Camber began to figure more prominently in the literature, genealogies and polemic of the period. Thus, in Llywelyn ap Gruffudd's eloquent rebuttal of the demeaning terms offered to him by Edward I in November 1282, the argument was repeatedly reiterated that his right (*ius*) in Wales (*in Wallia*) dated from the time of Brutus (*a tempore Bruti*). In short, his historical claim was neither to Britain nor to Gwynedd; it was to Wales.[43]

Even more important was it to instil this new (and restricted) Wales with a sense of a common political unity, in short to nurture a political culture of common purpose. Given the deep-seated regional and dynastic loyalties within this Wales and the federative character of such hegemonies as had been built in the past, this would be no easy task. Most of that task would be a matter of force, persuasion and power, but it was also underwritten by a self-conscious, if simple, ideology – that of unity (*unitas*). One Welsh native leader was to be 'of one war, counsel and aid' with Llywelyn ap Gruffudd; another was to be 'of one war and one peace' with him; his allies were warned of the consequences of withdrawing from his 'fealty and unity'; when his own brother was reconciled with him it was to his 'unity', and on his own terms, that he was restored. The recurrent use of the phrase suggests that Llywelyn and his advisers had a clear vision: the supremacy of Gwynedd was the prelude to the unity of a new-fangled political unit, a unitary native Wales.[44]

Above all what this new polity, Wales, needed if it was to develop and thrive as a credible political unit were the features of 'regnal solidarity' as identified by Susan Reynolds. This is precisely what the two Llywelyns sought to provide in so far as circumstances – and in particular the

---

[43] J. Beverley Smith, *The Sense of History in Medieval Wales* (Aberystwyth, 1989); Rachel Bromwich, 'Cyfeiriadau Traddodiadol a Chwedlonol y Gogynfeirdd' in Morfydd E. Owen and Brynley F. Roberts (eds), *Beirdd a Thywysogion: Barddoniaeth Llys yng Nghymru, Iwerddon a'r Alban* (Caerdydd, 1996), pp. 202–18; Martin (ed.), *Registrum . . . Johannis Peckham*, II, pp. 469–71.

[44] *LW*, pp. 35, 41, 79, 104, 138 (1261–78); Shirley (ed.), *Royal Letters of Henry III*, II, p. 312.

opportunities of English politics – allowed them to do so. They set out to do nothing less than to shape the new Wales into a streamlined, unitary polity. They demoted the other leaders of native society in this Wales to the status of 'magnates', 'lords' and (borrowing from English practice) 'barons'; they bound them to themselves by contracts, oaths, homage and threats; they presided over their territorial and marital ambitions; and they forged them into a political community – 'the magnates of Wales' – which was virtually a high court for the new polity and whose support could be cited as the sanction for their own actions, including defying the king of England. In short, they were attempting to create a 'community of the realm' in the new Wales.[45]

What measure of sustained and sustainable success would attend this exercise was still very doubtful. The events of 1240–55 and again 1277–82 showed the utter fragility and vulnerability of the experiment. But that should not lead us to underestimate what was being attempted. J. Goronwy Edwards, that most astute and measured of commentators, had no doubt on that score: Llywelyn ap Gruffudd, he remarked, 'was striving to make himself chief lord, in other words to establish a suzerain within Wales itself'. Prince Llywelyn made the same point with particular bluntness and directness in a famous letter to the king of England in July 1273: 'the rights of our principality are entirely separate from the rights of your kingdom, although we hold our principality under your royal power'. Llywelyn tended to overlook the force of the qualifying clause of his own statement; it was the initial claim of his declaration which was the political credo of the new polity he was attempting to establish.[46]

For us here it is the role of the word and concept 'Wales' in that credo which is of particular interest. It was, as we have seen, a word which the princes of Gwynedd had in effect hijacked – and been allowed to hijack – for their own purposes.[47] They assumed that Wales, *Wallia*, was theirs, though they could only do so by modifying the meaning of the word, and by replacing a geographical definition by a political designation. Their rhetoric echoed to the sound of the word: they spoke grandly, for example, of justice and equity according to the state of Wales (*status Wallie*); they referred to 'our principality of Wales' and 'its liberties'. The high-water mark of their success, both terminologically and substantively, was the Treaty of Montgomery in 1267, in which the king of England (albeit reluctantly) conceded to Llywelyn and his heirs the title 'prince of Wales'

---

[45] Smith, *Llywelyn ap Gruffudd*, pp. 285–309; Davies, *Age of Conquest*, pp. 318–20. For appeals to the sanction of 'the magnates of Wales', see *CACW*, p. 50; *BT, P20, s.a.* 1275; Shirley (ed.), *Royal Letters of Henry III*, II, pp. 284–5, 312.

[46] *LW*, p. xlvi; *CACW*, p. 86.

[47] See above, pp. 54–6.

and 'the principality of Wales', and added to this grant 'the fealty and homages of all the Welsh barons of Wales'.[48]

J. Goronwy Edwards had no doubt that Llywelyn had secured for himself and his heirs 'a position which legally was as near independence as they could hope to attain'.[49] That is to express Llywelyn's achievement in legal and constitutional terms. In terms of nation building and state formation it might not be too much to claim that the first tentative steps had been taken to establish a Wales as a unitary polity, to marry such regnal solidarity as had been achieved to an existing, if fractured, community of sentiment, law, language and ethnicity. In that process the word and concept 'Wales' (as interpreted by the two Llywelyns and their spokesmen and advisers) had been very effectively exploited, if also distorted. In Scotland likewise it was in the thirteenth century that 'the name Scotia, Écosse, "Scotland" . . . came finally and definitively to be synonymous with the kingdom of the Scots . . . the political entity to which all Scots belonged'.[50] But there the similarity between the new-born *principatus Wallie* and the much older *regnum Scocie* ended. The *principatus Wallie* was never co-extensive with geographical Wales; its regnal solidarity and political viability were only skin-deep. By 1282–3 it had been demolished. Though the concept of 'the principality of Wales' had a strange and utterly anomalous after-life as the term for the royal lands in north and west Wales,[51] the term 'Wales' reverted to what it had once been – a geographical expression for an area that was politically dependent on, and annexed to, England.

In truth, the Anglo-Normans and the English continued to use the word 'Wales' in a general geographical sense; they had certainly not surrendered to the political pretensions implied in the virtual annexation of the word by the princes of Gwynedd–Wales. 'Wales' was for them simply a geographical unit, part of the orbit of power of the king of England and his aristocracy. As to its pretensions to a separate political status, Gerald of Wales had succinctly expressed what was no doubt the official and universal view: 'Wales is a portion of the kingdom of England, and not a kingdom in itself'.[52] But such terminological clarity was clouded by at least two developments. The first, as we have seen, was the adoption of the term

---

[48] *CACW*, p. 9 (*status Wallie*); Shirley (ed.), *Royal Letters Henry III*, II, pp. 284–7; P. Chaplais (ed.), *Diplomatic Documents, I, 1101–1272* (London, 1964), no. 411 (liberties); *LW*, pp. 1–4 (Treaty of Montgomery, 1267); *CACW*, p. 52 (reluctance).

[49] *LW*, p. xlix.

[50] G. W. S. Barrow, *Kingship and Unity: Scotland 1000–1306* (London, 1981), p. 153. Cf. idem, *The Anglo-Norman Era in Scottish History* (Oxford, 1980), pp. 153–5; Dauvit Broun, 'Defining Scotland and the Scots before the Wars of Independence', in idem, R. J. Finlay and M. Lynch (eds), *Image and Identity: The Making and Re-making of Scotland through the Ages* (Edinburgh, 1998), pp. 4–19.

[51] See below, pp. 62–3.

[52] Brewer *et al.* (eds), *Giraldi Cambrensis Opera*, III, p. 166.

'March of Wales'.[53] Once that term was coined and regularly used, the meaning of the word 'Wales' would be subject to change, as the area came to be contrasted with the March of Wales. The second development was to slip into the usage – possibly for reasons of convenience and shorthand – of accepting the equation of Wales, *Wallia*, with the area which was directly or indirectly under native Welsh rule, that is, the area beyond the March of Wales. Particularly was this likely to happen when the fortunes of the prince of Gwynedd and his control of his fellow and client rulers were in the ascendant. The terminology in which an agreement was struck by the minority government of Henry III with Llywelyn ab Iorwerth and Worcester in March 1218 may serve as an example of how this usage took root and what were its implications. By its terms Llywelyn promised that he would strive that 'all the magnates of the whole of Wales' (*omnes magnates totius Wallie*) would come to the king, as their liege lord, to do homage and swear fealty; he also promised that he would not receive any enemy of the lord king 'in Wales' (*in Wallia*). We must not, of course, read too much into this choice of the use of the word; but it is clear that 'Wales' is now in some measure a specialized term of political and diplomatic art, not merely a geographical description (for Llywelyn self-evidently did not have power over all the magnates of geographical Wales).[54]

To that extent, the Welsh were winning the terminological contest, appropriating the term *Wallia* to describe that part of Wales which was still under their control. There were, broadly speaking, two – and to some extent supplementary – responses which the English government could adopt to this challenge. The first was the cornerstone of English policy towards the political pretensions of the princes of Gwynedd in the thirteenth century. It accepted the equation of the term *Wallia* with the native-controlled part of Wales; it also accepted, indeed encouraged, the notion that the leaders of this region should be called the magnates, nobles or barons (the increasingly preferred term) of Wales, *barones Wallie*, thereby distinguishing them from the barons of the March, *barones Marchie*.[55] But equally it insisted that the homage and services of these 'barons of Wales' (as well as those of the March) were owed directly to the king of England, *not* to or through the prince of Gwynedd. Such a policy accepted the new definition of the word 'Wallia', but vigorously denied the political pretensions of a unitary polity of native Wales which the princes of Gwynedd were seeking to build around the term.[56]

---

[53] See above, p. 52.

[54] Rymer (ed.), *Foedera*, I, pp. 149–50; for discussion, Smith, *Llywelyn ap Gruffudd*, pp. 21–3.

[55] For a contemporary list of the barons of the March, see *CR 1259–61*, pp. 23–4.

[56] J. Goronwy Edwards in *LW*, pp. xlvi–l.

This English policy was recurrently pursued and restated. It was acted upon when English power was in the ascendant – for example, in the Worcester accord of 1218 (cited above), in the famous letter dispatched from Tewkesbury in March 1238 to scotch Llywelyn ab Iorwerth's pretensions, in the series of demeaning treaties imposed on the house of Gwynedd in the 1240s, and frequently thereafter until the Treaty of Montgomery of 1267.[57] The implications of such a claim were potentially fatal to any concept of a unitary native principality of Wales. The native leaders could be classified quite simply as 'the barons of the lord king' (as was Gruffudd ap Gwenwynwyn in 1240); they could be collectively referred to as '*our* barons of Wales'; even the greatest of them, Llywelyn ap Gruffudd of Gwynedd himself, could be referred to as no more than the foremost of 'our magnates of Wales' and bracketed along with these other magnates.[58] When 'Wales' was interpreted in this fashion it became the term not for establishing a new polity for the Welsh, but for absorbing native Wales into the framework, language and mechanism of English power.

Such also was in effect the implication of the second method used by the English to neutralize any threat involved in the word *Wallia*. For the princes of Gwynedd, *Wallia* became the catchword for their attempt to establish a unitary polity in native Wales. Two events marked important stages in the realization of their dream: the assumption of the title 'prince of Wales' from 1258 and especially after 1262, and the formal acknowledge-ment of the title and with it of the existence of 'the principality of Wales' (*principatus Wallie*) by the English authorities in 1267.[59] Equally, it was the aim of the English, whenever they could, to frustrate this ambition. They did so pointedly by denying any title to the son and grandsons of Llywelyn ab Iorwerth until they were compelled to recognize the title 'prince of Wales' in 1267. Even more significant for the purposes of our argument is the way they sought to reappropriate, and demote, the term 'Wales' for their own purposes. It was quite simply 'our land' (*terra nostra*); as 'our land of Wales' (*terra nostra Wallie*), it was quite distinct in status from the kingdom (*regnum*) of England. Likewise the documents associated with the crushing English victory in 1277 could refer to 'the land of Wales' almost in the same breath as 'the land of Anglesey'.[60] Paradoxically, Llywelyn was allowed to retain the title 'prince of Wales' in the demeaning settlement

[57] *CR 1237–42*, pp. 123–4; *LW*, pp. 6, 8, 9; *CR 1261–4*, p. 143, etc.

[58] *LW*, p. 5; *CR 1242–7*, p. 348; *1256–9*, p. 107; Davies (ed.), *The Welsh Assize Roll*, p. 59.

[59] David Stephenson, 'Llywelyn ap Gruffydd and the Struggle for the Principality of Wales, 1258–82', *THSC* (1983), 36–47.

[60] *CR 1247–51*, p. 5; *1251–3*, p. 419; *1253–4*, p. 110; *LW*, p. 103.

imposed on him that year. It was now a mocking title. He had lost the battle for his vision of his Wales. His failure to come to terms with that loss and his desperate attempts to salvage some of the authority he had once enjoyed in his Wales in the struggle with Gruffudd ap Gwenwynwyn drove him eventually to revolt, or at least to join the revolt. In 1282–3 Edward I went in for the kill. *Wallia delenda est.*

The struggle in thirteenth-century Wales was, of course, much more than a dispute about a term; but as so often in human history the fortunes of language, concepts and terminology open a window onto the world of power and the constructions which men and women deploy to interpret it for their own ends. So it is with the word 'Wales'. The epilogue can be brief. For the Welsh, the events of 1282–3 were little less than apocalyptic. 'All Wales was cast to the ground' was the pithy comment of the native annalist. 'Ys terfyn byd?' (Is it the end of the world?) was the even more poignant question of the poet.[61] The poet's comment was, arguably, the more apt. A world had been shattered; a political vision had been brutally and utterly extinguished.

Terminologically, the English victory was complete. Wales was once more – as Scotland was to be after 1305 – simply a land, *terra Wallie*. It was not a kingdom nor a principality; it had no regnal solidarity, no unitary political or administrative existence; it was not even a country. It was united and annexed to the Crown of England as a parcel of the same. The problem of what was Wales and what Wales was had apparently been solved. But in fact the ambiguity remained. Edward I might issue a Statute of Wales; his chancery might open a new secretarial dossier called 'the rolls of Wales' (*rotuli Wallie*); and his documents could refer to a chancellor, treasurer and justiciar 'of Wales'.[62] But the Wales in question was not a geographical Wales, but such of Wales has had been under native rule until 1277–82. It is not least of the ironies of history that Llywelyn's native principality survived his death; it was reincarnated in the new, royal principality of Wales.[63]

By the same token Edward I did not, nor did he try to, reintegrate

[61] Thomas Jones (ed.), *Brenhinedd y Saesson or The Kings of the Saxons* (Cardiff, 1971), *s.a.* 1282; Rhian M. Andrews, N. G. Costigan (Bosco), Christine James, Peredur I. Lynch, Catherine McKenna, Morfydd E. Owen and Brynley F. Roberts (eds), *Gwaith Bleddyn Fardd a Beirdd Eraill Ail Hanner y Drydedd Ganrif ar Ddeg* (Caerdydd, 1996), no. 51, l. 23 (Bleddyn Fardd).

[62] *CACW*, pp. 118, 136; 'Calendar of Welsh Rolls', *Calendar of Various Chancery Rolls 1277–1326*, pp. 289, 293, 297, 305, etc.

[63] J. Goronwy Edwards, *The Principality of Wales 1267–1967: A Study in Constitutional History* (Caernarfon, 1969).

Wales. The March of Wales remained as a category. Indeed its geo-graphical area was greatly extended by the large lordships (notably Denbigh, Dyffryn Clwyd, Chirkland and Bromfield and Yale), which were now added to it through royal munificence. The duality that was now Wales was a duality which had been shaped by its history, notably in the twelfth and thirteenth centuries. The March of Wales was that area brought under English rule largely, though not exclusively, in the twelfth century by the private enterprise of Anglo-Norman lords and their followers. 'Wales' was the area beyond the March, the area where native authority retained its grip. It was also the area within which the princes of Gwynedd in the thirteenth century desperately tried to shape a unitary native principality of their own. They failed. The king of England was the residuary legatee of their efforts and of the usage of the word 'Wales' which they had exploited for that purpose. When geographical Wales eventually came to the experience of administrative and governmental unity in the sixteenth century, it would do so as a fully integrated annex of the English state.

5

A View from an Ecclesiastical Court: Mobility and Marriage in a Border Society at the End of the Middle Ages

LLINOS BEVERLEY SMITH

In October 1517 John Lippard of the parish of Norton, near Presteigne, was cited to appear before the commissary-general of the bishop of Hereford to answer a charge that, having set aside his lawful wife, Anna Goch, he had contracted a clandestine marriage with one Katherine without the required publication of banns and without seeking licence of his own parish priest or that of the bishop. In the course of the proceedings against Lippard, which took him to the churches of Leominster, Kingsland, Pembridge and Wigmore and ultimately to the august surroundings of the cathedral at Hereford, a tale of intriguing interest unfolded. Lippard could not deny that he had contracted a clandestine marriage with Katherine, an admission which earned him a penance of six whippings around Norton parish church and neighbouring churches. But in defence of his action he claimed that, although a contract of matrimony had been made and solemnized with Anna at Norton church, he had repudiated her because she had plotted his death. When Anna appeared in court, her testimony revealed that her marriage with Lippard had lasted for no more than six months, that she herself had been guilty of several adulterous affairs and that Lippard had sold her to one of her lovers, a Ieuan Dovey by name. Even so, the judge ordered that Lippard should restore full conjugal rights to Anna within three days on pain of excommunication. His response was to declare his intention to begin formal proceedings for a separation *a mensa et thoro* (from board and bed) against Anna, proceedings which were, indeed, commenced at the court of the bishop's official at Hereford in 1518.[1]

---

[1] Llinos Beverley Smith, 'Olrhain Anni Goch', in J. E. Caerwyn Williams (ed.), *Ysgrifau Beirniadol XIX* (Dinbych, 1993), pp. 107–26, and sources cited therein. For separation *a mensa et thoro*, Richard H. Helmholz, *Marriage Litigation in Medieval England* (Cambridge, 1986), pp. 100–7. I hope to undertake elsewhere a far more detailed treatment of many of the aspects touched upon in this chapter.

It so happens that two of the participants in this sordid novelette of marital misery and deceit can be identified more precisely. Ieuan Dovey or Ieuan Dyfi, one of the partners in Anna's *amours auxiliaires,* is undoubtedly the poet of that name, a native possibly of Aberdyfi in Merioneth, who flourished at the turn of the fifteenth century.[2] Although he may not perhaps be ranked among the foremost practitioners of his art, one of his *cywyddau* achieved considerable notoriety in his own day and among subsequent generations, judging by the numerous manuscript copies which survive. This was the *cywydd* addressed to a certain Anni Goch (the recipient also of his protestations of love in another of his poems) in which Ieuan, entering the lists of the *querelles des femmes,* vented his spleen on women and their treacherous wiles and invoked the memory of numerous heroes – Samson, Alexander and Aristotle among them – who had fallen prey to the wanton cruelty of the fair sex.[3] But, quite apart from the rare opportunity to marry a literary text with a historical record, John Lippard's matrimonial *imbroglio* neatly introduces the issues which this study sets out to explore. For the parish of Norton was one among several parishes situated on the borders of Wales – where the Merioneth poet had evidently dallied and where the marital problems of John Lippard were so cruelly exposed – which may be viewed through the eyes of a judge of the ecclesiastical court of the bishop of Hereford whose act books form the basis of what follows.

By the time that Lippard was making his frequent and tedious excursions to the courts of the bishop, the ecclesiastical fora were already encountering some of the virulent criticisms and challenges which would shake, although by no means undermine, the fabric of ecclesiastical justice in the ensuing decades. Yet, in the pre-Reformation period and for several generations thereafter, the church courts and their army of servants and functionaries were intrusive agents of discipline and correction as well as familiar tribunals for resolving disputes for a broad swathe of society.[4] Not that the church courts were by any means the sole arbiters of moral behaviour, nor the only vehicles for curbing breaches of seemly comportment. On the contrary, the regulation of morality was widely disseminated through a broad spectrum of agencies, and it may well be that the late

[2] Leslie Harries (ed.), *Gwaith Huw Cae Llwyd ac Eraill* (Caerdydd, 1953), pp. 28–31, 124–43; Gruffydd Aled Williams, 'The Literary Tradition to *c.*1560', in J. Beverley Smith and Llinos Beverley Smith (eds), *History of Merioneth, II, The Middle Ages* (Cardiff, 2001), pp. 598–9.

[3] Nerys A. Howells (ed.), *Gwaith Gwerful Mechain ac Eraill* (Aberystwyth, 2001), pp. 65–83, 132–47, and studies cited therein.

[4] Lawrence R. Poos, *Lower Ecclesiastical Jurisdiction in Late-Medieval England: The Courts of the Dean and Chapter of Lincoln, 1336–1349, and the Deanery of Wisbech, 1458–1484* (Oxford, 2001), pp. xi–lxiv, and sources cited therein.

medieval centuries in Wales, as elsewhere, witnessed an 'increased activism' on the part of secular powers in these matters.[5] Those who kept bawdy houses or stews, the pimps and the panderers as well as the inmates of such establishments, might be cited to appear and receive penance in the ecclesiastical courts. But equally the rectitude of the civic community could be protected by the secular courts, whose disciplinary actions against brothel-keepers and loose-living women are also recorded. A concern for communal peace and good governance, by curbing the tongue of the scold or regulating the behaviour of players at cards or at dice, might be a major concern of the parish community, but the secular fora were also engaged in the punishment of such misdemeanours. There were, moreover, several areas where lay and ecclesiastical jurisdictions overlapped and, on occasion, competed with one another. In the March of Wales the right of the ordinary to administer the goods of intestates was hotly contested by the secular powers who arrogated such rights to themselves. Suits for defamation or usury were brought to the secular and ecclesiastical courts indiscriminately, while the action of breach of faith (*causa fidei laesionis seu periurii*), that is to say, an action brought to enforce a promise made under oath, remained firmly within the jurisdiction of the church courts and offered an avenue alternative to that provided by the lay jurisdiction to bring cases of contract or debt to the court.[6] Beyond the sphere of courts and jurisdictions, much control over matters of sexual conduct and the ordering of personal relationships was certainly exercised by kinsmen or neighbours without recourse to any formally constituted tribunal, while, above all, there remained a persistent conviction that personal morality and the conduct of private affairs were matters to be determined, not by church officers or by the agents of secular powers, but by the parties themselves. This confidence in self-regulation was a permanent and enduring feature, deeply entrenched within Welsh society over several centuries.[7] Indeed, it has been commented more generally that, despite the precepts of canon lawyers and theologians, the impressive array of courts and the battery of sanctions developed by ecclesiastical powers, in practice the laity exercised a far greater control over marriage, separation and sexual behaviour than those in authority were prepared to admit.

Nevertheless, the organs of ecclesiastical justice retained a significant role in monitoring and disciplining matters of personal morality and in

[5] James A. Brundage, *Law, Sex and Christian Society in Medieval Europe* (Chicago and London, 1987), p. 487.

[6] Poos, *Lower Ecclesiastical Jurisdiction*, pp. lv, lxiii; see also A. T. Bannister, 'Visitation Returns of the Diocese of Hereford in 1397', *EHR*, 44 (1929), 279–89, 444–53; 45 (1930), 92–101, 444–63 at 453; Richard H. Helmholz, *Canon Law and the Law of England* (London, 1987), pp. 283–4, for some figures for the diocese of Hereford.

[7] See below, pp. 78–9.

providing a means for resolving parishioners' disputes. On the borderland between England and Wales ecclesiastical authority, like its secular counterpart, was complex and fragmented, and diocesan boundaries often cut across the boundaries of secular lordship. Three of the four dioceses of which the Welsh church was comprised, as well as the diocese of Hereford itself, exercised spiritual jurisdiction in the region but, although the prelates of the medieval Welsh sees undoubtedly exercised their duty to hold courts, very little of an archive that must once have been richly informative has survived.[8] Far more substantial are the court records of the consistory courts of the bishop of Hereford, a see whose detailed visitation returns survive for 1397, when Bishop Trefnant devoted two months of his vigorous and assertive ministry in close examination of the moral comportment of the clergy and laity of his see.[9] Although a consistent series of act books begins only in 1442, the organs of ecclesiastical justice, here described only in the broadest of outlines, were already in place. By then the prime forum was the bishop's consistory which, in so far as we can now establish, had subsumed within its own jurisdiction that of any lower ecclesiastical tribunal, and had bifurcated into two branches. The one, presided over by the bishop's official and normally meeting at the cathedral itself or within its precincts, was a court predominantly concerned with proceedings *ad instanciam partium,* that is to say, party and party litigation, its records reflecting the staple diet of the business of ecclesiastical courts within the period – breach of faith, defamation, tithes, ecclesiastical rights and matrimonial disputes – although the correction of clerics and occasionally of laymen might also be undertaken at this court. The other, the court of the commissary-general, was an itinerant court which travelled in circuit for the greater part of the year, holding its sessions at major churches and chapelries in each deanery and at the cathedral itself. While it, too, was competent to hear a broad range of suits between parties and to grant probate of wills, the greater part of its business comprised office or disciplinary jurisdiction over the miscreants of the diocese. The major sexual sins – fornication, adultery, prostitution, pimping and pandering among them – as well as offences against ecclesiastical

---

[8] H. D. Emanuel, 'Early St Davids Records', *NLWJ*, 8, no. 3 (1954), 258–63.

[9] Partly printed in Bannister, 'Visitation Returns'. See Poos, *Lower Ecclesiastical Jurisdiction*, p. xi, n. 3; P. E. H. Hair, 'Defaults and Offences of Clergy and Laity in Hereford Diocese, 1397', *Trans. Woolhope Naturalists' Field Club*, 47 (1991–3), 318–50. I have searched the act books for the deaneries of Clun, Pontesbury, Weobley, Leominster, Archenfield, Wenlock and Stottesden in the period 1442–1539 (Herefordshire Record Office (hereafter HRO) O/2–O/38); the other deaneries have been examined more cursorily. Act books of 'Instance', HRO I/1–I/6 (1491–1539), have also been consulted. References have normally been confined to the cases mentioned directly in the text.

discipline such as non-attendance at church, illicit trading or working on Sundays and holy days appear in abundance in the records of the Hereford courts. But whatever the reasons which brought people before the judge, the perambulant court of the commissary, no less than the bishop's own visitation, extended episcopal authority into the furthest reaches of the see and caught the inhabitants of the most distant Welsh parishes within the net of the bishop's consistory court.[10]

Moreover, whatever the deficiencies of ecclesiastical justice might have been, the judges of the courts should not be regarded as faceless automata implementing their rules in an impersonal and inflexible manner. Rather, the disciplinary authority exercised by the church depended on the co-operation and moral assumptions of ordinary laymen and women, for presentment of delinquent behaviour was made by representatives of the parish community, although common fame and gossip, sometimes malicious and unfounded, also played a part.[11] The work of the judges themselves, when they were concerned with marital cases, might often display a sensitivity and humanity in dealing with the disputes brought to their presence. At its best, ecclesiastical justice, through its encouragement of arbitration as a method of resolving disputes and the use of neighbours or fellow parishioners as conciliators or umpires, nurtured an ideal of harmony and communal peace within the communities which it served. In the March of Wales, too, the courts of the bishop of Hereford had a special significance since they provided a forum for dispute resolution which could transcend the particular, fragmented and jealously guarded liberties of the

---

[10] Brian L. Woodcock, *Medieval Ecclesiastical Courts in the Diocese of Canterbury* (Oxford, 1952), p. 82; Charles Donahue, Jr, *The Records of the Medieval Ecclesiastical Courts*, II, *England, Reports of the Working Group on Church Court Records* (Berlin, 1994), pp. 169–71. I have found no references to the archdeacon's court although his visitation is mentioned, for example, HRO O/3 (1445–6), pp. 89, 114. But see I/4, p. 476 (citation of official of archdeacon of Hereford for usurping bishop's jurisdiction by holding 'rural court' and exercising rights of correction). Some cases were heard by the bishop in person or by his commission, for example, HRO, O/8 (1468–9), p. 101; O/21 (1499–1500), p. 195. Occasionally, he presided at the consistory court, for example, O/8, p. 101; O/21, p. 195. The act books of the official's court survive from 1491, but the court was in existence much earlier. HRO I/2 is a record of the courts held by the commissary-general at the cathedral. The categorization of act books into those of 'instance' and 'office' is misleading. The city of Hereford and some peculiars lay outside the bishop's jurisdiction (Julia Barrow, 'Athelstan to Aigueblanche, 1056–1268', in Gerald E. Aylmer and John Tiller (eds), *Hereford Cathedral: A History* (London, 2000), p. 32; Robert Swanson and David Lepine, 'The Later Middle Ages, 1268–1535', ibid., p. 79).

[11] Helmholz, *Marriage Litigation*, pp. 188–9; but also Lawrence R. Poos, 'The Heavy-Handed Marriage Counsellor: Regulating Marriage in Some Later-Medieval English Local Ecclesiastical-Court Jurisdictions', *American Journal of Legal History*, 39 (1995), 291–309; idem, 'Sex, Lies, and the Church Courts of Pre-Reformation England', *Journal of Interdisciplinary History*, 25, no. 4 (1995), 585–607.

great lords of the March. The law of the episcopal court was canon law, the common law of the church. The authority of its judges derived from the powers of the ordinary and the unified system of justice and jurisprudence which his courts could provide.

The diocese revealed in the act books of the consistory court was by no means the largest or the wealthiest in England. Yet, within its bounds lay a social and physical landscape of vivid contrasts and diversity, features whose relationship with the religious practices of the region no less than with the efficacy of ecclesiastical discipline remains as yet undetermined. But the commissary, as he spent his long days in the saddle, riding 'to kepe his generallis' throughout the diocese,[12] would surely have noted the differences in the patterns of settlement, the modes of economic activity, the nature of parochial institutions and the quality of parish life within the countryside through which he laboriously journeyed. Leaving the Severn estuary with its small fishing communities (for the area known as the Deanery of Forest stood within the diocese until 1541 when the see of Gloucester was created), he would have entered the scattered industrial settlements of the Forest of Dean, where forges and bloomeries and small cloth-making centres lay in a terrain of deep valleys and ridges. To the north, at the heart of the diocese lay a benign landscape where compact riverine parishes such as Winforton, Bredwardine and Monnington-on-Wye, each centred on its own parish church, nestled within a gentle terrain of productive soils and rich pastures. Beyond, to the north and north-west, much of the region of which the archdeaconry of Shropshire was comprised lay within uplands, where undulating fields rose from the valleys to merge with rough pastures and inhospitable moorlands, such as those of Clun or the Clee Hills. Here, an economy with a pronounced pastoral character was reflected in a settlement pattern which was more dispersed and where parishes such as Old Radnor or Churchstoke, some with dependent chapelries within them, were often more extensive in size. The diocese was also studded with several towns. Apart from Hereford, 'the chief of all market towns from the sea to the banks of the Severn' as its mayor boastfully proclaimed, there was Ludlow. By the fifteenth century Ludlow was the headquarters of royal government, and its fine Perpendicular church, its well-to-do merchants and clothiers and the wide-reaching social constituency of its Palmers' Guild made it one of the larger

---

[12] Arthur T. Bannister (ed.), *Registrum Caroli Bothe, Episcopi Herefordensis A.D. MDXVI–MDXXXV* (London, 1921), p. 147. For chapelries, see P. E. H. Hair, 'Chaplains, Chantries and Chapels of North-West Herefordshire, *c.*1400', *Trans. Woolhope Naturalists' Field Club*, 46, parts 1 and 2 (1988–9), 31–64, 246–88.

provincial towns of the kingdom.[13] No less significant to the social composition of the diocese were smaller, but thriving, urban centres such as Monmouth, the *caput* of the Welsh marcher lordship, or Leominster which, although 'decayed' by the early sixteenth century, so John Leland claimed, was also 'meatly large [with] good buyldinge of tymbar' and had once flourished by 'great drapinge of clothe'. But Leland had also noted the numerous small boroughs and market towns of the far western limits of the see, each with its own parish church. He found at Presteigne 'a very good market of corne, to whiche very many folks of Melenith (Maelienydd) resorte to by corne'; at Knighton 'a praty towne after the Walshe buildinge', while Montgomery, once girded with walls whose 'great ruines' were still visible to the eye, was set in a 'good plentifull valley', its steep thoroughfares 'hillinge toward the castell'.[14] Whatever their spatial dimensions might have been, the small towns of the diocese have a special significance both for the nature of reported delinquencies and for the mechanisms by which the culprits were brought to the courts. The rapid turnover of population and occupational variety, two characteristics of medieval urban society, drew a number of migrants, both transients and new settlers, into the neighbourhood. Although we may well overstate the lack of a sense of privacy within medieval communities and the prurient eagerness of people to pry into one another's affairs, the intimate atmosphere of a small urban parish must have stimulated a close surveillance of moral comportment and sharpened a consciousness of the presence of newcomers in the town.

Small urban settlements such as Kington and Presteigne or rural townships such as Chirbury and Churchstoke were the natural foci for parishes which, straddling the historic border of England and Wales, lay within the lordships of the *seigneurs* of the March. This was truly a border society where the tenures, customs and laws of two peoples intertwined and where the Welsh and the English were 'i-medled to gidres' (mixed up together).[15] It was, moreover, a linguistically diverse and, in some important respects, a culturally syncretic society, as was notably demonstrated at Hergest, where a bishop of Hereford had once been made welcome by a

---

[13] Gervase Rosser, 'Conflict and Political Community in the Medieval Town: Disputes between Clergy and Laity in Hereford', in T. R. Slater and Gervase Rosser (eds), *The Church in the Medieval Town* (Aldershot, 1998), p. 22; Ralph A. Griffiths, 'Ludlow during the Wars of the Roses', in Ronald Shoesmith and Andrew Johnson (eds), *Ludlow Castle: Its History and Buildings* (Almeley, 2000), pp. 57–69.

[14] L. Toulmin Smith (ed.), *The Itinerary of John Leland in or about the Years 1535–1543* (5 vols, Carbondale, IL, 1964), II, p. 74; eadem, *The Itinerary in Wales of John Leland in or about the Years 1536–1539* (London, 1906), pp. 10–12.

[15] R. R. Davies, *Lordship and Society in the March of Wales 1282–1400* (Oxford, 1978), pp. 302–18; Churchill Babington and Joseph R. Lumby (eds), *Polychronicon Ranulphi de Higden Monachi Cestrensis* (9 vols, London, 1865–86), II, p. 35.

Welsh dignitary of his see, and where a fifteenth-century poet commended the use of two languages by his host.[16] Yet, the essential attributes of Welsh social practice remained strong. The vocabulary of renders and tenures might represent the residual legacy of an ancient Welsh past just as the framework of courts, which provided for separate tribunals for the Welsh and the English, reflected the ethnic contours of several communities. But the late survival of actions such as *sarhad* (trespass) and *galanas* (compensation for bloodfeud) also suggest the continuing vigour of processes deeply embedded in indigenous Welsh law. Above all, the vitality of the Welsh language was manifest. As he preached in the bishop's own lordship of Bishop's Castle in 1307, the saintly Thomas Cantilupe was obliged to make use of an interpreter among a seemingly monoglot Welsh population, while in the fifteenth century some of the gentry families of the March continued to use Welsh in their homes. At Churchstoke (Yr Ystog), in the very shadow of Offa's Dyke, the court of Gruffudd ap Hywel ap Dafydd was one which 'exalted the language', so one poet proclaimed, while at Brilley (Brilhau), far to the south, stood the home of a patron lauded as 'the best Welshman and speaker of Welsh'.[17] A frontier most certainly permeable to the influences of extraneous customs and practice, it was also a border society where some of the most tenaciously conservative communities of the period were to be found.

Apart from the palpably Welsh character of the western limits of the diocese, the border counties had long hosted Welsh communities within their bounds. The use of the Welsh patronymic or the identification of provenance by the use of locative surnames or toponyms are amply revealed both in the visitation returns of 1397 and in the act books of the consistory courts, evidence which suggests the widespread dispersal of Welsh men and women throughout the numerous parishes of the see. But small concentrations of Welsh settlements were also to be found. Thirteenth-century charters in the cartulary of Wormsley priory suggest, for example, that within the parishes of Wormsley and King's Pyon, barely 8 miles north-west of the city of Hereford, terms such as *villa Wallensica* were in use and communities identifiable as Welsh may have survived.[18] More significantly and certainly more thoroughly studied are the Welsh affinities of the extensive territory of Archenfield (Ergyng), an ancient Welsh kingdom whose customs, as Domesday records, were those of the

---

[16] John Webb (ed.), *A Roll of the Household Expenses of Richard de Swinfield, Bishop of Hereford, 1289–90* (London, 1854), p. 88; Davies, *Lordship and Society*, p. 446.

[17] Llinos Beverley Smith, 'The Welsh Language before 1536', in Geraint H. Jenkins (ed.), *The Welsh Language before the Industrial Revolution* (Cardiff, 1997), p. 20 and n. 17; Michael Richter, *Sprache und Gesellschaft im Mittelalter* (Stuttgart, 1979), pp. 184, 196.

[18] A. J. Roderick, 'Villa Wallensica', *BBCS*, 13, part 2 (1949), 90–2.

Welshmen of Archenfield before 1066. Although flanked from an early period to the north and north-west by settlements of the English, its place-names, church dedications, naming conventions and perhaps inheritance patterns evinced the survival of a distinctively Welsh texture to the region. Indeed, one of the few direct indications of the use of the Welsh language in the late Middle Ages is derived from the parish of Garway – dominated by its 'uncommonly interesting' Templar church – whose parishioners complained in 1397 of the deficiencies of their priest who, so they claimed, was unable properly to minister to their needs since he knew no Welsh, while many of his parishioners had no knowledge of English.[19] Yet the pastoral care of Welsh communities within the diocese was by no means as deficient as this comment might suggest. On the contrary, Bishop Lewis Charlton had earlier permitted the vicar of Welshpool (*ecclesia de Pola*) to hear the confessions of the Welsh members of his diocese, wherever they might be found; candidates for holy orders from the bishoprics of Llandaff, St David's and St Asaph regularly appear among ordinands of the diocese and Welsh names are frequently present among those instituted to benefices, not only in the western parts of the see but also in some of its eastern and more thoroughly English parishes.[20] That some measure of spiritual guidance in Welsh remained a necessity for some time to come is suggested not only by the sojourns of poets like Lewys Glyn Cothi (fl. *c*.1447–89) or Dafydd Benwyn (fl. *c*.1570) in gentry homes within Archenfield in the county, but also by the observations of Humphrey Llwyd (a man who by his birth and connections was ideally placed to provide accurate comment on the spoken languages of the border regions of England and Wales) that several parishes within Shropshire and Hereford-shire, and even of Gloucestershire, 'commenly used the Welsh tongue'.[21]

Even so, along with the intermingling of peoples, a legacy of conflict was also a feature of this border society. Even Hereford's late medieval bishops, who were by no means neglectful of the pastoral needs of the Welsh communities under their care, could on occasion espouse the flamboyant rhetoric of fear which the Welsh could arouse. In the orotund Latin of the episcopal chancery Bishop Thomas Charlton described the men of the March as a people 'out of whose unbridled fickleness many

[19] Bannister, 'Visitation Returns', 289; Nikolaus Pevsner, *Buildings of England: Herefordshire* (London, 1963), p. 135 (for Garway church).

[20] J. H. Parry (ed.), *Registrum Ludowici de Charltone Episcopi Herefordensis A.D. MCCCLXI–MCCCLXX* (London, 1914), pp. 45–6; P. E. H. Hair, 'Mobility of Parochial Clergy in Hereford Diocese, *c*.1400', *Trans. Woolhope Naturalists' Field Club*, 43 (1979–81), 164–80.

[21] Eirian E. Edwards, 'Cartrefi Noddwyr y Beirdd yn Siroedd Morgannwg a Mynwy', *LlC*, 13, nos 3–4 (1980–1), 205; Ieuan M. Williams (ed.), *Humphrey Llwyd: Cronica Walliae* (Cardiff, 2002), pp. 67, 82.

great evils have ensued' (*presertim homines Marchie Wallie ex quorum effrenata levitate visa sunt pluries mala plurima pervenire*) while, a century later, Bishop Thomas Spofford – that 'ideal of a bishop as a father in God' – excoriated the election of a prior of Chirbury as one perpetrated by his kinsmen 'the Welsh from the mountains, and of ferocious intent'.[22] Much of the ancient anxiety, it is true, had been rekindled during the Glyndŵr revolt and even the sober record of the clerk of King's Bench portrayed the city of Hereford in the mid-fifteenth century as 'almost a land of war' (*quasi in terra guerre*), with its loyalties riven between the English and Welsh. So also a fifteenth-century Welsh poet, in an elegy to one of his patrons, referred to the treachery of the 'villainous Englishman' (*bilain Sais*) who had murdered his benefactor in the town. This was, indeed, in Ralph A. Griffiths's evocative phrase, a 'sensitive interface' between the peoples of England and Wales, even if their interactions did not always fall neatly on either side of the geographical or ethnic divide.[23]

For the society which the Hereford act books reveal is one of significant mobility, where migration from towns and villages both in Wales and in England was under way. That the advent of Welsh migrants to the parishes of the diocese was by no means a novel phenomenon in the late fifteenth century is suggested by the evidence of the visitation returns of 1397 which, if locative surnames or by-names are an accurate measure of geographical provenance, show settlers from Elfael, Rhaeadr, Arwystli and Deheubarth within the localities of the shire. It may be that the political turmoil of the early fifteenth century had briefly created a less open and receptive climate for the migrant from Wales. Ralph A. Griffiths has noted the comparative rarity of Welsh names in the records of the mayor's courts of the city of Hereford during the early decades of the century, although after 1440 a substantial number, many of whom were engaged in the cloth trade or in victualling, appear as plaintiffs, defendants and sureties in the courts.[24] Turning to the evidence of the act books, which, as we have noted before, survive in substantial number only from 1442, the presence of Welsh migrants within the diocese is amply confirmed. Indeed, because the proceedings in court not infrequently record the earlier parish of residence

---

[22] *Registrum Thome de Charlton Episcopi Herefordensis MCCCXXVII–MCCCXLIV* (London, 1913), p. 59; Robin L. Storey, *Diocesan Administration in Fifteenth-Century England* (York, 1972), p. 18; A. T. Bannister (ed.), *Registrum Thome Spofford Episcopi Herefordensis A.D. MCCCCXXII–MCCCCXLVIII* (London, 1919), p. 242; R. R. Davies, *The Revolt of Owain Glyn Dŵr* (Oxford, 1995), pp. 107, 246–7.

[23] Ailsa Herbert, 'Herefordshire, 1413–61: Some Aspects of Society and Public Order', in Ralph A. Griffiths (ed.), *Patronage, the Crown and the Provinces in Later Medieval England* (Gloucester, 1981), pp. 110–11; Dylan Foster Evans (ed.), *Gwaith Hywel Swrdwal a'i Deulu* (Aberystwyth, 2000), pp. 23, 191–3; Ralph A. Griffiths, 'After Glyn Dŵr: An Age of Reconciliation?', *PBA*, 117 (2001), 143, 145.

[24] Griffiths, 'After Glyn Dŵr', 145.

of an individual or the parish where solemnization of marriage was claimed, the evidence of geographical movement which they provide may be far more reliable than that of a locative surname or patronymic alone. The larger towns, such as Ludlow or Monmouth, were evidently drawing new migrants from Wales, as was the case, for example, with Richard Carpenter of Ludlow, who claimed that his marriage had been solemnized 'at the church of Beaumaris in the diocese of Bangor', while John Gwynedd of Monmouth likewise claimed an earlier association with Holywell in the see of St Asaph.[25] Towns such as these were sufficiently attractive to encourage long-distance migration, but smaller urban centres such as Worthen, Montgomery or Wenlock also drew newcomers from afar. Thomas Pygot, whose marriage had taken place, so he claimed, at Denbigh (*apud Tynbize*), was by 1508 living at Worthen, his earlier sojourn in the marcher borough of the north-east being perfectly credible in view of the earlier presence of Pigots in the town. A Montgomery parishioner proffered proof of his marriage at Llangernyw within the lordship of Denbigh, while evidence of marriage and earlier residence at Bugeildy (Maelienydd) was provided when the parishioners of Wenlock began to entertain doubts of the marital status of a newly arrived couple in the town. Such evidence, a small sample which could easily be multiplied, suggests that the Welsh population within the diocese was being invigorated, even if it was not being numerically increased, through continuing migration by individuals and families from the towns and villages of the west.[26]

Not that the Welsh localities constituted the only source of migrants into the diocese. On the contrary, as the act books also reveal, settlers from other English communities were also to be found. With many of its southern parishes bounding the estuary of the Severn, the population of the diocese reflected the age-old cultural and commercial affinities with the counties of south-west England.[27] John Sebright (Sebrizt) of Monmouth, arriving alone in the town, had left a wife, so he claimed, 'in Devynshire' at Bridgwater; John ap Meredith, a tucker of Monmouth, had evidently sojourned for some time at Axbridge in Somerset where his first marriage was solemnized, while further north, at Presteigne, Hugh Capper successfully vindicated his legitimate marriage at Plympton in the diocese of Exeter. Moreover, whether their origins lay in Wales or in England, several

[25] HRO, O/3 (1445–6), p. 49; O/8 (1468–9), p. 139; O/21 (1499–1500), p. 199 (Maelienydd to Monmouth).

[26] HRO, O/3 (1445–6), p. 87; O/18 (1489–91), p. 187 (marriage of Archenfield couple at Corwen, Merioneth); O/25 (1508–9), pp. 148–9; O/27 (1517–18), p. 121.

[27] Ralph A. Griffiths, 'Medieval Severnside: the Welsh Connection', in R. R. Davies, Ralph A. Griffiths, Ieuan Gwynedd Jones and Kenneth O. Morgan (eds), *Welsh Society and Nationhood: Historical Essays presented to Glanmor Williams* (Cardiff, 1984), pp. 70–89; HRO, O/24 (1507–8), p. 247; O/27 (1517–18), p. 222; O/34 (1529–30), p. 70.

migrants, having arrived in the diocese, moved from parish to parish, as did George Sherman of Monmouth, who had arrived there from Salisbury, and went on to Ludlow. The short-distance migration of others is revealed in the movements of men such as David Hope, who moved residence from Worthen to Chirbury, or Geoffrey Carpenter of Montgomery, whose removal to the parish of Forden involved a journey of no more than 3 miles. Whether the mobile element thus revealed in the records is merely the tip of a very large iceberg it is impossible to decide; nor, indeed, are the age and occupation-specific characteristics of the migrant always made clear.[28] Adolescents in service may have accounted for some of the mobility. But, equally, people were moving into the area as adults, sometimes as single people, sometimes as couples, and sometimes quite separately from a partner who is known to have been resident elsewhere. Some of the movement is also explained by the itinerant lifestyle of a craftsman or artisan, as is suggested by the occupational labels – tucker, glover, turner or wright – which the court records sometimes supply.[29] Agricultural work may also have created a pool of migrant labour in a region known to attract seasonal workers from Welsh upland communities over several generations. Mobility and migration might clearly have had serious repercussions upon the effectiveness of ecclesiastical justice as miscreants slipped away and diocesan boundaries were breached. But judges, too, were by no means averse to encouraging culprits to depart and, for the affronted parishioner no less than for the functionaries of the court, the abscondment of a delinquent might often have been seen as an eminently satisfactory resolution of a difficult and troublesome case.

Lest it be thought that the mobile element within this society was disproportionately represented in the disciplinary proceedings of the courts, the presence of settled households and families is equally clear. Evidence of marriages which were endogamous, according to the canonical definition, was already visible in the returns of the bishop's visitation in 1397, but the act books reveal many more. Several couples were exposed to ecclesiastical censure on the grounds that they had married within the prohibited degrees, frequently in the remoter relationship of the third cousinhood or on the grounds of an affinal link.[30] The institution of godparenthood, also deemed an impediment to a valid canonical marriage, can be seen in the sources. For example, when Gutun Caereinion of Alberbury was accused

[28] HRO, O/4 (1447–8), p. 117 (Eardisley to Monmouth); O/21 (1499–1500), p. 199 (Ludlow to Clun); O/30 (1523–4), p. 21; O/18 (1490–1), p. 335 (Chirbury to Leominster); I/4 (1507–19), p. 113 (Burford to New Radnor).

[29] HRO, O/13 (1479–80), p.135; O/4 (1447–8), pp. 67, 76.

[30] For example, Bannister, 'Visitation Returns', 451, 460; HRO, O/17 (1487–9), pp. 22, 95; O/18 (1489–90), p. 63; O/20 (1494–5), p. 42; O/24 (1507–8), p. 134. Citations seem to be more numerous from the 1490s onwards.

of repudiating his first wife, he claimed that they had been legitimately divorced on the grounds that they were 'consobrini, anglice godbrothur et godsister', just as Llywelyn ap John of the parish of Shelve was cited for incest with Elena ferch Ieuan, 'whose child he had received from the font'.[31] Not infrequently, judges would use the knowledge of kinsmen to provide evidence of the family tree or, if consanguinity were denied, kinsmen might be required to act as compurgators to substantiate the claim. The choice of executors, no less than bequests in the last wills and testaments of the deceased, also suggests a stable network of kinsmen, and family members might also be called to act as proctors or representatives of their kinsfolk in court. Parents and kinsmen were frequently witnesses to marriage contracts entered into by family members and the habit, by no means superseded, of contracting marriage at home meant that relatives would be present when the exchange of consent was performed. Even clandestine marriages, that is to say, marriages celebrated without publication of banns outside the parish of one of the contracting parties and often at uncanonical seasons and hours, might often involve kinsfolk, present in some numbers, as several cases brought to the attention of the commissary reveal. Perhaps the western parts of the diocese, in close proximity to secluded churches and chapelries '*in Wallia*' – Llanbadarn Fynydd, Glasgwm or Penderyn – were especially vulnerable to the temptations of a clandestine wedding, just as the ready supply of an army of unbeneficed clergy, willing and anxious to turn a dishonest penny, provided the celebrants to officiate at such nuptials.[32]

It would be wrong, however, to suppose that the rituals of the full canonical marriage with publication of banns, an exchange of words of present consent (*verba de presenti*) and due solemnization in the church of the parish where one or both of the parties were normally resident were not widely respected within the diocese at this time. There were very good reasons why it should be so. The church setting imparted dignity and formality to an occasion which was perceived by many as a serious and prudent commitment, but there were also more immediately practical reasons for preferring a marriage in church. Solemnization in church before a priest and witnesses could, for example, provide authentication of marriage, a confirmation sometimes explicitly provided in writing, while the practice of dower at English common law required the bride's endowment *ad hostium ecclesie* (at the church door) and, likewise, encouraged people with landed property to marry in church. But the church wedding

---

[31] HRO, O/20 (1494–5), p. 123; O/24 (1507–8), p. 170; O/36 (1534–6), p. 2 (*sua le gossype*).

[32] E. J. L. Cole, 'Clandestine Marriages: the Awful Evidence from a Consistory Court', *TRS*, 46 (1976), 68–72.

had clearly become increasingly common at all social levels, and servants, carpenters and cobblers among others were claiming to have married in regular fashion in church. A further indication that the making of marriage was becoming an increasingly public affair, with solemnization in church at the centre of the proceedings, is the fact that suits to establish the existence of a contract of marriage were, by the late fifteenth century, in Hereford as elsewhere, on the wane. An important reason for their decline was the increasing tendency to enter into the contract of matrimony, not privately at home, but publicly and with due solemnity in a church. Indeed, it was the suit for the restitution of conjugal rights, an action which, by the fifteenth century, required the plaintiff not only to show the existence of a valid contract and consummation but also solemnization in church, which predominated in the matrimonial litigation initiated in the parishes with which we are concerned, testimony likewise to the ways in which popular practice in the western reaches of the diocese conformed to the requirements of the church. It is also the case that formal proceedings for nullity and divorce, and albeit less frequently, for separation *a mensa et thoro,* were instituted, often successfully. Most of the canonical grounds for divorce or separation – consanguinity, force and fear, impuberty, impotence and frigidity – might be pleaded, compelling evidence that parties were resorting to the decision of formally constituted tribunals, normally the bishop's consistory court. Clearly, in ending a marriage, no less than in its formation, the precise canonical requirements were being punctiliously observed.

Yet, the triumph of the ecclesiastical norm of marriage-formation was by no means complete. For many couples, living together without intention of matrimony was the preferred option, and such relationships (which were by no means always unstable and ephemeral arrangements) were widely regarded as a viable alternative to a regular marriage.[33] It was also the case that some couples who, by their own admission, had exchanged a contract of marriage, sometimes explicitly described as one 'by words of the present', and had entered into sexual relations but had not solemnized their union, might be cited to appear in court to answer a charge of fornication. Although it would be wrong to assume that such contracts were entered into without ceremony – indeed, the liminal state between contract and solemnization may well have enjoyed a measure of popular recognition – they were clearly defective in the eyes of the church. Thus, in cases in which a couple admitted the contract, the judge would enjoin a penance of whippings, together with an injunction that they should

---

[33] HRO, O/10 (1472–3), p. 45 (partnership for twenty years); O/17 (1488–9), p. 24 ('fornication' for more than twelve years); O/20 (1494–5), p. 123 ('fornication' for seven years and procreation of several children).

proceed to solemnization, meanwhile abstaining from the 'sin of consorting' with one another in suspect places. It may be that R. H. Helmholz is right to surmise that most of the persons who entered into such private agreements planned to have their unions solemnized at some later time and that long-standing marriage contracts were not commonly left in an unsolemnized state. Yet cases of an unsolemnized contract appear in the Hereford records, not in substantial numbers but sufficient to merit attention, as a few illustrative examples make clear. In 1468 a Worthen parishioner, cited for fornication, admitted the offence, but pleaded that a contract of matrimony had been made and submitted to penance, which was respited by the judge 'in the hope of a marriage' (*sub spe nubendi*); but he was still being cited for the same delinquency five years later and eventually left the diocese, thereby passing out of sight. The union of a Montgomery couple was also brought under similar scrutiny, with like penance and injunction, but it remained unsolemnized (if, indeed, it was ever solemnized) for six years and more.[34] What proportion of all marriages were vitiated by a failure to solemnize it is impossible to say, but the material strongly suggests that publication of banns and solemnization in church was by no means the acknowledged, accepted or universal practice among Welsh communities in the diocese at the end of the Middle Ages.

If, in the formation of unions, a considerable disjunction between ecclesiastical norms and popular practice existed, the ending of partner-ships also reveals how ecclesiastical precepts were often disregarded. Although, as we have seen, proceedings for a formal canonical divorce (albeit in small numbers) were being instituted in the consistory courts, it is also the case that a far larger number of unions were terminated without recourse to any authority. Time and again the court records reveal the citation of men and sometimes women who, having left their first partner, had taken up with another 'without judgement of the church' or 'on their own personal authority'. The marriage of a Churchstoke parishioner had been terminated, so we are told, 'without any decision of the church', and a subsequent clandestine marriage contracted. Margaret Kery of Worthen was another for whom the inconvenience of having a husband alive furnished no serious deterrent to her abandoning him and forming a second partnership, contracted in clandestine fashion at dead of night in the chapel of Woolston nearby.[35] It is true that many of those cited for

---

[34] Helmholz, *Marriage Litigation,* pp. 29–30. From a number of examples, see HRO, O/18 (1490–1), pp. 375, 380 (Monmouth man had contracted (*affidavit*) with woman *per verba de presenti* and promised to marry her by next consistory); O/30 (1523–4), p. 39 (woman admits fornication but claims contract and man ordered to answer woman in *causa matrimonialii* at Hereford).

[35] HRO, O/8 (1468–9), p. 20; O/12 (1474–6), p. 61; O/15 (1481–2), p. 91.

abandoning a legitimate spouse might offer a canonical reason in defence of their action and might even proffer or promise to produce pieces of writing (the majority of the ones which were produced were declared null and void) purporting to be records of a legitimate divorce.[36] In the majority of cases, however, steps to end a relationship were taken without the issue being ventilated in any formal tribunal. The lingering and enduring conviction that such matters were best regulated not by a court or by any superior authority is clearly displayed. The views that unions were ended 'by men's private authority' and that such matters should be left to individual choice were tenaciously held.[37]

Only a thorough analysis of a far wider range of materials than the act books alone can fully explain the contrasts in the practice of marriage which have been identified within this border society. It is tempting, however, to ascribe the persistence of habits deemed irregular, even illegal, in the eyes of the church, to the residual influence of a 'Welsh way of marriage' in the western reaches of the see, for the Welsh had long been identified as a people whose practice of marriage, no less than their sexual habits, were ones of singular repugnance and deviance.[38] The celebrated strictures of churchmen in the period of conquest can no doubt be explained in part by the age-old insistence of a conquering power on its moral predominance, in part by the fact that sexual imagery had often formed a significant component of the vocabulary of conflict and conquest, and in part by the efforts of churchmen, armed with a systematized body of law, to determine the regulation of an orderly Christian society. Yet their criticisms were not without substance and, for those trained in the ecclesiastical model of marriage, Welsh practices, as revealed in the native law texts, were seriously defective. Yet the contractual, non-sacramental character of marriage, its easy dissolution and the view that the termination of unions was a matter for the parties alone without recourse to any superior authority, are features by no means confined to the parishes of the western periphery of the diocese of Hereford. A residual Welsh influence is a matter of doubt, if not one that can be rejected outright.

Nor does the presence of religious dissent fully explain the secular and consensual view of marriage which has been encountered. For the Lollards, who were believed to be active within the diocese, as the spectacular trials at

[36] HRO, O/8 (1468–9), p. 38; O/22 (1501–2), p. 124.

[37] Martin Ingram, *Church Courts, Sex and Marriage in England, 1570–1640* (Cambridge, 1987), p. 147.

[38] R. R. Davies, 'Buchedd a Moes y Cymry' (The Manners and Morals of the Welsh), *WHR*, 12, no. 2 (1984–5), 155–79; Huw Pryce, *Native Law and the Church in Medieval Wales* (Oxford, 1993), pp. 82–112; Robin Chapman Stacey, 'Divorce, Medieval Welsh Style', *Speculum*, 77, no. 4 (2002), 1107–27 (for a new interpretation of the jurists' perception of the consequences of divorce).

the cathedral at Hereford reveal, the sacramental authority of the priest had been deemed an unnecessary intrusion and, indeed, at Lydney, on the edges of the Forest of Dean in the late fifteenth century, the view that 'solemnization of matrimony in a church was not necessary and could legitimately be omitted' was maintained.[39] However, in Essex, where tenacious adherence to Lollardy can be found, considered historical opinion prefers to view the rejection of the role of priests in forming the marital bond not as a consequence of Lollard influence, but as a belief that was entirely consonant with existing popular attitudes and 'meshed with and reinforced predispositions' within rural society.[40] The influences which helped to determine how the conjugal bond was formed or dissolved were undoubtedly complex. But some place should surely be given to the role of geographical mobility within this border society. For some, long-continued domicile apart from their spouse may well have produced genuine uncertainty whether the partner were dead or alive. For others, especially perhaps for the transient and rootless elements of society, the temptation to set up a new ménage in a new neighbourhood, far removed from old ties and acquaintances, must have proved irresistible.

The records of ecclesiastical justice undoubtedly penetrate parts of the human experience which other medieval sources cannot reach. Perhaps the western extremities of the diocese of Hereford were ones where the challenges posed to the organs of pastoral care and discipline were unusually severe. Perhaps, indeed, many of the miscreants who formed the regular clientele of the commissary's courts were drawn from a social stratum for whom sexual credit and honesty were of little concern and whose lifestyle and habits rendered them less amenable to control. But whatever the uncertainties raised by the Hereford act books, as the peccadilloes and frailties of men and women are exposed we are allowed to open a window not normally accessible to the historian of a Welsh medieval community and to explore a source which is of inestimable value.

[39] J. H. Parry (ed.), *Registrum Johannis Stanbury Episcopi Herefordensis A.D. MCCCCLIII–MCCCCLXXIV* (London, 1919), p. 119.

[40] Lawrence R. Poos, *A Rural Society after the Black Death: Essex 1350–1525* (Cambridge, 1991), p. 269.

6

The Interpretation of Late Medieval Houses in Wales*

RICHARD SUGGETT

Medieval buildings and documents provide direct links with the society which produced them. However, whereas documents are privileged as historical sources and for the most part are nowadays safely gathered in archives, we can be very negligent about our architectural heritage. The deliberate destruction of a unique medieval manuscript would be considered an act of lunacy, but the permitted demolition of medieval vernacular buildings has been commonplace in the post-war planning process. It is indeed somewhat ironic that the expertise of the Royal Commission on the Ancient and Historical Monuments of Wales in medieval houses has been acquired partly as a result of the emergency recording carried out at demolition sites.

The deplorable condition of Tŷ-draw, Llanarmon Mynydd Mawr, Denbighshire (Fig. 1), illustrates the fact that medieval houses are a diminishing historical resource. Tŷ-draw is important for students of vernacular architecture because it was here that it was realized that the plan of the upland medieval dwelling resembled that of the aristocratic hall-house.[1] Tŷ-draw is a house without a documented history; indeed, its name (which may reflect a historic shift in settlement) is a purely oral form unrecorded on any map. The building itself is the primary source for its own history, and it is apparent that its distinctive siting, cruck-framed construction and plan challenge modern conceptions of housing culture and raise important questions about late medieval society and economy. In particular, we need to appreciate that it was built as a durable house and has survived some 500 years. In much of medieval Europe the durable house was exceptional, and even today the majority of mankind live in

---

*It is appropriate to mention that research on the dating and context of medieval dwellings has been encouraged by Ralph A. Griffiths as a commissioner and latterly chairman of the Royal Commission on the Ancient and Historical Monuments of Wales.

[1] Peter Smith and D. B. Hague, 'Tŷ Draw: a Fourteenth-Century Cruck-Hall', *AC*, 107 (1958), 109–20. The plight of Tŷ-draw was reported in the *Transactions of the Ancient Monuments Society*, 45 (2001), 87–8, and happily it was subsequently bought by Mr Graham Moss who intends to restore the house.

houses that are impermanent and are periodically renewed.[2] I shall be arguing that the durable, largely cruck-framed houses of medieval Wales, whose professional craftsmanship still astonishes us, were built as acts of conspicuous display through which social identity was constructed and maintained.

Fig. 1 Tŷ-draw, Llanarmon Mynydd Mawr, Denbighshire, in 2000. Photograph by Iain Wright. RCAHMW: Crown Copyright.

Houses, like documents, are rather like texts that can be read once the necessary skills to do so have been acquired. It is plausibly argued by social anthropologists that a child learns some of the basic rules of a society through their architectural expression in a house. Likewise, the late medieval adult could no doubt read the text and subtext of a house at a glance; the historian after half a millennium has to work hard to frame the right questions that will unlock the implicit meanings of a dwelling like Tŷ-draw and reveal the social use of space.

First we should note – how can it be ignored? – the dramatic, platformed siting of Tŷ-draw on the open slopes of Mynydd Mawr. The location of a house and its relation to the surrounding landscape is an important aspect

---

[2] Paul Oliver, *Dwellings: The House Across the World* (Oxford, 1987), pp. 8–9.

of housing culture. We have to understand the siting of Tŷ-draw and other upland medieval dwellings in terms of the late medieval farming economy. The medieval upland house was characteristically sited on a very important boundary between wild and cultivated land. This boundary is no longer relevant to modern farming; throughout the early modern period farms were amalgamated and farmhouses relocated from the edge to the centre of farms, leaving a scattering of platforms along the old line of settlement which survive as archaeological features.

Fig. 2 Nannerth-ganol, Llansanffraid Cwmteuddwr, Radnorshire.
RCAHMW: Crown Copyright

In some of the steeper-sided valleys of Wales the characteristic siting of medieval houses can still be appreciated. Nannerth-ganol (Fig. 2) in the upper Wye valley, Radnorshire, sits on the margin of the enclosed fields that run up from the river. On a steep slope above the house are the remains of relict oak woodland and beyond is the open mountain. A distinctive vocabulary of medieval origin referred to this changing terrain – 'mynydd' (mountain), 'ffridd' (moorland), 'caeau' (fields), and 'dôl' (meadow) or 'gweirglodd' (meadow), and no doubt finer discriminations with regional variations. This terminology remains an important element in the underexplored inheritance of Welsh place-names.[3] The land use of the late medieval upland farm can be expressed diagrammatically (Fig. 3). The key to successful upland agriculture lay in achieving the right balance between open and enclosed ground. Even if a medieval farm had a relatively small acreage of enclosed land, as many seem to have had, access to the common gave the farmer the capacity to generate a surplus. There was often unlimited common for cattle on the mountain, and sixteenth-century documentation provides glimpses of temporary turf-walled summer dairy-houses (*lluestau*) there. Successful pastoral farming entailed maximizing the number of beasts that could be grazed on the common in the summer and then overwintered in the cowhouse. Once the subsistence grain requirement had been satisfied, the rest of the enclosed ground (as well as enclosures on the mountain) could be given over to hay production for winter-feed. But the pastoral farmer who miscalculated and was unable to feed his beasts in the winter would lose his livelihood.

Land use on medieval upland farms illustrates many boundaries of the binary type which social anthropologists like to identify: higher ground is opposed to the lower ground, as summer is opposed to winter; permanent dwellings are opposed to the impermanent huts of the higher ground; enclosed (cultivated) ground is opposed to open, wild ground. One can also say that wealth-producing was opposed to, or separated from, wealth-consuming. The wealth produced up on the mountain was consumed down in the houses on the edge of the enclosed land.

Medieval houses were sited in a particular way in order to take full economic advantage of the terrain. Late medieval upland farmers character-istically specialized in cattle rearing for the beef market. They chose to spend the surplus generated from this economy conspicuously on dwellings and these are the major artefacts of the material culture of the period. The cost of building a cruck-framed hall-house is not known, but the money required for such an enterprise would have been accumulated over a long

---

[3] David Jenkins, 'Rural Society Inside Outside', in David Smith (ed.), *A People and a Proletariat: Essays in the History of Wales 1780–1980* (London, 1980), pp. 121–2.

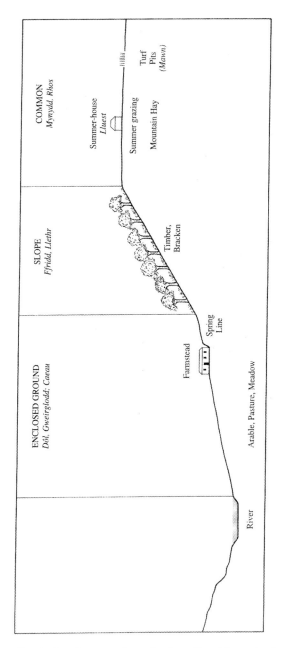

Fig. 3 Land use on the upland medieval farmstead.
RCAHMW: Crown Copyright

85

period, perhaps even over several generations if credit networks were not available. The money generated in the livestock market was spent on buying building materials and paying craftsmen to build durable houses. These professional craftsmen – it is important to emphasize – were carpenters rather than masons.

The medieval house in Wales was typically timber-built. In the twenty-first century many people, including contemporary architects, find this difficult to accept since it appears so contrary to common sense. After all, stone is present everywhere in Wales. Stone, especially slate, is now thought of as the quintessentially Welsh building material; slate has therefore been chosen for the facing of the Wales Millennium Centre in Cardiff. The use of stone to symbolize enduring Welsh identity would have been unintelligible to a medieval audience who associated stone building with the castles and boroughs of the Edwardian conquest. The medieval Welsh house was characteristically a timber house, even in areas which are now stone-built, including boulder-strewn Ffestiniog, the centre of Welsh slate production.

The best way to appreciate the former dominance of timber building in Wales is to examine Peter Smith's distribution maps of crucks and vaults in his enduring and inspirational *Houses of the Welsh Countryside*.[4] Full crucks are found largely in north and east Wales, but the scarfed crucks of south-west Wales extend the line of cruck framing much further west where it meets the stone-vaulting tradition of the south. The distribution map of vaulting shows that stone building was especially marked in the Vale of Glamorgan and south Pembrokeshire, historically areas of Anglo-Norman settlement and the nucleated village. The contrast between building exclusively in stone and building exclusively in timber is strongest between the north-east and the south-west. In Powys one actually encounters the all-timber house where every part of the dwelling, as far as was possible, including walls of solid post-and-panel construction, was built of timber. By contrast, in south Pembrokeshire there are buildings where every part, as far as was possible, was built of stone from vaulted floor to fireplace lintel to vaulted roof. The element of choice in these constructions must be emphasized. It was easier, and probably cheaper, to frame a floor or roof in timber rather than vault it in stone, but many Pembrokeshire builders chose the vault. The builder of the all-timber house (which was full of water traps) would have balanced the long-term durability of his house against the immediate prestige and pleasure that his timber bower would give.

The builders of vernacular houses can often surprise us by their choice and use of materials. But building is about choice, preferring one material

---

[4]   Peter Smith, *Houses of the Welsh Countryside* (2nd edn, London, 1988), maps 7, 12, 44.

to another and selecting one plan from many possible plans. Stone versus timber was a cultural tension deeply embedded in the historical experience of the Welsh people. To understand this fully we would need to look at castle building and the way in which stone was consciously employed as an imperial building material, especially in great castles like Caernarfon and Chepstow. In late medieval and Tudor Wales there was a clearly expressed sense in which stone and timber were in competition, but a sense also that the stonemason's craft was declining even as the carpenter's craft was improving. A tongue-twisting proverb of the period specifically says 'waethwaeth faensaer, gwellwell brensaer' (worse and worse is the stonemason, but better and better is the carpenter). George Owen, the Elizabethan historian of Pembrokeshire, explained the proverb by saying that the masons of his day were not as skilful as those who had built castles and other ancient vaulted buildings.[5] The perception that the carpenter's craft excelled that of the mason coincides with the development of the timber roof as a focus for decoration and display. The desire to enrich buildings with timber embraced churches as well as houses in late medieval Wales. Box-like stone-built churches were embellished with new timber-framed porches and towers, as well as ornate roofs, and occasionally a new church (as at Trelystan, Montgomeryshire) was constructed wholly in timber.

Timber building dominated late medieval Wales, but it was actually profoundly influenced by building in stone, though in ways that are not immediately obvious. The medieval timber house in Wales was characteristically a cruck-framed house. The origin of the cruck-truss has been a matter of controversy. Cruck-trusses were not a primitive form of construction, as has been argued, but rather the product of sophisticated carpentry at a particular historical period. The cruck-truss was an expression in timber of the international Gothic architectural vocabulary of the pointed arch, inspired no doubt by the great masonry churches and halls. A geographical scattering of tree-ring dates in England points to the translation of the Gothic stone arch into timber during the second half of the thirteenth century, and the earliest unambiguous documentary reference to crucks ('crokkes') occurs in a Welsh context in 1306.[6] The full cruck was widely adopted in Wales and the March, becoming the dominant form of roof truss in late medieval dwellings. Several hundred cruck-framed houses survive of the thousands that must have been built.

---

[5] Dillwyn Miles (ed.), *The Description of Pembrokeshire [by] George Owen of Henllys* (Llandysul, 1994), p. 78.

[6] A. J. Taylor, 'The King's Works in Wales, 1277–1330', in R. Allen Brown, H. M. Colvin and A. J. Taylor (eds), *The History of the King's Works: The Middle Ages* (2 vols, London, 1963), I, p. 364.

The cruck-trusses of the March were works of high craftsmanship and the centre of a distribution which stretched in a vast swathe from the north Wales coast to the east Midlands, where they became progressively less refined.[7]

Theoretically the cruck-framed medieval house has a pedigree that stretches back to the thirteenth century. But how old are Welsh cruck-framed houses and how can they be dated? Until a few years ago the dating of medieval houses was largely intuitive. However, dendrochronology now provides a secure way of establishing a chronology for medieval buildings. Tree-ring dating depends on the way in which hardwood trees lay down annual growth rings which vary in width according to the nature of the growing season. The growth-rings in a core taken from an historic timber are measured and computer-matched against a known dated series of tree-rings. If complete sapwood has survived, then the date and sometimes the season of felling can be calculated. The Royal Commission on the Ancient and Historical Monuments of Wales has undertaken a selective programme of tree-ring dating since 1995 and some thirty precisely dated sites now provide the basis for a secure chronology of medieval houses.[8] Tree-ring dating has transformed not only the study of buildings, but also the relationship between documentary-led history and architectural history. By assigning a precise date to a building one can contextualize it more securely. In the case of Tŷ-draw, we now know that the timber used to build it was felled in the winter of 1479/80, some two generations after Owain Glyndŵr's revolt and on the eve of Tudor rule in Wales.

The results have been somewhat surprising. No firm chronology has emerged in terms of timber styles. Late medieval Welsh carpenters employed diverse framing techniques, and cruck- and box-framed houses were being built at the same time. The real surprise has been in the date range of surviving structures. Despite the range of houses sampled, no dwellings earlier than 1420 have been identified, and standing houses of open-hall plan span the period 1430–1555. The early fifteenth-century cut-off for surviving houses seems to be fundamental. Although there are document-ary references to substantial fourteenth-century dwellings, houses of that date have not survived as standing structures, and we do not have a clear idea of their plan and appearance. The physical evidence for fourteenth-

---

[7] N. W. Alcock, 'The Distribution and Dating of Crucks and Base Crucks', *Vernacular Architecture*, 33 (2002), 67–70.

[8] The results have been regularly reported in lists of tree-ring dates published in *Vernacular Architecture* since 1996. All available tree-ring dates from Welsh sites have been listed in Richard Suggett, 'Dendrochronology: Progress and Prospects' in C. Stephen Briggs (ed.), *Towards a Research Agenda for Welsh Archaeology* (Oxford, 2003), pp. 153–69.

century and earlier houses is archaeological, but excavations of early houses sites have been disappointingly few.

If we take Owain Glyndŵr's revolt, which seems to have laid waste much of Wales between 1400 and 1410, as a defining event for late medieval Wales, we can say that surviving hall-houses are post-Glyndŵr rather than pre-Glyndŵr. The apparent absence of surviving structures before 1400 can be tentatively attributed to the devastating effects of Glyndŵr's revolt which set in train profound social changes. Both Glyndŵr and the Crown pursued a scorched earth policy and important houses were deliberately burnt, most notably of course Glyndŵr's hall at Sycharth. It cannot be doubted that there was a calamitous destruction of halls around 1400: 'the destruction was great and the recovery was slow', as Rees Davies puts it.[9]

Hoskins's famous phrase about 'the great rebuilding' (referring of course to seventeenth-century England) can be applied with even greater force to the rebuilding which occurred in late medieval Wales. A great quantity of enduring hall-houses sprang up after 1400. Survey work by the Royal Commission on the Ancient and Historical Monuments of Wales has identified *c*.500 standing (if often very fragmentary) medieval Welsh houses. It is not only the arrival of these houses that is impressive but also their steady accumulation. Dendrochronological analysis reveals that late medieval halls did not appear suddenly in one concentrated rebuilding, but were rather the cumulative result of a long process of 150 years or so, extending from the third decade of the early fifteenth century to the period immediately after the Reformation and the Acts of Union. These were professionally built houses, erected in large numbers, and they did not incorporate any reused material. This latter fact is surprising and revealing. Many post-medieval houses incorporated reused material, but the late medieval Welsh halls did not. It is clear that in Wales after 1400, following the years of plague and war, there was a late medieval transformation in housing which involved the complete rejection of earlier dwellings.

Although there was a wide variety of theme and variation in late medieval hall-house construction, it is clear from the dates obtained that the chronology of Welsh houses is related to the relative size of halls. In general terms large halls are earlier in date than small halls. This is perhaps the reverse of what might have been expected. It is evident from the results of tree-ring dating that great halls are generally older than gentry halls and these in turn are older than peasant halls. It must be emphasized that the small and simple house was not necessarily the earliest, although this seems to be a lesson that needs to be periodically relearned. Put another way, one

[9] R. R. Davies, *The Revolt of Owain Glyn Dŵr* (Oxford, 1995), p. 280.

can say that after Owain Glyndŵr's revolt those with greater resources built earlier and to a larger scale than those with lesser resources.

We can distinguish broadly between three types of hall-house, each type with a distinctive building chronology, and differing in size according to status. First are the 'great' hall-houses within lordships, or attached to religious houses; these generally have a hall of three bays. The great halls which have been dated belong to a short period between 1430 and 1450: they include Bryndraenog (Bugeildy, Radnorshire), dated 1436, discussed below, the abbot's house at Cymer Abbey (near Dolgellau, Merioneth), dated 1441, and the older part of Tretower Court (Tre-twr, Breconshire), dated *c.*1447. Second are the houses of the local gentry class, which generally had halls of two bays. The dated examples have a long chronology extending from *c.*1430 to *c.*1530, but they mostly belong to the second half of the fifteenth century. Finally, we can identify the halls of the free-tenants of the lordships. These, with some reservation, can be called peasant hall-houses, and have a hall of a single bay as a defining feature. The five examples dated by the Royal Commission on the Ancient and Historical Monuments of Wales were all built in the mid-Tudor period.

Identifying and assigning status labels to the builders of medieval houses in England has been fraught with difficulty. However, in Wales the class dimension of housing has unusual clarity because of the survival of a unique documentary source, the poetry and pedigrees relating to the gentry class.

One must begin discussion of the great halls with one which has vanished. One of the most remarkable poems, from the architectural historian's point of view, is the fifteenth-century *cywydd* by Lewys Glyn Cothi praising Ieuan ap Phylib, the constable of Cefn-llys castle.[10] It is clear that the hall at Cefn-llys was partly a court where the constable or steward of the lordship of Maelienydd exercised surrogate lordship on behalf of the marcher lord. The poet tells us that a master carpenter has been hired to make with his axe a new hall that will be like Arthur's hall in the lordship of Maelienydd. The new hall, the poet continues, will be a court for the country, like an earl's court, with three parts, and these will form one house. Pale oaks have been linked together to make the building. The hall has been roofed with close-fitting shields. The house is very wide, and white like an altar. From this poem we know uniquely that a named master carpenter, Rosser ap Ieuan, built the hall: while poets often praised carpenters, they rarely named them. It was timber-framed with a pale appearance, and tiled rather than thatched. It also had three parts or wings.

---

[10] Evan D. Jones, 'The Cefn Llys Poems of Lewis Glyn Cothi', *TRS*, 6 (1936), 20–2.

Fig. 4 A great hall-house: Upper House, Painscastle, Radnorshire.
Drawing by Harry Brooksby. RCAHMW: Crown Copyright

To understand the great hall-house we must retain the image of a triple court. The hall at Cefn-llys has long disappeared, but a hall-house with three parts has survived at Painscastle, Radnorshire. This hall, now known as Upper House, was probably the centre of the lordship of Lower Elfael. The hall has been built at the approach to the castle (which was the focus of the lordship) and it is reasonable to suppose that the house dates from the mid-fifteenth century when an attack on the castle would have seemed unlikely. A reconstruction drawing (Fig. 4) shows that the plan is essentially H-shaped, corresponding to the three parts of the hall described at Cefn-llys. The open hall is set between two wings, a service wing at the lower end and a parlour at the upper end. The interior splendour, even drama, of the hall must be emphasized. The hall was approached by an outside cross-passage and the entrance to the hall framed by the splendid spere-posts, creating an aisle-like effect which emphasized the width of the hall. On entering the hall, the eye takes in the ornate roof – especially the central arch-braced base-cruck truss – and looks beyond the central truss to the dais end of the hall where the bench and high-table were located. It may be noted that some aspects of the carpentry of the great halls were deliberately archaic (like the vocabulary of the poetry associated with them) and probably reflected the style of high-status halls which had been destroyed during Owain Glyndŵr's revolt. The base-cruck, in particular, was more or less obsolete in England by the second half of the fourteenth century, but examples were commissioned from Welsh master carpenters as late as 1460.

It proved impossible to tree-ring date Upper House, but at Bryndraenog in Bugeildy, north Radnorshire, tree-ring dating, survey and poetry have come together in a very satisfying way. The house was wholly timber-framed with an exquisite porch providing an entrance into the magnificent hall set between wings. The hall, with its wide base-crucks and elaborately decorated roof, is magnificent and remarkably complete. Dendrochronology has now established that the roof timbers were felled in spring 1436. This date enables us to link Bryndraenog with a recently edited praise-poem by Ieuan ap Hywel Swrdwal celebrating the new hall of Llywelyn Fychan ab Ieuan of Bugeildy, the chief lord of the district.[11] The poet praises the house for its richness and craftsmanship, especially the windows, which still survive. The poet continues by saying that those who come to the house would swear that it was an angel's work ('gwaith angel'), and asks was it really a man who made the house?

In fact, the administrative context of Bryndraenog is puzzling. It was not a historic centre of lordship administration within Maelienydd, yet it is so extravagant that it only makes sense in a lordship context. The poem makes a significant reference to the high status of the house by claiming that 'the duke' has many houses: 'I'r dug mae llawer o dai'. The duke may be identified as Richard Plantagenet, duke of York, heir to the vast Mortimer estates, and of course an unsuccessful claimant to the throne. Bryndraenog was built around five years after the duke had entered into his inheritance. Bryndraenog was not a lordship centre, but it was strategically sited midway between Ludlow (the duke's administrative centre) and the profitable lordships north of Maelienydd, whose income was important to Duke Richard. By using the route along the Teme valley, which passed in front of Bryndraenog, ducal officials could travel completely within Yorkist territory.[12] No doubt Bryndraenog accommodated lordship officials when travelling between lordships; and it was magnificent and vast enough to accommodate the duke himself and his retinue.

[11] Dylan Foster Evans (ed.), *Gwaith Hywel Swrdwal a'i Deulu* (Aberystwyth, 2000), pp. 98–100.

[12] Duncan James kindly pointed this out to me.

The second group of hall-houses belonged to members of the emerging gentry class, who might dominate a particular parish or township. They were wealthy and influential families at a local level, and they also partook of a national Welsh culture. They claimed descent from the Welsh lords of their regions and itinerant bards composed numerous praise-poems in their honour and preserved their genealogies. The poems generally follow the same pattern: they praise the lineage, house and generosity of the patron. The pedigree of the patron was important for his inherited gentility, but also as a statement of his claim to his inherited estate. The generosity of the patron was part of the idea of inherited gentility.

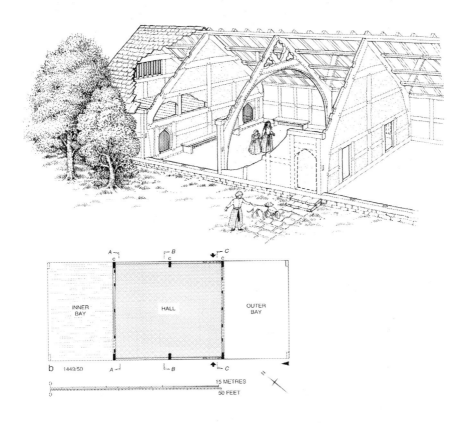

Fig. 5 A gentry hall-house: Great House, Newchurch, Radnorshire. Drawing by Jane Durrant. RCAHMW: Crown Copyright.

Working from the poetry and genealogies of the period, I have been able to calculate a survival rate of some 40 per cent for these halls in one particular area, north Radnorshire. Gentry halls are instantly recognizable because the central hall truss, the pride and joy of the owner of the hall, usually survives smoke-blackened and embedded in the inserted seventeenth-century chimney, and is usually only visible now at loft level. The cusped decoration (a quatrefoil flanked by trefoils) at Great House (Newchurch, Radnorshire) is characteristic (Fig. 5), and the trusses were shaped from timber felled in winter 1449/50. Llanshay, near Knighton (Radnorshire), dated to 1432/3, is the earliest of the dendro-dated gentry hall-houses, but it already has a mature plan form, and its decoration is virtually indistinguishable from that of Tŷ-mawr (Trefeglwys, Montgomeryshire) which was built sometime after 1510. Two points need to be emphasized about gentry hall-houses. First, there is the absolute regularity of the three-unit plan, which was hierarchically arranged with the two-bayed open hall set between lofted upper and lower ends. Secondly, the ornate central truss seems to have been the defining feature of a gentry hall and every gentry dwelling had a truss that was at least archbraced if not cusped. These ornate trusses are always striking and impressive, but the aesthetics of the decoration needs to be explored. Certainly at one level it should be appreciated that the quatrefoil emphasized the wealth of the owner of the hall because it echoed the cusping on the gold coinage of the period. It is very striking that there is not much variation between the plan and decoration of gentry hall-houses. The implication is probably that a fairly restricted type of status-related material culture made comparisons between houses easier and assertions of status relatively unambiguous.

Nevertheless, gentry halls developed in an interesting way. They were sometimes enlarged by the addition of a storeyed box-framed wing to the upper end of a cruck-framed hall (see Fig. 6). The open hall with its dais was left unaltered and presumably continued to provide the formal setting for meals. Some of these developments can be precisely dated. For example at Burfa (Evenjobb, Radnorshire), dendrochronology has demonstrated that the box-framed wing was added in 1502 to a cruck-framed hall constructed fifteen years earlier. In some respects the craftsmanship of these hall and cross-wing combinations of the first half of the sixteenth century was the supreme achievement of Welsh carpenters who combined the cruck- and box-framing traditions. In terms of planning, they seem to have been modelled on the hall and chamber blocks of aristocratic households, and there may have been some interesting social separation in the rooms of the cross-wings. Some solar cross-wings seem to have been elaborately decorated, although often only fragmentary wallpaintings survive. Uniquely at Althrey (Bangor-on-Dee, Flintshire) one is brought face to face with the owners of the hall. A remarkable mid-sixteenth-century double portrait of Elis ap Richard and his wife, Jane Hanmer, survives in the principal chamber.[13] The aristocratic pretensions of the Welsh *uchelwyr* are evident in this portrait and it was obviously based on contemporary royal 'power' portraits.

Fig. 6 Hall and cross-wing at Lower House, Walton, Radnorshire. Drawing by Jane Durrant. RCAHMW: Crown Copyright.

When reconstruction drawings of medieval dwellings are made, they are generally left unfurnished, as in the cutaway of the hall and cross-wing at Walton, Radnorshire (Fig. 6). There is not really much suggestion in the

---

[13] Smith, *Houses of the Welsh Countryside*, pl. VII; Peter Lord, *The Visual Culture of Wales: Imaging the Nation* (Cardiff, 2000), p. 23.

literature that late medieval houses had elaborate furniture apart from the fixed dais seat, which occasionally survives, and the associated table ('bwrdd tâl') which the poets sometimes mention. But the hall was not empty, despite the lack of furniture. Late medieval halls were certainly full of smoke from open fires, as the soot-encrusted trusses show today. Ideally the hall was also filled with the social personality of its owner. As the poets make clear, halls were expected to be full of praise, full of generosity and full of the high status of its owner. Building a hall established status, but there was a continual need to maintain status through entertainment. The inhospitable hall could be a matter for shame and satire. The status of the owner of the hall was periodically refreshed or renewed through feasts and through praise poetry. The genre is well known, but significant new examples have been brought to light by the current series on the poetry of the poets of the late medieval Welsh nobility (Cyfres Beirdd yr Uchelwyr) published by the University of Wales Centre for Advanced Welsh and Celtic Studies.

Two examples may be given here of poems of praise and dispraise because they are relatively early and short, and form something of a contrasting pair, one inverting the conventions of the other.[14] The first poem by Hillyn praises Ieuan Llwyd's new hall whose timber trusses have been 'raised' in south Ceredigion. The poet praises the dressed-stone walls, the posts of an aisle-truss within, and the whiteness of the building. Hillyn commends the extravagance of his patron who has spent so freely on a perfect house and who nourishes the bards within its hall.

> Dathlu codi Tŷ Ieuan Llwyd:
> Costes cun barddles, beirddlith,
> Ieuan rhan rhwydd, dŷ difeth,
> Naddfain a gwyngalch, filch fath,
> Neb ni'i cyst y rhyw byst byth!

Celebrating the building of Ieuan Llwyd's hall: A lord who benefits a poet, and who nourishes poets, [namely] Ieuan of generous portion has spent on a flawless house; he has spent on dressed stones and lime-wash of a splendid kind, no one else will ever [again] spend on such posts!

In the poem of dispraise (a rare survival) by Tudur Ddall, the poet satirizes the inhospitable hall of one Hywel. The fire within the hall is

---

[14] Ann Parry Owen (ed.), *Gwaith Llywelyn Brydydd Hoddnant, Dafydd ap Gwilym, Hillyn ac Eraill* (Aberystwyth, 1996), p. 104; R. Iestyn Daniel (ed.), *Gwaith Dafydd Y Coed a Beirdd Eraill o Lyfr Coch Hergest* (Aberystwyth, 2002), p. 203. I must thank Mary Burdett-Jones and R. Iestyn Daniel for discussing the texts with me.

sooting the crucks, but the door of the house is kept closed and there is no hospitality within. The poet, in a kind of curse, wishes that the house, although built of solid oak, would come tumbling down, and that fire from the unshared hearth would consume the house.

> Dychan i neuadd Hywel:
> Neuadd Hywel hygel hegl,
> Newydd-drwg: neud mwg a'i meigl,
> Ys dôr gaead, nid rhad rhugl,
> Os derw, ys diriaid na sigl,
> Ys oerffyrch anhygyrch hogl,
> Ys del drwy nen ei phen ffagl!

A satire on Hywel's hall: Behold the hall of Hywel with its hidden leg[s] (= hams *or* blades/feet of crucks), here is a new ill: smoke is soiling (= sooting) it; its door is closed, there is no open hospitality within. If it is made of oak, it is unfortunate that it doesn't sway; it is an inaccessible monstrosity with miserable forks (= crucks), may a flame come through the top of its roof!

The link between houses, status, liberality and hospitality is clear from these poems. There are abundant poetic references to feasts, of course, and even a specific reference by Lewys Glyn Cothi to sixty people who were present at a feast in Ieuan ap Phylib's hall in Cefn-llys (described above). There are no visual depictions of Welsh feasts. We have to imagine them from other sources like the famous drawing in the fourteenth-century Luttrell psalter which shows the trestle table, the ritual of serving, and the seating precedence at the dais end of Sir Geoffrey Luttrell's hall. Art historians have found it difficult to account for Sir Geoffrey's glum expression, although one cannot resist observing, with tongue only slightly in cheek, that establishing and maintaining one's status was undoubtedly a time-consuming, expensive and exhausting business.

As for minstrels, they are depicted in the famous panel now at Cotehele carved by a named Welsh carpenter.[15] The carving is broadly contemporary with the regulations prepared for the 1523 eisteddfod, which refer to the completion of a gentry house as one of the occasions when poets could embark on a circuit, suggesting of course that the practice was well established.[16] It must have been a remarkable occasion when a poem was

---

[15] Ralph A. Griffiths, *Sir Rhys ap Thomas and his Family* (Cardiff, 1993), p. 85 and pl. 7.

[16] Gwyn Thomas, *Eisteddfodau Caerwys: The Caerwys Eisteddfodau* (Caerdydd, 1968), pp. 68–9.

first recited in the house it praised. There are few certain details about performance but, in terms of the architecture of the medieval house, it needs to be emphasized that the preference for timber building was consistent with an emphasis on verbal culture. There were very good acoustic reasons for building a timber hall. The late medieval hall was the key auditory space in which poetry was sung or recited to the accompaniment of the harp and crwth. Recent work at the Globe Theatre has shown that the acoustic properties of wood helped to create an ambient sound.[17] A poem declaimed to the accompaniment of the hair-strung harp or crwth would have sounded better in a timber hall than in a stone hall because of the resonant properties of wood. It is probable that the lavish timber dais partition and associated canopy would have acted as sounding boards, throwing the sound back from performer (facing the dais) to the audience and filling the hall with sound.

Here we must emphasize the close connections between the two most significant surviving expressions of material culture in late medieval Wales – houses and the manuscript books which were kept in them. It is of remarkable interest that the chronology of manuscript production in the fifteenth century mirrors the chronology of house building. The hiatus in building in the early part of the fifteenth century was paralleled by a break in manuscript production. Daniel Huws has established that very few manuscripts dating from the first half of the fifteenth century have survived.[18] Moreover, there are no significant collections of poetry before *c*.1450. When poetry collections are made during the second half of the fifteenth century they are compilations of a new type of poetry, the *cywyddau* which praised the houses, gentility and generosity of the gentry patrons. It cannot be a coincidence that this new type of poetry (which had developed orally over the previous century) was given permanence at precisely the time when durable gentry hall-houses were being constructed.

I now turn to the less affluent free-tenants of the lordships, who may be called 'peasants' as a shorthand term for small-scale pastoral farmers. They are a class without a documented history and it is their dwellings which provide historical information about their *mentalité* and way of life. A few years ago the likelihood that a sixteenth-century peasant house would have survived seemed remote, but the evidence is now very strong that peasant halls form the structural core of many of the present-day farmhouses in much of Wales. Numerous fragmentary peasant houses with single-bayed halls have been identified and a few complete dwellings

---

[17] Bruce R. Smith, *The Acoustic World of Early Modern England* (London, 1999), chap. 8.

[18] Daniel Huws, *Medieval Welsh Manuscripts* (Cardiff, 2000), pp. 61–2, 86.

have been recorded, although regrettably several of the most complete examples have been destroyed during the past few years.

The contrast between houses with single- and two-bay halls probably corresponded to a very marked social contrast in terms of wealth. Wills and inventories from the very end of the hall-house period suggest that the owners of single-bay halls might leave goods worth between £15 and £30, while the occupiers of the two-bay halls were three or four times as wealthy, having goods which in some instances were worth £100. The parish gentry derived their income not simply from direct farming, but from other sources, often renting the parish tithes and exploiting the local mills. Sometimes their two-bay halls were sited near mills and the parish church. By contrast the single-bayed halls were often strung out on sloping ground between enclosed ground and the open mountain or common.

Fig. 7 A peasant hall-house: Tyddyn Llwydion, Pennant Melangell, Montgomeryshire. Drawing by Charles Green. RCAHMW: Crown Copyright.

There were probably many hundreds of these miniature halls in Powys, but their date range is uncertain. The single-bayed halls which have been dated were built in the mid-sixteenth century, but the sample is small and there are probably earlier examples. A range of single-bayed halls has been examined throughout Wales, but in many cases the timber was found to be fast-grown (probably derived from hedgerows rather than managed woods) and unsuitable for dating. There are only five secure dates, but they are remarkably close. Two box-framed single-bay halls from Montgomeryshire produced dates of late 1550 and 1552. Three cruck-framed examples have been dated: Llwyn (Llandrinio, Montgomeryshire) was built from timber felled in spring 1552, Tyddyn Llwydion (Pennant Melangell, Montgomery-shire) in 1554, and Nannerth-ganol (Cwmteuddwr, Radnorshire) in 1555.

A great deal is known about Tyddyn Llwydion because it has been exhaustively surveyed by the Royal Commission on the Ancient and Historical Monuments of Wales and excavated by the Clwyd-Powys Archaeological Trust.[19] The findings have been combined in a reconstruction drawing which shows the architectural interpretation of the house (Fig. 7). It has four bays hierarchically arranged: the inner room or parlour distinguished by close studding, a hall of a single bay, the passage and the lower-end bay. Excavation reached the parts inaccessible to architectural survey and refined the architectural interpretation. Crucially the location of the hall was established by the discovery of evidence for a large hearth. The interpretation of the lower-end bay as a cowhouse was confirmed by the discovery of the points of numerous stakes which defined the stalls. However, Tyddyn Llwydion produced few datable finds and it was the type of site that archaeologists tend to call 'aceramic'. The upland peasant hall in Wales was possibly completely dominated by a wood-based material culture.

Fig. 8 Reconstruction of a single-bayed hall at Upper Hem, Forden, Montgomeryshire. Drawing by Geoff Ward. RCAHMW: Crown Copyright.

The recovery of the single-bayed peasant hall is a most important step in our understanding of the range of late medieval dwellings. The peasant hall-house presented in miniature the hierarchy of the great hall complete

---

[19] W. J. Britnell and R. F. Suggett, 'A Sixteenth-Century Peasant Hallhouse in Powys: Survey and Excavation of Tyddyn Llwydion, Pennant Melangell, Montgomeryshire', *Archaeological Journal*, 159 (2002), 142–69.

with lower and higher ends and the sequence of cross-passage, hall and dais. The peasant hall-house was characteristically platformed with the socially superior end at a physically higher level than the outer room. Particular attention was paid to the entry into the hall from the cross-passage. The cutaway drawing (Fig. 8) shows a reconstruction of a single-bayed hall recorded before its demolition in Montgomeryshire. Here the entry to the hall was defined by special spere-posts, and the focus of the hall was clearly the dais where the farmer sat like a lord in his own hall with a canopy over the bench.

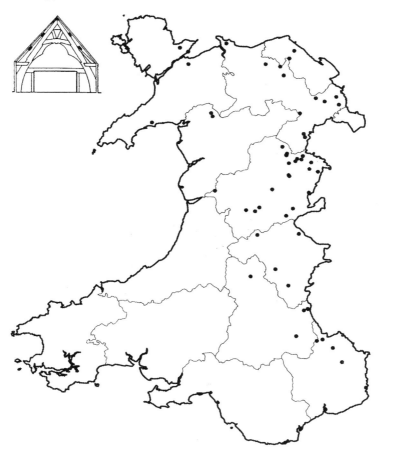

Fig. 9 Distribution map of dais canopies in Wales.
(Based on Smith, 'Houses of the Welsh Countryside', Map 24, with additions.)
RCAHMW: Crown Copyright.

It is of extraordinary interest that a range of Welsh hall-houses, many of modest status, incorporate as a structural architectural feature a canopy over the dais. The distribution map (Fig. 9) of surviving examples shows that this remarkable feature was widespread in the lordships of the March. The dais canopy has been interpreted in functional terms as an internal jetty designed to prevent soot from the open fire falling onto the high table. However, the canopy had greater symbolic significance as a representation of the cloth of estate which was present over the seat of the king and other great lords. Many canopies are more impressive than functional; most remarkably, the great trefoiled opening which frames the recessed dais seat of the gentry hall at Middle Maestorglwyd (Llanigon, Breconshire) seems to derive from the trefoiling of the roof of Westminster Hall, the supreme architectural expression of royal lordship.

The peasant hall-house was a scaled-down version of the aristocratic hierarchically arranged hall-house, complete with dais. The resemblances between hall-houses of different status have been observed before. Christopher Dyer rightly suggests that it raises difficult problems about the peasants' perception of their place in society.[20] Does it really mean, he asks, that peasants admired and imitated their lords' style? Was society so saturated with the aristocratic model that there were no alternative conceptions of housing? Or were peasant and gentry halls functionally different despite similarities in planning that were in fact superficial? This latter suggestion must be rejected. The hierarchical arrangement of the peasant hall complete with dais end is very revealing. The peasant who sat in his own seat at the upper end of his own hall was obviously his own master. Since there was social emulation in housing, there was surely emulation of the social life associated with the open hall. It is probable that many peasants in their durable halls imitated the gentry lifestyle, including the aristocratic practices of formal dining, hosting feasts, and patronizing and rewarding minstrels. The widespread adoption of the gentry lifestyle is consistent with sixteenth-century complaints that there were far too many untutored minstrels who devalued the calling of the expert poets and musicians. The uniform plan of the hall-house shows that there was in effect only one model of housing for lord and peasant in late medieval Wales. In one sense this was social conservatism, but for many peasants, especially those descended from the unfree, this would have been a social revolution. The changing nature of society in post-Glyndŵr Wales has been widely discussed, but the transformation in housing is the most revealing expression of a profound preoccupation with asserting free status through

---

[20] Christopher Dyer, 'History and Vernacular Architecture', *Vernacular Architecture*, 28 (1997), 6–7.

architecture and maintaining the style of living appropriate to the durable hall-house. We are, of course, the fortunate but unintended beneficiaries of conspicuous spending on the crafts of both poet and carpenter.

Locations of houses mentioned in the text:

Althrey Hall (Alrhe) (Bangor-on-Dee, Flintshire) SJ 3791 4408
Bryndraenog (Bugeildy, Radnorshire) SO 2040 7853
Burfa (Evenjobb, Radnorshire) SO 2794 6134
Cefn-llys Castle (Cefn-llys, Radnorshire) SO 092 630
Great House (Newchurch, Radnorshire) SO 2166 5066
Llanshay (Knighton, Radnorshire) SO 2970 7180
Llwyn (Llandrinio, Montgomeryshire) SJ 2460 1683
Lower House (Walton, Radnorshire) SO 2594 5976
Middle Maestorglwyd (Llanigon, Breconshire) SO 2125 3725
Nannerth-ganol (Cwmteuddwr, Radnorshire) SN 9424 7137
Sycharth (Llansilin, Denbighshire) SJ 2052 2586
Tretower Court (Tre-tŵr, Breconshire) SO 1857 2117
Tŷ-draw (Llanarmon Mynydd Mawr, Denbighshire) SJ 1282 2793
Tŷ-mawr (Trefeglwys, Montgomeryshire) SN 9573 8987
Tyddyn Llwydion (Pennant Melangell, Montgomeryshire) SJ 1077 2595
Upper Hem (Forden, Montgomeryshire) SJ 2343 0026
Upper House (Painscastle, Radnorshire) SO 1670 4612
Y Faner [Abbey Farm] (Cymer Abbey, Llanelltyd, Merioneth) SH 7208 1955

7

Wales and Hamburg: The Problems of a Younger Son

J. GWYNFOR JONES

On New Year's Day 1623 a dutiful younger son wrote to his father from Hamburg, where he was in his seventh year pursuing an apprenticeship as a merchant. At that time this younger son, Maurice Wynn of Gwydir in the Conwy valley, was advising his father, Sir John Wynn, how best to use his lead ore deposits for his own financial gain at Gwydir and for his merchant son's benefit in Germany. In his letter Maurice Wynn emphasized his complete reliance on his father's generosity in sustaining his commercial career:

> and by this meanes yow shall incourage mee much to goe forward in this course of life which I hardly beeleeve any of my breethren but myself would have undertaken but all this I did in obedience to yow with dutie vnto yow. What I have don in this kind I do not repent mee, god hath called mee vnto it & doubt not but will bless mee in the same, therefore I purpose, except some obstackle hinder, to proceed as I have beegun.[1]

Such a declaration of intent reflects three broad aspects of Maurice Wynn's outlook on commercial life and his motive for continuing along his chosen path. Despite the hindrances he was determined to make a success of his career. He was independent by nature and puritanically inclined, viewing his vocation as an accomplishment of divine will in his own life. Yet he was a son eagerly prepared to submit to his father's wishes.[2] When he unfairly rebuked Sir John for being niggardly towards him, he still sought and respected his advice and, referring to the two years' apprenticeship he had to serve, he stated:

> I will god willing, goe forwardes as I have beegunn. Yet though I had a mind to leave this course yet not presently would I do it . . . But if I find

---

[1] NLW MS 9058E, letter no. 1060 (1 January 1623).
[2] Ibid.

no hope at all of amending . . . I then will leave it & imbrace any honest course of life that yow shall wish me vnto . . . I shall willingly refer all things to your good discretion, not doupting with your fatherly care but yow will wish noething but for the best as ever hetherto I have found it.[3]

This was indeed a fulsome tribute to his father's benignity, a trait not often attributed by historians to that seemingly austere person. Such comments, however, reveal the frustrations which the younger son experienced in the early days of his career. Given his economic plight in Hamburg in the early 1620s, it appears that Maurice Wynn felt deep-seated resentment against his older and younger brothers and he reproached his father for attending more diligently to their needs than to his. He had expected a more generous response on this occasion but only obtained £100 although he had urgently requested double that amount:

I shall (god willinge) haue a tolleration to trade for my selfe freelie, & haueing noe more but soe much monney yt may proove to bee some disparadgment vnto yowr selfe (god haueing soe well blessed yow with meanes) to aford mee soe smale a some . . . yt hath pleased god to call mee vnto this vocation of a marchantt in w'ch (I praise him) I haue continewed vnto this time . . .[4]

In a broader context, studies of the Welsh gentry in the sixteenth and early seventeenth centuries have concentrated mainly on the fortunes of senior members of landowning families, chiefly because they, so it is believed, contributed the most to promoting the Tudor settlement (1536–43) as well as their own interests. By contrast the careers of younger sons have not been given the attention they fully deserve, perhaps because they were not normally eligible to inherit estates. On their father's death they were expected to fend for themselves and seek their livelihood elsewhere, chiefly as lawyers, administrators, clergymen, land speculators, moneylenders and commercial dealers.[5] Not that they abandoned their native countryside altogether when opportunities came their way. Indeed, many of them returned, married local heiresses and enjoyed relatively prosperous lives as minor country gentry. Among the most prestigious was John Salusbury, fourth son of Thomas Salusbury of Lleweni, who founded the Bachymbyd

---

[3] NLW MS 9058E, letter no. 1054 (5 December 1622).
[4] NLW MS 9057E, letter no. 964 (30 June 1621).
[5] For the social background, see J. F. Rees, *Studies in Welsh History* (Cardiff, 1947), pp. 54–5; W. Ogwen Williams, *Tudor Gwynedd* (Caernarfon, 1958), pp. 40–8; Glanmor Williams, *Renewal and Reformation: Wales c.1415–1642* (Oxford, 1993), pp. 418–19; J. Gwynfor Jones, *The Welsh Gentry, 1536–1640: Images of Status, Honour and Authority* (Cardiff, 1998), pp. 203–32.

branch towards the end of the fifteenth century.[6] Sir Roger Vaughan, third son of his namesake of Bredwardine, likewise succeeded in establishing the Vaughan family of Tre-tŵr;[7] and Francis Mansel, younger son of Sir Edward Mansel of Margam abbey, set up a junior branch at Muddlescombe, Carmarthenshire.[8] Examples could readily be multiplied, the most notable probably being the three younger sons of Thomas Morgan of Machen, namely Reynold, John and Edmund Morgan, who respectively became the founders of the cadet families of Llanfedw in east Glamorgan and Basaleg and Penllwyn-sarff in Gwent.[9] Ambitious sons of this type, each possessing shrewd business skills, established their fortunes through judiciously acquiring land and property and serving in local administration. Some of them, such as Sir Thomas Myddelton of Chirk Castle, a prestigious London entrepreneur, and his younger brother, Sir Hugh Myddelton, who also prospered in London, managed their affairs efficiently and subsequently broadened their interests.[10]

Many other younger home-keeping sons often associated themselves through marriage with well-established families of equal status, thereby coming to enjoy a local hegemony and achieving for themselves a status which served to perpetuate their own and the senior family's reputation and to increase their power. If a picture of society at gentry level is to be fully appreciated, further research is required into the lives and careers of Welsh gentlemen who, for far too long, have been regarded as inferior to their eldest brothers who enjoyed the benefits of primogeniture.[11]

One such younger son whose early career deserves consideration is Maurice Wynn, sixth son of Sir John Wynn of Gwydir, who held sway in north Wales for almost half a century between 1580 and 1627.[12] The Wynn papers are a mine of information on the attitudes and activities of family members and their inter-relationship with people of their own *milieu* in their locality and elsewhere. Judging by his correspondence with his father,

[6] *DWB*, pp. 900–1; W. J. Smith (ed.), *Calendar of Salusbury Correspondence, 1553–c.1700* (Cardiff, 1954), pp. 7–8, 13; table I, sheet A; table II, sheet A.

[7] *DWB*, pp. 1000–1.

[8] *DWB*, p. 611.

[9] L. Toulmin Smith (ed.), *The Itinerary in Wales of John Leland* (London, 1906), p. 14; G. T. Clark (ed.), *Limbus Patrum Morganiae et Glamorganiae* (London, 1886), p. 311; J. Gwynfor Jones, *The Morgan Family of Tredegar: Its Origins, Growth and Advancement c.1340–1674* (Newport, 1995), p. [6].

[10] *DWB*, pp. 675–6.

[11] For a discussion of the status of younger merchant sons, see Ruth Kelso, *The Doctrine of the English Gentleman in the Sixteenth Century* (Gloucester, MA, 1964), pp. 60–9 (esp. 66–7).

[12] For the background to the family, see J. Gwynfor Jones, *The Wynn Family of Gwydir: Origins, Growth and Development c.1490–1674* (Aberystwyth, 1995). For Sir John Wynn, see pp. 52–73, and for Maurice Wynn, pp. 63–7, 98–9, 100–1, 106–7, 128–9, 153–4, 202–3.

Maurice Wynn's period in Hamburg, a Hansa and Lutheran free imperial city in north-west Germany, between 1618 and 1624, was not entirely to his liking, mainly because of poor trade conditions. Although Hamburg was not seriously hit by the Thirty Years War, Wynn's letters reveal that its impact severely affected his prospects.[13] He was a self-motivated and tenacious younger son who, for several years, strove to overcome the obstacles which hindered his progress.[14] Sir John failed to give him sufficient allowance to complete his apprenticeship in order that he might set himself up as a merchant in his own right. His long and detailed letters, most of which he sent to his father, contain thorough accounts of the war and information on the commercial and political condition of Germany.[15]

In his youth Maurice Wynn was expected at one stage to pursue a university career. In his will in 1614 his eldest brother, Sir John Wynn junior, bequeathed to him £10 which he was to receive two years after entering on his bachelor of arts degree. He was not the only one among Sir John's sons to contemplate a career in trade and commerce, for it was expected that another, Owen, the third son, would become apprenticed to a London Merchant Adventurer. Soon after November 1608, when it was decided that he would be placed with a Mr Thorold, a merchant of the Staple, the arrangement was abandoned.[16] Whether or not Owen had the right aptitude to pursue such an apprenticeship it is difficult to say, but his father charged his heir, Sir Richard Wynn, to 'be curteouse & kynd unto hym so wyll he rune his head unto the fyre to do yow servyce'. The letter continued:

> Yowr brother Owen I have not so well provyded for as I was wyllynge . . .
> he ys fittest to lyve in the contrey & manadge the contrey affaers for I
> broght hym up in that sort of lyf becawse I saw yow w'th draw your self
> from a contrey lyf . . . your affayres wylbe but a trouble & an expence
> vnto hym & better wear hit for hym to draw to a retyred lyfe & to lyve of
> hys owen.[17]

---

[13] Hamburg shared the same privileges as Nürnberg and Augsburg. For its commercial status, see M. S. Anderson, *War and Society in Europe of the Old Regime, 1618–1789* (Leicester, 1988), p. 69; D. H. Pennington, *Europe in the Seventeenth Century* (London, 1989 edn), p. 355; Geoffrey Parker and Lesley M. Smith (eds), *The General Crisis of the Seventeenth Century* (London, 1997 edn), pp. 60, 98; Anthony F. Upton, *Europe, 1600–1789* (London, 2001), p. 62.

[14] Marjorie Foljambe Hall, 'The Wynn Papers (1515–1690): a Resumé and an Appreciation', *Y Cymmrodor*, 38 (1927), 110–11.

[15] For abstracts of Maurice Wynn's letters and others related to him, see John Ballinger (ed.), *Calendar of Wynn of Gwydir Papers, 1515–1690* (Cardiff, 1926), nos 696, 865, 883, 895–6, 898, 922, 964, 1013, 1023, 1031, 1054, 1060, 1078, 1083, 1088, 1132, 1154, 1205.

[16] NLW MS 9053E, letter nos 473 (15 January 1607–8); 487 (28 November 1608), 489 (12 December 1608), 494 (8 March 1608–9). Old style dates are retained in the notes but, in the text, the year is assumed to have begun on 1 January.

[17] NLW MS 9059E, letter no. 1188 (21 January 1623–4).

Although aware of his father's dire economic circumstances, Maurice was more concerned about his own miserable condition which caused him to complain to him in 1623 at a time when the most devastating of bad harvests occurred. His correspondence in that year reveals his desire for promotion to merchant status, offers prudent advice to his father on his financial circumstances, and supplies details of commercial fortunes and the course of the war. He was also anxious to help his father to come to terms with his economic plight and advise him on how he might improve the fortunes of the declining lead mines at Nant Bwlch-yr-haearn near Gwydir. Evidence from the Wynn papers reveals that some years previously Sir John had planned to experiment with the mineral resources he possessed on his estates, and in 1605 he also took a keen interest in the Mynydd Parys copper mines in Anglesey.[18] Although he did not realize his ambitions, his son Maurice became increasingly aware of the commercial potential of his father's estate and of the need to exploit it.

Despite the difficulties which Maurice Wynn experienced he can be regarded in some respects as one of the noblest of Sir John Wynn's sons. He possessed an adventurous spirit and, as an apprentice merchant, he learned much about the unsettled political and economic scene in Europe. He was attached to the fellowship of the Merchant Adventurers of England and became a factor for Rowland Backhouse, a London merchant who was reputed to be 'a very honest man'.[19] The chief export commodity was white or unfinished cloth. The trade was interrupted in 1614 when its privileges were transferred to Sir William Cockayne, whose new company produced dyed and finished cloth.[20] Wynn was disturbed by the crisis, but was promised by his master that if trade privileges were not restored within twelve months he would place him with another merchant so that he might serve the eight remaining years of his apprenticeship. With the collapse of the Cockayne project in 1617, trade was restored to the Merchant Adventurers, and it was then that Wynn settled in Hamburg, the European headquarters, where he served as Backhouse's agent.[21] In 1615 he testified to his master's kindness to him in purchasing apparel at a time when many

---

[18] NLW MS 9053E, letter no. 455 (6 November 1607); NLW Add MS 465E, letter nos 456 (9 November 1607), 460 (20 November 1607), 462 (30 November 1607); NLW MS 9053E, letter nos 467 (21 December 1607), 470 (1607), 471 (1607); Jones, *Wynn Family of Gwydir*, p. 68.

[19] NLW MS 9055E, letter no. 684 (14 February 1614–15); NLW MS 9056E, letter no. 896 (4 March 1619–20).

[20] Christopher Hill, *The Century of Revolution, 1603–1714* (Edinburgh, 1961), pp. 35–7; Astrid Friis, *Alderman Cockayne's Project and the Cloth Trade* (Copenhagen, 1927), *passim*; Barry E. Supple, *Commercial Crisis and Change in England 1600–42* (Cambridge, 1959), *passim*; Rees, *Studies in Welsh History*, p. 54.

[21] NLW MS 9056E, letter no. 896 (4 March 1619–20), NLW MS 9057E, letter no. 973 (24 August 1621); NLW MS 9055E, letter no. 696 (22 May 1615).

other merchants overseas were failing to meet their debts and expenses.[22] He found it extremely difficult, however, to maintain his position as a gentleman's son because of poor trading conditions and he constantly reminded his father of his duty to support him financially. As a merchant he would rank lower than a gentleman, a cause of considerable vexation to him. Because of his impoverished state he regarded the French crown (which was equivalent to an English groat), which he had received as a token from his father, as a mere pittance.[23] In the early summer of 1619 he began to feel the pinch and his comments reflected the condition of merchants in Hamburg generally:

> The barrenness of our trade at present is such that men are scarce able to liue upon yt & without a man hath very good menes indeed to beegin withall hee will neuer raise himself therby, both w'ch well considered will make a man awery of his prentiship considering there is noe better hope heerafter by yt to bee expected, but will rather growe with the wordle [sic], worse every day then other.[24]

Owing to Sir John Wynn's failure to meet his needs, Maurice Wynn considered himself to be socially placed among the less well-endowed.[25] In June 1621 he again approached his father, urgently requesting that he forward to him £200 as well as whatever lead deposits he had in his own mines so that the sum might be increased to £500 or £600.[26] Although he had served six and a half years of his apprenticeship and was about to pursue his chosen vocation, his circumstances forced him to think seriously about whether or not he should continue in trade. His view of his brothers' advancement served only to increase his annoyance:

> I fownde many times accidents w'ch caused mee to call my former life in mind & yet for all that I tooke resolution to goe forward in my vocation tho some thing contrary unto my mind (at some times) all to show my selfe an obedient sonn unto yow . . . but yet diuers doe daielie forget the same wch is to be pittied & withall in my education you have not bin at any great charge with mee noething soe much as to my younger breethren & thes thinges considered I hope it shall not bee forgott tho far distant in place from yow & withall wanting a frind to speke a good word for mee in due time.[27]

[22] NLW MS 9055E, letter no. 696 (22 May 1615).
[23] Ibid.
[24] NLW MS 9056E, letter no. 865 (31 May 1619).
[25] NLW MS 9057E, letter no. 964 (30 June 1621).
[26] Ibid.
[27] Ibid.

His words at the time showed no awareness of his father's own economic plight at home. The year 1622–3 was a period of scarcity which had damaging effects on the economy of Gwydir and prevented Sir John from attending to his son's needs. His urgent requirements led him to borrow money, which made him less self-assured in his correspondence with those from whom he expected help.[28] Writing from London in December 1621, his London-based son, Owen, informed him of the scarcity of money in the metropolis and of the fact that merchants failed to accumulate more than £200, whereas in the previous year they had easily raised £700 in a very short time.[29] He feared that his father's rents would be delayed and that expenditures relating to his lead mines would prevent him from being able to pay the drovers and make ends meet generally. This forced Sir John Wynn to take stock of his affairs in March 1623. He confessed that he was unable to satisfy Maurice's demands in Hamburg and complained how arduous his circumstances were:

> The thing w'ch annoyeth mee most is the decay of my rents & revenues w'ch have fallen above four hundreth pownds this yeare, & the next are like to fall also. I lose more then anie other . . . becawse my livinge consistes of great tenements & those mountayn land w'ch have noe corne growinge in them for these two yeares passed, neither cattel nor wooll nor sheepe nor butter cheese nor anie other comoditie that land yeldeth have borne anie pryce so as I am thousand pownds behynd of my last yeares rents & w'ch ys worsse my tenants have not wherewith to pay . . . the bread corne is at that exceedinge rate that a number doe die in this countrey for hunger w'ch is a lamentable thing to see, & the rest have the impression of hunger in ther ffaces exceedinge the memorie of anie man lyvynge.[30]

In such economic circumstances Maurice Wynn realized that his father was not in any position to assist him, and he was also increasingly aware that the war in Germany had had damaging effects on his trade. On New Year's Day 1623 he expressed his horror that the war showed no signs of subsiding:

> In these parts as yet we have wars & rumours of wars . . . all trade is much decayed: great hath bin the afliction of this country both with 4 years wars and base monneys w'ch hath been the undoing of many a honest man & indeed all the whole church of god at present is much perplexed . . . some with wars and our owne country with poverty . . .[31]

[28] NLW MS 9058E, letter nos 1075 (23 March 1622–3), 1085 (15 April 1623); NLW Add MS 466E, letter no. 1064 (18 January 1622–3).
[29] NLW MS 9057E, letter no. 993 (6 December 1621).
[30] NLW MS 9058E, letter no. 1075 (23 March 1622–3).
[31] NLW MS 9058E, letter no. 1060 (1 January 1622–3).

Cloth was scarce, yet merchants were unable to sell it. The number of ships used to transport the cloth had been reduced from eighteen to six, but the heavily laden vessels could not dispose of it. Debasement of the coinage had also led to a substantial increase in the price of all commodities and, according to Wynn, 200 merchants had been made insolvent because of the flourishing Dutch woollen trade.[32]

In these circumstances Maurice Wynn attempted to improve his own trading enterprises, to make his father's lead mines profitable, and to ensure that lead was quickly exported through London to Leghorn (Livorno) in Italy or Spain where there were better commercial prospects. Robert Geoffreys, a London Merchant Adventurer who was Sir John Wynn's financial adviser and a man whom Wynn trusted, became involved with the schemes he had devised to improve trading activities.[33] Circumstances, however, militated against Wynn and he admitted that 'ther is small hopes yt [i.e. lead] will raise in price in regard ther is much scarcitie of monney in the land wch causeth all commodities to bee at a low eb'.[34] In August 1620 he reported that since a large quantity of cheap lead ore had been imported into northern Germany from Poland it would be difficult to sell further quantities at a reasonable price there. If, as Sir John believed, the lead contained pewter or silver, it might be sold to Daniel Höchstetter (II) of Keswick, Cumberland. He was further advised to exploit what copper he had on his land so that it might go to Spain.[35] This advice coincided with a period of gradually improving economic conditions in Germany; harvests became more plentiful and the cloth trade more buoyant. War conditions, however, still had their devastating effects.

Maurice Wynn was a resilient person. His puritanical tendencies, doubtless cultivated during his stay in Hamburg, made him determined to persist in his plans. In response to his father's inquiry regarding what his future ambitions might be if his commercial interests were to cease, he replied:

> And in regard of the badness of trade you will mee to advize yow wither I will p'seed as I have beegoon either in this trade w'ch may mend or allter & fall into an other as divers have don or live a retired life in the countrie, But to resolve as yet I cannot . . . if I could receive content by it & a reasonable p'fit to maintain myself like an honest man w'ch if I find any

[32] NLW MS 9058E, letter no. 1023 (3 June 1622).
[33] Ibid.
[34] NLW MS 9055E, letter no. 684 (14 February 1614–15); NLW MS 9056E, letter nos 896 (4 March 1619–20), 898 (1 April 1620); NLW MS 9058E, letter nos 1021 (23 May 1622), 1023 (3 June 1622); NLW Add MS 466E, letter no. 1045 (18 October 1622); NLW Add MS 466E, letter no. 1184 (1 January 1623–4).
[35] NLW MS 9058E, letter no. 1031 (31 August 1622).

hope of during this time yt I have to serve being yet 2 years I will god willing, goe forwardes as I have beegunn.[36]

If his enterprise failed he would, according to his father's wishes, consider pursuing a 'retired life' as a gentleman. Sir John Wynn, however, entertained hopes of partly alleviating both their plights when he sent his son 20 tons of lead, and, in response, Maurice pressed his father to explore the possibilities of selling lead containing silver at a good price.[37] Sir John, however, was continually running his lead mines at a loss. The cost of mining and exporting was one problem; another was the expenditure laid out in smelting and purchasing the machinery needed for the work. Wynn constantly sought advice regarding how best to sell his lead. In 1622, for example, he approached Thomas Jones of Halcyn in Flintshire, an area well-known for its lead-smelting, but with little success.[38] Because of the urgent need for corn supplies in 1623, Sir John inquired whether corn could be exchanged for Welsh cottons in Newcastle upon Tyne, but the reply was negative because of the distance, the economic problems in Germany and the fact that many 'doe perrish daylie for wante of foode and . . . what corn is brought in to Newcastle . . . may not bee sent away for other partes'.[39]

Maurice also considered transferring his father's trade to Bristol because merchants there had close connections with France and might obtain corn in exchange for Welsh cloths, but this plan did not materialize either. He urged his father, however, not to abandon hope of reviving his lead mines and suggested using the port of Beaumaris, increasing the 24 tons already deposited there to 100 tons, and sending it with 100 tons of lead ore to him in Hamburg where he would inquire further where it might be sold, possibly in Lisbon, Leghorn or Málaga.[40] He mistrusted the Dutch and ceased trading with them because of their crafty dealings. If he succeeded in obtaining good-quality deposits, trading in alum and copperas (green non-sulphate crystals) was a prospect which Maurice Wynn was prepared to exploit. But losses were incurred in trading with Middelburg merchants, and he believed that his father should not sell lead and ore to the Dutch unless they offered reasonable terms. Indeed, in his view, his father's best course of action would be to sell them to him. Maurice also planned for the

---

[36] NLW MS 9058E, letter no. 1054 (5 December 1622).
[37] Ibid.
[38] Ibid. NLW Add MS 466E, letter no. 905 (11 July 1620); Jones, *Wynn Family of Gwydir,* pp. 65, 67; William Rees, *Industry Before the Industrial Revolution* (2 vols, Cardiff, 1968), II, pp. 421–2; W. J. Lewis, *Lead Mining in Wales* (Cardiff, 1967), pp. 58–63.
[39] NLW MS 9058E, letter no. 1078 (1 April 1623).
[40] NLW MS 9058E, letter no. 1060 (1 January 1622–3).

butter which his father obtained at Chester fair and markets to be sent to London, from where it could be exported to Lisbon where it was needed. In the following year he thought it possible that butter and lead ore might be exchanged for corn in Germany, and he pressed his father to use what influence he had to promote a parliamentary bill allowing butter and cheese to be directly exported from Wales to Germany.[41] Maurice feared, however, that war in Germany might have further serious consequences on his livelihood, for corn was still scarce and economic conditions were deteriorating. In response to his father's plea for imported corn in 1623, he offered no solution because of lack of money:

> for monny is the measure of wares, and where there is noe silver ther is leatle trade, and beesides corne is a commoditie that is bought for redy monny in all places, & consequentlie men will sell yt soe as they doe in Spain & England, & all other countries yet to have a good price will make a man give time of payment.[42]

Maurice Wynn did not regret entering the commercial trade and remained convinced that divine guidance had enabled him to face and overcome all adversities in his attempt to achieve success. Whether his father agreed with him is doubtful, but he was aware of his son's anxiety when trade was at a low ebb.

Maurice Wynn's puritanical disposition often revealed itself in varying degrees in his correspondence. When his father sent him a copy of Lewis Bayly's popular *The Practice of Piety* (*c.*1611) and Sir Francis Bacon's *Essays* (probably the 1619 edition, which consisted of thirty-eight essays), he expected him to meditate on their contents.[43] Both works contained much food for thought which a serious-minded young merchant like Maurice might have appreciated. Referring to these books in a letter, his brother William stated that Maurice should peruse them 'for the true use of diuinitie and morality', which 'laye well to [his] hearte'.[44] In one letter Maurice cautiously advised his father to promote preaching in his locality instead of spending his dwindling resources building a hospital for the poor at a time of pestilence:

> & nowe thinkeing of that dearth I presume to put yow in mind that there is annother Dearth that wch is worse by far w'ch is not soe sencible as the

---

[41] NLW MS 9058E, letter no. 1078 (1 April 1623); NLW Add MS 465E, letter no. 502 (14 August 1609); Rees, *Studies in Welsh History*, p. 55.

[42] NLW MS 9058E, letter no. 1060 (1 January 1622–3).

[43] NLW MS 9056E, letter nos 896 (4 March 1619–20), 898 (1 April 1620).

[44] NLW MS 9056E, letter no. 898 (1 April 1620).

other, but ought to bee far more and wee may insteid feare to bee the cause of the other, and that is the want of gods word preached amoungst yow by reson of w'ch Diuers soules perrish for want of knowledge; non can bee saued without ffaith and how is it wrought in mens hartes but by heareing his word ther; wher the words not hard ther cann be noe faith & without ffaith yt is vnposible to please god . . . I doe think yt to be a more pleaseing service to god to find one preaching minister, then to make 10 hospitalles for yt is not often seene that men perish for want of foode, but presumed . . . that many perish for want of eternal foode . . .[45]

It was clearly Maurice's faith which gave him the much-needed resilience to continue as a merchant in Hamburg. His master planned to extend his apprenticeship, but since he was totally dependent on his father for financial assistance he was uncertain whether he should continue with his chosen career or return home to become a country gentleman. His father urged him to consider marriage and suggested an unnamed heiress with £200 per annum, but Maurice showed little enthusiasm for her, claiming that her dowry was scarcely worth more than the allowance which he expected from his father.[46] If a suitable spouse could be found, however, he would accede to his father's wishes and comply with the conditions laid down by him:

it was my intent allwaies to liue a single life, & most on this side seas for more priuattnes & saueing of greate expences w'ch England will p'force draw a man unto, & so to have cut my cloke according to my cloth and with this kind of life I could well bee contented not that I hould it the best course of life but most fit for mee as matters stand & I doe not doupt but to be able by gods grace to liue as well & chast as I have done hitherto.

Wynn was not opposed to considering life as a country gentleman, but he was aware of the need to secure himself financially before considering any proposals. He was equally aware of the dangers besetting a merchant's life:

aduentureing diuers wayes, both at sea, & to men in giueing credit by both thes, men hath bin ouerthrowne, & many haue raysed ther fortunes acording as god hath blessed mens labours, a man may be now a ritch man & tomorrow a beggar, these lies in gods handes, to w'ch wee must refer ourselves, & therewith contented what casualltie soever comes to passe, & bee allwaies perswaded that yt is for good . . .[47]

---

[45] NLW MS 9058E, letter no. 1132 (23 August 1623).
[46] NLW MS 9058E, letter no. 1088 (19 April 1623).
[47] NLW MS 9058E, letter no. 1083 (9 April 1623).

'I am a man soe indifferent', he maintained when responding to Sir John's marriage plans, 'that I will doe as yow shall command me',[48] but, in view of financial constraints and the rent arrears which might be incurred, he feared that he would be unable to establish himself as an estate-owning gentleman at home. Only if he succeeded in building up his finances reasonably well in Hamburg would he be prepared to consider pleasing his father in these matters:

> I may heere during my abode with my Mr imploy yt in trade & soe gett a prettie some of monney together that heereafter I may imploy it in trade in the contrie such as I shall looke out for haveing not spent my time soe ill but that I can pick out a liueing ther & soe by thes meanes I shall haue two stringes to my bow that in case tennants make bad payment I may supplie my selfe out of the profit of my trade ther, & this is a certaine course if yt lykes yow I can searve my Mr a yeere after my yeeres are ended & not reject this ofer, for a yeere; hence yow may bee pleased to take her to yow to learne the English tongue & the yeere after I will god willing come home.[49]

In any event, he discouraged his father from reaching a hasty decision. He was happy to remain where he was and to make the best of his circumstances. He had set his heart on succeeding as a merchant, and his growing concern for his father's material welfare also cast light on his own ambitions. Offering advice on such matters, however, only served to exasperate further a perplexed father whose personal knowledge of how to handle his lead deposits was inadequate. Maurice Wynn believed that his father was capable of improving his economic circumstances in trade if only he could gain more reliable and trustworthy advice on how his lead might be mined, treated and prepared for export.

Maurice Wynn returned to his native country in the summer of 1624. Despite his previous suggestions to the contrary, his last known letter to his father from Hamburg contains advice on how to melt ore into lead.[50] According to his calculations, this would produce about 30 tons of lead, for which Maurice would seek a market on his return to Wales. His subsequent whereabouts are not known, but, according to his correspondence, it appears that he settled at Gwydir for some years.[51] Whether or not

---

[48] NLW MS 9058E, letter no. 1088 (19 April 1623).
[49] Ibid.
[50] NLW MS 9059E, letter no. 1219 (4 May 1624); NLW MS 9062E, letter no. 1626 (1638–9).
[51] NLW Add MS 467E, letter no. 1588 (19 November 1635), letter no. 1589 (1 June 1636).

he was disillusioned on his return is not known, but his experiences in Hamburg had not been encouraging. Judging by his activities, he seems to have decided to settle as a modestly placed gentleman, first at Gwydir and then, in 1649, at Crogen in Llandderfel, Merioneth.[52] He showed no further resentment over his brothers' advantages over him, and used his business capacities to exert some influence in local administration in his latter years, becoming a justice and commissioner of array for Caernarfonshire in 1642–3, justice of the peace and sheriff of Merioneth in 1651, and receiver-general for north Wales in 1653.[53]

Maurice Wynn's early career as a trade agent in Germany reveals features which were shared by many younger sons of gentry in the early modern period. Despite his affection for his father, his desire to advance his own career was frustrated in part because he considered that his brothers gained favour at Gwydir at his expense. He saw himself as an Orlando who proclaimed that in birth he differed 'not from the stalling of an ox',[54] and as an apprentice he faced stiff competition in Hamburg. It was no easy task for young men like him to enter the professions and, in the commercial world, circumstances often dogged their progress, as John ap Robert maintained in *The Yonger Brother His Apology* (1618).[55] Voicing his disapproval of the conduct of some eldest sons, John ap Robert favoured discarding primogeniture and granting equality to all sons.

> For an elder brother is found to spend more in a year idlie, then would prefer, or maintain a whole familie noblie; and to suffer their brothers and sisters to shift, which as these time shape, is oftentymes to liue either lewdly, or most miserably; being forced either to forget their good education, or to lay aside all badges of gentrie, who otherwise with some reasonable helps, might do God, their Countrey, and Family much honour.[56]

In his letters Wynn considered that he had been left with less to his name than his other brothers although, shortly before his death, Sir John Wynn

---

[52] NLW MS 9064E, letter nos 1903 (20 October 1649), 2032 (Maurice Wynn of Crogen's rental, 1653); Jones, *Wynn Family of Gwydir*, p. 101.

[53] NLW MS 9063E, letter no. 1764 (6 February 1645–6); J. R. S. Phillips (ed.), *The Justices of the Peace in Wales and Monmouthshire, 1541 to 1689* (Cardiff, 1975), pp. 30, 51; *PRO Lists and Indexes*, IX *List of Sheriffs for England and Wales* (New York, repr. 1963), p. 261; Edward Breese (ed.), *The New Kalendars of Gwynedd, 1284–1993*, ed. Hywel F. Richards (reprinted Denbigh, 1994), p. 91; B. E. Howells (ed.), *A Calendar of Letters Relating to North Wales, 1537–circa 1700* (Cardiff, 1967), no. 227, p. 137; W. M. Myddelton (ed.), *Chirk Castle Accounts A.D. 1605–1666* (St Albans, 1908), p. 44.

[54] *As You Like It*, Act 1, scene 1.

[55] Joan Thirsk, 'Younger Sons in the Seventeenth Century', *History*, 54 (1969), 365; John ap Robert, *The Yonger Brother His Apology by it selfe* (London, 1618).

[56] John ap Robert, *The Yonger Brother*, p. 33.

surprisingly admitted that, while economic forces had prevented him from adding to his son's portion, he cared more for his advancement than he did for his other children's welfare:

> the times are starke naughte for trade decreaseth exceedingly . . . Money is verie scante heere. The prices of Landes fall haulfe in haulfe of whatt they weare worthe heartofore. My father cannot receaue the third parte of his rents clearly these latter yeares besides hee is in dett and therfore payeth great interest, manie other allowances yssuynge alsoe yearly out of his livinge.[57]

These words were written by Maurice's brother William who, at the time, was serving the master of wards and wardrobe. He excused his father's inability to pay the merchant son his due portion. Although the country-side was devastated by famine and plague, he maintained that his father 'will not faile to adde still to yowr porcion, his care beinge now more for your preferment then anie of his children'. Despite the distance between Gwydir and Hamburg, he claimed that his father had vowed that he would assist Maurice, 'wherfor lett it not soe trouble yow that yow are out of his sight for surely yow are not out of his minde, and the longer hee hath [that is, to live] the better it wilbee for yow and all of us'. Sir John himself was fully aware that William and Henry had been better provided for than Maurice and Owen,[58] which suggests that he considered that something needed to be done to help them. In a letter of 21 January 1624 he charged his heir Sir Richard to care for 'poore Morice' who was 'utterly unprovyded for', and to 'lett hym have all that ys left hym by my wyll or eny other conveyance'.[59]

Maurice Wynn's desperation was caused largely by his failure to establish a reputation for himself as a merchant. On several occasions he considered himself to be so poorly treated that his fate was comparable to that of the younger sons of Italian merchants who were placed in monasteries so as not to be a financial burden on their families.[60] Maurice's respect for his father, however, was undisputed, as is revealed in a letter to him in December 1622:

> for . . . your great loue yow beare to mee w'ch I perceaue by this your leater receiued I doe most humblie thanke yow, & god blesseing mee I shall euer Indeuour soe to beehave my selfe as yt yow shall neuer haue

---

[57] NLW Add MS 466E, letter no. 1184 (1 January 1623–4).
[58] NLW MS 9059E, letter no. 1188 (21 January 1623–4).
[59] Ibid.
[60] NLW MS 9058E, letter no. 1132 (23 August 1623).

ocation otherwise to conceite of mee, and if I have ofended in beeing something to ernest for a greater stock I craue pardon for the same beeing inforced to doe yt beecawse I would doe as others more Inferiour . . .[61]

His declarations of obedience seemed on occasions to offset the bitter feelings which he often expressed about the lack of support given him. He believed on this occasion that his father had been unfair to him because, regardless of his efforts to please and be obedient, he had not been given means to prosper. His brothers' nests, he observed, 'are very well fethered allready by being soe neare at hand'.[62] On another occasion he claimed that he had gained more respect from an unnamed fellow merchant from Denbigh than from his own 'near kinred (to ther shame bee yt spoken)'.[63] In fact, most of his brothers had done well for themselves in education and in their subsequent careers. Sir Richard, the heir to Gwydir following his eldest brother's death in 1614, had been educated at Lincoln's Inn and had spent all his adult days at court.[64] Owen and Robert were sent to Westminster school and later Eton,[65] and Robert went on to Cambridge.[66] Ellis Wynn, who died in 1619, went to Gray's Inn, William Wynn entered Cambridge,[67] and Henry, the youngest of Gwydir sons, was educated at St Albans and the Inner Temple.[68]

Doubtless Maurice Wynn's concern for economic problems on the Gwydir estate caused him considerable distress and, in his opinion, impeded his progress in Hamburg's commercial world:

I thanke god I know not any cawse for yt, neither is the faulte in mee except yow thinke to much obedience (if I may soe tearme yt), a fault in takeing this course of life w'ch I know non of the rest of my brethren would ever have don.

---

[61] NLW MS 9058E, letter no. 1054 (5 December 1622).

[62] NLW MS 9058E, letter no. 1132 (23 August 1623).

[63] NLW MS 9056E, letter no. 865 (31 May 1619).

[64] Norman Tucker, 'Sir Richard Wynn of Gwydir, 2nd Baronet', *TCHS*, 22 (1961), 9–19.

[65] NLW MS 9053E, letter nos 429 (15 January 1606–7), 440 (12 April 1607), 449 (22 September 1607), 457 (10 November 1607), 464 (7 December 1607), 473 (15 January 1607–8).

[66] NLW MS 9053E, letter nos 476 (15 February 1607–8), 481 (28 June 1608), 487 (28 November 1608); NLW MS 9054E, letter no. 608 (1612).

[67] NLW MS 9054E, letter no. 571 (4 November 1611); NLW MS 9056E, letter nos 867 (10 August 1619), 878 (14 October 1619).

[68] NLW MS 9056E, letter nos 836–7 (19, 31 May 1618), 844 (7 October 1618), 886–7 (30 November, 6 December 1619); NLW MS 9058E, letter no. 1008 (12 February 1621–2).

Dependent though he was on his father's liberality and eager to demonstrate his obedience, he possessed an independent spirit which revealed itself in his statements on the essential needs of merchants: 'For one without monney (w'ch is the essens of a marchant) is but as a sipher in Arithmetick for of noething (as the saying is) noething can bee produced, and yt halfe repentes mee that I haue lost soe much time in my aprentiship.'[69]

Maurice Wynn's sheer determination to maintain his position as an apprentice merchant was a distinguishing feature of his character; so also was his aim to see his father improve his own economic circumstances in order that he might advance his own trading prospects. In June 1622 he commented on his own adversity and then observed the general economic distress which he reckoned was God's punishment for sin:

> yet I see no other remedie but for that w'ch cannot bee helped must with patience bee borne, & partake somewhat in my owne particular, with the misseries of thes present dayes w'ch greeues mee much to heere, & that ther showld bee such a want of monney throw the whole land, I pray god amend yt if it bee his will, and amend us all for whoes chasticment thes miseries are inflicted on us.[70]

His puritanism reinforced his determination to maintain whatever independence he could. It does not appear that he held extreme puritan views, but he did write with pietistic and moral fervour when considering his role as a merchant apprentice. When he heard that William was to become a lawyer, he commended him for abandoning an idle life at Gwydir so that he might do something worthwhile, and he hoped that both he and Ellis, another brother, once they had qualified as barristers, would charge their friends low fees:

> I am very glad of that yow showld take such a good course & far more to bee preferred then that Idle life w'ch at home yow did leade hoping yow will now recouer your loste time w'ch heretofore yow spent in the contry in idlenes . . . when yow & my brother Elis are barristers I hope yow will pleade the law for your frindes for smale consideration . . .[71]

As a Puritan, Maurice Wynn disapproved of idleness. To him, austerity, industry and the spirit of individualism were integral features of moral probity, and the reading and preaching of the Word of God were central to

---

[69] NLW MS 9058E, letter no. 1023 (3 June 1622); NLW MS 9058E, letter no. 1132 (23 August 1623).
[70] Ibid.
[71] NLW MS 9056E, letter no. 883 (19 November 1619).

his outlook on life.[72] His mother, Sydney Wynn, had prepared him well for that kind of life, and in her letter to him on 4 March 1620 she reminded him 'to serue god daily and hourely' and to eschew being 'seduced by any to yeeld to that vice of drunkenes' in Germany which, in her view, was 'most subject vnto of eny other nation'.[73] Although no evidence exists to show that Maurice Wynn had any connections with any religious sect, his views revealed deep-seated sobriety and gravity. He attended a church attached to a house set aside as living quarters for foreign merchant apprentices by the Hamburg senate, where he heard three weekly sermons delivered by a Dr Low, one of James I's chaplains, a 'rare preacher', he maintained, who was likely to add to Germany's 'credit'.[74] When he was informed that two of his brothers were about to enter St Albans school in 1615, he was concerned that they might be influenced by the licentious life led by scholars there:

> there is one fawlte ther that drowndes all the rest that is they are apt ther the scollers to take twobacco and to drinke and sweare and many other quallities ther beesides which I can not tell yow but hope per godes grace they will eschew all thos thinges and follow noe evill company.[75]

He went on to cite the example of his master's two sons, who had also been to St Albans and whose time there had been ruined by drinking and smoking.

Maurice Wynn's short career in Hamburg reveals the opportunities and frustrations which an ambitious merchant apprentice encountered in a period of war and economic stringency. As he himself admitted, his experiences were shared by many of his fellow merchants, who were similarly impeded by an unfavourable climate. It might be that Wynn had depended too much on his father. He knew very well that Sir John Wynn's industrial ventures had brought him poor returns and he was also aware that economic conditions on the continent would not enable him to prosper by trading in Welsh cloths, lead and copper which he so eagerly sought to promote. Quoting St Paul in 1623, he saw himself as one 'borne out of dew time',[76] and proceeded to vent his wrath on what he considered to be the

---

[72] John Marlowe, *The Puritan Tradition in English Life* (London, 1956), pp. 72–6; Geoffrey F. Nuttall, *The Puritan Spirit: Essays and Addresses* (London, 1967), pp. 85–7, 95–103; R. H. Tawney, *Religion and the Rise of Capitalism* (Harmondsworth, 1972 edn), pp. 227–51.
[73] NLW MS 9056E, letter no. 895 (4 March 1619–20).
[74] NLW MS 9056E, letter no. 865 (31 May 1619).
[75] NLW MS 9055E, letter no. 696 (22 May 1615).
[76] 1 Corinthians 15, 8.

galling experience of seeing his own kith and kin prospering while he was unable to prove his worth in his chosen profession:

> yt cannot thus but bee a crosse to a man not to bee able to follow his vocasion, if it were your owne case yow would say as much. I write not this as tho I would have yow take monney upon credit to furnish mee; god forbid I should doe soe, noe yt is not my intent. I will rather haue pasience a while but it stickes something in my stomak to see all my breethren both younger & elder seatled in such a course to liue all like gentlemen & my selfe not able to liue like a poore man.[77]

That which he failed to accomplish in the early stages, however, was compensated for in the latter half of his career. After settling on his small estate at Crogen, he assumed an active role as a local administrator and 'financial adviser' to several members of his family until his death on 28 September 1670.[78] Blessed with good health during most of his life, he persevered against all the odds, and his incisive mind and diligence assisted him greatly in contributing to local government administration. Moreover, his business skills also stood him in good stead. While in Hamburg he had frequently expressed unease regarding his position and his insecurity about the future but, within a short time after his return to Wales, his self-confidence and self-esteem were enhanced by his role as a much respected public figure.[79]

In a broader context, Maurice Wynn's hazardous years in Hamburg compared well with the experiences of merchant sons of other gentry families. His correspondence reveals social and religious traits which highlighted his desire to exploit what resources he had. He considered that his status was paramount in explaining his failure to achieve his aim of becoming a successful merchant. He was well aware of the status denied him as a younger son, a status reserved normally for the gentry and aristocracy. Like his peers, he enjoyed economic status and relied purely on his own initiative when conducting his commercial ventures. Maurice was fully aware that land meant wealth, and that wealth meant power and status, and that is why he was reluctant to consider marriage since he would not be able to maintain a wife who had inadequate financial means. His apprenticeship, however, as he realized, was a step towards citizen-ship,[80] but, although his master had offered him freedom to trade during

---

[77] NLW MS 9058E, letter no. 1132 (23 August 1623).

[78] NLW Add MS 469E, letter no. 2601 (28 September 1670); Myddelton (ed.), *Chirk Castle Accounts*, p. 44; Rees, *Studies in Welsh History*, p. 55.

[79] Rees, *Studies in Welsh History*, p. 55.

[80] Kelso, *Doctrine of the English Gentleman*, p. 65.

his last two years and to create him a freeman of the city, his stay in his profession was too short to have any permanent impact.[81] During his generation the cloth and mineral trades were important means of economic expansion, and he believed that sobriety and industry were the outcomes and not the causes of prosperity; hence his emphasis on prudence and probity. Despite his initial disabilities, his religious tendencies led him to believe that material prosperity was a mark of divine approval, and that by the same token economic failure was a mark of divine disapproval. Eventually he enjoyed in Wales the 'gentility' he had sought abroad.[82] To achieve success in trade he had to maintain a stable income, but wartime conditions abroad and famine and plague at home caused economic and financial setbacks. Although he was initially denied a status equal to that of the landed gentry, he eventually acquired it by purchasing an estate and adopting a gentrified lifestyle. Maurice Wynn's years after returning from Hamburg were occupied in strengthening his position as a younger son. He had already shown initiative which enabled him to put his practical skills to good use. He flourished as a modest landed proprietor and trusted county official and applied his resources well in north Wales in an era which saw military unrest, Puritan domination and a restored monarchy.

[81] NLW MS 9055E, letter no. 696 (22 May 1615).
[82] Kelso, *Doctrine of the English Gentleman*, p. 58.

8

A 'Poor, Benighted Church'? Church and Society in Mid-Eighteenth-Century Wales

ERYN M. WHITE

By the eighteenth century the Anglican Church had become widely accepted in Wales and seems to have been held in some affection. It was referred to by scholars and poets as 'y lân Eglwys olau' (the pure, bright Church). Ellis Wynne portrayed the Church in his *Gweledigaetheu y Bardd Cwsc* (Visions of the Sleeping Bard) wreathed in glory, with Queen Anne at its head, defending it with the shining swords of Justice and the Spirit.[1] The translation of the scriptures into Welsh during the sixteenth century had done much to associate the Protestant Anglican faith with the Welsh language and nation. The Welsh language was the only non-state language in Europe to acquire a translation of the Bible within the first century of the Reformation. The Welsh Bible and the introduction of Welsh-medium services under Elizabeth I helped to lay the foundation for the acceptance of the Anglican Church among the Welsh people. The Church was firmly linked to state and society and remained the religion of the majority, despite the freedom granted to Dissent by the Toleration Act of 1689. One consequence of the passing of this Act was a decline in the social and legal pressures impelling people to attend church regularly. Yet in spite of the fact that Anglicanism may well have been a purely nominal religion for many parishioners, it could still command considerable allegiance. At the beginning of the eighteenth century Dissent accounted for only a very small proportion of the population. The Test and Corporation Acts continued to discriminate against those who chose to dissent from the Church by excluding them from public office. All those who held office under the Crown in Wales had to produce sacramental certificates to confirm that they were indeed communicants of the Established Church. On the eve of the eighteenth century, therefore, the position of the Anglican Church seemed unassailable.

Despite its privileged position, however, the Established Church in Wales was beset by difficulties. Most studies of the Welsh Church in the

---

[1] Ellis Wynne, *Gweledigaetheu y Bardd Cwsc* (Llundain, 1703), pp. 45–6.

eighteenth century emphasize its crippling poverty, particularly in the south, its antiquated administration and the chronic lack of interest and leadership afforded by the bishops. Lay impropriation had deprived it of much of its revenue, particularly in the southern dioceses of St David's and Llandaff. Most of the perceived problems relating to the clergy arose from the fact that many of them were very poorly paid, particularly in comparison with their English counterparts. It is no great surprise that 'as ragged as a Welsh curate' became a popular gibe during this period. Those clergy whose benefices were worth less than £50 per annum technically qualified for assistance under Queen Anne's Bounty, which was intended to augment the salaries of the poorest paid clergy. However, the Bounty was poorly adminstered and haphazardly awarded for most of the eighteenth century.[2] It did not, therefore, adequately compensate the worst paid clergy and their meagre salaries drove many of them to pluralism and absenteeism. This was especially true in south Wales. In the northern dioceses of Bangor and St Asaph, where benefices tended to yield a more generous stipend, there was less frequent resort to pluralism. Evan Evans testified to this contrast and its implications for clerical standards when he stated that in north Wales there were 'a decent reputable set of clergy with good salaries' but that in Cardiganshire the clergy were ignorant and so poor as to make 'a despicable appearance in the eyes of the vulgar'.[3] It is undoubtedly true that the 'pure, bright Church' was not without faults. Yet its sternest critics were usually its own members, even its own clergy in the case of the likes of Moses Williams, Griffith Jones and Evan Evans.[4] They complained bitterly about the lack of support given by the church authorities to the Welsh language and the lack of opportunity of preferment for conscientious Welsh-speaking clerics.

The Church has also been subject to considerable criticism over the years from adherents of the Methodist cause. The Methodist revival and the growth of Dissent in general resulted in a radical change in the religious complexion of Wales by the end of the eighteenth century. One of the simplest explanations advanced for the Methodist revival has been that

---

[2] Eric J. Evans, *The Contentious Tithe* (London, 1976), pp. 2–3; S. R. Thomas, 'The Diocese of St David's in the Eighteenth Century, the Working of the Diocese in a Period of Criticism' (unpubl. University of Wales MA thesis, 1983), pp. 229–30; Peter Virgin, *The Church in an Age of Negligence: Ecclesiastical Structure and Problems of Church Reform 1700–1840* (Cambridge, 1989), *passim*. See also J. R. Guy, 'An Investigation into the Pattern and Nature of Patronage, Plurality and Non-Residence in the Old Diocese of Llandaff between 1660 and the Beginning of the Nineteenth Century' (unpubl. University of Wales Ph.D. thesis, 1983).

[3] Hugh Owen (ed.), *Additional Letters of the Morrises of Anglesey (1735–1786)* (parts 1–2, London, 1947–9), part 2, p. 689.

[4] Geraint H. Jenkins, 'Yr Eglwys "Wiwlwys Olau" a'i Beirniaid', *Ceredigion*, 10, no. 2 (1985), 131–46.

it was a response to the weaknesses of the Church in Wales. Over many generations Methodist apologists sustained an image of Wales as spiritually deficient prior to the advent of the Methodist revival. This interpretation of history has been effectively challenged by Geraint H. Jenkins in his work on the period 1660–1730.[5] It is a view of the past which first emerged in the writings of William Williams, Pantycelyn, from the 1760s onwards rather than during the initial stages of the revival itself. It was written retrospectively during a period when Methodism was gaining ground, establishing itself as a national force in Wales, and spreading beyond its original strongholds in rural south and mid-Wales. It is in this context that Williams developed his view of the history of the church. In *Ateb Philo-Evangelius* (1763) in particular, he outlined the history of Christianity as a recurrent cycle of revival and relapse.[6] Like John Foxe, he saw signs of hope in the deeds of heretics such as John Wycliffe in the later Middle Ages. The advent of Protestantism was naturally considered a period of revival, culminating in the Toleration Act of 1689. However, in Williams's view, this ushered in a period of lukewarmness and indifference amongst Anglicans and Dissenters:

> Gwŷr y cwrdd, cystal â gwŷr yr eglwys oedd yn diodde'r twmpath chwarae, anwybodaeth oedd yn goresgyn wyneb Cymru, nid oedd braint a safai i fyny yn erbyn llygredigaeth yr oes, nes oddeutu'r flwyddyn 1738 y torrodd y goleuni allan fel y wawr mewn llawer o ardaloedd y byd.

> Chapel men, like churchmen, suffered the play ground, ignorance prevailed in Wales, no privilege could stand against the corruption of the age, until around the year 1738 the light broke forth like the dawn in many areas of the world.[7]

It is not surprising that Williams wished to emphasize the impact of Methodism by painting an overly gloomy picture of the spiritual state of the country prior to the revival. The Methodists, however, were in the main extremely circumspect regarding the limitations of the Church in public, and professed their allegiance to it as well as urging members to attend Church communion. Methodist leaders, after all, were members of

---

[5] Glanmor Williams, 'The Diocese of St David's from the End of the Middle Ages to the Methodist Revival', *JHSCW*, 25, no. 30 (1976), 25–6; Geraint H. Jenkins, *Literature, Religion and Society in Wales, 1660–1730* (Cardiff, 1978); idem, '"Peth Erchyll Iawn" oedd Methodistiaeth', *LlC*, 17 (1993), 195–7.

[6] Eryn M. White, 'The People Called "Methodists": Early Welsh Methodism and the Question of Identity', *JWRH*, 1 (2001), 1–14.

[7] Garfield H. Hughes (ed.), *Gweithiau William Williams Pantycelyn, Cyfrol II Rhyddiaith* (Cardiff, 1967), p. 23.

the Church and most of them were ordained clergymen. In private, however, they were at times more critical. At a meeting of the Association, the ruling body of Methodism, Morgan John Lewis, a Methodist exhorter or lay preacher, proposed separation from the Church on the grounds that its foundations were Jewish, its canons contrary to the scriptures, its ministers God's enemies and its worship filled with Catholic superstition. The Association rejected the proposal and went on to discuss whether the Protestants had originally left the Catholic Church or had been ejected from it. Eventually, it was concluded that they had been expelled for denouncing errors within the Church. Howel Harris noted that 'we are guilty of none of the evils in our church as having all born our Testimony against them', the implication being that they should wait to be forced out of the Church rather than volunteer to leave.[8] Harris invariably spoke more in sorrow than in anger when addressing the deficiencies of the Church. He frequently referred to it as a 'poor, benighted Church', which he prayed might be reformed and enlightened.[9] On more than one occasion he and other Methodist leaders urged lay exhorters in the Association to bear with the church. During the monthly association held in October 1745 he said: 'I spoke home too of not giving offence to ye clergy etc. as much as possible as we are in ye Establishd Church & as it bore with us more than any church would.'[10] As a layman who preached extensively, Harris was frequently challenged regarding his attitude to the Church. He demonstrated a good deal of restraint in responding to the hostile letters of David Lloyd, the incumbent of Llandyfalle, Breconshire, before yielding to the temptation to justify his itineracy by citing the failings of the clergy:

they Preach some once a month others in English to a congregation of poor blind ignorant Creatures that understand little or no English that come and go as heedless as if they had been in a market & yet so are they blinded by the blind guides that they cry if we did after one half of what we hear in Church we would be safe how many scores of parishes may you go to and not find one man as much as Reformed much less inwardly changed by all the Preaching & yet the Cry is what need is there to go about have not we a Church and minister in every Parish and the generallity in the Parish as Ignorant as if they never heard a sermon what they hear being so slightly said & so slightly received & so profane as if there had been no Religion in the Country – for the fear of the Civil Law

---

[8] NLW, Calvinistic Methodist Archives, Diaries of Howel Harris, 103, 5 October 1743.

[9] For instance, NLW, Calvinistic Methodist Archives, Trevecka Letters 755, 916, 934; Diary of Howel Harris, 105, 2 December 1743.

[10] NLW, Calvinistic Methodist Archives, Diary of Howel Harris, 118, 21 October 1745.

would restrain from Publick Sins if there were no church ministry & that is all that is restrained in the Country & hardly that.[11]

Was there, however, any justification for this indictment? Were the clergy indeed 'blind guides' whose negligence drove their parishioners into the open arms of the Methodists and Dissenters? The quality of local clergymen was undoubtedly an important factor which determined attitudes to the church. There was certainly a good deal of criticism of the ineffectiveness of the parish clergy and of their unbecoming conduct. Serving two or three extensive rural parishes in order to earn a modest salary meant that it was virtually impossible for some of the clergy to fufil their duties to each church on Sundays. They were inevitably non-resident in some of their parishes, although many used the dilapidation of parsonages as an excuse, doubtless with some justification in several instances, for being so remiss.[12] A great many colourful stories circulated regarding their misdeeds, some of them certainly much embellished in the telling. A curate of Llan-y-crwys, Carmarthenshire, at the dawn of the century was said to leave the church on occasion during divine service to serve at the alehouse he had opened in the churchyard.[13] Howel Harris used to record in his diary some hair-raising tales about local clergymen, including the incumbent of Haverfordwest who allegedly sired and slaughtered a substantial number of illegitimate children whose bodies were buried in the garden of the parsonage.[14] Most of these tales were hugely exaggerated and it is not surprising that people enjoyed repeating them. As Evan Evans, whose own drinking habits were hardly above reproach, complained: 'The enemies of God's Church are always ready on all hands to take away any handle in these very evil days to speak ill of the Gospel and its ministers, how much more, when there is so much occasion given.'[15] Evan Evans and Goronwy Owen figure among the best-known of the eighteenth-century Welsh clergy and among the finest poets of the period; yet both were frustrated by their lack of advancement in the Church and were much inclined to seek solace in alcohol, which only served to hinder further any prospect of preferment.

[11] NLW, Calvinistic Methodist Archives, Trevecka Letters 343, 14 June 1741.
[12] Owain W. Jones, 'The Welsh Church in the Eighteenth Century', in David Walker (ed.), *A History of the Church in Wales* (Penarth, 1976), pp. 114–17; Nigel Yates, *Buildings, Faith and Worship: The Liturgical Arrangement of Anglican Churches 1700–1900* (Oxford, 1991), p. 48.
[13] G. Milwyn Griffiths, 'A Visitation of the Archdeaconry of Carmarthen, 1710', *NLWJ*, 19, no. 3 (1976), 319. See also J. R. Guy, 'Riding against the Clock: the Visitations of Edward Tenison in Carmarthen and Ossory in the Early Eighteenth Century', in J. R. Guy and W. G. Neely (eds), *Contrasts and Comparisons: Studies in Irish and Welsh Church History* (Llandysul, 1999), pp. 55–64.
[14] NLW, Calvinistic Methodist Archives, Diaries of Howel Harris, 54, 13 March 1740.
[15] NLW MS 2009B, p. 11.

Despite the proliferation of rumours, however, not many cases of neglect of duty were brought before the consistory courts. It is possible that many parishioners were inured to the effects of pluralism and only complained in extreme cases. A certain worldliness may not have been considered unusual amongst eighteenth-century clergy. Complaints against the clergy came under the jurisdiction of the consistory courts, though it is hard to discover firm evidence regarding clerical standards on the basis of these records since the evidence has not survived for all areas. There are no records for the period 1730–60 for the diocese of St Asaph or for the archdeaconries of St David's and Cardigan within the diocese of St David's. Apart from charges of conducting clandestine marriages,[16] only one accusation exists for neglect of duty in the archdeaconry of Brecon between 1730 and 1760.[17] Records are fuller for the archdeaconry of Carmarthen, where seventeen clergymen appeared between 1730 and 1760, mainly for neglect of duty. For example, John James, vicar of Meidrim, was charged with neglect of duty by one of his own churchwardens in 1740. The evidence of eleven witnesses, along with that of the vicar himself, was submitted to the court in this complicated case. Two of the chief charges levelled against James related to the family of William Brown, a 38-year-old butcher.[18] It was alleged that Brown had asked James to administer the sacrament to his wife, who was fatally ill, on 7 May 1739. The vicar's response was that he could not be expected to come that afternoon since it was already 4 p.m. Mrs Brown died without receiving the sacrament on 11 May. In addition, on 5 August 1739 Brown asked the vicar to bury his dead child the following afternoon, but he refused to do so unless he received payment beforehand. The body of the child was thus interred without Christian burial. The vicar's defence against the charge of failure to bury the child was that he had been taken prisoner by David Morgan, the under-sheriff of the county, just as he was on the point of conducting the service.[19] Witnesses testified that, following his release, he had requested that the grave be opened so that he might give the child a Christian burial, an offer which the father refused because the corpse had by then lain in the grave for a week.[20] David Lewis, vicar of Aber-nant, further testified that when he had been called to perform a burial service at Meidrim James had prevented him and taken away his surplice.[21] Meidrim, it would seem, was

---

[16] In this context this usually entailed conducting marriage ceremonies outside the hours permitted by law.

[17] NLW, Church in Wales Records, SD/CCB/G.

[18] NLW, Church in Wales Records, SD/CCCm(G)/289a.

[19] NLW, Church in Wales Records, SD/CCCm(G)/289k.

[20] NLW, Church in Wales Records, SD/CCCm(G)/289l–m.

[21] NLW, Church in Wales Records, SD/CCCm(G)/289o.

a less than happy parish, for John James had earlier in 1740 brought charges against his sexton, Thomas Rees John, for neglect of duty.[22]

In the diocese of Llandaff during the same period there are thirteen complaints against members of the clergy. One of these relates to clandestine marriage and the remaining twelve to drunkenness and neglect of duty, although in the case of John Powell of Aberystruth and Philip Thomas of Wenvoe this arose mainly from their association with the Methodist movement.[23] John Jones, curate of Coety, was accused in 1731 of unbecoming conduct and of being a scandal and a reproach to his order by resorting to alehouses and 'keeping company therein with ordinary Scandilous dissolute loose and profligate idle people, till you have got drunk & intoxicated your self with liquor there cursing swearing – fighting & quarrelling & generally behaveing your self as other drunken, dissolute & idle people do'.[24] He was also accused of neglecting his duty in order to occupy himself with farming and other lay employment. In addition Jones was said to be 'a fomenter a stirrer up of feuds, heats animosities strife quarrells & Discord'. His preference was apparently for teaching young men to fence and fight rather than catechizing the children of the parish. One witness, Richard Berry, heard Jones encourage one David Llew of Coety to fight: '"Dio, gwr wyti Myn Duw, pan bo ti yn taro, taro y dre myn Duw" signifying in English "Davey thou art a Man (by God) & whenever thou dost strike any body, strike home (by God)"'.[25] Another witness, Edward Nicholl, stated that nine years previously Jones had, out of sheer malice, refused to christen Nicholl's newborn child or to church his wife.[26] It is significant that several of the complaints involved failure to baptize or bury individuals, particularly young children, cases which would have caused parents genuine distress and prompted them to complain when other cases of neglect might have been excused.

It is remarkable that not a single complaint has survived in the consistory court papers for the diocese of Bangor during the same thirty-year period. There are references to accusations brought against the clergy in the surviving act books, but these do not provide any details. It is, therefore, difficult to know how much substance lay behind these cases. For instance, an accusation is listed against Ellis Wynne, rector of Llanfair near Harlech and author of *Gweledigaetheu y Bardd Cwsc*, for neglect of duty in 1730. The case was apparently the result of a parochial dispute over church seats, where the complainant was more at fault than the

---

[22] NLW, Church in Wales Records, SD/CCCm(G)/287.
[23] NLW, Church in Wales Records, LL/CC/G/918; LL/CC/G/952.
[24] NLW, Church in Wales Records, LL/CC/G/620.
[25] NLW, Church in Wales Records, LL/CC/G/620a.
[26] NLW, Church in Wales Records, LL/CC/G/620i.

ıe evidence for the dioceses of Bangor and St Asaph is obviously
to give a complete picture, but it seems to confirm Evan Evans's
. pastoral standards were higher among the clergy of north

r major cause for concern and criticism was the question of the
ıguage.[28] The Church was reckoned by its sternest critics, such as
Evan Evans and Moses and Samuel Williams, to be failing in providing
services and supporting publications in Welsh. Certainly the bishops
invariably offered less than wholehearted support for the native language.
The Act for the Translation of the Scriptures into Welsh in 1563 had
established the principle that Welsh should be the language of public
worship in parishes where it was commonly spoken. Yet it is clear that
valuable benefices, which were more common in the north of the country,
were awarded to non-Welsh-speaking incumbents by lay impropriators or
English bishops. In those cases, more often than not, Welsh-speaking
curates were appointed to carry out the day-to-day duties of the parish.
Most Welsh parishes were therefore served in Welsh, but that is not to say
that they were always adequately served. The Church had problems arising
from its responsibility to minister to all the souls within the parish. This
meant that if there was one non-Welsh-speaking person or family who
attended church, provision was required in English. Devising a suitable
formula of bilingual worship sometimes required a good deal of ingenuity.
The simplest solution was to conduct one Welsh and one English service
on a Sunday, which worked well in a large parish where two services were
held on a Sunday, but was beyond the means of a pluralist curate who
ministered to three or four churches. The latter would often conduct a
mixed service, with different elements in different languages.

Attempts to devise a fair linguistic policy often gave rise to complicated
arrangements, as was apparent in the the bilingual parishes of Gresford,
Marchwiel, Minera, Ruabon and Wrexham in Denbighshire, together with
an associated chapel at Delincourt.[29] The rural dean's report of 1749
explained that Minera was served entirely in Welsh and Marchwiel entirely
in English, except for the second lesson which was held in Welsh, as was
one service each month. At Gresford, the vicar always officiated in English
in the mornings, with the evening sermons alternating between Welsh and
English in the summer and the second lesson always read in Welsh. A
similar arrangement prevailed in Wrexham parish church and Delincourt

---

[27] Gwyn Thomas, *Ellis Wynne* (Cardiff, 1984), pp. 9–10.
[28] Eryn M. White, 'The Established Church, Dissent and the Welsh Language,
*c.*1660–1811', in Geraint H. Jenkins (ed.), *The Welsh Language before the Industrial
Revolution* (Cardiff, 1997), pp. 235–87.
[29] NLW, Church in Wales Records, SA/RD/26.

chapel: morning service was in English and evening service alternately Welsh and English in both. Whenever there was evening service in Welsh in one, there would be an English service in the other. The language at Ruabon church varied since, as the dean explained, 'The language used in church is about half Welsh half English, variable according to the congregation the vicar sees there.' It was not uncommon in bilingual parishes for the officiating clergyman to take a straw poll of Welsh- and English-speakers at the beginning of the service and then determine which language or mixture of languages to use. In addition, the clergy would in some cases be expected to conduct English services for the benefit of leading gentry families. English services were introduced into the Welsh-speaking parish of Llanycil, Merioneth, for the benefit of justices and lawyers who assembled at the Courts of Great Sessions in Bala.[30] Wherever the linguistic policy did not adequately cater for Welsh speakers, the Church was in danger of losing some of its members to Dissenting congregations which offered not only a fixed service but also in a language they could understand. Although few actual complaints were voiced by parishioners regarding the language provision, it was becoming an increasing problem for the Church in the light of competition from Methodism and Dissent.

Therefore, there is evidence of pastoral shortcomings in the records of the Church, but it needs to be viewed with caution. Several complaints seem to have arisen after a lengthy period of tension within the parish between incumbent, sexton and churchwardens. It is difficult to judge how many cases were unfounded and malicious since the judgements have not always survived to reveal whether the clergy involved were exonerated or not. These are obviously the most extreme examples in any case and represent only a minority of the clergy. For each clergyman guilty of neglect of duty, one could cite a decent, conscientious counterpart like Griffith Jones, Thomas Ellis, Daniel Rowland and David Havard, who took seriously the care of souls in their charge.

If there is no conclusive evidence that the clergy were 'blind guides', what then of the perceived impact on their parishioners? Is there any evidence to substantiate Howel Harris's accusation that lack of clerical guidance had an impact on the behaviour and attitude of parishioners in general? Matters of discipline, in the case of parishioners as well as clergymen, were the province of the church courts. Since there were no archdeacons' courts in the Welsh dioceses, cases were heard by the bishops' consistory courts. The consistory courts retained the right to grant marriage licences and probate, as well as overseeing discipline 'for

---

[30] NLW, Church in Wales Records, SA/RD/21; SA/RD/23; SA/RD/26; SA/QA/12.

the reformation of morals and the soul's health'.[31] The courts had played an important role in ensuring religious conformity during the initial phases of the Protestant Reformation,[32] but by the eighteenth century they were less concerned with ensuring regular attendance and more preoccupied with cases relating to morality, conduct in church, defamation and payment of church tithes and rates. The courts had only limited power to punish and could not inflict physical or financial punishments by this period. They could, however, insist on costs being paid, as in the case of Anne Parry of Nefyn, Caernarfonshire, who was excommunicated for failing to pay the costs of £6 10*s*. for the judgement awarded against her for assaulting Lowri Jones during divine service in Nefyn church.[33] There were three major sanctions available: excommunication (often temporary), admonition and penance. Excommunication was a frequent sentence in the church courts of early and mid-eighteenth-century Wales. It was often imposed on those who failed to pay church rate and on those who failed to appear to answer charges, usually on a temporary basis until the error was corrected. It entailed exclusion from the Church and its communion – in effect from the Christian community – but it could be revoked if the sinner showed contrition. Penance had traditionally involved a public apology before the assembled congregation in church. The offender had often been required to wear a white sheet as a symbol of penitence and a form of public shaming. However, quoting John Penry's statement, Glanmor Williams suggests that, even during the late sixteenth century, these rituals did not constitute any great deterrent: 'The punishment hereof in our bishop's court is derided of our people. For what is it to them to pay a little money or to run through the church in a white sheet?'[34]

By the eighteenth century penance had become less public and less obviously humiliating. For instance, in 1739 Joan, wife of William David Lewis of Llanddingad, Carmarthenshire, was found guilty of defamation and was ordered to apologize in the church porch before the witnesses in the case and at least one churchwarden, rather than the entire congregation. There was less shame involved in such a sentence, but even so Joan was subsequently excommunicated for refusing to carry out the penance.[35] The

---

[31] Martin Ingram, *Church Courts, Sex and Marriage in England, 1570–1640* (Cambridge, 1987), p. 43; idem, 'Reformation of Manners in Early Modern England', in Paul Griffiths, Adam Fox and Steve Hindle (eds), *The Experience of Authority in Early Modern England* (Basingstoke, 1996), p. 54. See also Walter T. Morgan, 'The Consistory Courts in the Diocese of St David's, 1660–1858', *JHSCW*, 7, no. 11 (1957), 5–24.

[32] J. A. Sharpe, *Crime in Early Modern England 1550–1750* (London, 1984), pp. 26–7, 85.

[33] NLW, Church in Wales Records, B/CC/(G)/14.

[34] Glanmor Williams, *Wales and the Reformation* (Cardiff, 1997), pp. 323–4.

[35] NLW, Church in Wales Records, SD/CCCm(G)/285.

diocese of Bangor developed a printed form for penitents, which included an apology which they were expected to read out, and space for their minister to confirm that penance had been carried out before returning the form. In 1755, for instance, Lewis Owen confirmed that Owen Roberts, one of his parishioners at Penrhosllugwy, Anglesey, had duly read the following confession:

> Good People, I do hereby in the Presence of God, his Minister, and this Congregation, Acknowledge, Confess and Bewail my Guilt and Wickedness in committing the unlawful and abominable sin of Fornication with Catherine Edward for which I am most heartily sorry; as having thereby offended God, and all well-disposed Christians, and wounded my own soul. And I do earnestly and sincerely repent of this and all other heinous Sins, and Offences, and do beseech God of his infinite Goodness, for the sake of Jesus Christ, who came to the world to save sinners, to have Mercy upon me, and to forgive me this and all other my Transgressions. And I do also beg the Pardon of the Church, and all good Christians, whom I have by the said Sin offended, and desire this Congregation to join with my in Prayers to God for his Mercy.[36]

He was then required to kneel and recite the Lord's Prayer. In this case, however, he was ordered to perform the penance in his clergyman's house, which made it a private rather than a public apology. As the eighteenth century progressed, church courts seemed increasingly less able to enforce their discipline through public penance.

Church records in general reveal a substantial degree of apathy towards the Established Church. Visitation returns from many parishes suggest that a large number, if not a majority, of parishioners only attended church once a year, usually during Easter communion, if then. John Richards, rector of Coety, Glamorgan, admitted that, of the 600 or so potential communicants in his parish in 1763, 'not above twenty or thirty at most usually receive the holy communion at church'.[37] Of some 350 families in the parish of Abergavenny in 1763, no more than eighty communicants attended the major festivals.[38] Attendances appear to have been more healthy in north Wales, however, if the figures given by the clergy are to be believed. Of 400 families in the parish of Denbigh in 1738, there were some 100 regular communicants and around 500 communicants at Easter.[39] Thomas Ellis of Holyhead reported in 1749 that 500

---

[36] NLW, Church in Wales Records, B/CC/G/63.
[37] NLW, Church in Wales Records, LL/QA/1. 1763 is the earliest set of visitation returns to survive for the diocese of Llandaff.
[38] NLW, Church in Wales Records, LL/QA/2.
[39] NLW, Church in Wales Records, SA/QA/1.

parishioners from the 290 families in the parish attended Easter communion, and up to 200 took communion regularly.[40] In Llanfechell, Anglesey, also in 1749, Richard Bulkeley listed ninety families in the parish, among whom there were seventy regular communicants, rising to around 190 at Easter.[41] The evidence of his relative, William Bulkeley, suggests that the incumbent of Llanfechell was by no means exaggerating, since his diary notes that 300 people received sacrament in the parish church at Easter 1741.[42] Yet, even where attendance was low, the local parish still played an important role in the community. The Church maintained its virtual monopoly over baptisms, marriages and burials, which meant that it inevitably played an essential part in the rites of passage of most of its parishioners. Since few Dissenting chapels had graveyards during this period, the majority of people were buried in churchyards. The Church was generally judged to be more important for baptism and burial than for marriage, as many parishioners favoured clandestine or unofficial marriages. These were preferred because they were quicker and more convenient than the process of calling the banns and, of course, they were easier to terminate after a trial period.[43]

The parish church was also firmly associated with a wide range of popular customs. For instance, the practice of 'churching' women after they had given birth continued during this period. The religious calendar set by the Church marked the passage of time for many people and provided a framework for various superstitions and customs. Some days held special significance. In particular, the *gwylmabsant*, or patron saint's day, also known as a wake, was a major holiday in most parishes. It was not always celebrated on the actual saint's day – in many instances the festivities were moved to the summer if the saint's day fell in winter – but it usually maintained a strong association with the relevant saint. Originally an occasion for religious observance, it had evolved into a festival celebrated by eating, drinking and playing games, much of which took place in the churchyard. The festivities still frequently began with a church service, which duly ushered in the more secular celebrations.[44] The clergy would in many cases attend wakes, although the formidable Thomas Ellis, vicar of Holyhead, was reputed to have have prohibited wakes in his jurisdiction and to have bullied his parishioners into attending church

[40] NLW, Church in Wales Records, B/QA/2.

[41] NLW, Church in Wales Records, B/QA/2.

[42] G. Nesta Evans, *Religion and Politics in Mid-Eighteenth Century Anglesey* (Cardiff, 1953), p. 71.

[43] David W. Howell, *The Rural Poor in Eighteenth-Century Wales* (Cardiff, 2000), pp. 146–8.

[44] Ibid., p. 28.

instead of frequenting 'filthy interludes'.[45] Williams Pantycelyn decried the tendency among Anglicans and Dissenters in early eighteenth-century Wales to tolerate the *twmpath chwarae* or playground.[46] Howel Harris, the Methodist leader, was incensed by the predilection of some of the clergy for the 'harmless Recreations' of cockfighting, gaming and dancing and for attending wakes:

> so to the memory of that saint still there must be annual feast kept of gaming Drunkeness Fighting etc. Many poor families thereby reduc'd to ruin – nay the very Holy Days which our good Reformers Laid aside for to be kept Holy to the Lord to be spent to his service now so become Days of all vanities that tis as it were Lawful to give our selves Liberty then to indulge our selves in all pomps and vanities.[47]

Thomas Davies of Ystradyfodwg, Glamorgan, used to chase away Methodist preachers who sought to disrupt the festival.[48] In all fairness, the presence of the clergy may actually have prevented the celebrations from degenerating into complete disorder in some instances. An anonymous English visitor to Llandrindod in 1744, who later published an account of his visit, was surprised to find the churchyard full of people in their best clothes, drinking cider and eating mutton during the *gwyl-mabsant*. Those not eating and drinking were dancing to music provided by fiddlers, while others were playing tennis or fives against the church wall. The visitor found it all rather quaint and charming, an example of the 'happiness and simplicity of the ancient Britons'. 'Long may they continue', he said, 'their innocent customs, manners and recreations!'[49] The churchyard in general was frequently the venue for sport and entertainment. It was believed to be an ideal venue for cockfights because it was more difficult for opponents to curse a cockerel when on holy ground. There are also eighteenth-century accounts of people attending Sunday services before emerging to play fives or tennis against the walls of the church.[50]

The *gwylmabsant* was also frequently the occasion of contests between parishes, especially games of football or *cnapan*. These were often fiercely fought battles which lasted an entire day, with many of the players nursing

[45] Prys Morgan, *The Eighteenth Century Renaissance* (Llandybïe, 1981), p. 34.
[46] Garfield H. Hughes (ed.), *Gweithiau William Williams Pantycelyn*, p. 23.
[47] NLW, Calvinistic Methodist Archives, Trevecka Letters 343, 14 June 1741.
[48] Roger L. Brown, *An A–Z of Welsh Clerics* (Llanrwst, 2002), p. 64.
[49] Anon., *A Journey to Llandrindod Wells* (London, 1746), pp. 56–66.
[50] NLW, Church in Wales Records, B/CC/(G)/44; LL/CC/G/825; Emma Lile, 'Chwaraeon Tymhorol yng Nghymru cyn y Chwyldro Diwydiannol', in Geraint H. Jenkins (ed.), *Cof Cenedl XVIII: Ysgrifau ar Hanes Cymru* (Llandysul, 2003), p. 75.

bruises and broken limbs at the end. Richard Suggett and David Howell have argued that these competitions became more intense during the eighteenth century as a sense of parochial identity and solidarity grew following the imposition of the 1662 Act of Settlement, which made the parish the unit responsible for the poor.[51] This gave a new significance to the parish boundaries and an added financial dimension to their importance. No parish wanted to maintain paupers from elsewhere. Disputes arose between parishes over the responsibility for some paupers and the ferocity of football matches may have been an opportunity to retaliate for some perceived inter-parochial wrong. This may have been prompted by a sense of community solidarity and by loyalty to the parish as one's locality rather than as a territorial unit of the Church, but the church was at least indirectly associated with these customs.[52]

Therefore, the churchyard was in essence a public space which lay at the heart of the community, even for those who seldom or never attended divine service. When Benjamin Malkin published an account of his visit to south Wales in 1803 he expressed his horror at the misuse of the church at Fishguard, a town which he suggested was 'so filthy, so illbuilt and so uncivilized, as to be interesting on these very accounts'. He commented further:

> There seems here to be nothing of decency, no alienation from common purposes, attached to the idea of a church. The churchyard affords, in some sort, a market place. There are hooks all along its wall, on which the meat is exposed; there is no market house; the churchyard wall, and the door of the public house opposite, seem the principal stations of traffic.[53]

Attitudes towards conducting a market or cockfight in the churchyard were markedly different from those of nineteenth- and twentieth-century Nonconformists in Wales regarding acceptable behaviour in what was frequently called 'God's house'. Nevertheless, complaints were evident from the Restoration period onwards concerning the disrespectful behaviour of church congregations. Reports appeared in publications like the *Tatler* regarding the reprehensible conduct of the upper orders of

---

[51] Richard Suggett, 'Festivals and Social Structure in Early Modern Wales', *PP*, 152 (1996), 103–5; Howell, *Rural Poor*, pp. 140–1.

[52] See Robert W. Malcolmson, *Popular Recreations in English Society 1700–1850* (Cambridge, 1973), pp. 71–4; Bob Bushaway, *By Rite: Custom, Ceremony and Community in England, 1700–1880* (London, 1982), p. 126; John M. Golby and A. William Purdue, *The Civilisation of the Crowd: Popular Culture in England 1750–1900* (London, 1984), pp. 22–8.

[53] B. H. Malkin, *The Scenery, Antiquities, and Biography, of South Wales* (London, 1804), p. 239.

society in church, who were partial to taking snuff and ogling members of the opposite sex. Consistory court evidence from Wales also reveals what appears to be a distinct lack of reverence on the part of many parishioners. Brawls and assaults within churches and churchyards were by no means uncommon. In September 1750, for example, it was said at the consistory court that David Griffith of Myddfai, Carmarthenshire, did 'strike push kick and beate' Margaret, wife of David Phillip, in Myddfai church. His response was that he had possibly brushed against her clothes accidentally while sitting on the same bench. Witnesses, however, insisted that he had certainly squeezed Margaret's shoulder and pushed her against the next seat. Whatever the truth or indeed the cause of the dispute, David Griffith was excommunicated for failing to appear to answer the charge.[54]

It would seem then that either quarrels arose in church or that parishioners brought their quarrels with them to church. In this respect the clergy certainly did not always set an appropriate example to their parishioners. For example, a fierce disagreement occurred in the parish of Llan-y-crwys, Carmarthenshire, in 1750 between the curate, Lewis Lewis, and his supporters on one side and the churchwardens and their followers on the other. This quarrel developed over a long period of time, culminating with the churchwardens barricading themselves into the church on a Sunday in order to prevent Lewis Lewis from conducting services. His response was not to appeal to the church authorities but to take the law into his own hands. He appeared on the following Sunday, 14 October, with several supporters, including his son-in-law, Marmaduke Bowen, equipped with axes to break down the doors. The result was a pitched battle within the church and the churchyard. Accusations and counter-accusations in the consistory court included instances of individuals being battered over the head and threatened with swords, guns and axes during the fracas.[55] Given the number of weapons allegedly used in Llan-y-crwys church that Sunday, it is surprising that no one was fatally injured and that most of the participants escaped serious injury. After breaking into the church, Marmaduke Bowen allegedly threatened to kill William Thomas, uttering 'brawling Terrifyeing Chideing Words & Expressions not fitting mor becomeing in the Holy Church'. William Thomas was subsequently beaten unconscious by Marmaduke Bowen, but he survived to bring the case to the consistory court, where Bowen was accused in the following terms:

> you the said Marmaduke Bowen haveing then and there at the time and place aforesaid a Naked Sword or Semitor in your hand at the Church of

---

[54] NLW, Church in Wales Records, SD/CCCm (G)/347.
[55] NLW, Church in Wales Records, SD/CCCm (G)/348–54.

Llanycruise aforesaid on the Day aforesaid. And you the said Marmaduke Bowen made Severall attempts to runn the said William Thomas through his body with the said Naked Sword or Semitor which you had in your hand as aforesaid. And also that you the said Marmaduke Bowen did on the Day and year aforesaid at the Church of Llanycruise aforesaid with a Great Oaken Cudgell which you had then and there in your other hand you Gave the said William Thomas Severall Blows with the said Cudgell upon his head by reason of which said Blows so by the said William Thomas received from you the said Marmaduke Bowen he was thereby Deprived of his Senses for a Considerable time.[56]

Although the consistory court dealt with cases of assault and affray in churches, the churchwardens, John Edwards and David Thomas, also indicted Lewis and Bowen before the court of Quarter Sessions, where they pleaded guilty to charges of riot and assault and were fined 2*s*. 6*d*. each.[57] It is surprising to learn that this was the same Lewis Lewis who conducted the marriage ceremony of Howel Harris, the Methodist leader, and his wife, Anne, in 1744. Harris admitted that, although Lewis seemed 'full of Power & Life', yet he 'falls abominably'.[58] His periodic falls from grace were demonstrated also in 1750 when he became so inebriated on Easter Sunday that he lost his horse on his way home and was incapable of conducting service on the morning of Easter Monday.[59]

Mercifully, this kind of violence was rare in Welsh churches, but there were several other, more minor, quarrels. These may have occurred simply because the parish church was a public place of assembly. There was obviously a sense that this was improper conduct in a place of worship since complaints were brought before the consistory courts. Church seats in particular were a frequent bone of contention. Perhaps the phenomenon of 'pew rage' needs to be examined as the eighteenth-century equivalent of road rage, since feelings certainly ran high in some cases. In 1739 Richard David of Y Castellnewydd, Glamorgan, brought a complaint against Gwenllian Richard relating to the rights to a particular pew in the parish church. The case as presented involved a lengthy account of the history of the ownership of the pew, dating back generations to a time when it existed merely as a 'bench with a back to it'. The right to sit in the pew was attached to a house which Richard David had bought from a Sir Thomas Jones but, although the tenants of the house in the past had shared the pew

---

[56] NLW, Church in Wales Records, SD/CCCm(G)/348.
[57] Carmarthen Record Office, QSI/1, 123.
[58] NLW, Calvinistic Methodist Archives, Diaries of Howel Harris, 109, 16 April 1744.
[59] NLW, Church in Wales Records, SD/CCCm(G)/349.

with Gwenllian Richard, she now contested that right by locking herself in the pew.[60] Similarly, in 1740, David Lewis of Llanboidy, Carmarthenshire, brought a complaint against Thomas Howells senior and Thomas Howells junior, gentlemen. Lewis, the owner of Cilbrenin, stated that traditionally a church seat went with that holding. However, the Howells family consistently attempted to prevent his family from sitting there. Matters came to a head when David Lewis's wife, Jane, was forced to leave the seat in some consternation after Thomas Howells junior joined her in the pew and squeezed her hand.[61] It is worth noting that many of these disputes seem to have arisen between parish gentlemen or more substantial farmers in the community. There were certainly territorial aspects to these quarrels. Seats tended to be attached to houses and their holdings, and they changed ownership with those houses. There were also social implications. Those who paid the highest church rate were usually allocated the best seats in church. Seating in church was therefore an indication of wealth and social standing, as Richard Gough showed in his *History of Myddle*. It was not surprising then that powerful individuals were willing to argue their case in a church court rather than acknowledge a rival as a social superior by allowing him the better seat.[62]

There were also numerous cases of non-payment of tithe or church rate, which could be interpreted as a protest against the Church. On closer examination, however, most of these demurrals did not arise from resentment towards having to pay tithes to a church which one did not attend or support. People on the whole refused to pay tithes or rates whenever they felt it had been unfairly assessed rather than as a matter of principle. In 1742, for instance, Alex Ferguson was summoned before the consistory court for failure to pay the church rate in the parish of St Peter's in Carmarthen. His defence was that he had been taxed $1s$. $1d$. for a field called 'Parc y Conduit', for which he had never been taxed previously.[63] It appears that most people were less concerned about having to contribute to the upkeep of the church than having to pay more than their fair share towards its upkeep. The church rate in particular was problematic since it was assessed on the basis of an estimate of the annual value of dwelling houses in towns and the annual income of agricultural land in rural areas. As with all estimates, there was room for error. In addition, there were claims that a piece of land had been rated in the wrong parish, so the parish boundaries would have to be examined before the problem could be

---

[60] NLW, Church in Wales Records, LL/CC/G/887.
[61] NLW, Church in Wales Records, SD/CCCm(G)/291.
[62] See Walter T. Morgan, 'Disputes Concerning Seats in Church before the Consistory Courts of St David's', *JHSCW,* 11, no. 16 (1961), 65–89.
[63] NLW, Church in Wales Records, SD/CCCm(G)/303.

resolved. Consequently, although a number of cases of non-payment occurred, in none do we find a statement of refusal to pay as a matter of principle.[64]

In conclusion, therefore, it is hard to detect any signs of real resentment or discontent on a large scale. Some individual clergymen were perceived as failing in their duty. Many people rarely attended services, but that does not necessarily mean that they attended other places of worship instead. Despite the shortcomings of the Church as an institution, the local parish church still had a place at the centre of the community, even if fewer and fewer parishioners chose to attend it regularly. The sense of loyalty which the Church could still command is evident in the hostility expressed by mobs towards Methodist preachers. The early Methodists awakened echoes of those Puritan groups who had been associated with turning the world upside down, executing the king and subverting existing religious practices and traditions. Often egged on by local clergymen, angry crowds attacked the Methodists in order to defend the unity of the Church.[65] The fact that the Methodists themselves insisted on remaining within the Church until 1811 is further evidence of an abiding sense of loyalty towards the Established Church.

The Methodist movement, however, may well be seen as a response to the continued inability of the Church to offer adequate spiritual provision for its parishioners. The growth of Methodist societies sounded a warning for Church authorities, had they but ears to hear. Perhaps the greatest failure of the Church was in not rising to the challenge presented by Methodism and Dissent or making better use of the talents of men such as Howel Harris and William Williams, Pantycelyn. But the sad truth is that the eighteenth-century Church was in no condition to respond effectively. The blame lay not so much with individual clergy, who were frequently aware of deficiencies, but with the overwhelming problems facing the Church as an institution. Wholesale reform of the finances of the Church, including the abolition of lay impropriation, would also have been required to eradicate many of the difficulties. To have formulated a centralized, consistent policy towards the Methodist challenge would also have required a far greater measure of leadership and vision from the Welsh bishops. There seemed little prospect that this could be achieved during the eighteenth century. Oliver Cromwell had attempted such radical reform of

[64] See Walter T. Morgan, 'Cases of Subtraction of Church-Rate before the Consistory Courts of St David's', *JHSCW*, 9, no. 14 (1959), 70–91.

[65] John Walsh, 'Methodism and the Mob in the Eighteenth Century', in G. J. Cuming and Derek Baker (eds), *Popular Belief and Practice: Studies in Church History*, VIII (London, 1972), pp. 216–19; Eryn M. White, *Praidd Bach y Bugail Mawr: Seiadau De-orllewin Cymru 1737–50* (Llandysul, 1995), pp. 189–96.

Church finances, but it was unlikely that such an experiment would be repeated in the climate of the eighteenth century.

Nevertheless, the fact remains that, in the mid-eighteenth century, the Established Church still commanded a substantial amount of goodwill among the population at large. Much of that goodwill was squandered during the century which followed. As the Methodists went on to ordain their own ministers from 1811 onwards, clergymen were not needed to baptize, marry and bury parishioners to the same degree as before. The customs which had bound the Church to the community had also declined. The vacuum created by their disappearance was to a large extent filled by the *seiat*, the prayer meeting, the *cymanfa ganu* and the chapel eisteddfod. Over time, therefore, many Welsh people came to regard the chapel denominations, rather than the mother church, as their spiritual home, but this was by no means a foregone conclusion during much of the eighteenth century.

9

Was there a Welsh Enlightenment?

R. J. W. EVANS

My question seems rarely to have been asked. The latest reference books remain as silent on the subject as do – so far as I can see – writings within Wales.[1] Until recently there was no issue. The Enlightenment was traditionally regarded as a continental phenomenon for the most part, associated with certain specific, mainly French, thinkers, and with a programme taken to be iconoclastic, Deist, and, at least intellectually, subversive.[2] However, several decades of work have now greatly expanded the bounds and substance of the movement. Alongside a geographical expansion to the very edges of Europe has gone recognition of its different incidence and character in different countries or regions.[3]

The place of Britain in the historiography of Enlightenment was long a curious one. The term was applied to the Scottish school – which as such constitutes a major academic growth industry in the present era of devolution.[4] It has increasingly come to be applied to an American one too. English thinkers were acknowledged as models in the Enlightenment's early phase. But England – so it was largely assumed – did not thereafter

---

[1] John W. Yolton (ed.), *The Blackwell Companion to the Enlightenment* (Oxford, 1991), includes only Richard Price. Werner Schneiders (ed.), *Lexikon der Aufklärung* (Munich, 1995), and Michel Delon (ed.), *Dictionnaire européen des Lumières* (Paris, 1997), include both countries and persons, but appear to make no reference to Wales or the Welsh.

[2] Ernst Cassirer, *The Philosophy of the Enlightenment* (1932; Eng. trans., Cambridge, 1951); Paul Hazard, *The European Mind, 1680–1715* (1935, as *La Crise de la conscience européenne*; Eng. trans., London, 1953); Alfred Cobban, *In Search of Humanity: The Role of the Enlightenment in Modern History* (London, 1960); Peter Gay, *The Enlightenment: An Interpretation* (2 vols, New York, 1966–9); Norman Hampson, *The Enlightenment* (London, 1968).

[3] See the influential collection Roy Porter and Mikuláš Teich (eds), *The Enlightenment in National Context* (Cambridge, 1981), and the huge enterprise of Franco Venturi, *Settecento Riformatore* (5 vols in 7, Turin, 1969–90).

[4] Cf., most recently, Paul Wood (ed.), *The Scottish Enlightenment: Essays in Reinterpretation* (Rochester, NY, 2000); Alexander Broadie, *The Scottish Enlightenment: The Historical Age of the Historical Nation* (Edinburgh, 2001); Arthur Herman, *The Scottish Enlightenment: The Scots' Invention of the Modern World* (London, 2001).

need a critique of privilege, despotism, religious intolerance, superstition, etc., and did not seem to have been fired to the same high pitch of analysis and conjecture, or justification of rational enquiry. Only the changing conception of the whole movement has at last brought England fully into the picture, above all through the monumental and virtuoso new treatment by the late Roy Porter. Ireland, meanwhile, is also being drawn into the same field of investigation.[5] Yet Wales still earns hardly any mention.

Britain can thus be accommodated, and prominently, within an Enlightenment which now – despite the latest masterful reassertion by Jonathan Israel of an essentially earlier set of priorities[6] – appears less dominated by *philosophes* or by radicals. Current emphasis is on its empirical methods, its active pursuit of tolerance, its utilitarian and practical goals, its sociable and educative functions, its tendency to operate with the grain of state action. The roles of human and of natural history within it are acknowledged; similarly those of reformist agendas within the churches, directed towards more reasonable and personal forms of religion. All this occupied enquiring minds across the continent in the middle decades of the eighteenth century: its centre of gravity lay closer to Germany's *Aufklärung* – for all the high metaphysicians there – than to France's *lumières*.[7] Where then does Wales stand, against such a background?

It might be claimed that the concept of 'Welsh Enlightenment' is really a kind of contradiction. On the one hand, for our purposes, enlightened culture played itself out in a British – mostly English – or occasionally a European sphere. Those of Welsh origin who participated in it, even (or particularly) if they were notables like Richard Price or David Williams or Sir William Jones, lived elsewhere, mainly in London. They would hardly be perceived at all as Welsh; nor would Welshness have much direct

---

[5] Roy Porter, *Enlightenment: Britain and the Creation of the Modern World* (London, 2000), a vastly expanded version of his chapter in Porter and Teich (eds), *Enlightenment in National Context*, pp. 1–18. He disclaims coverage of 'internal debates' in Ireland or Wales. Graham Gargett and Geraldine Sheridan (eds), *Ireland and the French Enlightenment, 1700–1800* (London, 1999).

[6] Jonathan I. Israel, *Radical Enlightenment: Philosophy and the Making of Modernity, 1650–1750* (Oxford, 2001).

[7] Recent surveys on these lines are Ulrich Im Hof, *The Enlightenment* (Eng. trans., Oxford, 1994), Dorinda Outram, *The Enlightenment* (Cambridge, 1995), and Thomas Munck, *The Enlightenment: A Comparative Social History, 1721–94* (London, 2000). For Germany see, most accessibly, Richard van Dülmen, *The Society of the Enlightenment: The Rise of the Middle Class and Enlightenment Culture in Germany* (Eng. trans., Cambridge, 1992). A fresh and nuanced view of the French in L. W. B. Brockliss, *Calvet's Web: Enlightenment and the Republic of Letters in Eighteenth-Century France* (Oxford, 2002), esp. pp. 1–19.

relevance to them either, at least in respect of their enlightened activities.[8] On the other hand, Wales itself was arguably, by the same token, an unenlightened world. It witnessed during these years change, revival, even renaissance. But those occurrences were chiefly *sui generis*, or at least apprehended as such, a private debate about changing national values.

Yet Enlightenment, in its broader senses, surely does have relevance for an understanding of the contemporary Welsh situation. It is not so much that Welsh backgrounds were putatively of some significance, even for those who chose to be expatriates. More importantly, the whole theme of national identity is now seen to have been squarely addressed by Enlightenment; indeed, patriotism became one of its keywords, as a balance to the cosmopolitan notions with which it stood in regular debate. Besides, the very fact that Wales was remote, marginal, often ignored or disdained – the more so as an active and mostly willing ancillary to such a master state as Great Britain – perforce gave her a distinctive place. And we can find some clear similarities – as well as important contrasts – with European territories in parallel circumstances. What follows is a mere *ballon d'essai* (Montgolfier-style), to venture a few reflections on those themes.

That modest otherness of Wales appears very clearly in the episode which is agreed to represent the genesis of a modern Welsh cultural renewal: the circle which formed around the Morris brothers, and especially the founding in the early 1750s of the Cymmrodorion, a society based among comparatively prosperous London exiles, but also drawing in natives to its membership. The society's constitution, the so-called *Gosodedigaethau*, lays great stress upon the 'British or Welsh' language as key to the early history of Britain and the recovery of literary traditions. The outside world, particularly the English, had failed to understand or appreciate these; but no less responsible was the 'supineness and neglect' of the Welsh people, as the Morrises' friend, Evan Evans, put it. Evans, moreover, saw the process of emergence into 'this enlightened age' more or less explicitly in the same terms as Immanuel Kant would later formulate the nature

---

[8] Porter, *Enlightenment: Britain*, pp. 239–41, 365–6: members of the 'Enlightenment first team' were happy to move to England (whereas native thought was illustrated by Iolo Morganyg (*sic*)). He lists titles (only) of Evan Evans, *Some Specimens of the Poetry of the Antient Welsh Bards* (1764) (below, n. 68), and Rhys Jones, *Gorchestion Beirdd Cymru* (1773).

of Enlightenment itself, as 'man's emergence from his self-incurred immaturity'.[9]

The Cymmrodorion initiative, a single association, along with its later offshoots like the Gwyneddigion, in a foreign city, reflected the limited range of the intellectual culture it sought to promote: 'so few persons are there in this country [of Wales] that relish any thing of learning'.[10] Superior nations and provinces already had their institutions at home. They included not just Scots and Irish, with their capitals, universities, societies: the Select Society of Edinburgh a contemporary counterpart, perhaps, to the Cymmrodorion, but only one among several; the Royal Irish Academy a highly urbane equivalent to the later Gwyneddigion. Nearly 300 works of broadly enlightened persuasion by French authors alone were published in eighteenth-century Dublin.[11] Comparable continental peoples, too, achieved more: for example, the Danes, roughly twice as numerous as the Welsh at the time and likewise experiencing a degree of cultural subordination. In Denmark tension between ethnic Danes and dominant German elites did much to generate the local Enlightenment; but it operated on a secure base in Copenhagen, and with a Royal Danish Society for History of the Fatherland as early as 1743.[12]

If the Welsh therefore stood very far below any Enlightenment premier league, they were nevertheless not in its third division either. Wales possessed a more vigorous native literary language and culture than many another peripheral area. This manifested itself in the pre-Cymmrodorion era with savants like Edward Lhuyd, Moses Williams, or William Jones Sr, even if such men were associated with English institutions in Oxford and London. Indeed English agrarian, commercial and industrial development – strong, relatively speaking, even within Wales – yielded a surplus for cultural objectives. That was one cause of the extraordinary success of Griffith Jones and his circulating schools, which delivered remarkably high

[9] R. T. Jenkins and Helen M. Ramage, *A History of the Honourable Society of Cymmrodorion* (London, 1951), esp. pp. 227–30. Cf. Caryl Davies, *Adfeilion Babel: Agweddau ar Syniadaeth Ieithyddol y Ddeunawfed Ganrif* (Caerdydd, 2000), pp. 170–201. Aneirin Lewis (ed.), *The Correspondence of Thomas Percy and Evan Evans* ([Baton Rouge], 1957), pp. 1–2, 9, 55. Cf. H. Reiss (ed.), *Kant's Political Writings* (2nd edn, Cambridge, 1991), pp. 54–60. The basic sources for the Morrises are J. H. Davies (ed.), *The Letters of Lewis, Richard, William and John Morris of Anglesey* (2 vols, Aberystwyth, 1907–9 (hereafter *LM*)), and Hugh Owen (ed.), *Additional Letters of the Morrises of Anglesey, 1735–86* (Parts 1–2, London, 1947–9 (hereafter *ALM*)).

[10] *ALM*, II, p. 620.

[11] Listed in Gargett and Sheridan (eds), *Ireland*, pp. 243–84.

[12] Klaus Bohnen and Sven A. Jørgensen (eds), *Der Dänische Gesamtstaat: Kopenhagen – Kiel – Altona* (Tübingen, 1992). Cf. B. J. Hovde, *The Scandinavian Countries, 1720–1865: The Rise of the Middle Classes* (2 vols, Ithaca, NY, 1948), I, pp. 89–149.

levels of basic literacy by the standards of eighteenth-century vernacular teaching. In its quaint statistical precision, Jones's publicity organ, *The Welch Piety,* claimed 3465 school terms and 314,051 day pupils over the period from 1737 to 1777.[13] Partly as a consequence, book production had become distinctly robust, particularly but not solely in religious genres; from dictionaries to practical handbooks, a surprising amount of information was already available in Welsh.[14]

Speakers of other Celtic languages had far less scope. Persecution and discrimination in Gaelic Ireland and Scotland notoriously left the cultures of the indigenous languages isolated and their carriers largely unlettered. In Brittany, too, a closer match with Wales in many respects, the bounds of the native culture were narrowly circumscribed. Sharply divided by dialect, it was overwhelmingly Catholic, its publications restricted almost exclusively to devotional works and a few dictionaries compiled by priests. Economic stagnation contributed to depressing the number of schools, and literacy in Breton remained very low (according to some estimates it was little more than 1 per cent). Both at home and still more in Paris, educated Bretons assimilated.[15] What would metropolitan French *lumières* have been without Lesage, Duclos or La Chalotais?

About as limited, if we move to slightly remoter analogues, was the Basque situation, where some enterprise, regional identity, and growth in literacy subsisted within a deeply traditional, Catholic and Spanish matrix.[16] Even the Catalans, in their eighteenth-century trough after the Bourbon conquest, lost all traditional centres of learning and were reduced to rudimentary cultural expedients.[17] Castilian domination here matched that of Swedish in Finland, which had a domestic university, but where Finnish-speakers, about equally as numerous as the Welsh, remained in the shadows. In similar or worse case were Slovaks or Slovenes or Sorbs –

---

[13] David Jones, *Life and Times of Griffith Jones of Llanddowror* (London, 1902), p. 162 and *passim.*

[14] Eiluned Rees, *Libri Walliae: A Catalogue of Welsh Books and Books Printed in Wales, 1546–1820* (2 vols, Aberystwyth, 1987); Prys Morgan, *The Eighteenth Century Renaissance* (Llandybïe, 1981), pp. 40 ff., 65 ff.; Geraint H. Jenkins, *The Foundations of Modern Wales: Wales 1642–1780* (Oxford, 1987), pp. 215–17, 409–10 and *passim.* Cf. R. J. W. Evans, 'Ieithoedd dan Orthrwm Ymerodraeth', *Y Traethodydd,* 154 (1999), 91–100.

[15] J. Delumeau (ed.), *Histoire de la Bretagne* (Toulouse, 1969), pp. 352 ff.; Yann Brekilien, *Histoire de la Bretagne* (Paris, 1985), pp. 263 ff.; Rhisiart Hincks, *I Gadw Mamiaith Mor Hen: Cyflwyniad i Ddechreuadau Ysgolheictod Llydaweg* (Llandysul, 1995), esp. p. 86 re literacy.

[16] R. L. Trask, *The History of Basque* (London, 1997); José María Jimeno Jurío, *Navarra: Historia del Euskera* (Tafalla, 1997), pp. 147–78.

[17] Francisco Canals Vidal, *La tradición catalana en el siglo XVIII: Ante el absolutismo y la ilustración* (Madrid, 1995); Miquel Batllori, *Obra completa, IX, La Illustració* (Valencia, 1997), pp. 165–209.

not to speak of smaller peoples within the Orthodox world. And considerable tracts of Europe probably supported no denser a network of writers than Wales. In the whole of the Habsburg territories, a survey of 1776 revealed only 437 authors, and they had no academy, even in Vienna.[18]

Viewed in such European terms, the activity of the Morrises represented a classic enlightened step. Where there had been little beyond an occasional local eisteddfod or reading group, the three brothers, Lewis, Richard and William, established a loose organizational structure, at once learned but convivial, which maintained continuity both by meetings and by correspondence. Thus in the Habsburg Monarchy – to stay with that example – they had counterparts in the equally pioneering Societas Incognitorum Eruditorum, a more sober scholarly cluster which flourished around 1750 at Olomouc/Olmütz in Moravia, and then its successor, the Learned Society of Prague from 1772. If the Bohemian lands furnish the closest intellectual parallels, arising as they did in the shadow of a dominant (German) culture, and displaying a first hesitant enthusiasm for the Czech vernacular by the end of the century, rather nearer to Wales in organizational terms was Hungary, where various short-lived attempts were made to found indigenous enlightened associations, but only exiles in Vienna actually succeeded.[19]

The Morris brothers derived from a semi-educated artisan background, their father a studious cooper on Anglesey. This would be a standard pattern on the continent, too, for first-generation proponents of Enlightenment. Then with their career choices they fitted into another paradigm, as middle-class officials: Lewis and William in the customs service and Richard in the Navy Office. The occupational information which the brothers diligently brought together about their fellow Cymmrodorion points in the same direction.[20] Many of their equivalents abroad were government employees – including military officers – with some share in implementing policy, and some consequent sense of moral and charitable responsibility. That went with the Morrises' markedly practical bent, and

---

[18] [Ignaz de Luca], *Das gelehrte Oesterreich: Ein Versuch* (1 vol. in 2, Vienna, 1776–8), II, pp. 481 ff.

[19] The fullest account for Bohemia is Josef Haubelt, *České osvícenství* (Prague, 1986); cf. Walter Schamschula, *Die Anfänge der tschechischen Erneuerung und das deutsche Geistesleben* (Munich, 1973), on the German models. For Hungary: Domokos Kosáry, *Művelődés a 18. századi Magyarországon* (Budapest, 1980), pp. 562–71 (for academy projects) and *passim*; summarized in idem, *Culture and Society in Eighteenth-Century Hungary* (Budapest, 1987).

[20] For the family biography, see Hugh Owen, *The Life and Works of Lewis Morris (Llewelyn Ddu o Fôn) 1701–1765* (n.pl., 1951), based on *LM* and *ALM*. Cf. the excellent discussion in Jenkins, *Foundations*, pp. 389 ff.; Jenkins and Ramage, *History of the Cymmrodorion*, pp. 252–73 (occupations).

their eagerness for the 'propagation and Improvement of any . . . Branch of Learning and useful knowledge', as the *Gosodedigaethau* put it. Not by accident was the first of the Welsh agricultural societies, that at Brecon, founded in the same year, 1755.[21] Lewis Morris, who functioned for years as agent of the crown mines in Ceredigion, was an inveterate projector and experimenter; he would have felt at home in the Prague Learned Society, devoted to 'mathematics, history and natural history of the fatherland', and founded by a mineralogist.[22]

In its relation to the establishment, too, the Morris circle was typical. While being ready enough to act on their own, its members sought to appeal to their social betters. We now know how pivotal was the role of European nobilities in the process of Enlightenment, not least in France.[23] The likes of William Vaughan of Corsygedol, who presided over the Cymmrodorion, were abundant in similar societies elsewhere. At the same time there was a substantial involvement across Europe of clergy, usually of those inclined to more tolerant and reformist opinions, and plenty of them – particularly Catholics – bitterly critical of their own churches. Wales was notable for the absence of prelates from the ranks of native culture. Instead, her Anglican pastors and curates, though they might well share the negligent and latitudinarian attitudes of their superiors, sometimes nursed fierce resentments of them, none more so than Evan Evans.[24] Abroad, the proliferating freemasonic lodges would have catered for much polished socializing between classes. Welsh masonry appears (from what we know of it) to have played a less creative or progressive part, at least until late in the century.[25] Perhaps, however, the rejuvenated vogue for bardic names – Ieuan Fardd for Evans etc. – may carry echoes of the masonic sobriquets so popular elsewhere.

Striking among the Morrises is a prime devotion to language and history, in that order, as mutually supportive pillars of a national cultural edifice in need of renewal. Their impulse was restorative, a recreation of older Welsh literature and language on classical models. Saunders Lewis labelled

---

[21] Jenkins, *Foundations*, p. 282.

[22] Much on this can be found in *LM*, *ALM*, and Owen, *Life and Works of Lewis Morris*. Ignaz Born (ed.), *Abhandlungen einer Privatgesellschaft in Böhmen* (6 vols, Prague, 1775–84); cf. Haubelt, *České osvícenství*.

[23] See esp. Daniel Roche, *Le siècle des lumières en province: Académies et académiciens provinciaux, 1680–1789* (Paris, 1978).

[24] Evan Evans, *The Love of our Country* (2nd edn, Carmarthen, 1773), pp. 27–8; cf. Lewis (ed.), *Correspondence of Thomas Percy and Evan Evans*, pp. xxiv–xxv.

[25] J. P. Jenkins, 'Jacobites and Freemasons in Eighteenth-Century Wales', *WHR*, 9, no. 4 (1979), 391–406.

this 'Augustan', given the English influences on Lewis Morris, Goronwy Owen, Edward Richard, or Evan Evans.[26] Typologically, it could just as well be thought of as neo-humanist, like the *œuvre* of (say) Josef Dobrovský among the Czechs. The distaste for popular, debased linguistic forms (for example, many of those in Thomas Richards's dictionary) likewise had many continental parallels in an age of rising purism.[27] Yet the Morris brothers themselves still used English for many purposes, even in their correspondence, as contemporary devotees of Hungarian or Finnish would have employed German or Swedish respectively, and so on. To a second, overlapping, kind of Enlightenment the language question anyway meant much less and the national history correspondingly more. This asserted its Welshness rather through a territorial focus. Its paragon was Thomas Pennant.

Pennant's tours of Wales provide rich evidence of a warm regard and active concern for his country and its past, but one largely shorn of a linguistic base, and certainly of a political one, despite his enthusiasm for medieval eisteddfodau – at least those of his native Flintshire – and for Owain Glyndŵr, whom Pennant did much to rescue from oblivion.[28] At the same time he was an eminent figure of the English and European Enlightenment, as appears certified in his characteristically whimsical and contrived autobiography.[29] Pennant travelled extensively in almost every corner of the British Isles, and most of this he wrote up in book form, alongside much other work on geography and natural history, from the *British Zoology*, which was sold under the auspices of the Cymmrodorion for the benefit of the London Welsh school, to the multi-volume, un-published 'Outlines of the Globe'. Most of all he left his name as a naturalist, especially an ornithologist. In that guise he was a patron of fellow aficionado William Morris on Anglesey, as the correspondence of the *Morrisiaid* reveals, but more famously of Gilbert White, who wrote the first half of the *Natural History of Selborne* as letters to Pennant.[30]

Continental links were equally significant. Decisive was his early association with Linnaeus, who arranged his election to the Royal Society of Uppsala when Pennant had only just turned the age of 30, the first of several Scandinavian honours. A recent reinterpretation of Linnaeus as practical enterpriser, amateur theologian and national activist helps bring

---

[26] Saunders Lewis, *A School of Welsh Augustans* (Wrexham, 1924); cf. Ceri Davies, *Welsh Literature and the Classical Tradition* (Cardiff, 1995), pp. 91–111.

[27] For Dobrovský, see Jaroslav Ludvíkovský, *Dobrovského klasická humanita: Studie o latinských vlivech na počátky našeho obrození* (Bratislava, 1933).

[28] Thomas Pennant, *A Tour in Wales* (2 vols, London, 1784), II, pp. 325–94, 456–78. Cf. R. R. Davies, *Owain Glyn Dŵr* (Talybont, 2002), p. 136.

[29] *The Literary Life of the Late Thomas Pennant, Esq., by Himself* (London, 1793).

[30] Richard Mabey, *Gilbert White: A Biography* (London, 1986), pp. 104 ff.

him closer for us to the world of Pennant – and of the Morrises.[31] Pennant was also a friend of *philosophe*-scientists such as Buffon, and of the great German-born naturalist-explorer of Russia, Peter Pallas.[32] Among other German acquaintances he forged a special bond with the brilliant but wayward duo of Forsters, father and son, Linnaeans, and classic *Aufklärung* figures. The elder, Johann Reinhold, paid extensive visits to Pennant's estate at Downing, translated his work, and sponged off him, both before and after his voyage with Cook to the South Seas – an experience in which he was followed by one of the prominent Welsh intellectuals of the late-century generation, David Samwell.[33]

Several of Pennant's fellows among the cultivated Welsh gentry shared his combination of allegiance to place of birth and dwelling beside a broader assimilation into British or international society.[34] So did their peers within the continental lesser nobilities. Even if few of them would have been able or desirous to write verse, like William Vaughan of Corsygedol, in such a low-status vernacular as Welsh, they were, in the spreading parlance of the time, patriots. The subject gave rise to an entire genre of enlightened literature, including an English poem on *The Love of our Country* by 'a curate from Snowdon', alias Evan Evans. His treatment is strikingly intense, being directed specifically against English detractors of his motherland. He tells how the 'Cambrian' Asser brought learning to Alfred and the Saxons. He lauds the 'ancient British verse' as 'more manly and heroic than the wretched rhimes of the English'.[35] This is hardly the pure notion of *ubi bene ibi patria*, as subscribed to by cosmopolitans; it is much more virulent than, for example, Josef von Sonnenfels' simultaneous

---

[31] Pennant, *Literary Life*, pp. 4 ff. Lisbet Koerner, *Linnaeus: Nature and Nation* (Cambridge, MA, 1999).

[32] Carol Urness (ed.), *A Naturalist in Russia: Letters from Peter Simon Pallas to Thomas Pennant* (Minneapolis, 1967).

[33] Michael E. Hoare, *The Tactless Philosopher: Johann Reinhold Forster, 1729–98* (Melbourne, 1976); Pennant, *Literary Life*, pp. 36, 40. For the burgeoning literature on his son, see Thomas P. Saine, *Georg Forster* (New York, 1972) and, most recently, C.-V. Klenke, J. Garber and D. Heintze (eds), *Georg Forster in interdisziplinärer Perspektive* (Berlin, 1994), and *Georg-Forster-Studien* (Berlin, 1997–).

[34] I am quite unclear how many. There is good material from south Wales in Philip Jenkins, *The Making of a Ruling Class: The Glamorgan Gentry, 1640–1790* (Cambridge, 1983) and David W. Howell, *Patriarchs and Parasites: The Gentry of South-West Wales in the Eighteenth Century* (Cardiff, 1986).

[35] Evans, *Love of our Country, passim*, Exactly this view of early English verse had already been expressed to Evans by his correspondent Thomas Percy: Lewis (ed.), *Correspondence of Thomas Percy and Evan Evans*, p. 52.

treatment of the same theme in Austria, with its stress on disinterested service to the state from its citizens, after the Roman model.[36]

In Germany as a whole the vogue for patriotic writings emphasized civic freedoms, public spirit and a moderately national political and cultural tendency still compatible with wider horizons, though not immune to military heroization, particularly of Frederick the Great. It is fitting that Evans, too, wrote a pair of odes to the Prussian king, the second on his victory over the French at Rossbach, deliciously Cymricized by the poet as 'Rhosfach'.[37] The Danish 'burgher' patriotism advocated by Tyge Rothe was so anodyne as actually to unleash the resentment of his aggrieved fellow 'natives'.[38] By 1767 even the unregarded Sorbs of Lusatia had a printed celebration of their patriotic credentials.[39] Elsewhere on Europe's western peripheries there was a Société Patriotique for all of Brittany, and in the Basque provinces a Real Sociedad Vascongada de Amigos del País from 1764.

Territorial identity in the eighteenth century could involve different layers of loyalty and delicate balances, especially where largely divested of institutions, as in Wales. It is – as already suggested – a moot point how far people like Pennant were perceived as Welsh at all outside the country. By the same token, outsiders could be attracted to such an identity. Witness the activities of Daines Barrington, an avid naturalist and the other recipient of White's letters from Selborne, an Englishman drawn in as judge on the Welsh circuit, a patron of Evans, and an enthusiast for the country's traditions and antiquities in general.[40] From these beginnings would grow by the years around 1800 the writings of county topographers – indebted, of course, to their English equivalents, and correspondingly strongest in the eastern border areas – and such patriotic-statistical work

---

[36] For analyses of Sonnenfels's *Uiber die Liebe des Vaterlandes* (1771), see Grete Klingenstein in *Judentum im Zeitalter der Aufklärung* (Wolfenbüttel, 1977), pp. 211–28; Harm Klueting in G. Birtsch (ed.), *Patriotismus* (Hamburg, 1991), pp. 37–51; R. J. W. Evans, 'Über die Ursprünge der Aufklärung in den habsburgischen Ländern', *Das Achtzehnte Jahrhundert und Österreich*, 2 (1985), 9–31; Ernst Wangermann in H. Reinalter (ed.), *Josef von Sonnenfels* (Vienna, 1988), pp. 157–69.

[37] Christoph Prignitz, *Vaterlandsliebe und Freiheit: Deutscher Patriotismus von 1750 bis 1850* (Wiesbaden, 1981), pp. 7–38. D. Silvan Evans (ed.), *Gwaith y Parchedig Evan Evans (Ieuan Brydydd Hir)* (Caernarfon, 1876), pp. 83, 157n.

[38] Tyge Rothe, *Tanker om Kærlighed til Fædrelandet* (Copenhagen, 1759); cf. Ole Feldbaek, in Bohnen and Jørgensen, *Dänischer Gesamtstaat*, pp. 7–22, and in O. Dann and J. Dinwiddy (eds), *Nationalism in the Age of the French Revolution* (London, 1988), pp. 87–100.

[39] Simon Brězan, *Deutsche Aufklärung und sorbische nationale Wiedergeburt* (Bautzen, 1993).

[40] Lewis (ed.), *Correspondence of Thomas Percy and Evan Evans*, pp. 6n., 8n., 11n., 49, 54, 142; Mabey, *Gilbert White*, pp. 119 ff; Evans (ed.), *Gwaith y Parchedig Evan Evans*, pp. 173ff.

as the agricultural surveys of Walter Davies (Gwallter Mechain), which had continental counterparts in numerous governmental and regional agencies. For Wales the enlightened commitment to territory and heritage arguably led to the first signs of an Anglo-Welsh literary allegiance with immense implications for the future.[41]

From the Bible editions of Richard Morris through to these 'learned old parsons' (*hen bersoniaid llengar*) of the next era, both our – intersecting – networks, Morris and Pennant, had the same religious complexion: they were firmly Anglican. So was Griffith Jones and his whole campaign for educational improvement which grew out of earlier London-based initiatives for Wales, as a 'dark corner of the land', particularly through the work of the Society for Promoting Christian Knowledge. The fame of the circulating schools extended as far as Russia, precisely because so many others in Enlightenment Europe launched similar programmes. Elsewhere these tended to be more state-directed enterprises, as in the Prussia of Frederick William I, the Austria of Maria Theresa and Joseph II, the Denmark of Frederick V, the Russia of Catherine II, the Sweden of Gustavus III – though the 'ambulatory' schools of the 1760s in that country show a family likeness. Almost everywhere the agenda was one of practical and graded instruction, within existing social confines, as the Breton educator La Chalotais recommended for pre-revolutionary France.[42]

Besides reformist Anglicanism, Dissent is now recognized as a key element in the English Enlightenment. Its rational spirit became a significant factor in Wales too, exercising, for example, a powerful influence on the intellectual formation of Richard Price.[43] Yet what of Wales's classic mid-century revival, Methodism, which both coincided and notoriously collided with the movement of the Morrisians? Surely this was neither Welsh nor enlightened in aspiration: its defence of the language merely a means to an end; its 'illumination' understood as a rival source of authority? The paradoxical role of the Methodists as prime but accidental contributors to a distinctive Welsh culture has been familiar at least since the subtle analysis by R.T. Jenkins.[44] It is, nonetheless, not entirely without links to our theme.

[41] This is well treated in Morgan, *Eighteenth Century Renaissance*, pp. 85ff., 136ff.

[42] H. A. Barton, 'Popular Education in Sweden: Theory and Practice', in J. A. Leith (ed.), *Facets of Education in the Eighteenth Century* (Oxford, 1977), pp. 523–41 and *passim*; James Van Horn Melton, *Absolutism and the Eighteenth-Century Origins of Compulsory Schooling in Prussia and Austria* (Cambridge, 1988).

[43] D. O. Thomas, *The Honest Mind: The Thought and Mind of Richard Price* (Oxford, 1977), pp. 4 ff.

[44] R. T. Jenkins, *Hanes Cymru yn y Ddeunawfed Ganrif* (2nd edn, Caerdydd, 1931), pp. 70 ff.

The Methodist awakening formed part of a European movement, with roots especially in Germany, in the Pietist and (to a lesser extent) Moravian revivals.[45] These displayed priorities which clearly matched some of the concerns of the early Enlightenment. A series of major studies since the pioneering diagnosis by Koppel Pinson, published in 1934, has shown how, on the one hand, the emotional, spiritual, and subjective values of the Pietists fed into early German patriotism, along with a new valuation of vernacular language and a confessional tolerance which promoted loyalty to the secular state.[46] On the other hand, the central Pietist experiences of conversion and rebirth were placed, above all by Francke at Halle, in the service of social and pedagogical amelioration: a form of altruism rather different, it has been argued, from puritan regard to individual improvement.[47] However that may be, the *pietas Hallensis* played a large role as international stimulus, particularly among smaller nations in the east of Europe (in the extreme case, Sorbian 'Enlightenment' seems to have grown directly out of it),[48] but also further west. It shared common ground on the Catholic side with Jansenism, at least in its Italian and central-European forms. Even in Spain it was rival traditions within Catholicism which allowed some continuing scope to Catalan individuality.[49]

Protestant renewal in Wales certainly belonged to the same picture. Griffith Jones's programme of vernacular instruction, the model for Methodist pedagogy, was itself modelled on Halle, and he also had links with the Moravian church. Richard Morris was invited to translate Zinzendorf.[50] Yet it is probably more a matter of correlation than contact. Whereas we might wonder whether the Methodists' unofficial *seiadau* could constitute any real part of enlightened sociability, there is no doubt that their attack on superstition as well as dogma had a liberating effect within eighteenth-century Wales. Their styles of charity, too, like those of the Cymmrodorion, need to be seen in a larger context. The same applies

---

[45] The best survey is now W. R. Ward, *The Protestant Evangelical Awakening* (Cambridge, 1992).

[46] K. S. Pinson, *Pietism as a Factor in the Rise of German Nationalism* (New York, 1934); Gerhard Kaiser, *Pietismus und Patriotismus im literarischen Deutschland: Ein Beitrag zum Problem der Säkularisation* (Wiesbaden, 1961); Klaus Deppermann, *Der hallesche Pietismus und der Preußische Staat unter Friedrich III. (I.)* (Göttingen, 1961). For an English summary of this literature, see Richard L. Gawthrop, *Pietism and the Making of Eighteenth-Century Prussia* (Cambridge, 1993), esp. pp. 275–9.

[47] There is a powerful but slightly overdrawn evaluation in Carl Hinrichs, *Preußentum und Pietismus: Der Pietismus in Brandenburg-Preußen als religiös-soziale Reformbewegung* (Göttingen, 1971). Cf. Melton, chap. 2.

[48] Brězan, *Deutsche Aufklärung*.

[49] Canals Vidal, *Tradición catalana en el siglo XVIII*.

[50] W. Moses Williams (ed.), *Selections from the Welch Piety* (Cardiff, 1938), p. 8; R. T. Jenkins, *The Moravian Brethren in North Wales* (London, 1938); *ALM*, I, p. 99.

to early Welsh Methodism's greatest writer. If William Williams could only be turned into a real European figure, as the first Romantic, through some very special pleading by Saunders Lewis, nevertheless he stands comparison with some continental contemporaries both for his psychological insights and as hymnodist: the German poet Gellert, for instance. Moreover, Pantycelyn's *Pantheologia*, a 'history of all the religions of the world', published in parts between 1762 and 1779, was a didactic compilation to combat popular ignorance very much in the spirit of folk educators in remoter foreign realms.[51]

Such work was Enlightenment at its most rudimentary. Among the movement's international heavyweights, by contrast, 'Welshness' was always at far more of a premium. Take Henry Lloyd from Cwm Bychan – primeval Wales, as it was depicted by his close contemporary Pennant. Lloyd pursued a standard career, including Jesus College, Oxford, until he broke with his family and traditions and went abroad. He associated with Jacobites (and compiled British coastal charts for Paris, just when Lewis Morris was making them for London). Having picked up much military experience and theory, Lloyd – another admirer of Frederick the Great – became the leading author of the age on war as an exact science, as well as writing on government and finance and providing a strong stimulus to his Lombard friend, Pietro Verri.[52]

The same question arises about the Welsh share in that advanced Enlightenment which, at the time of the French Revolution, turned briefly into an international cause. It included David Williams and Richard Price as cosmopolitan figures, with names made earlier: Williams as a known *philosophe*, translator of Voltaire and Montesquieu (and another friend of the Forsters), and a practising Deist in London; Price as a moral and economic philosopher and a Dissenter with a European reputation.[53] They definitely retained some Welsh identity. Even if Williams, in his fragmentary autobiography, betrays a sense of his origins only in connection with his temperamental reaction when insulted by Edmund Burke, his history

---

[51] Saunders Lewis, *Williams Pantycelyn* (London, 1927), esp. pp. 17, 30; cf. R. Tudur Jones, *Saunders Lewis a Williams Pantycelyn* (Abertawe, 1987). William Williams, *Pantheologia, neu Hanes Holl Grefyddau'r Byd* (6 parts, Caerfyrddin, 1762–78). Cf. Alwyn Prosser, 'Diddordebau Lleyg Williams Pantycelyn', *LlC*, 3, no. 1 (1954–5), 201–14; Gomer M. Roberts, *Y Pêr Ganiedydd [Pantycelyn] Cyfrol II. Arweiniad i'w Waith* (Aberystwyth, 1958), pp. 221–5.

[52] Franco Venturi, *Le vite incrociate di Henry Lloyd e Pietro Verri* (Turin, 1977). For Cwm Bychan, cf. Pennant, *Tour in Wales*, II, pp. 114 ff.

[53] Whitney R. D. Jones, *David Williams: The Anvil and the Hammer* (Cardiff, 1986); Thomas, *The Honest Mind*.

of Monmouthshire a few years later provides evidence of a kind.[54] Price – like Lloyd perhaps – less so, for all his continuing familial connections with Glamorgan. Price's *Discourse on the Love of our Country*, delivered in London in November 1789, became the most celebrated in the whole genre, since it gave rise to a far more serious insult from Burke, eloquent but thoroughly intemperate, in the shape of his *Reflections on the Revolution in France* (1790). But Price's 'country' is Great Britain: there is no mention of Wales.[55]

Others of Price's general persuasion at home made up for that: Morgan John Rees, with his evangelical and chiliastic mission; Thomas Evans (Tomos Glyn Cothi), John Jones (Jac Glan-y-gors) and William Jones of Llangadfan. The Gwyneddigion acted as a focus. Welsh-language publication included a flurry of radical pamphlets, even journals. There was a belated direct acquaintance inside Wales with some work of the *philosophes*.[56] Gwallter Mechain's 1790 medal-winning eisteddfod essay on the progress of *rhyddid* (freedom), for all its crudeness, signals the role of British 'liberty' – and the need for further extension of it – as a siren to all Welsh enlightened thinkers.[57] Edward Williams (Iolo Morganwg) belongs here, with his enthusiasm for Voltaire, Rousseau, the French language and even the Linnaean system, with his Unitarianism, populism and modernism.[58] Altogether Wales in the Jacobin years seems to resemble rather the Rhineland, where Georg Forster led the supporters of revolution, or Poland and Hungary, where democrats were forced into conspiratorial action, than the run of other small language homelands.

From the mid-1790s Welsh public life largely relapsed into channels of conservative British loyalty, as indeed did the term 'patriotism' itself.[59] That included even David Williams, who foreswore his French connections. In his Monmouthshire history he remained a sort of Voltairean, attacking the follies of the clergy – but Williams required subscriptions from the local gentry too. There were many European parallels for this

---

[54] Peter France (ed.), *Incidents in my own Life which have been Thought of Some Importance*, by David Williams (Brighton, 1980), esp. pp. 45–6, 80 ff., 120–2.

[55] Richard Price, *Discourse on the Love of our Country* (London, 1789). Cf. Roland Thomas, *Richard Price: Philosopher and Apostle of Liberty* (London, 1924), pp. 122ff., 152–3; Thomas, *The Honest Mind*, pp. 296 ff.

[56] J. J. Evans, *Dylanwad y Chwyldro Ffrengig ar Lenyddiaeth Cymru* (Liverpool, 1928) is useful, essentially on political writing. Cf. Gwyn A. Williams in Trevor Herbert and Gareth E. Jones (eds), *The Remaking of Wales in the Eighteenth Century* (Cardiff, 1988), pp. 111–47.

[57] Reprinted in D. Silvan Evans (ed.), *Gwaith y Parch. Walter Davies (Gwallter Mechain)* (3 vols, Caerfyrddin, 1868), II, pp. 1–109.

[58] Ceri W. Lewis, *Iolo Morganwg* (Caernarfon, 1995), pp. 16, 30, 129 ff.

[59] Dinwiddy, 'England', in Dann and Dinwiddy (eds), *Nationalism in the Age of the French Revolution*, pp. 53–70.

kind of *volte-face*.[60] At the same time an intellectual shift took place right across the political spectrum, with the reception in Wales, as all over the continent, of a new Romantic sensibility: among the pointers to it are the legend of Prince Madoc, the linguistic imaginings of William Owen Pughe, and above all Iolo Morganwg as an over-creative antiquarian and fabricator of the Gorsedd of Bards. Such fancies were typical of the day, forming a kind of anti-Enlightenment which is no concern of this essay. Yet in the Welsh case its fit with earlier ideas might seem a little too close for comfort. Had not the previous generation's thinking about the country and its past always been rather too uncritical to gain sound enlightened credentials? Had it ever outgrown the fables of a Theophilus Evans, or an obsession with druids and mythical ancestors?

The Morrises assuredly had, as the *Gosodedigaethau* put it, a 'high idea of the national and acquired abilities of the Antient Britons . . . a polite and learned people'. Thus they espoused an idealized view of Celtic prehistory which chimed in with the contemporary Irish – but not Scottish – approach, and which anticipated Herder's notions, subsequently taken up particularly by Slav ideologues.[61] Associated with this were primordial claims for the Welsh as true Britons, partly within their own given territory, partly beyond it: again, some Slav assertions come to mind, and Romanian ones even more.[62] On the whole, however, the Morris circle took a reasonably measured view, Evan Evans notably so. They inherited an antiquarian and comparatively sober history, in the spirit more of Edward Lhuyd than of the fanciful Breton abbé Pezron.[63] And at least, on the greatest literary scam of the period, they took the crucial point about the implausibility that the Ossianic poems could represent genuine continuity with a primal Celtic tongue – despite the avowal of modern Welsh's pristine credentials in the *Gosodedigaethau* and by such as Griffith Jones.[64] Wales probably produced no more than her fair share of the linguist cranks of the time.[65]

The druids were a general British craze, fuelled by much English writing too – think of Stonehenge! – and above all by the curious but immensely

[60] Lewis, *Iolo Morganwg*, pp. 137 ff.; Jones, *David Williams*, pp. 136 ff.; and for Wales in general, Evans, *Dylanwad y Chwyldro Ffrengig*. One continental case: Jacques Droz, *L'Allemagne et la Révolution Française* (Paris, 1949).

[61] Jenkins and Ramage, *History of the Cymmrodorion*, p. 230. Cf. Colin Kidd, *British Identities before Nationalism: Ethnicity and Nationhood in the Atlantic World, 1600–1800* (Cambridge, 1999).

[62] Adolf Armbruster, *La Romanité des roumains: Histoire d'une idée* (Bucharest, 1977).

[63] For Evans's views, cf. Evans (ed.), *Gwaith y Parchedig Evan Evans*, pp. 255–301. Cf. now the excellent discussion in Davies, *Adfeilion Babel*, esp. pp. 60ff.

[64] Contrast Lewis, *Welsh Augustans*, pp. 133 ff., with Jenkins and Ramage, *History of the Cymmrodorion*, p. 229, and Williams (ed.), *Selections from the Welch Piety*, p. 51. Cf. Lewis (ed.), *Correspondence of Thomas Percy and Evan Evans*, pp. 35ff., 100, 121–2.

[65] Like Rowland Jones: see Davies, *Adfeilion Babel*, pp. 202–30.

influential misconceptions of Pezron about Celtic languages, including that spoken in Wales ('qui est dans l'Angleterre'), as a source of all the rest.[66] Whereas Henry Rowlands, an etymological day-dreamer but archaeological pioneer, followed up clues from Tacitus on his native Anglesey, it was the French who inclined to regard the druids as proto-*philosophes*, a belief consonant with their fervour for the higher, more mystical masonic rites which became an important concomitant of advanced Enlightenment on the continent.[67] By these standards it was not so absurd to regard the Welsh bards as carriers of some kind of ancestral truths, as in the discriminating – and Latinate – text of Evan Evans; and the supposed massacre of them by Edward I, though first asserted in print in the Gwydir edition by Barrington and not disowned in Wales, tended to be taken up beyond her frontiers.[68] By the time of (say) Peter Roberts after 1800 the historical view has become even-handed and staid, even if he still gives Merlin, Arthur and company the benefit of the doubt.[69] Roberts's distance from Theophilus Evans is great – if not as far as that between (say) Daniel Juslenius (d. 1752), the wild chronicler of pristine Finnish greatness, and Henrik Porthan (d. 1804), the founder of Kalevala studies.

It seems appropriate, in moving towards my coda, to invoke the foremost linguist – anywhere – of the late Enlightenment. Sir William Jones had family links to the Morrises and became a member of the Cymmrodorion; he served his turn, like Barrington, on the Welsh legal circuit and revealed an affection for the scenery and people of Wales. However, with his Harrow education and metropolitan graces he seems for our purposes to have been manifestly an 'Oriental', and at best a 'semi-Welsh' Jones.[70] The ground area between activities not really Welsh, on one side, and those not

[66] T. D. Kendrick, *The Druids: A Study in Keltic Prehistory* (London, 1966 edn), pp. 17ff.; A. L. Owen, *The Famous Druids* (Oxford, 1962); Stuart Piggott, *The Druids* (London, 1968), pp. 131 ff. For Pezron, see Davies, *Adfeilion Babel*, quoted on p. 65.

[67] On Rowlands, see Owen, *Famous Druids*, pp. 73–82; Davies, *Adfeilion Babel*, pp. 110 ff. For masons, see René Le Forestier, *La franc-maçonnerie templière et occultiste aux XVIIIe et XIXe siècles* (Paris, 1970); J. M. Roberts, *The Mythology of the Secret Societies* (London, 1972), esp. pp. 90 ff.

[68] Evans, *Some Specimens of the Poetry* [including 'De Bardis Dissertatio']; cf. Lewis (ed.), *Correspondence of Thomas Percy and Evan Evans*, pp. 11–12. and n., 15 and n.; Sir John Wynn, *The History of the Gwedir Family*, ed. Daines Barrington (London, 1770); cf. Morgan, *Eighteenth Century Renaissance*, pp. 101ff. *passim*.

[69] Peter Roberts, *The Cambrian Popular Antiquities* (London, 1815).

[70] Contrast [John Shore] Lord Teignmouth, *Memoirs of the Life, Writings, and Correspondence of Sir William Jones* (London, 1807), with Caryl Davies '"Romantic Jones": The Picturesque and Politics on the South Wales Circuit, 1775–1781', *NLWJ*, 28, no. 3 (1993–4), 254–78, and eadem, 'Syr William Jones: Hanner Cymro', *Y Traethodydd*, 149 (1995), 156–70.

really enlightened, on the other, was always narrow. Subsequently it disappeared from sight completely.

By 1850 an alliance of Romantic legacy with Nonconformist religiosity had come to obscure the enlightened and secular features of eighteenth-century culture. The period was perceived as having delivered a national awakening, what Nefydd in 1852 already styled 'cyffrawd Cymreigyddawl', now divorced from any wider contemporary context. This view persisted through to the influential statement in R. T. Jenkins's standard work of 1928, and beyond.[71] As late as 1970 *Geiriadur Prifysgol Cymru* recorded no usage for either of the terms 'Goleuedigaeth' or 'oes oleuedig'.[72] Iolo Morganwg's very success as forger and obfuscator both showed the limits of Welsh Enlightenment – in that he went undetected – and helped close it off to posterity.

Yet that 'vertical' section, locating the phenomenon within Wales's own historical evolution, surely needs to be balanced also by 'horizontal' coordinates, to show parallels as well as distinctiveness in European terms, and set Wales alongside other nascent 'national movements'. The most special feature lay in politics – or the absence of them. The precocity of England's cultural advance had caught up Wales in its wake, not least (as the Cymmrodorion show) since the role of London as metropolis was not replicated elsewhere, even by Paris. In Britain a broad, reasonably inclusive sense of 'nation' operated from the start, blending the individual and the communitarian: contrast the still estates-based movements on the continent. By the same token, however, these circumstances also accelerated Wales's semi-autonomous cultural development as compensation for, and justification of, its lack of separate political clout.

From the Welsh side, enlightened interplay with England involved a discernible ethnic *ressentiment*, as in the complaints from the 'ancient inhabitants', the *cymmrodorion*, that the English had got Welsh traditions wrong, and corrupted their historical sources. But it was clear that they had also been helpful to Wales, for example as subscribers to Bible editions and schools, or as curious and sympathetic outsiders like Thomas Percy.[73]

---

[71] William Roberts [Nefydd], *Crefydd yr Oesoedd Tywyll, neu, Henafiaethau Defodol, Chwareuyddol a Choelgrefyddol* (Caerfyrddin, 1852). Cf. Morgan, *Eighteenth Century Renaissance*, pp. 145 ff. According to R. T. Jenkins, 'ailenedigaeth yr iaith a'r llenyddiaeth a'r traddodiad Cymraeg' was indigenous, whereas all the rest – the educational, industrial and religious transformations on which he concentrated – was imported.

[72] *Geiriadur Prifysgol Cymru*, part 23 (Caerdydd, 1970), p. 1450, gives 'goleuedig', with an example from 1792 in a clearly religious context. It gives a cross-reference for 'oes oleuedig' to the word 'oes', but in part 42 (1992) there is no relevant entry.

[73] Cf. *ALM*, I, pp. 320–4, II, pp. 445–53. W. Moses Williams, *The Friends of Griffith Jones: A Study in Educational Philanthropy* (London, 1939). Lewis (ed.), *Correspondence of Thomas Percy and Evan Evans*.

This state of affairs sufficed to lend a national accent to Enlightenment; but furnished no territorial or institutional basis for that reaction, any more than for the radicalism which succeeded it. The eighteenth century anyway brought a nadir in mutual perceptions of north and south, further impeding any overall Welsh political identity. Hence Welshness remained a *cultural* force within a *British* context. The lack, even in Iolo Morganwg, of any kind of Welsh political programme stands markedly at odds with what happened in many other parts of Europe, but in a direct line from the 'enlightened patriotism' of the Morrises and the loyalist verses bawled out at Cymmrodorion meetings.[74]

Those Cymmrodorion, more rowdy than studious, disappointed their founders (could most of them read at all?, wondered Lewis Morris in a black moment).[75] Certainly, not many people in Wales ever read even Voltaire – as William Jones Llangadfan did – let alone Spinoza. The Enlightenment there produced little of original quality which could be called distinctively Welsh, beyond the outstanding correspondence of the *Morrisiaid* (and the role of letters in spreading *lumières* is plain across the continent).[76] Its linguistic priorities also reduced its amplitude, cutting out any wider readership for Welsh texts, whereas English-language publishing in Wales was correspondingly stunted. So our subject remains a marginal one, perhaps; but as one of the greatest scholars of the Enlightenment has argued, such cases yield special insights into its nature.[77]

[74] Jenkins and Ramage, *History of the Cymmrodorion*, pp. 73–4. No wonder Saunders Lewis was so scathing about them: Lewis, *Welsh Augustans*, p. 18.

[75] Jenkins and Ramage, *History of the Cymmrodorion*, p. 82.

[76] Cf., most recently, Brockliss, *Calvet's Web*.

[77] 'Enlightenment was born and organized in those places where the contact between a backward world and a modern one was chronologically more abrupt and geographically closer': Franco Venturi, *Utopia and Reform in the Enlightenment* (London, 1971), p. 133.

10

A Private Space: Autobiography and Individuality in Eighteenth- and Early Nineteenth-Century Wales

PRYS MORGAN

In his essay contrasting Tom Ellis and Lloyd George, and, through them, highlighting the fractured consciousness of late nineteenth-century Wales, Kenneth O. Morgan refers to Tom Ellis's belief that the Welsh had a natural genius for cooperation: 'The Welsh, Ellis believed, had a natural capacity for local collective association. Theirs was the land of *cyfraith, cyfar, cyfnawdd, cymorthau* and *cymanfaoedd*, all of them concepts which embodied the co-operative ethic.'[1] No doubt the spirit of Tom Ellis would be delighted by the completion in 2002 of the great Welsh-language dictionary of the University of Wales, *Geiriadur Prifysgol Cymru*, and be especially pleased to see that the sections beginning with 'cyd-', 'cyf-', and 'cym-' are among the longest in the dictionary. But it would also be surprised to see that, while there are in Welsh around 348 words beginning with the cooperative prefix 'cyd-' (co- or together with), there are 358 words listed beginning with the individualistic prefix 'hunan-' (self-).[2] By far the greater proportion of these words expressing selfhood emerge in the eighteenth and early nineteenth centuries. In other words, while it may well be true that the collective and the cooperative traditions of the Welsh reach far back into history, there is at least some evidence of a rise of individualism in eighteenth- and early nineteenth-century Wales, which would help to explain a fractured consciousness – a rift between the collective and the individualistic – which dates from well before the generation of Tom Ellis and Lloyd George.

The evidence to be discussed in this chapter consists of a selection of some thirty autobiographies which were written by Welshmen, mainly in

---

[1] Kenneth O. Morgan, 'Tom Ellis *versus* Lloyd George: the Fractured Consciousness of *Fin-de-Siècle* Wales', in Geraint H. Jenkins and J. Beverley Smith (eds), *Politics and Society in Wales, 1840–1922* (Cardiff, 1988), p. 104.

[2] *Geiriadur Prifysgol Cymru* (4 vols, Cardiff, 1950–2002), I, pp. 658–73 for words beginning with 'cyd-'; II, pp. 1912–23 for words beginning with 'hunan-'.

the late eighteenth century and the period up to the 1840s; the great expansion of the number of portraits in Welsh houses during the eighteenth century; the change in architectural fashions in the same period, which saw the emergence of houses with private rooms, as opposed to communal living quarters; the rise in the fashion after 1700 for commemorating individuals with gravestones in Welsh churchyards; the rising demand for personal or individual religion, as seen in Dissent and Methodism; and lastly, the lexicographical revolution designed to meet the great demand, not only for words beginning with 'hunan-' (self-), but a Welsh vocabulary to express each individualistic nuance of the human personality. It should be made clear at the outset that the emergence of individualism is an immensely complex subject, and this short chapter does not deal with the great social and economic changes of the period, such as the emergence of the 'middling sorts' and the craftsmen during the eighteenth century, although they are relevant to the subject.[3]

The autobiography did not become a significant phenomenon in Wales until the last quarter of the eighteenth century. It is true that several Welshmen had previously written accounts of their lives: John Gwynne of Trelydan's memoirs of the civil wars, Lord Herbert of Cherbury's autobiography, the famous account by the Quaker Richard Davies of Cloddiau Cochion, which was published in 1710,[4] the autobiography of a smuggler William Owen of Nevern (who was hanged at Carmarthen on 2 May 1747),[5] which was presumably dictated as a sort of scaffold confession, and in the same year, but far away in New Jersey, the Welsh-language ballad by David Evans of Pencader, relating his life story as an emigrant to America.[6] But these are all single swallows, wheeling about in a cold and lonely autobiographical spring, never quite making a summer.

Following a gap of some thirty years we have a few autobiographies at the end of the 1770s: the Wesleyan itinerant preacher, Thomas Olivers of Tregynon near Newtown, published in 1779 an account of his life in *The Arminian Magazine,*[7] and in the same year the journal of the life of John Griffith, a Quaker from Radnorshire (who had died in 1776), was also

---

[3] For the middling sorts and the craftsmen, see Geraint H. Jenkins, *The Foundations of Modern Wales: Wales 1642–1780* (Oxford, 1987), pp. 257–99, esp. 269–76, 386–8.

[4] Richard Davies, *An Account of the Convincement, Exercises, Services, and Travels of . . . Richard Davies* (London, 1710).

[5] Glyn Parry, 'Autobiography of a Smuggler', *NLWJ*, 24, no. 1 (1985), 84–92.

[6] Gareth Alban Davies, 'Y Parch. David Evans, Pencader: Ymfudwr Cynnar i Pennsylvania', *NLWJ*, 14, no. 1 (1965), 74–96, esp. 84–92. See also David Evans, *A Short Plain Help for Parents and Heads of Families,* ed. Boyd S. Schlenther (Aberystwyth, 1993).

[7] Glyn Tegai Hughes (ed.), *Thomas Olivers of Tregynon: The Life of an Early Methodist Preacher Written by himself* (Gregynog, 1979).

published.[8] There are strong autobiographical elements in the pioneering local history *A History of the Parish of Aberystruth* by 'The Old Prophet', the Independent minister, Edmund Jones, published at Trefeca in 1779, but it appears that a preliminary autobiography by him was either lost or neglectfully destroyed. Jones was an associate and friend of the Methodist pioneer Howel Harris, though they deeply disagreed on some matters. Harris, as is well known, left extremely lengthy diaries and also began to write an autobiography in 1744, one of the earliest written in Wales.[9] After his death in 1773, his followers used the diaries and other autobiographical material to publish memoirs of Harris in English in 1791 and in Welsh in 1792.[10] Harris was a protégé of a pioneering Independent family, the Joneses of Pencerrig, Radnorshire, who encouraged him, although he was a Methodist, to preach in farm buildings which they owned around Llandrindod. One of the sons of Thomas and Elizabeth Jones of Pencerrig, Captain Frederick Jones, served in India in 1778 and kept an account of his life there, which he eventually published at Brecon in 1794.[11] Another son of Pencerrig was the famous painter Thomas Jones (1742–1803), who lived in Italy from 1776 to 1783, and who tells us that he kept careful accounts and diaries throughout his life, parts of which he recomposed as a 'Memoir' to circulate among friends. This he did in the 1780s after returning for a few years to live in London, and before retiring to Pencerrig to settle down to the life of a Radnorshire squire. He did so, believing that a genuine account of real events would be more interesting to people than any work of fiction. The 'Memoirs' remained in manuscript until they were published in 1951, since when they have been recognized as a remarkable document, the first autobiography by any British artist.[12] Frederick and Thomas Jones were both members of the Independent congregation at Cae Bach chapel, on the outskirts of Llandrindod Wells – the Jones family were

[8] *A Journal of the Life, Travels and Labours . . . of John Griffith* (London, 1779). Griffith's manuscript journal is in NLW MS 23002A.

[9] Geraint Tudur, *Howell Harris: From Conversion to Separation 1735–1750* (Cardiff, 2000), pp. 1–12 on Harris's diaries and their importance as 'spiritual autobiography', and pp. 65–6, 93, and 256, n. 18, for Harris's autobiography. For Edmund Jones's autobiography, see G. F. Nuttall, 'Cyflwr Crefydd yn Nhrefddyn, Sir Fynwy, 1793, gan Edmund Jones', *Y Cofiadur*, 46 (1981), 23–8.

[10] Howell Harris, *A Brief Account of the Life of Howell Harris, extracted from Papers Written by himself* (Trevecca, 1791), and idem, *Hanes Ferr o Fywyd Howell Harris* (Trefecca, 1792).

[11] Frederick Jones, *A Brief Account of the Tullaugaum Expedition from Bombay* (Brecknock, 1794). See also R. C. B. Oliver, 'The Diary of Captain Frederick Jones (Part I: 1789 to 1799)', *TRS*, 53 (1983), 28–56.

[12] Paul Oppé (ed.), *The Memoirs of Thomas Jones of Pencerrig* (London, 1951). See also Prys Morgan, 'Thomas Jones of Pencerrig', *THSC* (1984), 51–76; R. C. B. Oliver, 'Pencerrig: House at the Top of the Rocks', *TRS*, 39 (1969), 36–46; idem, *The Family History of Thomas Jones the Artist, of Pencerrig, Radnorshire* (Llandysul, 1970).

responsible for the development of the spa and its hotels – and around the year 1788 the minister of Cae Bach, a great friend of Howel Harris and a protégé of Mrs Jones of Pencerrig, the Independent minister Ioan (or John) Thomas, was also busying himself with writing the story of his life in Welsh.[13] This was eventually published following his death in 1810 under the title *Rhad Ras* (Free Grace), which, perhaps not quite accurately, has been supposed to be the earliest autobiography in Welsh.

Yet another friend of Howel Harris was the famous Bible expositor and author, Peter Williams who, some time before his death in 1796, compiled an autobiography which was eventually published together with that of his son, the Anglican schoolmaster Eliezer Williams (d. 1820), in the latter's collected works.[14] Peter Williams was considered to be the 'stormy petrel' of the Methodist movement and was excommunicated for heresy. A more conventional Methodist who left an autobiography was Thomas Jones of Denbigh, who led Methodism after the death of Thomas Charles of Bala in 1814, and this was published by Gee of Denbigh in 1820.[15] In 1799 the Methodist magazine *Y Drysorfa Ysprydol* began publishing a remarkable series of dialogues between 'Scrutator' and 'Senex', the former being Thomas Charles of Bala, the latter the then aged Methodist pioneer, John Evans. They continued in various numbers up to 1813, and are probably unique in the annals of Welsh autobiography since they take the form of an interview, in which the old man is persuaded to recount his memories of the beginnings of Methodism in mid-eighteenth-century Merioneth.[16]

It should not, however, be imagined that only Dissenters or Methodists followed the fashion for autobiography: in 1793 the famous zoologist and travel-writer Thomas Pennant of Downing in Flintshire published his curiously titled *The Literary Life of the Late Thomas Pennant Esq. By Himself*, which contained not only his memoirs but also reprints of pamphlets he had written on topics of the day.[17] A year later, as a short preface to his two volumes of English verse, Edward Williams ('Iolo Morganwg') penned a charming, but rather misleading, autobiography, a self-portrait of a poor lonely untaught 'Bard of Nature', who was, nevertheless, the heir to the centuries-old lore of the Glamorgan druids.[18]

[13] John Thomas, *Rhad Ras*, ed. J. Dyfnallt Owen (Caerdydd, 1949); for John Thomas, see *DWB*, s.n. John Thomas of Rhayader (1730–?1804).

[14] St George Armstrong Williams (ed.), *The English Works of the Late Rev. Eliezer Williams . . . with a Memoir of his Life* (London, 1840), and see the appendix, pp. clviii et seq. for 'Life of Peter Williams, written by Himself'.

[15] Idwal Jones (ed.), *Hunangofiant y Parch. Thomas Jones* (Aberystwyth, 1937).

[16] Goronwy P. Owen (ed.), *Atgofion John Evans Y Bala: Y Diwygiad Methodistaidd ym Meirionnydd a Môn* (Caernarfon, 1997).

[17] *The Literary Life of the Late Thomas Pennant, Esq., by Himself* (London, 1793).

[18] Edward Williams, *Poems, Lyric and Pastoral* (2 vols, London, 1794): the autobiography forms a short introduction to vol. I.

One of the most entertaining of all the autobiographies of this period is that of Thomas Edwards 'Twm o'r Nant', best known as a poet and composer of plays or interludes, in which he described his life as an actor, woodcutter and innkeeper, and how he got into all sorts of scrapes and fights, but with few regrets. Although born into an extremely poor family in Nantglyn, Denbighshire, he was writing plays by the age of nine. Their poverty as a family could be judged by the fact that Twm had to gather the knots of an elder tree to boil down into ink, and had to write on scraps of charred packing paper bought for a song from a burned-out shop. He probably prepared the memoir around 1800, but it first appeared in *Y Greal* in 1805 and was then published in 1810 as a separate work.[19]

When he penned his short autobiography in 1794, Iolo Morganwg was already well-known as a religious and political radical. He may have been deeply influenced by the anti-trinitarian views of Richard Price, the famous philosopher and spokesman for the American and French Revolutions. Price spent part of each year at Bridgend and Southerndown in Glamorgan, and was a leading local freemason. He wrote the outline of his autobiography in the summer of 1790, hoping to complete it following his return to London in October that year. He apparently never completed it and died in 1791.[20] One Unitarian minister who did succeed in completing an autobiography was the eccentric Charles Lloyd (1766–1829), who published his memoirs in 1813.[21] A great friend of Iolo Morganwg and a man who played a far more active part in the events of the Revolution in France was the Deist and historian, David Williams of Caerphilly. Several years later, around 1810, he also wrote an autobiography, which remained unpublished until 1980.[22]

In a sense, it can be seen that by the 1800s the pattern to be followed through the first half of the nineteenth century had been set. There were a handful of autobiographies from curious eccentrics, such as the four-volume memoirs of the somewhat improbable Llewellin Penrose of Caerphilly (born *c*.1725), published in 1815,[23] or the delightful Welsh memoir (first published in 1826) of David Williams of Landore, Swansea, describing his life working in silver mines in Mexico – it contains the first

[19] Thomas Edwards, *Gwaith Thomas Edwards, yn nghyd a Hanes ei Fywyd* (Merthyr Tydfil, 1849): the autobiography is on pp. i–xxxi. See also G. M. Ashton (ed.), *Hunangofiant a Llythyrau Twm o'r Nant* (Caerdydd, 1948).

[20] David Davies, *The Influence of the French Revolution on Welsh Life and Literature* (Carmarthen, 1926), p. 209.

[21] Anon., *Particulars of the Life of a Dissenting Minister* (London, 1813).

[22] David Williams, *Incidents in my own Life which have been Thought of Some Importance*, ed. Peter France (Brighton, 1980).

[23] John Eagles (ed.), *The Journal of Llewellin Penrose, a Seaman* (4 vols, London, 1815).

164

reference in Welsh to tortillas[24] – or the military memoirs (published in 1839) of David Price of Brecon, describing his career as a field officer in India, which curiously re-echo the career of his neighbour in Brecon Frederick Jones.[25] There were also one or two rare examples of memoirs by simple peasants: that of Rhys Cox of Anglesey, which, one suspects, contains a good dose of fantasy, was published in *Lleuad yr Oes* in 1827,[26] and another by Matthew Owen of Anglesey, a more plausible historical account, was eventually published in 1908.[27]

The majority of autobiographies – as was true of biographies also – were by ministers of religion. John Hughes of Brecon, a Wesleyan minister and historian, and author of *Horae Britannicae*, left a manuscript of his memoirs, which was later used by Gwilym Lleyn (William Roberts) as a basis for a biography of Hughes which he published in short snippets in *Yr Eurgrawn* in 1848 and 1849.[28] Christmas Evans, one of the greatest preachers of his day, appears to have compiled a manuscript memoir *c.*1836, which formed part of his Welsh biography published in 1840.[29] Hopkin Bevan of Llangyfelach was a Methodist but, like Christmas Evans, he died in 1839, and it was left to his son in 1840 to publish his auto-biography.[30] John Elias, the dominant figure in Welsh Calvinistic Method-ism up to his death in 1841, also left an autobiography.[31] Yet another Methodist, John Dafis of Nantglyn, had an autobiography published just after his death in 1843.[32] The famous hymn-writer Azariah Shadrach incorporated in 1840 a piece of autobiography in his collection of hymns

---

[24] David Williams, *Llythyrau Cymro yn Mexico (Dafydd Williams) at ei gyfeillion yn Glandwr, wrth Abertawy* (Abertawy, 1826). See also *DWB*, s.n. David Williams (?1793–1845).

[25] David Price, *Memoirs of the Early Life and Service of a Field Officer . . . of the Indian Army* ed. Edward Moor (London, 1839).

[26] 'Ymddiddan rhwng gwr ieuanc o Arfon, a gwr hen o Fon . . . yn anialdir America', *Lleuad yr Oes*, 1, part 6 (1827), 316–18, 374–6.

[27] 'Hanes Bywyd Matthew Owen o'r Flwyddyn 1769 hyd y Flwyddyn 1836', *Cymru*, 34 (1908), 253–7.

[28] The manuscript memoirs are in NLW MS3501. See *DWB*, s.n. John Hughes (1776–1843), and R. T. Jenkins, 'John Hughes, the Antiquary (1776–1843)', *Brycheiniog*, 8 (1962), 67–82. For the biography by Gwilym Lleyn, see *Yr Eurgrawn Wesleyaidd*, 40 (1848), and 41 (1849), in twenty-one short sections.

[29] William Morgan, *Cofiant, neu Hanes Bywyd y Diweddar Barch. Christmas Evans* (Caerdydd, 1839); D. Rhys Stephen, *Memoirs of the Late Christmas Evans, of Wales* (London, 1847). See also D. Densil Morgan, *Christmas Evans a'r Ymneilltuaeth Newydd* (Llandysul, 1991).

[30] Hopkin Bevan, *Ychydig o Hanes Bywyd y Parch. H. Bevan, Cilfwnwr, Llangyfelach* (Abertawy, 1840).

[31] Goronwy P. Owen (ed.), *Hunangofiant John Elias* (Pen-y-bont ar Ogwr, 1973).

[32] Thomas Parry, *Cofiant Y Parch. J[ohn] Davies o Nantglyn, ynghyd a Byr-ddywediadau, Traethodau, a Phregethau o'i eiddo* (Caerllion, 1844).

entitled *Cerbyd o Goed Libanus*.[33] William Jones of Gresford died in 1846, and his son, with filial piety, published his father's autobiography in the same year.[34] Jones was a 'Scotch Baptist' preacher and although the pioneer of the sect in Wales, J. R. Jones, Ramoth, had mocked 'Y Fi Fawr Fethodistaidd' (The Great Methodist Ego), his followers felt that there was room for individuality and self-writing.[35] The fashion for auto-biography meant that by the 1840s there were many more examples than can be mentioned here.

It can be seen, therefore, that, with a few rare exceptions such as Thomas Pennant, the great bulk of the autobiographical writing came from Dissenters and Methodists. Of course there was a fashion in England in the Romantic age for the writing of autobiography – Southey noted in 1807 that in that period everyone had become an autobiographer.[36] It may be that Dissent and Methodism drove Welsh people of poor and humble origins to keep diaries and journals, and it was but a short step from these to writing an autobiography. A 'spiritual autobiography', after all, could be urged upon one's fellow believers as a means of instruction and edification. It has been remarked on many occasions that, although the Methodists often had social concerns, their chief concern was their own movement, and central to their preoccupation was the spiritual welfare of the individual. The popular ballads of the seventeenth and eighteenth centuries had emphasized the communal and ritual aspects of life, congregational devotion, expressed in the plural person. By contrast, the hymns and lyrics of Methodism consisted of a dialogue between the singer and his or her own soul.[37] Derec Llwyd Morgan has emphasized the startling quality of the new Methodist literature, such as William Williams's *Aleluia* in 1744, with its intense, direct first-person colloquial style, its individualism and sensuousness of style.[38] Others have also drawn attention to Methodist self-expression and self-analysis: hence the need for journals and diaries kept meticulously by the convert and enthusiast. They felt a constant need to define the boundaries between society in general – 'the world', as they called it – and their own private society, and to define

---

[33] See *DWB*, s.n. Azariah Shadrach (1774–1844).

[34] See *DWB*, s.n. William Jones, Gresford (1762–1846).

[35] E. G. Millward (ed.), *Blodeugerdd Barddas o Gerddi Rhydd y Ddeunawfed Ganrif* ([Felindre, Abertawe], 1991), p. 19.

[36] Iain McCalman (ed.), *An Oxford Companion to the Romantic Age: British Culture 1776–1832* (Oxford, 1999), p. 411.

[37] Millward (ed.), *Blodeugerdd Barddas o Gerddi Rhydd*, p. 17.

[38] Derec Llwyd Morgan, *Y Diwygiad Mawr* (Llandysul, 1981), pp. 134–6. For Methodism, see Jenkins, *Foundations*, pp. 342–85, esp. 354, 356, and 361.

the boundaries of the individual soul. The result was their need for a vast new and complex vocabulary in Welsh.[39]

It goes without saying, probably, that Dissenters and Methodists strove to convert people who were largely illiterate. Methodists certainly converted large numbers by the sheer eloquence and enthusiasm of preaching, and sustained their converts with vast numbers of hymns, learned off by heart, and by constant conversation and listening in the *seiat*, or society. There was nevertheless a close association between the preaching movements and the revolution in literacy in the eighteenth century brought about by the Welsh circulating schools. Dissenters and Methodists actively encouraged their converts to learn to read, and even to write. The fact that so many of them by the late eighteenth century kept journals and wrote autobiographies is, therefore, the result not merely of Methodism but also of the advance of popular education. In the light of the struggle of Twm o'r Nant to find even ink and paper in the mid-eighteenth century,[40] it must be admitted that it was the gradually rising tide of material prosperity during the century that also enabled increasing numbers of humble people to find time for education and leisure to write, and the means of purchasing the wherewithal for writing. It is indicative of this change in Wales that while *myfyrgell* (study) appears as a word in the middle of the seventeenth century, the Welsh word *desg* usually refers to a lectern in church until it first appears in a domestic context in the letters of the Morris brothers in 1763.[41] This presumably was one of the desks on which those indefatigable letter-writers wrote their colourfully idiosyncratic letters in the middle decades of the eighteenth century.

The three Morris brothers of Anglesey were Anglicans. They had little patience with Methodists: Lewis Morris painted a most disparaging portrait of Howel Harris, whom he had heard preaching at Builth. This reminds us that we should not lose sight of the fact that selfhood or individuality in Wales in this period was not merely the concern of evangelicals. There were signs of it throughout Welsh life and there is space here only to deal with one or two aspects, such as the rise of the fashion for portraiture. In the 1940s John Steegman carried out a survey of portraits preserved in Welsh houses, which provides invaluable evidence because most of the collections have by now been dispersed.[42] Steegman's survey reveals that the very greatest families, such as the Myddeltons of

[39] Glanmor Williams, *The Welsh and their Religion* (Cardiff, 1991), pp. 54–5, for individual personal religion; see Glyn Tegai Hughes, *Williams Pantycelyn* (Cardiff, 1983), p. 8, for 'spiritual autobiography'.

[40] Edwards, *Gwaith Thomas Edwards*, pp. vii–viii.

[41] *Geiriadur Prifysgol Cymru*, s.nn. 'myfyrgell' and 'desg'.

[42] John Steegman, *A Survey of Portraits in Welsh Houses* (2 vols, Cardiff, 1957, 1962).

Chirk or the Morgans of Tredegar, had collections of portraits before 1700. The great majority of houses, which were homes either of the greater or minor gentry, contained portraits painted in the eighteenth century. Steegman admitted that his survey, which was confined to gentry houses, omitted the portraits of the middle and lower classes. Paul Joyner's recent survey of artists in Wales from the 1740s to the 1850s draws attention to the appearance of travelling portrait painters in the eighteenth century, and notes the attempts by Giuseppe Marchi to set up a permanent portrait studio in Swansea *c.*1770–2. Marchi was a friend of the autobiographer Thomas Jones, and is today perhaps best remembered for his portraits of the Jones family of Pencerrig.[43]

Steegman's survey begins with the eleven collections in Anglesey, and while Plasnewydd had a very large number of portraits dating from before 1700, the more typical Anglesey houses such as Carreglwyd had five before 1700 and eight from the eighteenth century. In Caernarfonshire, which had eleven collections, Glynllifon had only one before 1700 and nine in the eighteenth century, while Nanhoron had two before 1700 and seventeen dating from the eighteenth century. Denbighshire recorded a total of twenty-one collections, several of which, such as Chirk, Erddig and Bryncunallt, had a preponderance of portraits before 1700. But even Brogyntyn, near Oswestry, which was included in Wales for the purposes of this catalogue, had eighteen before 1700 and sixty-two from the eighteenth century. This reflects the pattern in the lesser houses. In Flintshire the great gentry houses such as Leeswood and Mostyn had large collections of portraits dating from before 1700, but the general pattern was represented by Rhual, which had only five before 1700 and thirty dating from the eighteenth century. The pattern is repeated in Merioneth, with a few great houses such as Nannau and Peniarth having substantial numbers of portraits predating 1700, but the majority of houses had a preponderance of portraits dating from the eighteenth century. The twelve collections listed for Montgomeryshire again repeated the pattern: even the immense Powis Castle collections had thirty-two portraits before 1700 and as many as fifty-five dating from the eighteenth century.[44]

Steegman's second volume, devoted to south Wales, corroborates the evidence of the north Wales volume. Old Gwernyfed in Breconshire had ten portraits before 1700 and nineteen from the eighteenth century, while Llwyn Madog had only one from before 1700, and nine from the eighteenth century. This pattern was again repeated in the Cardiganshire collections,

---

[43] Paul Joyner, *Artists in Wales, c.1740–c.1851* (Aberystwyth, 1997), pp. 77–9; Peter Lord, *The Visual Culture of Wales: Imaging the Nation* (Cardiff, 2000), pp. 127–8, for Giuseppe Marchi in Wales.
[44] Steegman, *Survey of Portraits*, I, *passim*.

one exception being the noble family of Trawsgoed, where there were fourteen before 1700 and only eight from the eighteenth century. Carmarthenshire collections showed a similar pattern: Golden Grove, belonging to a noble family, had eleven from before 1700 and only six dating from the eighteenth century. More typical was Tre-gib, with three from before 1700 and twenty from the eighteenth century. Of the sixteen Glamorgan collections examined, only two, Penrice Castle and Tythegston Court near Porth-cawl, had important collections of portraits made before 1700. Typical was Coedrhiglan, near Cardiff, which had four from before 1700 and eleven from the eighteenth century. In Monmouthshire's fifteen recorded collections, even at Llan-arth and Tredegar, where there were large numbers of portraits before 1700, they were outnumbered by those from the eighteenth century. Trewyn was an exception in so far as it had large numbers of early portraits, but these were from the Molyneux family and from outside Wales. Pembrokeshire collections showed an almost total absence of portraits dating from before 1700: even the great noble collection at Stackpole had only one from before 1700 compared with twenty-six from the eighteenth century. Radnorshire followed exactly the same pattern as other Welsh counties: typical was Llysdinam with two from before 1700 and five from the eighteenth century.[45]

This general pattern of development is confirmed by the valuable studies of Peter Lord on the visual culture of Wales, in which he reveals the spread of portrait collections down from the noble families in the seventeenth centuries to the lesser gentry by the end of the eighteenth. Lord has also charted the rise of artisan painters during the first half of the nineteenth century, notably the career of Hugh Hughes (1790–1863), and these researches make it perfectly clear that there was a demand for portraits among the Welsh middle classes in that period.[46] These were the people who bought Welsh dictionaries and the memoirs and autobiographies of Welsh worthies in this period. Lord's researches are particularly pertinent here since they show that several of the autobiographers mentioned above also sat for their portraits, and that, in some cases, there was a demand for copies of the portraits which were hung in Welsh homes almost as icons. He discusses the portraits of Twm o'r Nant, the aged Methodist pioneer John Evans of Bala, and Thomas Jones of Denbigh, as well as heroes of the pulpit such as John Elias and Christmas Evans, all of whom were autobiographers. In many cases these portraits were produced at the same time as the later autobiographies mentioned above, and they underline the great fascination of the middle classes with expressions of individuality.

[45] Ibid., II, *passim.*
[46] Peter Lord, *Hugh Hughes, Arlunydd Gwlad, 1790–1863* (Llandysul, 1995).

The poor had to make do with engraved portraits and it is no surprise that the picture of Peter Williams, the Bible expositor and autobiographer, hung on the walls of so many Welsh homes, even within living memory.[47]

The spread of the fashion for painting portraits down from the noble families to the gentry and then the minor gentry by the end of the eighteenth century, and from them to the middle classes in the first decades of the nineteenth, is surely connected not only to a growing desire to commemorate individuals but also with the growing material prosperity of the age, which allowed commemoration to be concretely expressed. Another field in which individual commemoration was increasingly expressed was God's acre, the churchyard, and by the early nineteenth century, the chapel graveyard. Studies of Welsh gravestones are few and far between: A. O. Chater's detailed study of Cardiganshire churchyards shows that, while there were few stones of any kind before 1688, monumental stones appear in most places soon after 1700.[48] They reveal considerable individuality and local character until around 1820, when the spread of the fashion for commemorative stones for all kinds of people became so great that a kind of conventionalizing process takes over. The change of fashion was intimately connected to the ability of large numbers of people to read and thus was dependent to some extent on the spread of popular literacy. Even so, it seems fair to adduce commemorative stones as evidence of a rising sense of selfhood and individuality during the eighteenth century.

If this tendency can be seen in graves of the dead, it should also be possible to gauge it in the houses of the living. Various architectural historians, of whom the best-known is Peter Smith, have studied Welsh houses from the sixteenth to the eighteenth centuries and have pointed out the significance of the coming into Wales, even in a simple and humble form, of the 'Renaissance-type centralized plan', and to emphasize that the ultimate achievement of this plan was privacy for the dwellers.[49] Among many other changes in building styles there was the development of the medieval hall-house into a many-roomed dwelling, and among humble farms and cottages a development from a single cell into a multicellular dwelling. But Smith and others emphasize that there was little real privacy in seventeenth-century houses, even for kings and princes, because one

---

[47] Idem, *Imaging the Nation* (Cardiff, 2000), pp. 167–244, esp. p. 203 (Twm o'r Nant), p. 204 (Thomas Jones of Denbigh), p. 206 (John Evans), p. 211 (John Elias), and pp. 216–17 (John Elias and Christmas Evans), for portraits of autobiographers.

[48] A. O. Chater, 'Early Cardiganshire Gravestones', *AC*, 125 (1976), 140–61; *AC*, 126 (1977), 116–38.

[49] Peter Smith, *Houses of the Welsh Countryside* (London, 1975), pp. 222–63, esp. 234–63.

room led into another, and a lack of corridors meant that no one could be private unless they were hidden behind screens or within the curtains of a four-poster bed. The great blessing of a private chamber derived from the Renaissance axial plan, with its central stairwell, with rooms opening off a 'hall' which was, of course, no longer a real medieval communal hall, but rather a kind of lobby. The fashion for these centrally planned houses spread through Wales from the late seventeenth century onwards, first of all for the gentry, then for the middle classes, and finally for the lower orders by the early nineteenth century. Even the fairly humble 'two-up two-down' dwelling had at least two private rooms upstairs. This protracted architectural transformation, dating from *c.*1660 to *c.*1840, was caused partly by growing material prosperity and partly by a desire for comfort and privacy, both those aims being achieved by more exact specialization of the functions of rooms and the subdivisions of the living space. It is likely that the furniture inside the houses developed also to enable the individual to sit where he or she pleased. Anyone who has visited antique salerooms during the last fifty years will confirm that Welsh chairs before 1700 are exceptionally difficult to find, whereas one can still discover in large numbers in any saleroom Welsh oak chairs made in the latter half of the eighteenth century. In any case, it will be clear that the architectural process, with its growing emphasis on privacy, runs in parallel with the other developments towards the definition of personality and individuality given above.[50]

Perhaps the most profound evidence of all for the development of self-awareness and individuality in the eighteenth and early nineteenth centuries is that provided by the vast expansion of Welsh vocabulary.[51] As with the developments mentioned above, here again the most rapid advances took place in the last quarter of the eighteenth century, with a complex and subtle vocabulary appearing in the dictionaries of John Walters of Llandough near Cowbridge (from 1770 onwards), William Richards of Lynn in 1798, and William Owen Pughe in 1803, as well as in the periodicals of the same period. Many of their words fell by the wayside, and Pughe's excessively elaborate inventions in particular – such as 'gogoelgrefyddusedd' (some degree of superstitiousness) – have caused mirth and mockery. But an examination of the words dating from this

---

[50] *An Inventory of the Ancient Monuments in Glamorgan*, IV, *Domestic Architecture from the Reformation to the Industrial Revolution. Farmhouses and Cottages* (London, 1988), pp. 1, 2, 29–30 of the introduction. For furniture, see L. Twiston-Davies and H. J. Lloyd-Johnes, *Welsh Furniture: An Introduction* (Cardiff, 1950) and Luke Millar, 'Late Georgian Wooden-Bottomed Chairs in South Wales', *Regional Furniture*, 5 (1991), 1–15.

[51] Prys Morgan, 'Dyro Olau ar Dy Eiriau', *Taliesin*, 70 (1990), 38–45.

period, and which have remained in use in Welsh ever since, shows that it would be difficult to hold an intelligent conversation without them, and that, taken all in all, they enabled Welsh speakers, who constituted the overwhelming majority of the population, to reveal and discuss the subtleties of the human personality and the relation of the self to society.[52]

Quaker and Puritan writers in Welsh had, as might be expected, shown the way by inventing such words as *allanol* (outward) (1657), *myfyrdodol* (contemplative) (1676) and *bwriadol* (intentional) (1657). In some cases eighteenth-century writers simply twisted an old word to give it a contemporary meaning: thus *personoliaeth* had generally been used to discuss the personality of Christ up to the early eighteenth century, but by 1793 periodicals were using it to discuss the 'personality of the language'. The old word *treth* (tax) was adapted to give *trethu* (to tax one's powers) by 1793. *Siomedigaeth* was an old word, meaning a trick or deception, but by 1740 it had taken on an emotional meaning of 'disappointment', which it still retains. *Diwylliant* had originally meant the cultivation of the wild ground, but by 1795 it had taken on the modern meaning of 'culture' or 'civilization'. In most cases authors or lexicographers simply took their cue from the language theorists of the day, who showed that Welsh words were made up of particles, and added suffixes and prefixes to create new words.[53] Only a tiny selection can possibly be listed here out of several hundreds.

Taking a short alphabetical selection, together with the year in which they first appear, we have *awyrgylch* (atmosphere) (1770), *arddegau* (teens) (1794), *babandod* (babyhood) (1762), *beirniadaeth* (criticism) (1772), *camdriniaeth* (maltreatment) (1765), *cenedligrwydd* (nationality) (1798), *cydraddoldeb* (equality) (1797), *cydymdeimlad* (sympathy) (1725–6), *cyfrifoldeb* (responsibility) (1814), *dathlu* (to celebrate) (1794), *diddorol* (interesting) only takes on its modern meaning in 1828, *dyfeisgar* (inventive) (1771), *dylanwad* (influence) (1716), *gwladgarwch* (love of one's country) (1776), *gwreiddioldeb* (originality) appeared as 'radicalness' in the late eighteenth century and did not take on its modern meaning until 1847–8, *mewnol* (interior) (1803), *myfiaeth* (egotism) (1777), *mynegiant* (expression) (*c.*1785–90), *nodwedd* (characteristic) (1803), *odrwydd* (singularity, oddity) (1778), *oerfelgarwch* (apathy, indifference) (1737), *parchusrwydd* (respectability) (1783), *pencampwr* (champion) (1807), *pendantrwydd* (positiveness) (1780), *penderfynol* (determined) (1710),

---

[52] All the examples listed below are taken from *Geiriadur Prifysgol Cymru* and are given with the earliest known dates of their use, as noted in the dictionary.

[53] Caryl Davies, *Adfeilion Babel: Agweddau ar Syniadaeth Ieithyddol y Ddeunawfed Ganrif* (Caerdydd, 2000) for a valuable survey of linguistic theories as they influenced Welsh: pp. 253–69 for eighteenth-century lexicographers, pp. 202–30 for linguistic particles and word invention, and pp. 267–94 for the circle of William Owen Pughe.

pleidlais (vote) around 1785–90, *poblogrwydd* (popularity) (1780), *pwyslais* (emphasis) (1800), *rhesymol* (rational, reasonable) (1776), *rhwyddineb* (facility) (about 1730), *rhywiol* (sexual) (1803), *segurdod* (idleness) (1790), *swildod*; (shyness) (1793), *swynol* (charming) (1793), *sylweddoli* (to realize) (1783), *teimladrwydd* (sentiment) (1773), *torcalonnus* (heartbreaking) (1735), *trafodaeth* (discussion) (1757), *trefniant* (arrangement) (1803), *treiddgar* (penetrating) (1808), *unigedd* (solitude) (1776), *unigolyn* (individual) (1793), *unigryw* (unique) about 1785–90, – this, appropriately enough, from Iolo Morganwg, one of the autobiographers – *ymddiheuro* (to apologize) (1803), *ymgomiwr* (conversationalist) (1753), *ymosodol* (offensive) (1778), *ymwybodol* (conscious) (1772), *ystrydeb* (stereotype, cliché) (1806).

In addition to those there are well over 300 words in Welsh beginning with the word 'hunan-' (self-), the great majority of which first appeared in the eighteenth and early nineteenth centuries.[54] Again, only a very short selection need be offered here to indicate broadly the concern of the period for defining individuality. Taking them alphabetically, we have *hunanadnabyddiaeth* (self-knowledge) (1771), *hunanaddoliad* (worship of the self) (1773), *hunanallu* (self-sufficiency) (as early as 1740), *hunan-barch* (self-respect) (1797), *hunanbwysig* (self-important) (1800) – this was a term invented by the autobiographer and preacher Christmas Evans – *hunander* (egoism) (1771), *hunan-dwyll* (self-deception) (1728), *hunan-dyb* (conceit) as early as 1688, *hunanfeddiant* (self-possession) (1757), *hunan-fudd* (self-interest) (1740), *hunangar* (selfish) (1770) – this was an invention of the autobiographer and biblical expositor Peter Williams – *hunangofiant* (autobiography) which surprisingly comes as late as 1852, *hunangyfiawn* (self-righteous) (1775), *hunanhyder* (self-confidence) (1741), *hunanol* (selfish) (as early as 1683), and, lastly, *hunanymwybodol* (self-conscious) (1792).

The above short selection of vocabulary does not really do justice to the inventiveness of the Welsh writers of the period or to their determination to enable the Welsh to map out the newly discovered territory of the self in the language of the common people. Yet the new vocabulary, with all its richness and subtlety, serves to echo the developments I have mentioned above: the plethora of self-writing, the obsession of the age for a warm personal religion, the portraits on the walls, the individual gravestones, the private rooms in the houses, all add up to a discovery and cultivation of the self, personality and individuality, which must have been one of the most profound changes of the age and which must have had serious consequences. Many aspects of this change have not been touched upon in

---

[54] *Geiriadur Prifysgol Cymru*, II (1912–23) for words beginning with 'hunan-'.

this chapter, for example, the growth in specialization of knowledge, crafts and professions, in this period.[55] The Welsh were clearly expressing themselves personally through language and the arts in the eighteenth century, and were beginning to demand that each soul should be taken seriously, that each person should have religious rights, and have the opportunity to develop his and her personality through education. As a result, by the middle of the nineteenth century the individual would have seen himself as a political personality and demand political rights.

The world of the early nineteenth century was that of the grandparents of men such as Tom Ellis and Lloyd George, the world of sturdy independent craftsmen, who had so often subscribed to Welsh books and dictionaries, and founded chapels and meeting-houses, literary clubs and societies, and the world of independent farmers and doughty tenants who tried to wriggle out of the grasp of the landowners. Such was the culture of Dafydd Llwyd (1800–34) and his son Richard Lloyd, shoemakers of Llanystumdwy, grandfather and uncle of Lloyd George.[56] Such, too, was the culture of the ancestors of Tom Ellis, Owen M. Edwards, J. Puleston Jones, D. R. Daniel and others at Cefnddwysarn. The profound seismic shift which has been sketched in this chapter appears to have been closely associated with other economic and social changes, and to have been connected in some ways with material prosperity of some sort, and yet it predated the coming of large-scale industrialization during the nineteenth century, with all its emphasis upon the communal shared experience. Welsh radicalism, for all the rhetoric about the shared experience, also owed much to individualism. The search for a private space had arisen much earlier than industrialism, and yet its consequences were to be felt profoundly in the struggles for political and religious rights in the age of Tom Ellis and Lloyd George.

[55] Keith Thomas, in his foreword to R. T. W. Denning (ed.), *The Diary of William Thomas, of Michaelston-super-Ely, near St Fagans, Glamorgan 1762–1795* (Cardiff, 1995), p. 8, refers to the specialization and division of knowledge in this period as the greatest aid to the formation of human individuality.

[56] W. R. P. George, *The Making of Lloyd George* (London, 1976), pp. 15–16, and for Dafydd Llwyd, pp. 17–29.

11

'A Very Horrid Affair': Sedition and Unitarianism in the Age of Revolutions[*]

GERAINT H. JENKINS

For the best part of thirty years George Hardinge, grandson of a chief justice and formerly solicitor-general to the queen, served as senior justice for the Courts of Great Sessions in the counties of Brecon, Glamorgan and Radnor. Widely admired for his extensive learning and brilliant wit, this urbane and somewhat dandyish figure, later to be immortalized as the 'waggish Welch Judge, Jefferies Hardsman' in Byron's *Don Juan*, found himself in the third week of August 1801 in the busy and turbulent town of Carmarthen, on the fringe of the anti-trinitarian fiefdom known to Calvinistic Methodists as 'Y Smotyn Du' (The Black Spot).[1] It was Hardinge's practice to choose appropriate music for Sunday worship at St Peter's church and, having listened intently to the Assize sermon, he might well have strolled along the banks of the Tywi in the evening (he composed several poems on Welsh rivers) to brood over some of the issues, among them the lamentable state of civil order in the rapidly industrializing county of Glamorgan and the baneful influence of republicans and levellers, which had preoccupied him since his appointment in 1787. With the ruinously expensive war against France in its ninth year and fears of either Jacobin republican rule or arbitrary Napoleonic rule very much alive, he was in no mood to undermine confidence in the British government by showing any sympathy towards those who appealed either to reason or revelation in pursuing subversive goals. Throughout the 1790s he had been adamantly hostile towards those suspected of fomenting sedition

* I should like to record my general debt to the team of research fellows – Mary-Ann Constantine, Andrew Davies, Cathryn Charnell-White, David Jones and Ffion Jones – who are working under my direction on a major AHRB research project entitled 'Iolo Morganwg and the Romantic Tradition in Wales 1740–1918' at the University of Wales Centre for Advanced Welsh and Celtic Studies.

[1] *Gentleman's Magazine*, 86 (1816), 469–70; W. R. Williams, *The History of the Great Sessions in Wales 1542–1830* (Brecknock, 1899), p. 149; Hilary M. Thomas (ed.), *The Diaries of John Bird: Clerk to the First Marquess of Bute, 1790–1803* (Cardiff, 1987), p. 32.

or committing public disorder in urban communities.[2] The auguries, therefore, must have been alarming for those pugnacious Welsh Unitarians who
rallied that week to the defence of Thomas Evans, known locally as Twm
Penpistyll and nationally as Tomos Glyn Cothi, who had been indicted for
sedition. The first Welsh Unitarian minister, Evans was widely supposed to
be an ardent revolutionary who, in his sermons and through the printing
press, had delighted in bloodying the noses of kings, bishops and clergymen. Carmarthen was one of the fastest-growing towns in south Wales,
and its printing presses, Dissenting academy, grammar school, book
societies and masonic lodges had nurtured a literate and highly politicized
society. Readers of the *Welsh History Review* – to whose editors this
chapter is dedicated with gratitude – will be familiar with accounts of the
way in which relatively affluent radical Unitarians established a strong
Jacobin tradition in Merthyr,[3] but we need to restore the balance by
reminding ourselves that the fountain-head of anti-trinitarianism was
located in south-west Wales, where well-read intellectuals and daring
thinkers challenged the theological certainties of the times, openly discussed
seditious ideas and made them available to the swinish multitude.

Wartime Britain was characterized by invasion scares, clandestine activity
and show trials, and the progress and outcome of the case against Thomas
Evans in 1801 kept the town of Carmarthen and Unitarian congregations in
south Wales in a state of ferment for many weeks. Unitarianism might not
have been numerically strong in Wales during the Age of Revolutions, but
the possible consequences of its liberal-minded radicalism increasingly
preoccupied local magistrates, patriotic societies and orthodox trinitarians.
By the turn of the eighteenth century, many believed that the time had come
to clip its wings. The bizarre story of this show trial, a case which involved
spirituality, sedition and sexual favours, as well as its profound implications
for rational Dissent in Wales, have never been fully analysed.[4] It highlighted, among other things, an intriguing tangle of liaisons and depend-
encies which brought together people who were as deeply interested in the
cultural inheritance of Wales as in its religious and political future.

---

[2] Cardiff Central Library MS 2.716, I, pp. 5, 12[r–v], 18v; II, pp. 13[v], 26, 46[v], 47[r], 57–8,
81; NLW, Bute L48/57i; David J. V. Jones, *Before Rebecca: Popular Protest in Wales
1793–1835* (London, 1973), pp. 215–20.

[3] Gwyn A. Williams, 'The Making of Radical Merthyr, 1800–1836', *WHR*, 1, no. 1
(1961), 161–92; D. J. V. Jones, 'The Merthyr Riots of 1831', *WHR*, 3, no. 2 (1966),
173–205; Gwyn A. Williams, 'The Merthyr Election of 1835', *WHR*, 10, no. 3 (1981),
359–97.

[4] For previous short and incomplete narrative accounts in Welsh, see Geraint
Dyfnallt Owen, *Thomas Evans (Tomos Glyn Cothi)* (n.pl., 1963), pp. 32–43; G. J.
Williams, 'Carchariad Tomos Glyn Cothi', *LlC*, 3, no. 2 (1954), 120–2; D. Elwyn
Davies, 'Helynt Carchariad Thomas Glyn Cothi', *Yr Ymofynnydd*, 64, no. 8 (1964),
129–42.

We must first consider the events which paved the way for the arraignment of a Unitarian minister who had a reputation as a scourge of government and an unflinching friend of liberty. On 5 March 1801 a 'cwrw bach' (bid-ale) was held at Brechfa, Carmarthenshire, to raise funds to assist an indigent parishioner, Thomas Joseph. During such convivial events neighbours habitually organized a raffle and on this occasion lots were drawn for the disposal of a watch owned by Joseph himself. Each participant was invited to contribute sixpence and abundant fresh ale was made available. Thomas Evans recorded the names of the contributors on a sheet of paper, but before the draw could be made he was distracted by an invitation to visit the next-door neighbour Henry Williams. In his absence George Thomas, a shoemaker who had been excommunicated by Evans from the local Unitarian church for some unspecified immoral deed and wilful atheism, cut out the names of the participants and conducted the draw. When Evans and his friends returned they were incandescent on finding that the lots had already been drawn and that one of Thomas's associates had pocketed the watch. The assembled throng cried foul, the draw was declared null and void, Evans rewrote the names of the participants, and a young boy was enlisted to draw the name of the winner. By this stage the beery gathering had become noisy and fractious. Several rousing hymns and satirical songs were sung, and such wounding barbs were directed at George Thomas that he left in high dudgeon. Determined to wreak his revenge, he filed a complaint against Thomas Evans, Daniel Evans (a husbandman) and Daniel Jones (a victualler) with a local magistrate, the gist of which was that they had sung loudly a seditious English version of the Carmagnole during the bid-ale which included the inflammatory verse:

> And when upon the British shore
> The thundering guns of France shall roar,
> Vile George shall trembling stand
> Or fly his native land,
> With terror and appal,
> Dance Carmagnol, Dance Carmagnol.

The three accused were allowed bail and were bound over to keep the peace until their appearance at the Court of Great Sessions in August.[5]

On 21 March Evans wrote to his friend Edward Williams, universally known as Iolo Morganwg, outlining the charge against him, protesting his

---

[5] NLW, Great Sessions 4/753/1–3; NLW MS 21373D, f. 5^{r-v}; NLW MS 21411E, no. 26.

innocence – 'My Innocency is My Shield' – and inviting him, at his cost, to hasten to Penpistyll farm at Llanegwad to advise him how to proceed and to alert his brother Rees to his predicament.[6] Never one to spurn a brush with the law (seven years earlier he had maintained that 'hardly an instance can be produced where a poor man unbacked by wealthy friends ever obtained justice in our Law-Courts'),[7] Williams duly complied and spent several weeks preparing on behalf of embattled local Unitarians a petition seeking the financial support of Unitarian societies in London, Bristol and south Wales to defray the expenses of the forthcoming trial and to support their minister, his wife and nine children. The twenty-two petitioners, seven of whom could not write, vigorously defended the good name of Thomas Evans against the 'villainously false' accusation conjured up by hostile trinitarians and a disgraced atheist.[8] It is unlikely, however, that Evans's predicament provoked a sympathetic response from the Calvinist majority. For he and his mentor Edward Williams were known to have spent the previous decade propagating anti-trinitarianism, *sans-culottism* and the rights of man. This background must now be examined.

Thomas Evans and Edward Williams are fine exemplars of the craftsman-artisan tradition which contributed so richly to the cultural, spiritual and political life of late eighteenth-century Wales.[9] Both were of journeyman stock, scraped a living and had very little formal education. Born in 1747 in the hamlet of Pennon in the Vale of Glamorgan, Williams was the son of Ann Matthew and Edward Williams, a stonemason. Evans, born in 1764, was seventeen years younger: the son of Hannah and Evan John, a weaver, he hailed from Capel Sant Silyn, Gwernogle, Carmarthenshire.[10] Both followed their fathers' trade. Whereas Williams's mother, a demanding figure who showered him with English literature, was the most powerful early influence on his cultural mindset, Evans's mentor was his father, who plied him with scriptural material, encouraged him to think liberally, and improved his mind and stamina by walking him each Sunday to Alltyblaca to listen to the spellbinding sermons of the Arian minister David Davis (who later became known as Dafydd Dafis Castellhywel). In their teens both apprentices developed a taste for poetry in English and

---

[6] NLW MS 21281E, Iolo Morganwg Letters no. 174.

[7] Edward Williams, *Poems, Lyric and Pastoral* (2 vols, London, 1794), I, p. xi.

[8] NLW MS 21373D, pp. 1–4.

[9] David Jenkins, 'The Part played by Craftsmen in the Religious History of Modern Wales', *Welsh Anvil*, 6 (1954), 90–7; Geraint H. Jenkins, *The Foundations of Modern Wales: Wales 1642–1780* (Oxford, 1987), pp. 386–9.

[10] Glamorgan Record Office, P/36/CW/1. Llancarfan PR; G. J. Williams, *Iolo Morganwg* (Caerdydd, 1956), chap. 2; Ceri W. Lewis, *Iolo Morganwg* (Caernarfon, 1995), chap 2; *Gardd Aberdar, yn cynwys y Cyfansoddiadau Buddugol yn Eisteddfod y Carw Coch, Aberdar, Awst 29, 1853* (Caerfyrddin, 1854), pp. 89–110.

Welsh, though Evans's toe-curling juvenilia do not bear comparison with the pastoral poems or the medieval *cywyddau* which Williams composed from the early 1770s onwards.[11] Both were voracious readers and delighted in their bardic pseudonyms. Having initially flirted with the pen-names 'Iorwerth Gwilym' and 'Iorwerth Morganwg', Williams eventually and happily settled upon 'Iolo Morganwg', while Evans, who was born on the banks of the river Cothi, became the Romantic age's equivalent of Lewys Glyn Cothi, the famous fifteenth-century poet. The two men do not seem to have met until the first bardic moot was held on Welsh soil at Stalling Down, near Cowbridge, on 21 March 1795, but from then onwards these squat, unkempt, intelligent and quizzical rational Dissenters became the leading torchbearers of the Unitarian movement in Wales.

Thomas Evans's spiritual odyssey took a different course from that of the Glamorgan stonemason. It was both swift and straightforward. Raised close to Llwynrhydowen, the epicentre of Welsh anti-trinitarianism, and heavily influenced by his father's spiky individualism and the progressive sermons of David Davis, who lent him books and laced his homilies in the pulpit with indelicate comments about local Methodists and snatches of ribald sedition,[12] Evans soon warmed to the cause of religious and civil liberty and came to believe that Calvinism, the predominant theology, represented tyrannical authority and closed minds. Though he greeted the revolution in France with enthusiasm, Evans never seems to have ventured far from his native patch (except to sell flannel at fairs and markets in Glamorgan and possibly Bristol) and he relied heavily on middle-class Dissenters in England for cerebral and material support. It was their munificence which enabled him to build Cwm Cothi meeting-house, the first Unitarian chapel erected in Wales. On 11 September 1794 Evans was ordained its first minister.[13]

As might be expected in the case of such an enigmatic figure, the curve of Edward Williams's theological path was anything but straightforward. He was baptized and married within the Established Church but, as a result of fraternizing with a small group of plebeian radicals and free-thinkers which included John Bradford and Edward Evan, he kept his

---

[11] NLW MSS 7362–3B; Owen Jones and William Owen (eds), *Barddoniaeth Dafydd ab Gwilym* (Llundain, 1789); Williams, *Poems, Lyric and Pastoral, passim.*

[12] See *Telyn Dewi sef Gwaith Prydyddawl y Parch. David Davis, o Gastell-Hywel, Ceredigion* (Aberystwyth, 1927).

[13] Thomas Evans, *Datganiad Ffydd, a gafodd ei Thraethu yn Gyhoeddus gerbron Gweidogion (sic) ac Eraill, gerllaw y Gwarnogau, yn Sir Gaerfyrddin, Medi 11, 1794* (Caerfyrddin, 1795). Iolo Morganwg carved a tablet of stone for the new meeting-house (NLW MS 13103B, p. 300; NLW MS 21406E, p. 12).

mind open.[14] Having developed a taste for electioneering during the county election in Glamorgan in 1789,[15] he went up to London to seek subscriptions for his *Poems, Lyric and Pastoral*, which, after much heart-searching and mental stress, saw the light of day in two volumes in 1794. During 1791–4 his head became filled with a rich array of ideas based on druidism, Quakerism, Brahminism, Paineism, freemasonry, millenarianism, Romanticism and Rationalism, some of which he vented publicly in the boisterous meetings of the Gwyneddigion Society or in the Gorsedd of Bards which, from its inception on 21 June 1792, became a totemic image inextricably associated with his name. Convinced that druidic bardism was the patriarchal religion of ancient Britain, he maintained that the Welsh bards had 'at all times espoused the sacred doctrine of a belief in one God, the Creator, and Governor of the Universe'.[16] Throughout the decade he remained strongly attracted to Quakerism. 'I am of the same sentiments with the Quakers',[17] he informed war-mongering William Pitt in December 1796 and, two years later, reflecting the theological flux of the times, he referred to himself as a Unitarian Quaker.[18] He prided himself on his independence of mind, his detestation of 'scoundrelism', and his faith in peace, benevolence and liberty. And by means of his druidic moots he peddled his own peculiar brand of Unitarianism.

One of the principal theological influences on both Evans and Williams was Joseph Priestley, the leading standard-bearer of Enlightened Dissent in England. Priestley's association with Wales, though modest, predated Thomas Evans's birth. At Wrexham in 1762 he had married Mary, sister of the powerful ironmaster John Wilkinson, and by the 1770s he was corresponding on matters such as metaphysics with Richard Price, the most internationally celebrated Welshman of the day.[19] Edward Williams knew Price, who lived in nearby Bridgend, and also his uncompromisingly republican nephew George Cadogan Morgan, as well as Priestley himself.

---

[14] Iolo used to refer to them as 'Gwŷr Cwm y Felin' (NLW MS 13121B, pp. 335–8); Ceri W. Lewis, 'The Literary History of Glamorgan from 1550 to 1770', in Glanmor Williams (ed.), *Glamorgan County History, IV, Early Modern Glamorgan* (Cardiff, 1974), pp. 614–16, 618–19.

[15] NLW MS 13091E, p. 323.

[16] William Owen, *The Heroic Elegies and Other Pieces of Llywarç Hen* (London, 1792), p. xxviii. For further discussion, see D. Elwyn J. Davies, 'Astudiaeth o Feddwl a Chyfraniad Iolo Morganwg, fel Rhesymolwr ac Undodwr' (unpubl. University of Wales Ph.D. thesis, 1975).

[17] PRO 30/8/190/83LH.

[18] NLW MS 21285E, Iolo Morganwg Letters no. 863. See also Geraint H. Jenkins, *Facts, Fantasy and Fiction: The Historical Vision of Iolo Morganwg* (Aberystwyth, 1997), pp. 14–15.

[19] *Autobiography of Joseph Priestley*. Introduction by Jack Lindsay (Bath, 1970), p. 16; D. O. Thomas and W. B. Peach (eds), *The Correspondence of Richard Price* (3 vols, 1748–91, Durham, NC, and Cardiff, 1983–94).

He claimed that he owed his nomination as a member of the London Philosophical Society to Priestley and he was horrified when Priestley's home, laboratory and library were rendered 'a burnt-offering to the Moloch of intolerance' by a furious 'Church and King' mob in Birmingham on (by a grotesque irony) Bastille Day 1791.[20] Williams's papers contain a printed copy of Priestley's letter, addressed to the inhabitants of Birmingham five days later,[21] and he applauded his Arian friend David Davis for persuading the Presbyterian assembly at Llechryd in 1791 to condemn the attack on Priestley's home even though Davis himself, as his amusing mock epitaph reveals, balked at Priestley's thoroughgoing materialism:

> Here lie at rest,
> In oaken chest,
> Together pack'd most nicely,
> The bones and brains,
> Flesh, blood and veins
> And *soul* of Doctor Priestley.[22]

Although Elijah Waring claimed that Williams was 'a partial, though not an implicit disciple' of Priestley, he tantalizingly failed to expand on this generalization.[23] We know that he championed Priestley's experimentalism and that he admired his bravery. If anecdotal evidence is a reliable guide, he also approved of Priestley's abridged version of David Hartley's views on necessarianism (a philosophical theology which stressed the invariable succession of cause and effect and denied the arbitrariness of Calvinism). As he walked on one occasion from Flemingston to St Hilary in the company of Rees, Thomas Evans's brother, who was a successful weaver and Unitarian at Tonyrefail, Edward Williams became involved in a heated dispute over the autonomy of the individual and the determining power of personal considerations. Probably in a deliberate attempt to provoke his interlocutor, Rees Evans queried the difference between necessarianist theology and the Calvinist doctrine of election. The old bard ground to a halt in the middle of the road and, beating his stick on the

---

[20] NLW MS 21285E, Iolo Morganwg Letters no. 861; NLW MS 21406E, no. 12; Elijah Waring, *Recollections and Anecdotes of Edward Williams* (London, 1850), p. 134.
[21] NLW MS 21401E, no. 38.
[22] NLW MS 13129A, p. 448; Thomas Griffiths, *Cofiant am y Parch. David Davies* (Caerfyrddin, 1828), pp. 10–11, 48. Iolo was certain that he would meet in heaven 'my excellent friends George Morgan, D[r]. Kippis, D[r]. Priestley, banish by persecution, and Gilbert Wakefield where neither King nor Bishop can persecute' (NLW MS 13174A, pp. 61[v]–62[r]).
[23] Waring, *Recollections and Anecdotes*, p. 134.

ground in exasperation, cried: 'What difference? There is as much difference between them as there is between Heaven and Hell. The one begins in every evil and ends in every pain; the other begins in all wisdom and goodness, and ends in total bliss.'[24] Such was Williams's respect for Priestley that he attended his final sermon at the Gravel Pit meeting-house, Hackney, prior to his departure for America in 1794. Around three years later he urged Theophilus Lindsey to write to Priestley to inform him that 'the Welsh Bard presents him with the most affectionate compts . . . and has also joyfully felt the high respect that D[r]. Priestley has met with in a far better part of the world than ours'.[25]

Yet, for all Williams's affection for 'Gunpowder Joe', Joseph Priestley's name has always been associated in Wales with Thomas Evans, or 'Priestley bach' (little Priestley), as his friends and enemies dubbed him. This is entirely appropriate since Evans was the first to disseminate Priestley's doctrines in the Welsh language. In 1792 he published a Welsh translation of Priestley's *An Appeal to the serious and candid professors of Christianity*, in which he called on his supporters to defend their theological principles in a spirit of Christian charity but also to suffer persecution if and when required.[26] In the same year he published *Amddifyniad o bennadwriaeth y Tad*, the first Unitarian sermon in Welsh. Both works, printed by John Ross at Carmarthen, sold well and were reprinted regularly in response to public demand. In 1793 Evans published a Welsh translation of *The Triumph of Truth*, an account (with a preface by Priestley) of the trial of Edward Elwall, who had been accused of blasphemy in 1726. His aim was to encourage his followers not to fear Welsh clergymen, the chief enemies of freedom and truth.[27] In his hard-hitting but shortlived periodical *The Miscellaneous Repository, neu y Drysorfa Gymmysgedig* (1795) the imprint of Priestley's works is unmistakable and no one in the parish of Llanegwad was surprised when, in 1799, Evans christened one of his sons Joseph Priestley Evans (who also became a weaver). In several ways, therefore, Priestleyism not only took root in 'Y Smotyn Du' but also nurtured its own folklore.

From a practical point of view, however, Evans's debt was much greater to Theophilus Lindsey, the founding father of English Unitarianism. Lindsey had resigned his Anglican living to establish the first Unitarian chapel in Britain at Essex Street, London, in April 1774, where he steadily

---

[24] See *Yr Ymofynydd*, 4, no. 51 (1851), 243. For Rees Evans, see Morien and Thomas Morgan, *Hanes Tonyrefail* (Caerdydd, 1899), pp. 36, 50–2, 60–4, 66.

[25] NLW MS 21406E, no. 12.

[26] Thomas Evans, *Appêl at Broffeswyr Difrifol a Diduedd Cristianogrwydd* (Caerfyrddin, 1792). A 2nd edn was published at Merthyr in 1812.

[27] Thomas Evans, *Gorfoledd y Gwirionedd* (Caerfyrddin, 1793). For unpublished sermons preached by Evans, see NLW MSS 3637–8A.

built up an affluent and distinguished congregation. When Evans wrote to Lindsey in 1792 to introduce himself and solicit financial support for a proposed meeting-house at Cwm Cothi he was so 'struck and delighted' to receive such a winsome letter from 'one so educated or rather without education, and so young' that he persuaded William Tayleur of Shrewsbury, a prosperous Unitarian philanthropist, to come to his aid.[28] Lindsey, too, contributed handsomely and Evans responded by building the meeting-house, translating Lindsey's influential *The Catechist: or, An Inquiry into the Doctrine of the Scriptures, concerning the only True God*, which he published in 1796, and naming another of his sons Theophilus Lindsey Evans.[29] From December 1796 the Dr Williams's Trust helped to sustain his preaching ministry with annual sums of four or five pounds, and the enormously wealthy duke of Grafton sent him ten pounds in 1798.[30]

It is possible that the good offices of Edward Williams proved critical in securing this financial lifeline, for Williams was not only worshipping at Essex Street by 1793–4, where John Disney had succeeded Lindsey, but had also befriended an extraordinarily gifted and erudite group of middle-class Cambridge-trained Dissenters – George Dyer, Robert Robinson and Gilbert Wakefield – who shared his passion for literature and freedom and who found the printing press of Joseph Johnson (William Blake's publisher) a congenial meeting place. Dyer's pamphlets, especially *The Complaints of the Poor People of England* (1793) and *A Dissertation on the Theory and Practice of Benevolence* (1795), made a profound impression on Williams and he much enjoyed conversing with him about 'Politics, republicanism, Jacobinisms, Carmagnolism, Sansculololisms, and a number of other wicked and trayterous *isms*'.[31] Robinson was the founder of the Cambridge Constitutional Society and Dyer, in his memoir to him, praised his eloquence and political adroitness. Wakefield, who saved his most waspish comments for persecuting prelates, once memorably accused Samuel Horsley, bishop of St David's, of 'rude and contemptuous buffoonry' and so angered Richard Watson, bishop of Llandaff, for denouncing him as an

---

[28] John Rylands University Library, Manchester. Theophilus Lindsey to William Tayleur, 14 June, 1 July, 26 July 1792.

[29] Thomas Evans, *Yr Egwyddorwr* (Caerfyrddin, 1796); *The Biographical Index of W. W. Price Aberdâr* (reproduced at NLW), pp. 255–66.

[30] Dr Williams's Library, Dr Williams's Trust, General Meeting of Trustees Minute Book 1786–1814, pp. 163, 193, 229, 249, 267; Dr Williams's Library MS 12.57, letter no. 20. Theophilus Lindsey to Thomas Belsham, 26 August 1800. For Lindsey, see G. M. Ditchfield, *Theophilus Lindsey: From Anglican to Unitarian* (London, 1998).

[31] NLW MS 13221E, p. 49; NLW MS 21280E, Iolo Morganwg Letters no. 132–6. For Dyer's warm appreciation of Iolo on the occasion of his death, see the *Monthly Repository*, new series, 1 (1827), 582.

absentee and a pluralist and for arguing that a French invasion would improve the lot of the poor that he found himself behind the bars of Dorchester prison.[32] Although there was a considerable social gulf between Welsh-speaking Unitarian craftsmen and middle-class liberal Dissenters in England, Edward Williams's reputation for bluntness meant that the Essex Street congregation could not ignore the needs and aspirations of their counterparts in south Wales. With their assistance, Williams maintained, 'I shall live to see *a Glorious Unitarian Church in Wales*, emerging out of that Wilderness into which we have been driven by the fury of the Great Dragon. Many of us however are yet but children that must be fed with milk.'[33]

Gwyneth Lewis has vigorously argued that Edward Williams returned to Wales late in 1795 in order to give the Gorsedd of Bards a much wider and safer opportunity of becoming an influential Welsh-medium academy of letters and also a conduit for radical Unitarianism.[34] During his sojourn in London he had acquired first-hand experience of the ugly 'Church and King' mobs who roamed the streets and who hanged, shot and burned effigies of his great hero Tom Paine.[35] Edward Jones, the loyalist King's Bard, effectively threw Williams to the wolves by betraying him to the Privy Council. His papers were confiscated, though not before he had taken the precaution of removing incriminating evidence.[36] The self-publicist in him continued to invite close surveillance. In 1795 he wrote to William Pitt to defend the reputation of Richard Brothers, an eccentric pseudo-prophet who was eventually locked up in a lunatic asylum. Having sat in the public gallery during the famous treason trials he published a rousing song, entitled *Trial by Jury, the Grand Palladium of British Liberty*, to celebrate the acquittal of Hardy, Thelwall and Tooke.[37] The suspension of habeas corpus, the banning of radical societies, and the infamous 'gagging acts' were painful indicators of the government's determination

---

[32] George Dyer, *Memoirs of the Life and Writings of Robert Robinson* (London, 1796); Gilbert Wakefield, *An Address to the Right Reverend Dr Samuel Horsley, Bishop of St David's* (Birmingham, 1790), p. 7; Gilbert Wakefield, *Memoirs of the Life of Gilbert Wakefield* (2 vols, London, 1804), II, p. 119; NLW MS 21408E, no. 10.

[33] NLW MS 21285E, Iolo Morganwg Letters no. 861.

[34] Gwyneth Lewis, 'Eighteenth-Century Literary Forgeries with Special Reference to the Work of Iolo Morganwg' (unpubl. University of Oxford D.Phil. thesis, 1991), part II.

[35] NLW MS 21285E, Iolo Morganwg Letters no. 838; NLW MS 21401E, no. 34; NLW, Bute L46/30; Hywel M. Davies, 'Loyalism in Wales, 1792–1793', *WHR*, 20, no. 4 (2001), 687–716.

[36] NLW MS 21282E, letter no. 39; NLW MS 21285E, Iolo Morganwg Letters no. 824, 837, 842.

[37] NLW MS 21280E, Iolo Morganwg Letters no. 49; Waring, *Recollections and Anecdotes*, pp. 82–6; NLW MS 13221E, p. 1; NLW MS 21335B, pp. 14–16.

to crack down on Jacobins and clearly figured prominently in Williams's decision to quit the capital for what he hoped would be the peace of Wales. But he continued to compose in English as well as in Welsh, and his work in both languages was just as incendiary as it had been in London. Moreover, there were strong personal factors drawing him home. He still nursed a deep sense of guilt following the death of his daughter Elizabeth (Lilla) in 1793 and the acute economic downturn had brought his family close to destitution.

Whatever the reasons for Williams's return to Wales may have been, he seized every opportunity to pursue his radical agenda at gorseddau and impromptu eisteddfodau, and in Thomas Evans he found a kindred spirit: he, too, was a champion of the Welsh bardic tradition (Williams's eyes lit up when he saw Evans's copy of 'Tlysau'r Beirdd'),[38] a tireless transcriber of manuscripts, and an avid collector and disseminator of combustible political material. Williams's voluminous correspondence and personal papers provide incontestible evidence of his determination to keep the flame of religious and civil liberties alive in Wales. In a striking and sometimes bewildering maze of essays, satires, burlesques, squibs and trifles, many of which were either left incomplete or reshaped according to his mood, he provides a vivid depiction of his own agonies as well as the turmoil of the times.[39] Though much more slender, Thomas Evans's writings also portray a witty, sceptical libertarian who was not prepared to be cowed into submission by 'Church and King' mobs.[40] Although Williams liked to convey the image of a tea-drinking vegetarian, on tipsy evenings he could raise a glass with the best of them, and in private these leading Welsh Unitarians discussed the works of John Milton, Tom Paine, William Godwin and Thomas Spence, thumbed the pages of the *Cambridge Intelligencer* and the *Manual of Liberty*, exchanged examples of the homespun parables of Benjamin Franklin, collected a devastating array of charges against English monarchs who sent innocent victims to fields of slaughter 'which they most blasphemously call the field of *glory*',[41]

---

[38] NLW MS 5474A. For some of these literary links, see Cardiff Central Library MS 1.133; NLW MS 13096B, p. 171; NLW MS 13115B, p. 88; NLW MS 13150A, pp. 273, 294; G. H. Hughes, *Iaco ab Dewi 1648–1722* (Caerdydd, 1953), p. 51.

[39] I am currently preparing a work, based on the voluminous papers in the National Library of Wales, devoted to the religious and political writings of Iolo Morganwg. For a shrewd initial assessment of his political Jacobinism in 1791–5, see Damian Walford Davies, *Presences that Disturb: Models of Romantic Identity in the Literature and Culture of the 1790s* (Cardiff, 2002), chap 4. See also Geraint H. Jenkins, 'The Bard of Liberty during William Pitt's Reign of Terror', in Leslie E. Jones and Joseph F. Nagy (eds), *Heroic Poets and Poetic Heroes in Celtic Traditions: Studies in Honor of Patrick K. Ford* (forthcoming).

[40] See NLW MSS 3281D, 6238A, 6868B, 7893A.

[41] NLW MS 21392F, p. 5; NLW MS 21401E, nos 1–3; NLW MS 21433E, no. 4.

dissected translations of speeches by Robespierre and Napoleon, penned stanzas about the 'Right Dishonourable William Pitt' which depicted him as a butcher, an oppressor and a traitor,[42] deplored the mariners, merchants and slaving agents who traded in human cargo, and reserved their greatest scorn for absentee bishops, tithe-grabbing clergy and wild-eyed cater-wauling Calvinistic Methodists whose fervent revivalism exposed their lack of intellectual muscle. Among the terse aphorisms which they exchanged, the triad 'Parsonism, Kingism and Devilism, the three grand curses of the world'[43] was a special favourite.

Yet, despite the wild rhetoric and intemperate rants against bloody tyrants, canting priests, pettifogging lawyers, rich monopolists and all other 'Fiends of the Bottomless Pitt',[44] there is no direct evidence that these Welsh *sans-culottes* were involved in any kind of insurrectionary conspiracy or that they had established liaisons with dangerous foreigners. Thomas Evans was swift to condemn in verse the French landing at Fishguard in 1797 and in his encomium to the Glamorgan Volunteers (a song which he later sent to George Hardinge) Edward Williams heartily approved of their efforts to 'vanquish all foes that would Britons enthrall'.[45] But the fact that clandestine meetings, coded messages and druidic moots were couched in Welsh – a potentially seditious tongue[46] – meant that spies and informers kept them under regular surveillance. On his return to Cowbridge Williams swiftly realized that his reputation had preceded him and that he was almost universally dubbed 'a Democrat, a Jacobin, a plotter against Gov^t.'[47] His riposte was to denounce 'Bully' Pitt's servants as the most 'loathsom swarm of the vilest bloodsucking insects that ever dishonoured the Creation'.[48] For his part Thomas Evans discovered that Pitt's repressive policies could easily cut off the oxygen of publicity on which libertarians depended: after three issues, no press would handle *The Miscellaneous Repository*, his purveyor of uncomfortable truths.

---

[42] NLW MS 3281D, p. 35; NLW MS 6238A, pp. 104, 107–8, 117–19, 123–5, 181–97, 246–8, 281–2, 315–17, 410; NLW MS 13158A, p. 87; NLW MS 13159A, pp. 200–3; NLW MS 21399E, p. 20.

[43] NLW MS 13174A, p. 21. See also NLW MS 13110B, pp. 129–31 and NLW MS 13124B, pp. 315–17.

[44] NLW MS 21281E, Iolo Morganwg Letters no. 264. See also Geraint H. Jenkins, '"A Rank Republican [and] a Leveller": William Jones, Llangadfan', *WHR*, 17, no. 3 (1995), 373–4.

[45] NLW MS 3281D, p. 36; NLW MS 13116B, pp. 292–9; NLW MS 13144A, p. 175; NLW MS 13221E, letter no. 21, pp. 107–10.

[46] Geraint H. Jenkins, 'The Cultural Uses of the Welsh Language 1660–1800', in idem (ed.), *The Welsh Language before the Industrial Revolution* (Cardiff, 1997), pp. 403–5.

[47] NLW MS 21319A, p. 7. See also NLW MS 21414E, no. 17.

[48] NLW MS 13112B, p. 367.

All the evidence then points to the fact that Thomas Evans and Edward Williams were marked men long before 'the great trial' of 1801, and presumably George Thomas's file of complaint provided the authorities with their first clear-cut opportunity to single out a known dissident for exemplary punishment. A year earlier Evans had complained to John Disney that Unitarianism 'meets with violent opposition from the Clergy of the Establishment and Dissenters', and the Arian David Davis confirmed that the 'activity and artifice' of anti-trinitarians had made pariahs of them.[49] David Peter, senior tutor at the Presbyterian academy at Carmarthen (traditionally a hotbed of criticism), refused to admit young Unitarian students and the appointment in February 1801 of Bishop George Murray brought to St David's a man whose animus against 'Socinians' matched that of his predecessor Horsley.[50] Boneyphobia was rife among the gentry and the clergy following the abortive French landing at Fishguard, and turbulent corn riots in 1800–1 scarcely soothed their frayed nerves. In both Lancashire and Yorkshire magistrates were expecting a rebellion in the summer and, in spite of the defeat of the United Irishmen, there were fears that Irish agents were heavily involved in promoting sedition in south Wales. Small wonder that Senior Justice George Hardinge, a proven scourge of troublemakers, was fêted by local governors on his arrival at Carmarthen in mid-August 1801.

Hardinge had never made any secret of his contempt for those who propagated Priestleyism and who posed a direct challenge to law and order. To him, Jacobins were 'Fiends of Hell', 'men of blood' and 'many-headed wolves', and he warned the ironmaster Richard Crawshay to exercise the greatest vigilance against the 'evil Spirit' which prevailed among Dissenters led by 'the Damnable Doctrines of D[r]. Priestly & Payne'.[51] He was so perturbed by the lamentable state of civil order in Glamorgan that he threatened to go before the king himself to warn him of the contagion spread by immoral in-migrants and political incendiaries in south Wales.[52] As the 1790s unfolded his addresses to the Grand Jury became increasingly political. While praising the prompt exertions of the

[49] Aneirin Lewis, 'Tomos Glyn Cothi a'r Dr John Disney', *LlC*, 6, nos 3–4 (1961), 220; NLW MS 5497E, unpaginated. Letter dated 2 February 1803.

[50] R. T. Jenkins, 'Nonconformity after 1715: Methodism', in J. E. Lloyd (ed.), *A History of Carmarthenshire* (2 vols, Cardiff, 1935–9), II, p. 241; T. Oswald Williams, *Undodiaeth a Rhyddid Meddwl* (Llandysul, 1962), chap. 10; D. Eurig Davies, *Hoff Ddysgedig Nyth* (Abertawe, 1976), p. 82; F. C. Mather, *High Church Prophet: Bishop Samuel Horsley (1733–1806) and the Caroline Tradition in the Later Georgian Church* (Oxford, 1992), p. 168.

[51] John Nichols (ed.), *The Miscellaneous Works, in Prose and Verse, of George Hardinge* (3 vols., London, 1818), II, p. 411, 419–20; Gwent Record Office, MS D2.162, fo. 130. Letterbook of Richard Crawshay.

[52] Cardiff Central Library MS 2.716, vol. 2, p. 13[v].

Welsh in repulsing the French in 1797, he still felt duty-bound to warn them against associating with persons who had 'imbibed the principles of Thomas Pain' and, having extolled the 'Glorious achievement' of Lord Nelson at the battle of the Nile in 1798, he urged the 'ancient Britons' to remain loyal and vigilant.[53] Four months before Thomas Evans was brought before him, Hardinge had branded three rioting Merthyr iron-workers levellers and incendiaries whose plundering deeds opened the way to anarchy and rebellion. 'For you my heart bleeds', he declared, as he coolly sentenced them to death.[54] Five years later, 17-year-old Mary Morgan, the last female to be publicly hanged in Radnorshire, became another of Hardinge's victims. His heart once more bleeding at the infanticide committed by the defendant, he described the sentence and her death as a mercy to her and a warning to 'many *other girls* like *you*'.[55] Confronted by a senior justice who believed that delivering a sentence of death was a piece of enlightened benevolence, Thomas Evans must have feared for his future.

By a curious irony, Edward Williams was known to Hardinge. In August 1786 Williams had been incarcerated in Cardiff prison for debt, where he and his pregnant wife were so grossly abused and beaten by the gaolkeeper and turnkey that he petitioned Hardinge and Abel Moysey, newly appointed senior justices, for redress.[56] They also had common cultural interests. Given his obsession with authenticity debates, it is more than likely that Williams was familiar with Hardinge's *Nugae Antiquae et Novae* (1782), his contribution to the fierce controversy over Chatterton's authorship of the poems of the medieval monk Thomas Rowley.[57] In 1794 Hardinge had subscribed to six sets of Williams's *Poems, Lyric and Pastoral*, and his correspondence with the likes of William Owen Pughe and Edward 'Celtic' Davies reveals that he was deeply interested in etymology, philology, Celticism and druidism, themes which deeply pre-occupied the Glamorgan stonemason.[58] But the dissemination and declam-ation of inflammatory seditious writings was another matter, and in previous verdicts Hardinge had served notice of his determination to silence friends of the Revolution.

Judge Hardinge cut an impressive figure in his full-bottomed wig and

---

[53] Ibid., pp. 47[r], 57–8, 81.

[54] NLW, Bute L48/57ii–iii; Nichols (ed.), *Miscellaneous Works*, I, pp. 12–22.

[55] Nichols (ed.), *Miscellaneous Works*, I, pp. 51–64; Patricia Parris, 'Mary Morgan: Contemporary Sources', *TRS*, 53 (1983), 57–64.

[56] NLW MS 21389E, no. 10.

[57] [George Hardinge], *Rowley and Chatterton in the Shades Or, Nugae Antiquae et Novae* (1782) (William Andrews Clark Memorial Library, UCLA, 1979).

[58] Cardiff Central Library MSS 3.79, 3.82, 3.86; NLW MS 145C. See also a letter from Iolo to Hardinge (Cardiff Central Library MS 3.104, no. 41).

scarlet robes, and his frosty eloquence on 17 August rendered the atmosphere in the Guildhall, Carmarthen, even chillier than usual. Much to his discomfort, there was considerable support for the beleaguered defendant (the charges against his colleagues had been dropped) within and without the court precincts. The presence of the Welsh Bard, who scribbled furiously throughout the proceedings, must also have disconcerted him. Four witnesses were called by the prosecution, the chief of whom was George Thomas. According to Edward Williams, none of his evidence was credible and he recorded his view of him with brutal frankness: 'Informers are *state lights* made of base stuff who, when they've burnt themselves down to the snuff Stink and are thrown away, – *and fair enough.*'[59] Following the trial it came to light that several witnesses at Brechfa claimed that Thomas had often declared that the Bible was a fiction and that he had wilfully altered the form of fast-day prayer sent to Thomas Evans in 1795 and that this had prompted Churchmen to draw unmerited 'reproaches and imputations of disaffection to Government'.[60] But with a score to settle, George Thomas and his fellow witnesses doggedly insisted that a seditious version of the Carmagnole had been sung by Evans and his friends on the night in question.

There are grounds for believing that the case for the defence was badly botched, probably as a result of ambiguous or misleading information supplied by Edward Williams to leading Unitarians in Bristol and London who, in the light of this material, had sought legal advice from George Erskine, the brilliant London barrister who numbered Tom Paine and Thomas Hardy among his clients. Williams had claimed that twenty witnesses would swear that Evans had not sung the seditious song, but on the day of the trial only three were called. It is possible that George Hardinge had expedited matters by urging the defence counsel to 'save the time of the Court without prejudice to their Client',[61] but it is more likely that Evans's barrister had realized late in the day that only three of the witnesses had been present at the bid-ale. John Prior Estlin, the Presbyterian-Unitarian minister of the affluent Lewins Mead congregation at Bristol, sharply upbraided Williams for prejudicing Evans's case by supplying false information:

> Not that I believe he sang the song, but I can conceive that the Judge & Jury might think he did. His conduct was constantly imprudent, as ours has since been. Had the case been as stated by M[r] [Josiah] Rees & yourself

[59] NLW MS 21373D, fo. 7; NLW MS 21411E, p. 26.
[60] NLW MS 21373D, fo. 6, nos 1–23.
[61] PRO 40 47/27, p. 299.

there can be no doubt but he would have been liberated with honour and with a fortune.[62]

It appears, therefore, that Williams's penchant for exaggeration had inadvertently jeopardized his friend's case and played into the hands of the prosecution.

Having heard the evidence and approved the Grand Jury's verdict against Evans, Judge Hardinge was not disposed to set free a Unitarian minister with a reputation for political incendiarism and whose local dens of dissidents offered a convenient hiding place for Jacobins who, in his view, deserved to be shot like rabid dogs. In his address to the Grand Jury, which he always used as a means of educating the multitude, he infuriated Edward Williams by describing George III as the 'most innocent and the best man, the best character, in the kingdom', by gratuitously lamenting the growth of sectarianism in Wales, and by claiming that Evans's witnesses had been suborned by him. In spite of his undoubted gifts, he went on, the defendant was irredeemably 'of a very bad and dangerous disposition' and if he and his views were given free rein murder and bloodshed would prevail. Amid widespread consternation, Thomas Evans was sentenced to two years' imprisonment, to be pilloried annually in public, and to be bound over to keep the peace for seven years after his release.[63] Denied the right to seek postponement of the sentence, the first Unitarian minister in Wales was frogmarched to Carmarthen prison. Four days later Edward Williams, writing from Carmarthen to Owain Myfyr, referred to the trial as 'a most lamentable occasion . . . a very horrid affair'.[64] Yet, compared with the harsh punishments suffered by his Unitarian counterparts in Scotland – Thomas Muir and Thomas Fyshe Palmer (with whom Iolo Morganwg corresponded) – both of whom were bundled off to Van Diemen's Land in 1794, Thomas Evans was treated relatively leniently.

To his dying day, however, Evans denied having sung seditious songs in English during the ill-starred bid-ale, and it is surely inconceivable that either he or his friends, however inebriated, would have caroused in English in a community where Welsh was overwhelmingly the medium of communication. That is not to say that Jacobin choruses in Welsh were not declaimed as the night got increasingly rowdy, among them (as Edward Williams suggested) 'Cân Rhyddid' (Song of Liberty), a version of the

[62] NLW MS 21281E, Iolo Morganwg Letters no. 153.
[63] NLW MS 21373D, fo. 8.
[64] British Library MS 15031, Letter 6, fos. 29–30. During the same Sessions, two prisoners were sentenced to death, one for sheep-stealing and the other for stealing a yoke of oxen. Another was ordered to be transported for seven years. *Bristol Journal*, 29 August 1801.

Marseillaise which Williams had published under a pseudonym in David Davies's radical magazine, *Y Geirgrawn,* in May 1796.[65] To his credit, Thomas Evans warmly appreciated his colleague's exertions on his behalf and did not hold against him the confusion caused by his skewed account to the Bristol Unitarians.[66] In a vain bid to make amends, Williams assembled seventeen witnesses and arranged for them to make sworn affidavits before a magistrate at Carmarthen on 24 October, presumably as a basis for an appeal against the verdict. None of the witnesses could recall their minister singing English verses at the bid-ale and several of them pinpointed George Thomas's murky past and his alleged atheism. Evan John, a Llanegwad tanner, claimed that he had heard Thomas sing the song which referred to 'vile George' at the Angel Inn, Carmarthen, and that John Jones, Thomas's co-witness, had told him: 'It is a very good song. I love it in my heart. I have sung it a hundred times and will sing it a hundred times again, for I am a Republican by God.'[67]

By this stage, however, such evidence, reliable or otherwise, was of little use to the gaoled minister and his family. More reassuring was the solid support received from influential Unitarians, though Estlin feared that a royal pardon was unlikely 'unless we could persuade persons of different sentiments to interest themselves in his favour'.[68] Charles Lloyd of Coedlannau Fawr, a Unitarian minister and farmer, launched an appeal for financial support and once more Evans's traditional benefactors – the Estlins and the Lindseys in particular – were not found wanting.[69] When David Jones, 'The Welsh Freeholder' who, following his acerbic dispute with Horsley in the early 1790s, had trained as a barrister, prepared an appeal to the Crown, the imprisoned minister was persuaded to throw himself on the mercy of the king by affirming his total loyalty to his Majesty, the government and the 'happy constitution'.[70] But his loyal protestations, delivered through gritted teeth, made no impression on John Lloyd of Lincoln's Inn, who was invited by Lord Pelham, the Home Secretary, to review the evidence in March 1802. Lloyd informed Pelham that the verdict had been sound and that it had subsequently come to light that the prisoner was in the habit of 'composing singing and teaching

---

[65] *Y Geirgrawn: Neu Drysorfa Gwybodaeth* (May, 1796), pp. 127–8; NLW MS 21373D, p. 5; NLW MS 21401E, no. 29.

[66] NLW MS 21281E, Iolo Morganwg Letters no. 176.

[67] NLW MS 21373D, fo. 6, no. 7.

[68] NLW MS 21281E, Iolo Morganwg Letters no. 154.

[69] NLW MS 21373D, fo. 10.

[70] NLW MS 21281E, Iolo Morganwg Letters no. 154; NLW MS 21373D, p. 15; PRO HO 47/27, pp. 297–301.

others to sing songs in the Welsh Language of very seditious Tendency'.[71] Unsurprisingly, Pelham rejected the appeal.

Having been built by the architect John Nash on Howardian principles in 1789–92, Carmarthen county gaol and Bridewell was hardly Guantanamo Bay, but, without the generous support of benefactors, Thomas Evans's lot would have been appreciably harder. Regular funds not only helped him to feed his family but also to grease the palm of the gaoler John Thomas, who allowed him to smoke and drink, play football in the courtyard, bring in and read books, and compose an English–Welsh vocabulary for Welsh learners, which, on his release, was published at Merthyr in 1804.[72] By winning over the gaoler, too, Evans blunted the sharp public sanction – corporal punishment and ridicule in a pillory – which Hardinge had imposed upon him. The gaoler executed a procedure by which the defendant was placed virtually out of sight in the pillory and two of his daughters, fetchingly dressed in white frocks, were allowed to stand on either side of him in order to engage the sympathy of bystanders.[73] Tradition has it that one old lady spattered his face with an egg, only to beg his forgiveness for insulting a minister of the gospel, and the assembled throng broadly took the view that the public shaming of a Dissenting minister was both improper and vindictive. Bishop George Murray, confirming how ill-informed prelatical birds of passage were in the see of St David's, complained bitterly of the 'farcical' procedure employed by the gaoler and suggested to Lord Pelham on 23 November 1802 that this 'Anabaptist teacher' was involved in the conspiracy of Colonel Edward Despard, an Irish soldier who had been arrested a week earlier for allegedly plotting to assassinate the king on his way to Parliament.[74] In his reply Pelham pointedly noted that the Welsh Unitarian had been safely under lock and key when the Despard plot was hatched.[75] Undeterred, Murray continued to complain of the trivial manner in which Evans's sentence was being conducted and, under the circumstances, it is not surprising that the prisoner became increasingly bitter and resentful. He wrote peevish letters to the infirm Theophilus Lindsey which deeply hurt his old benefactor and prompted his redoubtable wife Hannah to deplore his 'high conceit of himself, his talents & title to distinction' and even to wonder whether a long confinement might well improve his morals.[76]

[71] PRO HO 47/27, pp. 297–301.

[72] PRO HO 42/66, pp. 74–5; Thomas Evans, *An English–Welsh Vocabulary* (Merthyr, 1804). Further edns were published in 1805, 1816 and 1820.

[73] PRO HO 42/66, p. 437; Dr Williams's Library MS 12.57, no. 33.

[74] PRO HO 42/66, pp. 74–5.

[75] PRO HO 43/13, p. 436.

[76] Dr Williams's Library MS 12.57, no. 33. Letter from Hannah Lindsey to Thomas Belsham, 27 September 1802.

In the event, the opposite occurred. During the course of 1802 Evans had received messages from neighbours informing him that the tanner Evan John (who had previously given evidence on his behalf) was in the habit of paying nocturnal visits to Penpistyll farm. When he confronted her with this accusation, Evans's wife Ann promised to end the liaison. Early in 1803, however, John's libido got the better of him and he was spotted at Penpistyll both late at night and early in the morning. To be cuckolded by a neighbour and a worshipper at his church was a much greater humiliation for Evans to bear than being publicly pilloried, and he wrote to Thomas Evans, a breeches-maker at Carmarthen, pleading with him to inform Evan John that he was forbidden from visiting Penpistyll again. When Evans complied, both Evan John and Ann Evans exploded with rage and began spreading slanderous statements about the behaviour of the embattled minister. We have no means of knowing with any certainty whether this was an adulterous affair, but wagging tongues had convinced Thomas Evans that the Llanegwad tanner and his own wife were 'most infamous creatures'. 'Taking all things together', he informed his namesake at Carmarthen, 'I can almost say that I am wearied of life and that I wish to be in a silent grave.'[77] In his turmoil he himself sought comfort, and presumably sexual favours, from a thoroughly unexpected quarter: he became besotted with a fellow prisoner, a Welsh convict girl awaiting transportation to New South Wales.[78] There were four convict girls – Martha Daniel, Rachel Griffiths, Ann Lloyd and Sarah Smith – awaiting transportation in Carmarthen prison between 1801 and 1803, any one of whom might have been the object of Evans's affections before slipping off 'the social map into the void of the antipodes'.[79] When Edward Williams got wind of the affair he immediately sought confirmation from David Davis of Neath, the Unitarian son of the Castellhywel school-master. The revelation which followed stunned Williams and the whole Unitarian fraternity in Wales:

All his old friends, that I have talked to upon the subject, firmly believe that their fears and apprehensions were too well founded – His conduct latterly affords more than probably evidence of the truth of the reports which have been in circulation – Evan Harris, who, you know, was a fellow-prisoner with T. Evans call'd on me in school last Saturday . . . He informed me, with which information thro' several other channels well

[77] NLW MS 21281E, Iolo Morganwg Letters no. 179.
[78] NLW, Great Sessions 4/753/3–4; Deirdre Beddoe, 'Carmarthenshire Women and Criminal Transportation to Australia 1787–1852', *CA*, 13 (1977), 65–71. There were four convict girls awaiting transportation in Carmarthen prison between 1800 and 1803, any one of whom might have been the object of Evans's affections.
[79] Robert Hughes, *The Fatal Shore* (London, 1988), p. 137.

accords, that he is still in Gaol, sacrificing every thing that is dear to man, in a state of rational society, to that female convict which is detained there but till she can be conveniently transported to the land of infamy – His wife is in an agony of distress – She has lost not only the affections of her husband, but also those means, of supporting herself and numerous family above indigence, which the charity of Compassionate plentifully afforded . . . can it be believed, that a man in possession of reason could have quietly witnessed a convict, tho' his mistress, throw a shovelful of live embers into the breast of a woman that was the mother of nine of his own legitimate children . . . This convict woman has her purse full of Silver and Gold – He continues in Gaol not from want of sureties . . . but, it is believed, from attachment to the girl and perhaps a shame of shewing his face to the world.[80]

By this stage, Evans's extraordinary fall from grace had brought Welsh Unitarianism into grave disrepute. David Davis's brother Timothy admitted in his diary that Evans emerged from prison a discredited man,[81] but he continued to believe that he was more sinned against than sinning and assured Edward Williams that his release from the 'House of Bondage' had been delayed by a writ instigated by 'that Beast of a fellow' John Thomas, the former gaoler, who had sought redress for a debt of ten pounds, which he eventually paid by parting with several of his cherished books.[82] Coldly received in his native patch, Evans resumed his trade as a weaver. But for his children, he would have parted from his wife and sought asylum in America. Barred from taking part in what might be construed as dangerous religio-political activity, he found solace in transcribing medieval Welsh poetry, translating Unitarian tracts and compiling a substantial *English–Welsh Dictionary* (1809).[83]

By imprisoning, shaming and securing assurances of future good behaviour from Thomas Evans, Judge Hardinge must have hoped that the sentence would prove to be a severe, perhaps mortal, blow to radical Unitarianism in the south-west. In the short term, it certainly blighted Evans's family life and career, but in the long term it energized the Unitarian campaign. When Edward Williams had arrived in Carmarthen in mid-August 1801 to witness the trial, he had other cards up his capacious sleeve. He spent part of the time successfully rummaging in the

---

[80] NLW MS 21280E, Iolo Morganwg Letters no. 102. For a petition by the imprisoned Evan Harris, see NLW, Great Sessions, 4/753/3.

[81] NLW MS 5490C, unpaginated. Diary entry, 14 January 1833.

[82] NLW MS 21281E, Iolo Morganwg Letters no. 177, 178.

[83] NLW MS 21281E, Iolo Morganwg Letters nos 180, 181; NLW MS 21315A, pp. i, 56; Thomas Evans, *An English–Welsh Dictionary; Neu, Eir-lyfr Saes'neg a Chymraeg* (Merthyr, 1809).

storerooms of the printer John Ross for the Welsh manuscripts of Evan Evans (Ieuan Fardd), but his major achievement was to persuade fourteen Unitarians to support his aim of establishing a society to defend, maintain and disseminate Unitarian doctrines in south Wales.[84] Shocked by what he reckoned was a concerted attempt to bring about the demise of the anti-trinitarian cause and embarrassed by the need to go cap in hand for support from Unitarians outside Wales, he was determined to set up a robust regional infrastructure. As a result, at Gelli-gron on 8 October 1802, the Unitarian Christian Society of South Wales was founded.[85] It became very much his pride and joy, and he derived great satisfaction from 'the happiness of laying the first foundation stone of it'.[86] The erstwhile 'Bard of Liberty' transmogrified himself into the 'Bard to the Theo-Unitarian Society of South Wales', and launched a progressive campaign which included supporting local churches and ministers, organizing lecture tours, and translating and distributing Welsh books.[87] By the 1820s he was proudly referring to himself as the oldest Unitarian in Wales and it is both poignant and reassuring to note that the final sentence which he wrote to his son before his death in December 1826 was 'Remember that there is a God'.[88] Never at any stage did Edward Williams renounce his political radicalism or retreat from the political arena, and, living up to his father's reputation, Taliesin ab Iolo led the campaign to urge Lord Melbourne to spare the lives of Dic Penderyn and Lewsyn yr Heliwr following the Merthyr Rising in 1831.[89]

As for the disgraced Thomas Evans, he blossomed once more as a radical Unitarian minister, this time in the rapidly industrializing parish of Aberdare where he became pastor of Hen Dŷ Cwrdd from 1811, two years before Unitarians were granted liberty to worship in public.[90] He laboured on behalf of the 'Resurrection of Rational Christianity', played a full part in the programmes of the Unitarian Association, helped to organize Richard Wright's epic ten-week mission in south Wales in 1816, and rejuvenated eisteddfodau in the Aberdare–Merthyr area.[91] His relationship

---

[84] British Library MS 15031, Letter 4, fos. 25–6; NLW MS 13152A, p. 350.

[85] NLW MS 13145A, pp. 159–74, 278–98; Cardiff Central Library MS 2.1020; *Rheolau a Threfniadau Cymdeithas Dwyfundodiaid yn Neheubarth Cymru* (Llundain, 1803).

[86] NLW MS 21286E, Iolo Morganwg Letters no. 952.

[87] NLW MS 13145A, p. 450; *Monthly Repository*, 2 (1807), 444.

[88] NLW MS 21286E, Iolo Morganwg Letters no. 1013.

[89] Gwyn A. Williams, *The Merthyr Rising* (London, 1978), p. 182.

[90] Owen, *Thomas Evans (Tomos Glyn Cothi)*, pp. 46–7; A. C. Davies, 'Aberdare 1750–1850: a Study in the Growth of an Industrial Community' (unpubl. University of Wales MA thesis, 1963).

[91] Cardiff Central Library MS 4. 207, letter nos 2, 3, 4; *Monthly Repository*, 11 (1816), 680–4, 735–6; Anon., *Awenyddion Morganwg neu Farddoniaeth Cadair Merthyr Tudful* (Merthyr Tudful, [1826]), pp. 24–6, 127–31.

with Edward Williams, however, had cooled considerably following his
moral indiscretion and it deteriorated still further when his colleague, who
resented the fact that Evans was much more prolific, accused him of
plagiarizing some of his unpublished hymns and psalms.[92] Williams was
also in the habit of lacing the margins of some of Evans's printed translations with annotations like 'camsyniad!!!' (error!!!) and 'ffaeledd ha ha!'
(fault ha ha!).[93] Williams could be a deeply unpleasant and vindictive man
at times, and he both ridiculed and anathematized his colleague in private.
In 1820 he warned the Revd William Davies, Cefncoedycymer, that Evans
was 'a man of very bad principles. I strongly suspect him to be at heart a
rank infidel'.[94] The fire-eating Jacobin of the 1790s had clearly lost none of
his fondness for incendiary deeds, and the Merthyr Rising of 1831, which
Evans certainly witnessed and may even have helped to foment, was
attributed by the marquis of Bute to 'the construction put by the workmen
upon the political instructions of their Spiritual advisers'.[95] Indeed,
Thomas Evans's soul seems to have gone marching on. Nearly two years
after his death in January 1833 the *Merthyr Guardian* printed a letter from
'The Ghost of the late Reverend Thomas Evans, Aberdare' urging the
voters of Merthyr and Aberdare to protect the 'right of free enquiry in
matters of religion',[96] and in 1846, when his grave was reopened on the
occasion of the death of one of his daughters, his body was found lying
face downwards, which convinced local people that the fiery Unitarian had
been buried alive.[97] Even in death the innocent victim of a show trial in
sans-culotte Carmarthen was the talk of south Wales.

---

[92] NLW MS 13145A, pp. 321–3; NLW MS 13159A, pp. 253–4; NLW MS 21352A,
p. xii; Edward Williams, *Salmau Yr Eglwys yn yr Anialwch* (2 vols, Aberystwyth, 1857),
I, p. v.
[93] Cardiff Central Library MS 2. 1020. Annotations to Thomas Evans's translation
Traethawd Byr ar yr Athrawiaethau o Ryddid ac Angenrheidrwydd Philosophyddawl
(Caerfyrddin, 1809).
[94] NLW MS 21286E, Iolo Morganwg Letters nos 973, 974, 975.
[95] Jones, 'Merthyr Riots', 200.
[96] *Glamorgan Monmouth and Brecon Gazette, and Merthyr Guardian*, 13 December
1834. See also *Hereford Times*, 16 February 1833; *Seren Gomer*, 16, no. 217 (1833),
299–300, 306; *Greal y Bedyddwyr*, 9, no. 101 (1835), 221.
[97] *The Biographical Index of W. W. Price*, p. 255.

12

A Tolerant Nation?
Anti-Catholicism in Nineteenth-Century Wales

PAUL O'LEARY

In a Welsh treatise on the British Constitution, published in 1864, William Hughes of Llanelli argued that toleration was an essential companion to the liberties enjoyed by British citizens.[1] In making this argument he was in agreement with those of his contemporaries who saw the toleration of belief systems alternative to those of the state religion as a necessary underpinning of constitutional freedoms. Writers of the 1850s and 1860s who discoursed on the theme of liberty, like the philosopher J. S. Mill, also emphasized the importance of toleration. For most liberals, toleration of different beliefs was in essence a question for the individual. However, such individual rights also had implications for group identities. As the dominant expression of national identity in Wales was increasingly equated with Nonconformity from the mid-nineteenth century onwards, the question of how to deal with beliefs that the majority considered objectionable surfaced regularly in public debate.

The dilemma for nineteenth-century liberals was how to reconcile tolerance of diversity with a commitment to what was axiomatically believed to be the innate superiority of Protestantism and the civic and religious institutions it had created. In this respect, they faced one of the central questions of all modern liberal democracies, that is, how to preserve the institutions that are believed to embody the core values of society while at the same time restraining a tendency to penalize apparently 'wrong' beliefs. Since 1945 the issue of toleration in Britain has been inextricably enmeshed in the politics of race relations.[2] But the recent rise in Islamophobia is a reminder that, in a longer historical perspective, religion has been a much more important feature of the debate about cultural pluralism.

---

[1] William Hughes, *Y Cyfansoddiad Prydeinig* (Caerfyrddin, 1864), pp. 108–40.
[2] Colin Holmes, *A Tolerant Country? Immigrants, Refugees and Minorities in Britain* (London, 1991); Neil Evans, Paul O'Leary and Charlotte Williams (eds), *A Tolerant Nation? Exploring Ethnic Diversity in Wales* (Cardiff, 2003).

One of the most important indicators of toleration in nineteenth-century Britain was attitudes to Catholicism. Hostility to the Catholic Church had been one of the defining features of British national identity for centuries, and Welsh Protestants shared this prejudice.[3] However, one recent commentator has claimed that 'Wales did not participate in the fervent anti-Catholicism of the Victorian era' that had been so characteristic of the wider British experience,[4] while another historian has drawn attention to the lack of Welsh participation in militant anti-Catholic movements.[5] Given the fact that Wales was acknowledged to be one of the most Protestant parts of the kingdom in the mid-nineteenth century, these judgements imply that Welsh Protestants adopted very different attitudes to their brethren in the remainder of the United Kingdom and elsewhere. At the very least, these claims require further scrutiny. Furthermore, such confident generalizations prompt questions about the extent to which anti-Catholicism in Britain was a uniform phenomenon.

During the first half of the nineteenth century a series of political controversies ensured that the position of Catholics in British society remained at the forefront of public attention. The first of these was the debate about extending full civil rights to Catholics which followed the end of the Napoleonic Wars. Arguments for and against emancipation were avidly rehearsed in Welsh publications, but the evidence of sustained opposition to legal concessions is compelling, and the language in which this opposition was couched was often violent and uncompromising. A constant theme running though this literature is that Catholicism was instinctively oppressive and that it mercilessly persecuted its enemies. This was exemplified by the claim that priests prevented ordinary people from reading the scriptures. The theme of persecution was mentioned frequently as a justification for denying civil rights to Catholics: if Catholic countries denied civil rights to Protestants, why should Protestant countries not reciprocate in the same spirit? Moreover, it was maintained that allowing Catholics a voice in the government of the land would inevitably lead to the curtailment of the rights of free-born Protestants. Anglicans were prominent in defence of the Protestant constitution, with two bishops in Welsh dioceses, Thomas Burgess of St David's (1803–25) and William van Mildert of Llandaff (1819–26), occupying a leading role among the Ultra-Tories.[6] However, the agitation also encompassed many – probably a

[3] Philip Jenkins, 'Anti-Popery on the Welsh Marches in the Seventeenth Century', *Historical Journal*, 23, no. 2 (1980), 275–93.

[4] Trystan Owain Hughes, 'Anti-Catholicism in Wales, 1900–1960', *Journal of Ecclesiastical History*, 53, no. 2 (2002), 313.

[5] John Wolffe, *The Protestant Crusade in Great Britain, 1829–1860* (Oxford, 1991), p. 311.

[6] Ibid., p. 24.

majority of – Nonconformists. While some argued in favour of toleration to all religious denominations, most were fearful of relaxing prohibitions against 'papists'.[7]

Meetings were held throughout Wales to protest against the claims of Roman Catholics in 1807 and 1813,[8] and Sir William Paxton claimed that his electoral defeat in Carmarthenshire in 1807 was due in part to a cry of 'No Popery'.[9] A Welsh translation of John Foxe's *Book of Martyrs* appeared in 1813.[10] Much of the debate between 1815 and 1829 carries the strong whiff of the war patriotism that had dominated public life in Britain for a generation after 1793. The influence of the anti-Catholic editor of the Baptist journal *Seren Gomer* on that journal's contents was particularly obvious. In December 1818 the periodical calculated that throughout history the Catholic Church had been responsible for the deaths of 16,390,277 people,[11] and in 1822 a correspondent insisted that a hundred Irish Catholic MPs at Westminster would be 'a more terrible band . . . than one hundred thousand armed French soldiers in our country'.[12] A great deal of ink was spilt in the religious press – emanating from both church and chapel – on the iniquities of popery. Writers constantly drew attention to 'the Beast' and 'the Whore', as they described the Catholic Church, and 'the Anti-Christ' and 'Man of Sin', as they described the pope. In their lurid descriptions of the Inquisition they underscored the bloody and persecutory history of the Church. More than anything else, they were determined to demonstrate that the character of Catholicism remained the same as it had been at the time of the Reformation. The implication was clear: the Catholic Church remained intolerant of those who disagreed with its doctrines and, given the opportunity, would repress such dissent as violently as it had done in previous centuries.

Petitions from Wales during these years were notable for opposing emancipation. In 1825 the overwhelming majority were hostile to Catholic ambitions,[13] and news of Parliament's rejection of the Bill of that year was met with 'lively demonstrations of joy' and the ringing of bells at Carmarthen.[14] This agitation had an impact on several parliamentary contests during the general election of 1826. In Pembrokeshire John

[7] R. T. Jenkins, *Hanes Cymru yn y Bedwaredd Ganrif ar Bymtheg* (Caerdydd, 1972 edn), pp. 74–7.

[8] *The Cambrian* (11, 15 April 1807, 16, 30 January, 6, 13 February 1813).

[9] R. D. Rees, 'Electioneering Ideals Current in South Wales, 1790–1832', *WHR*, 2, no. 3 (1965), 240.

[10] A. H. Williams, *Efengyliaeth yng Nghymru, c. 1840–1875* (Caerdydd, 1982), p. 21.

[11] *Seren Gomer* (December 1818), 373.

[12] *Seren Gomer* (August 1822), 236.

[13] *The Cambrian* (19 March, 2, 30 April 1825).

[14] *The Cambrian* (11 June 1825).

Hensleigh Allen lost his seat in the Commons because of his 'advanced views' on emancipation.[15] In Anglesey the issue divided the more liberal landed magnates from the squires and Nonconformists, who were diametrically opposed to relief measures. In neighbouring Carnarvon Boroughs there was a similar divide between the anti-Catholic burgesses and the more liberal Pagets of Plasnewydd.[16] In some cases, such as that of Lord James Stuart in Glamorgan Boroughs, a pro-emancipation candidate was able to ride out the hostility to his views.[17]

The volume of anti-Catholic publishing in Welsh increased during the 1820s as emancipation edged closer to becoming reality. During these years there appeared translations of anti-Catholic tracts into Welsh from other languages as well as a variety of indigenous publications.[18] The crescendo of anti-emancipation agitation reached its climax in 1829. More than twenty petitions hostile to emancipation were sent to Parliament from Anglesey alone, a number that has been attributed to the island's proximity to Ireland and its role as a gateway to Britain for many Irish migrants at this time.[19] The Calvinistic Methodists of Caernarfonshire sent a petition bearing 11,000 signatures in opposition to the measure.[20] In such cases, opposition was actuated by a fear of the unknown; in fact, outside the border counties of Flintshire and Monmouthshire, few of those who opposed the measure with such vehemence would have encountered a Catholic. The potential of 'No Popery' rhetoric to inflame passions was demonstrated by events at Haverfordwest in Pembrokeshire in March 1829, when an anti-Catholic meeting organized by the sheriff to collect signatures for a petition ended in violence.[21] Few petitions supported emancipation.[22]

Despite the fact that emancipation was achieved in 1829, anti-Catholicism did not disappear from public life. On the contrary, the following decades witnessed the true heyday of 'No Popery' sentiment. These were years when organized religion made great advances in Wales and the relationship between the Anglican Church and the Nonconformist

---

[15] Roland Thorne, 'Pembrokeshire and National Politics, 1815–1974', in David W. Howell (ed.), *Pembrokeshire County History,* IV (Haverfordwest, 1993), pp. 229–31.

[16] G. I. T. Machin, 'Catholic Emancipation as an Issue in North Welsh Politics', *THSC* (1962), 81–92; Frank Price Jones, *Radicaliaeth a'r Werin Gymreig yn y Bedwaredd Ganrif ar Bymtheg* (Caerdydd, 1975), pp. 135–6, 150–3.

[17] Rees, 'Electioneering Ideals', 241.

[18] For example, John Williams, *Y Chwil-lys* (Llanrwst, 1825); David Owen, *Cwymp Babilon Fawr* (Llanymddyfri, 1829); Anon., *Ymddiddanion am Grefydd rhwng Thomas a William* (Merthyr Tydfil, 1829); Anon., *Hanes Cywir am Gyflwr Arswydus Francis Spira* (Caernarfon, 1817).

[19] Linda Colley, *Britons: Forging the Nation, 1707–1837* (London, 1992), p. 330.

[20] *Lleuad yr Oes* (January 1829), 52–3.

[21] *The Cambrian* (21 March 1829).

[22] *The Cambrian* (7, 14 March 1829).

chapels deteriorated markedly. One theme in the conflict between church and chapel in these decades was who represented the most reliable defender of the country against popery.

Similar responses to those witnessed during the debates on emancipation between 1815 and 1829 can be discerned at other notable times of tension, such as during the bitter and protracted debate over the government subsidy to Maynooth College in Ireland, a topic which greatly exercised the press during the 1830s and 1840s. The idea that a Protestant state should subsidize the training of Catholic priests was anathema to many. Moreover, the vocal presence of Anglo-Catholics in the Church of England provoked outrage among evangelicals, both inside and outside the Church. During these years many Nonconformist commentators came to view the Church of England as a halfway house to 'Popery', rather than as a bulwark against it, which previously it had seemed to be. In this context, the significance of fulminations by influential Methodist intellectuals like Lewis Edwards against the influence of the Oxford Movement should not be underestimated. The term 'Puseyaeth' (Puseyism) to describe such tendencies was a term of abuse in the Welsh press. In fact, the influence of the Oxford Movement has been identified as one of the reasons why Methodism detached itself from an alignment with the Anglican Church and developed a greater affinity in political outlook with the other Protestant Nonconformist denominations.[23]

During the 1840s anti-Catholicism was clothed in appeals to Welsh nationality. Thus, when Henry Wilcox of St David's implored the different denominations to unite against the errors of Rome in 1847, he made his appeal specifically to the Welsh as a people, declaiming: 'God preserve the Welsh, as a nation, from "BELIEVING IN ERRONEOUS SPIRITS AND DEVILISH PHILOSOPHIES".'[24] That same year the infamous government reports on the state of education in Wales produced a wave of indignant protest after they attributed the prevalence of sexual immorality to the influence of the chapels. This incident, the 'Treachery of the Blue Books', had nothing whatsoever to do with the Catholic Church and is properly seen as an episode in the widening gulf between church and chapel. And yet the principal defender of the Nonconformist cause, the Congregational minister Ieuan Gwynedd, warned that divisions in Nonconformist ranks held out the prospect of Catholic triumphalism.[25] Anti-Catholicism developed hand in hand with a developing national

---

[23] Peter Freeman, 'The Response of Welsh Nonconformity to the Oxford Movement', *WHR*, 20, no. 3 (2001), 435–65.
[24] Henry Wilcox, *Cyfeiliornadau y Grefydd Babaidd yn cael eu Dynoethi* (Llanidloes, 1847), p. 48.
[25] *Y Dysgedydd* (September 1847).

consciousness in the mid-century. It was emblematic of a world-view that interpreted political change in terms of fundamental theological and denominational divisions. It is somewhat surprising, therefore, that a brief attempt in 1847 by one of the English Protestant societies to establish an anti-Catholic agent in Swansea was unsuccessful.[26]

Further evidence of the intensity of anti-Catholic sentiment can be found in the response of Protestants to the news of revolution on the continent in 1848. Their reactions were heavily coloured by the implications of this upheaval for the temporal power of the Catholic Church in the Vatican states. Some writers saw the fall of the church's temporal power in millenarian terms.[27] Consequently, most Protestant commentators had more to say about the impact of revolutionary activity in the Italian states than they did about the events in Paris. In a poem titled 'Cwymp Babilon' (The Fall of Babylon), written in 1848, the popular journalist and lecturer William Rees ('Gwilym Hiraethog') celebrated 'the destruction of this great whore'.[28]

Since it was believed that the temporal power of the papacy had been destroyed in 1848, the news of 'Papal Aggression' in November 1850 was greeted with dismay. Newspapers and periodicals in both languages responded vigorously to the news that a Catholic hierarchy of bishops with territorial dioceses had been created for England and Wales in place of the system of vicars apostolic, who had been responsible for different 'regions' of the country. The assumption of territorial titles was interpreted as an attempt to usurp the legitimate authority of a Protestant state over its own territory. The triumphal tone of the announcement in Rome incensed British Protestants and reinforced their suspicions about the papacy's intentions. The agitation was sparked by the publication of a letter by the prime minister, Lord John Russell, denouncing the initiative and calling in vague, but inflammatory, terms for actions against the papacy.[29] The letter, which was published in early November 1850, was reproduced or summarized in most English-language newspapers in Wales and appeared

[26] Wolffe, *Protestant Crusade in Great Britain*, p. 181.

[27] Robert Fleming, *Mynegiadau Prophwydol tra Hynod mewn Perthynas i Gwymp Teulu Bourbon a'r Babaeth yn 1848* (Caernarfon, 1848).

[28] O. M. Edwards, *Gwaith Gwilym Hiraethog* (Llanuwchllyn, 1911), pp. 39–40.

[29] D. G. Paz, *Popular Anti-Catholicism in Mid-Victorian England* (Stanford, CA, 1992); W. G. Rawls, 'The Papal Aggression Crisis of 1850: A Study in Victorian Anti-Catholicism', in James R. Moore and Gerald Parsons (eds), *Religion in Victorian Britain*, IV, *Interpretations* (Manchester, 1988), pp. 115–34.

in translation in Welsh-language publications. The controversy provided a stimulus for a wave of new anti-Catholic publications in Welsh.[30]

Many Welsh Protestants responded with vehemence to Russell's letter. A series of well-attended protest meetings was arranged throughout the country to arrange petitions of protest to be sent to Parliament. What is striking about these meetings is that they attracted the support of a cross-section of society, in terms of social status, language and religious affiliation. Some newspaper editors and Nonconformist ministers were wary of joining an agitation that seemed to be defending the privileged position of the Established Church. The position of different denominational magazines was unequivocal on this point. In some public meetings, such as those at Swansea, the claims of the Church were hotly contested. But it is also clear that in many other cases individual Nonconformist ministers and laypeople of all denominations joined with supporters of the Establishment in demanding the curtailment of civil rights for Catholics.[31] The Methodist divine, Dr Lewis Edwards, wrote of 'the man of sin making a new effort to re-possess England and Wales'.[32]

At least 112 petitions were organized from twelve of the thirteen Welsh counties (Radnorshire was the exception). It is difficult to calculate how many individuals supported these petitions because in some meetings a representative individual signed on behalf of the whole meeting. But where the number of signatories is known, there is evidence of widespread and deep-seated hostility to the establishment of Catholic bishoprics. Small rural villages, like Llan-gain in Carmarthenshire and Aberdyfi in Merioneth, each collected hundreds of signatures in protest, while small towns, such as Amlwch in Anglesey and Dolgellau in Merionethshire, produced even more. Signatures to petitions from each of the larger urban centres, such as the iron-manufacturing townships of Merthyr Tydfil and Dowlais, were numbered in their thousands.[33] By any standards, this was an impressive political mobilization and it offered evidence of how anti-Catholicism in Wales responded to the same stimuli as those that excited public opinion in the rest of Britain. The protests of 1850–1 also provide evidence of how easily such controversies bridged the divide between formal politics and

---

[30] For example, Evan Davies, *Pabyddiaeth a'r Bibl* ([Treffynnon], 1850); Owen Williams, *Drych yr Oen a'r Bwystfil* (Caernarfon, 1851); D. D. Roberts, *Y Dichell Offeiriadol* (Caernarfon, 1851); John Owen, *Annghrist* (Caernarfon, 1851); Anon., *Ychydig Eiriau Plaen ynghylch Pabyddiaeth a'r Pab* (Treffynnon, 1851); John Rees, *Y Drych Pabyddol* (Llanelli, 1852).

[31] This paragraph is based on a systematic reading of the local newspaper press for 1850–1.

[32] Lewis Edwards, *Traethodau Duwinyddol* (Wrexham, 1867), p. 631.

[33] *Parliamentary Papers LIX 1851, Return of the Number of Addresses . . . on the Subject of the Recent Measures taken by the Pope, passim.*

popular culture, with some evidence of a revival of interest in Guy Fawkes celebrations.[34]

Anti-Catholic agitation would never again reach the same heights as it did in 1850–1, but nor did it disappear from politics. Several developments during the 1870s infused new life into anti-Catholic sentiment in Britain and, once again, Wales was no exception. The Vatican Council of 1870 and the Pope's promulgation of the doctrine of Papal Infallibility caused Protestants considerable anxiety.[35] That year an Anglican journal reminded its readers that 'The Welsh have been taught to hate Popery since they were on their mothers' breasts.'[36] Nonconformists clearly shared this view: Henry Richard, the Liberal MP for Merthyr Tydfil, who denounced the Cowper-Temple clause in the Education Bill, described the Anglo-Catholic movement in the Church of England as 'bastard Catholicism', and raised the spectre of Catholic priests gaining access to their own denominational schools to influence the minds of children.[37] Despite representing a town with a significant Irish population, his criticism of denominational education in these terms was clearly acceptable to the majority of voters. His speech confirms the view that education was the main battleground for opponents of Catholicism in Wales by the 1870s.

By this juncture the majority of Welsh Nonconformists supported the Liberal Party and the chapels exercised a powerful influence over its political programme. As Kenneth O. Morgan demonstrated in his seminal work on nineteenth-century Welsh politics, support for disestablishment, temperance and non-denominational education are evidence of this.[38] As a High Church Anglican, William Gladstone's support in Wales was potentially precarious. Indeed, one nineteenth-century Welsh biographer noted that Gladstone's standing among Nonconformists during the early 1870s was jeopardized by accusations that he was a closet sympathizer with Catholicism.[39] The basis for this claim was that he was a well-known High Churchman at a time when evangelical Protestants increasingly saw the Established Church as an unreliable bulwark against Roman influence. In fact, a Calvinistic Methodist journal asserted that it was difficult to distinguish between Anglican ritualism and the ritualism of Rome.[40] Nonconformists viewed Gladstone's position on state education with great

---

[34] *Carnarvon and Denbigh Herald* (9 November 1850); *North Wales Chronicle* (9 November 1850).

[35] E. R. Norman, *Anti-Catholicism in Victorian England* (London, 1968), pp. 80–104.

[36] *Yr Haul* (June 1870), 189.

[37] *Baner ac Amserau Cymru* (18 December 1872).

[38] Kenneth O. Morgan, *Wales in British Politics, 1868–1922* (Cardiff, 1980 edn).

[39] Griffith Ellis, *William Ewart Gladstone: Ei Fywyd a'i Waith* (Gwrecsam, 1898), 289–95.

[40] R. Buick Knox, *Wales and 'Y Goleuad'* (Caernarfon, 1968), p. 137.

suspicion. However, he reinforced his credibility among doubters by publishing attacks on the pope and the Vatican decrees in the mid-1870s, pamphlets which found a receptive audience when translated into Welsh.[41] Gladstone subsequently reacquired heroic status among the Welsh people, but the only other publication of his to be translated was the Midlothian speeches. Greater numbers of anti-Catholic publications of his were translated into Welsh than on any other subject.[42] The force of public opinion on this topic should not be underestimated.

It has been shown that Welsh Protestants responded to the perceived threat of Catholicism at the same time that Protestants in other parts of Britain did during the nineteenth century. That antipathy to Rome occupied a central place in the culture of Nonconformity can be seen from the work of prominent intellectuals as well as the popular journalism which appealed to less cerebral passions. At one end of the spectrum was the Methodist divine Dr Lewis Edwards, editor of the weighty religious periodical *Y Traethodydd*, the premier Welsh periodical of its day. Lewis was an essayist and theologian who exercised considerable influence on Welsh intellectual life. During the 1840s and 1850s he wrote a series of articles ferociously attacking Catholicism from the standpoint of theology and politics. In 1845 he asserted that the government grant to Maynooth seminary in Ireland would mean that a portion of the fruit of the daily labour of Welsh paupers would now be spent on maintaining 'Popery of the worst kind'.[43] He followed this with articles on the dire influence of the Jesuits, the cruelties of the Inquisition and the insanity of monasticism. In his response to the Papal Aggression crisis of 1850 he stressed the deception, oppression, injustice and villainy of Catholicism, and implored Nonconformists and Anglicans to unite against a common foe.[44] In his determined and vocal opposition to 'Popery', Edwards was at one with the majority of his Nonconformist contemporaries. Their view of the world was informed by what they saw as the dire moral and political consequences of the influence of the Catholic Church.

In this respect Edwards was representative of educated Protestants more widely. However, the character of anti-Catholic writing in Victorian Wales varied considerably in tone and content from the closely argued scholarly

---

[41] W. E. Gladstone, *Dedfrydau Llys y Pab yn eu Heffaith ar Deyrngarwch Gwladol* (Wrexham, [1875]); idem, *Faticaniaeth: Atteb i Geryddon ac Attebion* (Wrexham, [1875]).

[42] W. E. Gladstone, *Anerchiad Mr Gladstone at Etholwyr Midlothian* (Dolgellau, [1885]).

[43] Lewis Edwards, 'Maynooth', *Y Traethodydd*, 1 (1845), 327.

[44] Lewis Edwards, 'Yr Ymgyrch Pabyddol', *Y Traethodydd*, 7 (1851), 129–32.

discussion of theological differences to the bigoted rant. Books, pamphlets and articles in religious periodicals which dealt with the perils of popery might be considered a minority taste, even if their messages were disseminated more widely through lectures and sermons. Of greater significance was the pervasive presence of anti-Catholic statements, often of a casual kind, in newspapers in both Welsh and English languages. Among these must be considered the large body of verse that lyrically denigrated the pope and everything he stood for. Much of this output was no better than doggerel, but its lack of literary quality did not prevent it from both reflecting and reinforcing popular attitudes.[45]

The growth of literacy and the press, in both English and Welsh languages, ensured that antipathy to Rome was disseminated more widely than ever before. The fact that many newspaper editors were Nonconformist ministers is of some relevance here. While the attitudes of readers cannot be assumed to mirror those published in newspapers in any simple or straightforward way, the sheer pervasiveness of anti-Catholic comment in apparently secular as well as in religious publications was surely significant. As might be expected, reports of religious matters frequently made reference to the depredations of the Roman Church, but so, too, did analyses of international politics. Developments in Italy, France, Spain and Germany in the 1860s and 1870s were scrutinized for their implications regarding the influence of Catholicism. In the years before 1869 Ireland was included in this category of countries imperilled by Roman influences, although that attitude began to change, albeit slowly, after Irish disestablishment in 1869.

Fear of the 'evil Jesuits' featured strongly in this journalistic output. They were condemned as a group of secretive and scheming clerics, who conspired against civil authority to achieve their own ends.[46] As one writer insisted in 1880: 'The Pope has his treason being carried out by the Jesuits in nearly every state.'[47] The 'treasonable' nature of Catholicism was widely accepted, so much so that the church was described as 'a kind of religious Fenianism'.[48] This reference to the armed Irish republicans who had terrorized some British towns during the 1860s had powerful resonances for many contemporaries, even in those areas free from Irish migration.[49]

Similar themes are discernible in the anti-Catholic literature of the

---

[45] For example, *Y Gwyliedydd* (September 1828), 282; *Y Gwyliedydd* (November 1828), 346; *Y Diwygiwr* (February 1872), 50–1; *Y Tyst a'r Dydd* (19 April 1878).

[46] For example, *Baner ac Amserau Cymru* (17 July, 30 October, 20 November, 18 December 1872).

[47] *Y Diwygiwr* (December 1880), 378.

[48] Ibid.

[49] Paul O'Leary, *Immigration and Integration: The Irish in Wales, 1798–1922* (Cardiff, 2000), p. 253.

remainder of Britain, and it is clear that there was considerable cross-fertilization of ideas and motifs between English, Scottish and Welsh Protestants. It is difficult to determine how much of the literature published in English circulated among bilingual Welsh men and women, but it is reasonable to assume that at least some tracts and books did. A few English-language publications were demonstrably a product of activity in Wales;[50] nor should the growth of the local English-language newspaper press be discounted.

How did the attitudes expressed in these publications and petitions influence behaviour towards Catholics? Linking words and thoughts to specific acts or patterns of behaviour is a difficult enterprise. It is tempting to correlate the upsurge in anti-Catholic sentiment in the 1840s and 1850s to the increase in Irish migration during those years arising from the famine. The arrival of tens of thousands of destitute and starving migrants, many of whom were baptized if not practising Catholics, appeared to bring the threat of popery closer to home.[51] And yet there is no simple causal relationship between the number of Catholics in a particular town or region and the incidence of anti-Catholic comment or behaviour. Indeed, as has been seen, the significance of anti-Catholicism in Welsh life pre-ceded the arrival of significant numbers of Irish migrants, and it makes more sense to view mid-century developments as a continuation and intensification of a tradition rooted in the early modern period.

It is true that some people saw the establishment of Catholic places of worship as a tangible and immediate threat to the freedoms of a Protestant people. During the 1830s and 1840s there was an increasing tendency to warn Protestants against the spread of Catholicism in Wales. Catholics in Cardiff encountered difficulties in acquiring land for the construction of a chapel because of opposition to their religion.[52] In 1839 the Reformation Society warned against the presence of Catholics in Holywell,[53] while in 1840 the bishop of Llandaff preached against the spread of Catholicism in Newport.[54] In 1851 the Revd B. Richards published a Protestant catechism for the use of schools and families in order to counteract the influence of a

---

[50] Anon., *Letters on the Roman Catholic Question by a Protestant* (Aberystwyth, 1828); Hugh Jones, *The Evil of Consenting to Popery* (Holywell, 1849); A. Mursell, *Romanism and Liberty: A Sermon for the Times* (Cardiff, 1870).

[51] O'Leary, *Immigration and Integration*, chap. 3.

[52] John V. Hickey, *Urban Catholics* (London, 1967), p. 125.

[53] *Statistics of Popery in Great Britain and the Colonies* (London, 1839), p. 63.

[54] *Monmouthshire Merlin* (14 November 1840); Edward Copleston, *False Liberality and the Power of the Keys* (London, 1841).

Catholic seminary that had been established in north-east Wales.[55] In 1853–4 Catholics at Newport encountered so much determined opposition to their request for a separate portion of the new municipal burial ground that the issue was only settled by the intervention of Lord Palmerston.[56] And in 1854 Lewis Edwards issued a dire warning about the establishment of a Catholic monastery at Pantasaph in north Wales. Many other examples of friction during the mid-century decades could be added to this list.

One index of tension between the different sections of society is inter-communal violence. There can be little doubt about the intensity of hostility shown towards Irish migrants in different parts of Wales; at least twenty ethnic riots of various sizes and degrees of violence occurred between 1826 and 1882.[57] However, only one of these was explicitly sectarian and few of the others included a religious dimension. A Catholic chapel was sacked during the anti-Irish riot at Cardiff in 1848 and the priest was forced to flee the town, but this can probably be explained by the crowd's determination to find an escaped Irish murderer, whom they believed had sought sanctuary in the chapel. The disturbance was not motivated by religion as such. An incident in Mold in 1850 was more explicitly anti-Catholic. Following a meeting to protest at 'Papal Aggression', a crowd paraded the town before burning an effigy of the pope, as well as effigies of several local people who had expressed support for Catholics. They then attacked houses occupied by Irish migrants, breaking windows and destroying furniture, before moving on to attack the local priest's lodgings.[58] At neighbouring St Asaph the police steered an anti-Catholic crowd away from the houses of Irish immigrants.[59] During the last major anti-Irish disturbance in Wales, at Tredegar in 1882, the church was attacked and the priest was forced to flee for safety; however, this target appears to have been chosen because it was a symbol of the Irish community more generally rather than being a symptom of sectarianism.[60] Other anti-Irish disturbances arose from workplace tensions or more diffuse community tensions in which religion did not play an obvious or documented part.

By the mid-1880s Irish integration in Welsh life was progressing apace. Increasing numbers of Irishmen were joining and organizing some of the

---

[55] Benjamin Richards, *Holwyddoreg Protestanaidd* (Ruthyn, 1851).

[56] O'Leary, *Immigration and Integration*, pp. 232–3.

[57] Paul O'Leary, 'Anti-Irish Riots in Wales, 1826–1882', *Llafur*, 5, no. 4 (1991), 27–36.

[58] *Liverpool Mercury* (13 December 1850)

[59] *Carnarvon and Denbigh Herald* (9 November 1850).

[60] O'Leary, 'Anti-Irish Riots in Wales', *passim*.

mass trade unions that grew up as part of the 'New Unionism' of that decade, while the decision of the overwhelming majority of Welsh Liberals to support Irish Home Rule ensured that Irish Catholics appeared on political platforms with Nonconformist politicians. During the election of 1886 Liberal Unionism created tensions within the Liberal Party in Wales, but it was rapidly eclipsed thereafter. Attempts were made by a minority to advance the 'Home Rule equals Rome Rule' message, but it found few sympathetic listeners.[61] In the fields of sport and other leisure activities there is no evidence of the 'ghetto' existence which some believe persisted among the Irish until the Second World War.[62] A clear conceptual distinction needs to be made here between assimilation and integration. Assimilation implies that a minority increasingly takes on the characteristics of the majority, in the process diluting or effacing cultural characteristics which mark them out as different. According to this definition, the evidence for Irish assimilation in nineteenth-century Wales is patchy. By contrast, integration allows for the possibility that a minority can participate fully in public life without necessarily discarding those characteristics which mark them out as different. Indeed, some institutions which shore up cultural difference can, under certain circumstances, become conduits for integration. This was increasingly the case in Wales from the mid-1880s onwards. Direct opposition to Catholics must be sought in other areas.

When compared with the evident strength of anti-Catholicism in Welsh culture, the relative absence of violent sectarianism raises broader questions about the nature and meaning of anti-Catholicism. The inability of militantly Protestant societies to recruit in Wales would appear to be a telling fact. In his study of the 'Protestant crusade' in mid-nineteenth-century Britain, John Wolffe noted the 'almost total absence' of organized anti-Catholicism in Wales.[63] As this chapter has shown, this cannot be read to mean that anti-Catholicism itself was absent. In this context, Wolffe's explanation of the difference between Wales on the one hand and England and Scotland on the other requires further consideration. His suggestion that the weakness of Anglicanism in Wales might have affected the strength of 'No Popery' agitation is inadequate. In fact, from the late 1840s Nonconformists' fear of the Romanizing tendencies of the Church of England helped to create a sense of solidarity between the Methodists and Old Dissent and stiffened their resolve to campaign for severing the link

---

[61] Kenneth O. Morgan, *Modern Wales: Politics, Places and People* (Cardiff, 1995), pp. 36–45; O'Leary, *Immigration and Integration*, pp. 297–313.
[62] Hughes, 'Anti-Catholicism in Wales', 320.
[63] Wolffe, *Protestant Crusade in Great Britain*, p. 311.

between Church and state. Rather than Church–chapel tensions undermining or displacing antipathy to Catholicism, 'No Popery' agitation was assimilated to that divide. As late as 1885 the Liberal MP Henry Richard described Anglicanism as 'Popery in disguise'.[64]

The concern with achieving disestablishment of the Church of England in Wales had an important impact on one feature of anti-Catholicism which distinguished Wales from England. From the 1860s support in Wales for disestablishment of the Church of England as a whole increasingly narrowed to the demand for disestablishment of that part of the establishment which covered Wales first. This was a product of the strength of Nonconformity and the decisive intervention of the Liberation Society in Welsh politics during the 1860s.[65] Because there was no separate Welsh church to disestablish, the debate revolved around the question of precedents for recognizing the strength of non-establishment religions. The obvious example was Irish disestablishment in 1869, a development which was warmly welcomed in Wales. Whereas Ireland had customarily been depicted as a symbol of the worst moral effects of a priest-ridden country, it slowly came to be seen as an exemplar for constitutional change in Wales. By the 1880s, when Gladstone renounced his earlier opposition to Welsh disestablishment, it was increasingly difficult to defend Irish disestablishment *and* emphasize the perils of Home Rule for Protestantism.[66]

The comparative weakness of the Catholic Church in large parts of the country did not affect the strength of anti-Catholicism in Wales. It is clear that proximity to Catholics, whether Irish or Welsh, was not a necessary precondition of hostility to Rome. This point was made explicit in an anti-Catholic tract by Thomas James of Carmarthen published in 1829: 'No Catholics live in my district', he wrote, 'and I have not seen them worship either.'[67] This did not prevent him from taking an impassioned interest in the subject. In such cases, it was not contact with Catholics as much as the absence of such contact which prompted individuals to write on the subject or to support a petition. For people such as this, it was either disagreement with the tenets of Catholicism on an abstract theological level or a fear of the unknown which prompted them to act.

The intensive petitioning of 1825–9 and 1850–1 would appear to support

---

[64] *South Wales Daily News* (8 November 1885).

[65] Ieuan Gwynedd Jones, 'The Liberation Society and Welsh Politics, 1844–1868', *WHR*, 1, no. 2 (1961), 193–224.

[66] Paul O'Leary, 'Religion, Nationality and Politics: Disestablishment in Ireland and Wales, 1868–1914', in J. R. Guy and W. G. Neely (eds), *Contrasts and Comparisons: Studies in Irish and Welsh Church History* (Llandysul, 1999), pp. 89–114; Morgan, *Modern Wales*, pp. 142–76.

[67] Thomas James, *Anghyssondeb Daliadau Eglwys Rhufain a Gair Duw* (Caerfyddin, 1829), p. 5.

Wolffe's contention that the absence of the Reformation Society and the Protestant Alliance from Wales was a product of cultural, as opposed to organizational, considerations. One factor here might be the reluctance of Protestant societies based outside of Wales to translate their material into Welsh. Equally, however, it might be argued that there was little need for additional translated material, given the vigorous publishing activity that already occurred in Wales, producing both indigenous material and translations from other languages. Outside assistance was superfluous. Other English-based contemporary campaigning organizations, such as the Anti-Corn Law League and the Liberation Society, appointed Welsh agents and translated their propaganda for dissemination among Welsh speakers. The difference between these and militant Protestant societies is that the former were attempting to create a public opinion in favour of their causes, whereas the case against 'Popery' was already well established. There was no need for outside activity to shore up the cause.

In this context, the fact that the famous anti-Catholic lecturer Alessandro Gavazzi toured the other countries of the British Isles but not Wales is of questionable significance. Other anti-Catholic lecturers found fertile ground for their message in Wales,[68] although the extent and influence of such activity is difficult to judge. Without a sustaining local public opinion in favour of an issue, visiting lecturers were little more than fleeting sources of information and entertainment. On the other hand, popular indigenous lecturers often wove anti-Catholic themes into their treatment of individuals like Martin Luther and the Italian nationalist Giuseppe Mazzini.

A crucial factor in explaining why such anti-Catholic rhetoric did not prompt Protestants to organize militant anti-Catholic societies was the increasing fixation of Nonconformists on the Church of England as a fifth column which was allegedly introducing 'popish' influences into Wales, an anxiety that was not decisively assuaged until the disestablishment of the Church in 1919. This did not reduce the intensity of anti-Catholic feeling, but it did provide an alternative target for it and diffused its impact. While disestablishment remained a significant issue in political life, the 'No Popery' cry could be levelled at the Church of England as much as the Catholic Church.

In addition, the absence of the Orange Order from Wales is of some importance in explaining the lack of support for militant Protestant societies. Irish migrants in south Wales hailed overwhelmingly from the Catholic south of Ireland and, unlike the west of Scotland and the north of England, which attracted migrants from Ulster, south Wales did not

---

[68] See *Western Mail* (5, 6, 7 March 1883).

import the sectarianism which became endemic in cities like Liverpool and Glasgow.[69] Moreover, the Orange Order's links with Toryism made it an uncongenial movement to the Nonconformist Welsh. This is a salutary reminder that the language of hatred can only become a systemic problem when adopted and nurtured by social institutions and movements, despite the unsavoury atmosphere such language creates. Thus it was that anti-Catholicism achieved its greatest longevity in the politics of education, which focused debate on the role of different religious beliefs in the state system. This was mainly because candidates in the elections for school boards divided on denominational lines. In many cases parish priests would stand for election in order to defend the Catholic interest, just as representatives of the other Nonconforming denominations and of the Anglican Church stood as representatives of their constituencies.[70] The full extent and significance of such attitudes can be gauged only by detailed local studies. Catholics at Cardiff mobilized politically in order to defend Catholic schools and to ensure Catholic representation on the Board of Guardians, but this 'sectarianism' was not a barrier to holding a large annual Corpus Christi procession in the city's main streets and suggests that religious rivalry in educational politics was somewhat self-contained. The experience of Cardiff, with a large and well-organized Catholic community, must be compared with regions like the north-east, where specifically anti-Catholic schools were established, despite a low level of Irish settlement.

The only sustained attempt at establishing a militant Protestant society came with the inception of the Welsh Protestant Alliance at Cardiff in the 1890s. Information about this organization is scarce, but it prompted a great deal of publishing activity by Catholic organizations in the city in response. Perhaps the Alliance's lack of impact is best judged by local responses to the annual Corpus Christi processions, when thousands of Catholic children established the right of Catholics to use public space by parading the main thoroughfares of Cardiff. The general attitude was summed up by one newspaper's comment in 1891 that Corpus Christi had 'literally become the event of the year in the town'.[71]

As this chapter has shown, a study of anti-Catholicism in nineteenth-century Wales sheds revealing light on the meaning of toleration and the

---

[69] On the Orange Order in Britain, see Donald M. MacRaild, *Irish Migrants in Modern Britain, 1750–1922* (Basingstoke, 1999), pp. 109–22, 148–50.

[70] O'Leary, *Immigration and Integration*, pp. 256–8; Gareth V. Williams, 'Wrexham School Board Elections 1871–1901', *TDHS*, 40 (1991), 43–59.

[71] *Western Mail* (29 May 1891).

way in which the 'Nonconformist nation' dealt with cultural difference. Torn between a commitment to religious equality and resistance to cultural pluralism, it navigated attitudes to Catholicism with great difficulty. The question of whether toleration related only to an *individual*'s freedom of conscience or whether it encompassed the rights of minority *groups* was never resolved satisfactorily. Even though legal equality for Catholics was established in large part in 1829 – in the teeth of determined opposition in Wales – popular attitudes to Catholicism were slower to change. During the 'Papal Aggression' agitation, some Protestants from a variety of denominations publicly regretted the emancipation of Catholics and demanded a curtailment of their civil liberties. It was a reminder that, ultimately, toleration always holds in reserve the threat of withdrawal of acceptance.

Significantly, Nonconformists would use the slogan 'From Toleration to Equality' in their battle with the Established Church.[72] For them, toleration of their freedom to worship was insufficient by itself and needed to be bolstered by a removal of the privileges of the Established Church. However, the case for disestablishment was increasingly argued largely on the grounds that the Welsh were 'a nation of Nonconformists' and that the Anglicized minority Church was an institution which oppressed the majority. The popularity of this 'majoritarian' argument from the 1860s turned Liberalism into a national crusade which grafted a sense of national identity onto religious differences. This added to the difficulties of accepting another religious grouping – Catholicism – which Protestants already considered anathema. Consequently, the demand for 'civil and religious freedom' for Nonconformists was accompanied by an enormous volume of anti-Catholic writing and rhetoric. In many cases, this antipathy derived from a combination of ignorance and a legitimate disagreement with the doctrines of the Catholic Church, but in some few cases it was clearly a product of pathological hatred. The fact that such antipathies did not tear apart the fabric of Welsh society and politics, as they did elsewhere in the British Isles, is one of the unheralded successes of the Liberal hegemony of the late nineteenth and early twentieth centuries.

[72] See next chapter.

13

'A Nation in a Nutshell':[1]
The Swansea Disestablishment
Demonstration of 1912 and the Political
Culture of Edwardian Wales

NEIL EVANS

> Swansea was . . . a centre of civic liberalism which national leaders of the
> party had to take seriously . . . in . . . venues like the Albert Hall and the
> Elysium . . . Lloyd George and others came to denounce the bishops, the
> brewers, the peers, the landlords and other proven enemies of mankind,
> and to proclaim the old imperishable creed of economic freedom and civic
> and religious equality.[2]

This apt quotation, drawn from an essay by Kenneth O. Morgan in a
book edited by Ralph A. Griffiths, seems a particularly appropriate
introduction to a chapter written in honour of these two fine historians. The
concept of political culture assumes that there are coherent patterns in
public life, and one of the ways in which they can be revealed is through the
ceremonies which display the idea. Some claim more for the idea and see
it as a set of orientations to political action, and therefore as having some
explanatory power in political analysis.[3] In early nineteenth-century Britain
there were two chief elements in the political culture: the rituals of elections
and extra-parliamentary campaigning, undertaken both by pressure groups
like the anti-slavery movement and the Anti-Corn Law League and by the

---

[1] *Cambria Daily Leader* (28 May 1912). I'm grateful to Paul O'Leary for his comments
on a draft of this chapter.
[2] Kenneth O. Morgan, 'The Challenges of Democracy', in Ralph A. Griffiths (ed.),
The City of Swansea: Challenges and Change (Gloucester, 1990), p. 56.
[3] Jean H. Baker, 'The Ceremonies of Politics: Nineteenth-Century Rituals of
National Affirmation', in William J. Cooper Jr, Michael F. Holt and John McCardell
(eds), *A Master's Due: Essays in Honor of David Herbert Donald* (Baton Rouge, 1985),
pp. 161–78; Ronald P. Formisano, 'The Concept of Political Culture', *Journal of
Interdisciplinary History,* 31, no. 3 (2001), 393–426.

radical mass platform.[4] Extra-parliamentary agitations were inspired and supported by the emerging newspaper press. In the mid-Victorian period this position changed dramatically. The mass platform collapsed in 1848 and popular radicalism became absorbed into Liberal politics, while many of the election rituals became inappropriate for the enlarged electorate from the 1860s.[5] Much ritual and street theatre gave way to organized, respectable and indoor forms of activity.[6] Gladstone fused these remnants together and developed them in new ways from the 1860s onwards. The Bulgarian agitation joined an extra-parliamentary campaign under a major parliamentary leader, while the Midlothian Campaign of 1879–80 initiated a dialogue between Westminster politicians and voters which crystallized in autumn speaking tours. Speeches were extensively reported in the press, aided by the electric telegraph, thereby providing another connection between politicians and public.[7] Mass meetings and demonstrations, which had originated in radical politics, fused with the local expressions of Westminster politics in revised forms of election rituals suited to the newer technical and social circumstances of the late nineteenth century. The political culture – the framework of values and expectations within which political action was taken – had been decisively transformed.

Within this changed situation Wales had a distinctive position. From 1868 it was dominated by a single party rather than by meaningful two-party competition. This was celebrated as a central value in Welsh politics. In introducing the Disestablishment Bill in 1912 Reginald McKenna, the Home Secretary, referred to it as being the key issue which underlay the huge majorities which he and his colleagues enjoyed in Wales and to the lack of materialism and the religious spirit of what he called a homogeneous people. In the same year W. Llewelyn Williams, in celebrating his by-election victory, praised the consistency of the Welsh people whom he claimed were less fickle than the English and stood by their principles. The dominance of the Liberal Party in Wales was an expression of this.[8] The

[4] Frank O'Gorman, 'Campaign Rituals and Ceremonies: the Social Meaning of Elections in Britain, 1780–1860', *PP*, 135 (1992), 79–115; John Belchem, 'Republicanism, Popular Constitutionalism and the Radical Platform in Early Nineteenth-Century England', *Social History*, 6, no. 1 (1981), 1–32.

[5] John Belchem, '1848: Feargus O'Connor and the Collapse of the Mass Platform', in James Epstein and Dorothy Thompson (eds), *The Chartist Experience: Studies in Working-Class Radicalism and Culture, 1830–1860* (London, 1982), pp. 269–310.

[6] John Belchem, *Popular Radicalism in Nineteenth-Century Britain* (Basingstoke, 1996), esp. p. 6.

[7] Richard Shannon, *Gladstone and the Bulgarian Agitation, 1876* (2nd edn, London, 1975); H. C. G. Matthew, 'Rhetoric and Politics in Great Britain, 1860–1950', in P. J. Waller (ed.), *Politics and Social Change in Modern Britain: Essays Presented to A. F. Thompson* (Brighton, 1987), pp. 34–58.

[8] *Hansard*, 1912, XXXVII, 23 April, cols. 947–9, 960; W. Llewelyn Williams, 'The Consistency of Wales', *Wales,* 2, no. 3 (March 1912), 139–41.

Liberal Party identified with the religious and cultural values of Wales, through the appeals it made to electors as Welsh people and through the policies which it embraced. It forged the Welsh language into a political weapon tempered for the enlarged electorate. The Conservatives effectively conceded this national ground to the Liberals by offering themselves as the party of the English or British nation.[9]

Disestablishment was the longest-lived cause for which Welsh Liberalism fought. Sabbatarianism and temperance won a joint victory in 1881 with the Welsh Sunday Closing Act. Many of the educational concerns of Wales had been addressed by the mid-1890s. But disestablishment remained log-jammed behind the veto of the House of Lords. The constitutional crisis of 1909–11 broke the dam and by the spring of 1912 Irish Home Rule was lined up to ride out on the flood tide with Welsh disestablishment in its wake. Having lost their aristocratic bastion, supporters of the Established Church turned to democratic arguments. They were aided by the fact that Nonconformity had slipped a little from the dominance it had exercised in the mid-Victorian period – despite the impact of the revival of 1904–5 – and the Established Church had undergone its own less spectacular but sustained revival to redeem its moribund state. The Royal Commission on the Church (1906–10) initiated a debate on the relative numbers of supporters of church and chapel. It was claimed that Welsh people – apart from some 'faddist' leaders – did not really desire disestablishment. Nor was this simply an opposition which came from Conservatives and the church. Many English Liberals were at best lukewarm about the cause and felt there were more pressing concerns.

Welsh Liberal politics had been in the doldrums at the turn of the century, indeed since the Conservative victories of 1895. The campaigns against the 1902 Education Act and the religious revival had done much to change that. The elimination of all Tory representation in 1906 was well-predicted before the event and almost seems to have been achieved as an act of will by Liberal leaders. In the wake of this success – proclaimed from platforms and in the press as 'Cymru Gyfan' (The Whole of Wales) – there were suggestions that a large political rally should be held to celebrate what a later age would call a Tory-free Wales. By 1912 expressions of the strength of Welsh national feeling and ideas of a renaissance in Welsh national and political life were legion.[10]

Welsh National Liberal Conventions emerged from a parallel strand of thought, and stretch back at least as far as 1898. They were simply

---

[9] Neil Evans and Kate Sullivan, '"Yn Llawn o Dân Cymreig" (Full of Welsh Fire): The Language of Politics in Wales, 1880–1914', in Geraint H. Jenkins (ed.), *The Welsh Language and its Social Domains, 1801–1914* (Cardiff, 2000), pp. 561–88.

[10] *Cambria Daily Leader* (3 May 1912); See *Wales*, 2 (March 1912), *passim*.

meetings of the Welsh National Liberal Council, but what marked them out strongly was the idea of the political unity – almost the general will – of a nation. The term 'convention' arose out of the American Revolution and the Constitutional Convention of 1787, which produced the draft constitution. That led to ratifying conventions at state level which seem to have been expressions of the national will – a kind of Lockean device to redraw the social contract. Little wonder, then, that it was this term which was used in France for the elected body of the First Republic in 1792 and it would also be adopted by the Chartists for their anti-parliament of the 1830s and 1840s.[11] The excluded asserted their right to remodel the constitution and redraw the social contract. In December 1876 the national meeting to protest against the Bulgarian Massacres had been called a conference since it was essentially party political, though it had originally been hoped that a cross-party convention might be held.[12] It is indicative of the type of political thinking that in Wales these lines were blurred. Liberals called their party gatherings a convention. They claimed to be the political nation.

This stress on unity was, at least partly, a response both to the revival of the church and to the emergence of the labour movement as a potential challenger to Liberal hegemony. Never did Liberals in Wales, it seems, assert national unity more strongly than when the first cracks began to appear in the edifice built in the mid-Victorian period. After the war this element would rise to a crescendo of invective which defined Labour as being outside the nation and a threat to it.[13] In 1912 there was outrage that the opposition to the Disestablishment Bill was denigrating the national status of Wales. Bishop John Owen of St David's, the Liberals' favourite enemy, referred to it as 'an obscure part of the country'. The Conservative argument was that the real concern was with Britain, or rather with the legal entity, England and Wales. Almost inevitably they denigrated Welsh national aspirations in this context, claiming that the issue was not one for Wales alone but one which affected the whole shape and structure of the Established Church. Some raised the spectre of what would later be called the West Lothian question, protesting that Wales, Scotland and Ireland were being given self-government in some spheres while their MPs were

[11] T. M. Parssinen, 'Association, Convention and Anti-Parliament in British Radical Politics, 1771–1848', *EHR*, 88, no. 348 (1973), 504–33.

[12] Shannon, *Gladstone and the Bulgarian Agitation,* pp. 141–6.

[13] Robert Griffiths, *Turning Towards London? Labour's Attitude to Wales, 1898–1956* (Abertridwr, 1981); Peter Stead, 'The Language of Edwardian Politics', in David Smith (ed.), *A People and a Proletariat: Essays in the History of Wales 1780–1980* (London, 1980), pp. 148–65; Christopher Howard, 'Reactionary Radicalism: the Mid-Glamorgan Bye-Election, March 1910', in Stewart Williams (ed.), *Glamorgan Historian IX* (Barry, n.d), pp. 29–42.

free to reshape English national education.[14] As so often after 1847, there was a close association between Welsh national assertion and metropolitan barbs.

In 1911 the celebrations of the investiture of the prince of Wales in Caernarfon provided one kind of seal of approval for the achievements of Liberal Wales. The reforged nation was old enough to have its pantheon of heroes. The memory of Gladstone echoed around the streets of Swansea in 1912, for his visit there in 1887 was a constant source of comparison. His progress from Hawarden to Singleton Park had resembled a whistle-stop tour in an American election. His special train had stopped at many places for him to greet crowds and give speeches. Sixty thousand people greeted him as they enjoyed politics in the park.[15] Henry Richard was also remembered in 1912 on the centenary of his birth. If he had been the pioneer as 'Member for Wales', many saw Tom Ellis as 'the Parnell of Wales'. In the spring of 1912 his speeches and essays were published, providing an occasion to reflect on a lost leader.

Others chose to celebrate the evicted martyrs of 1868, who sometimes came to mind when commemorating the more ancient martyrs of 1662, the evicted Puritan ministers. Celebrating the bicentenary of the latter had been a critical act in the birth of Nonconformist Liberalism in 1862, and in 1912 both the original event and its commemoration were recalled. It is surely a sign of a rich political culture that there were so many intersecting points in the public memory.[16] The early death of Tom Ellis was counter-balanced by the fact that David Lloyd George had achieved the highest office yet held by a Welshman in modern times as chancellor of the exchequer. He appeared to many to be the inheritor of Ellis's mantle, a fulfilment of the promise which seemed to have been denied. In 1912 J. Hugh Edwards published his *Life of D. Lloyd George*: the first volume is a history of the Welsh people, culminating in a chapter on Ellis. The second volume is devoted to the early life of Lloyd George. It presents Lloyd George as the highest embodiment of the nation, and Ellis –'The Herald of a New Era' – as his John the Baptist. Lloyd George was very much a living politician, but he was already in the pantheon. A Tory satirist imagined 'a home-ruled, unchurched Wales . . . [with] a golden image of the Chancellor of the Exchequer . . . placed on the summit of

---

[14] The general arguments can be followed in the debates on the first and second readings of the bill, and in the press. The 'West Lothian' point was made by W. Joyson Hicks, *Hansard*, XXXVI, 25 April 1912, cols. 1311–12.

[15] Richard Shannon, *Mr Gladstone and Swansea, 1887* (Swansea, 1982); H. C. G. Matthew (ed.), *The Gladstone Diaries, XII, 1887–1891* (Oxford, 1994), pp. 38–9.

[16] *Cambria Daily Leader* (8, 28 May, 24 June, 8 July 1912); *Rhondda Socialist* (1, 25 May, 6, 20 July 1912); S. Trevor Jones, 'The Henry Richard Centenary, 1812–1912', *Wales*, 2 (May 1912), 241–2.

Snowdon, to which at the sound of Tôn-y-botel, all Wales shall bow the knee'.[17] The extent of Liberal adulation of Lloyd George rendered such comments not entirely unfair. A cartoon in the magazine *Wales* showed him in a bishop's regalia as 'St-David-up-to-date'. He suffered no loss of popularity from his involvement in the Marconi Affair in 1913 and rallies were held in his constituency which amounted to a popular refutation of the charges. Some of the savagery of anti-suffragette violence in north Wales in 1912–13 stemmed from their targeting of this Welsh national icon.[18]

Swansea was a fitting arena in which to place the Welsh political nation on display. Though eclipsed by Cardiff in the size of its population and lacking the leading role which Cardiff's elevation to city status in 1905 had given it, it was a large town and the one with which Liberal Wales was most comfortable. It was much more Welsh in speech than was Cardiff and it was enjoying its own civic renaissance in the Edwardian high noon. The disappointing census figures for Cardiff in 1911 – it scraped 182,000 inhabitants whereas 200,000 had been widely predicted – coincided with Swansea's schemes for municipal progress and enlargement as 'Greater Swansea'.[19] Perhaps the leadership of Wales and the status of capital had not been lost to its larger rival after all.

In this context Swansea was chosen as the site for the central demonstration in a series for and against the Disestablishment Bill. The first was in Caernarfon for the visit of the archbishop of Canterbury – the first such archiepiscopal visit to Wales since Archbishop Pecham's attempt to mediate between Llywelyn ap Gruffudd and Edward I in 1282. This meeting was a huge success and was particularly well-organized. It appears that there were church defence secretaries in each parish in north Wales and this created a framework of organization.[20] The pavilion, which held 10,000 people, was so full that overflow meetings became necessary. Unusually for Church and Conservative propaganda, a Welsh national claim was asserted: 'Here was a body representative of the national life of Wales. No other religious body could bring together so representative a gathering.'[21]

Demonstrations often display their nature in the shapes they assume on the ground. The platform at the pavilion was packed with church

[17] 'Glendower' [J. W. Wynne-Jones], *Welsh Notes* (Bangor, 1913), pp. 6–7.
[18] Kay Cook and Neil Evans, '"The Petty Antics of the Bell-Ringing Boisterous Band"? The Women's Suffrage Movement in Wales, 1890–1918', in Angela V. John (ed.), *Our Mothers' Land: Chapters in Welsh Women's History, 1800–1939* (Cardiff, 1991), pp. 159–88.
[19] W. St John Hancock, *A Greater Swansea* (Swansea, 1912).
[20] The main sources are the *North Wales Chronicle*, and the *Carnarvon and Denbigh Herald*, April–May 1912.
[21] *North Wales Chronicle* (26 April 1912).

dignitaries and landowners, clearly placing the social hierarchy at the head of the popular demonstration. Something like 7000 people arrived by special trains, while the remainder of the crowd came by carriage, brake, car and on foot. Following the archbishop's speech, the demonstrations continued around the town for some hours. It was observed that a majority of the people present were women – as were many of the church's voluntary workers. Even the Liberals had to concede the success of the Church event. The local Liberal newspaper contented itself with observing that the real reason for such an unexpectedly large turnout was the novelty of seeing an archbishop of Canterbury. The fact that six centuries had elapsed since the previous visit was another indicator of the neglect of Wales by the Established Church.

The following month the Liberals had their opportunity to counter this with their own demonstration when Lloyd George and other ministers promised to attend a meeting in the same building. At best it only equalled the Conservative demonstration (so the Liberals claimed) and it was probably smaller (so the Tories claimed). The array of talent on the platform was smaller than had been promised; quarrymen were suffering from a period of unemployment and their own annual demonstration in the town a few weeks earlier had been something of a damp squib. The Liberal meeting turned out to be overshadowed by suffragette interventions, which disrupted it from the beginning. It was linked with a Welsh National Convention meeting in the town, but it was not a demonstration in the modern sense of the term. That term was applied (as was frequently the case at the time) to the mass indoor meeting during which speeches were made. Certainly the Liberals had not outshone the Church in the first round of this battle to influence Parliament and public opinion. Much would depend on the Swansea meeting, the south Wales younger twin of Caernarfon, to be held the following week. That, too, was allied to a Welsh National Convention meeting, but it was to be followed by a demonstration through the streets and a series of public platforms in Victoria Park. Here there would be an opportunity to demonstrate support and enthusiasm.

Clearly the Swansea meeting was hastily organized, and this needs to be borne in mind when assessing its meaning and significance. Swansea Borough Council granted permission on 3 May 1912 and the event took place just over three weeks later on 28 May in the Albert Hall and in Victoria Park.[22] It was an intelligent move to hold it at a holiday time – on Whit Tuesday – so that it could join and resonate with the burgeoning

---

[22] West Glamorgan Archive Service, TC 2/1 Swansea Borough Council Minutes, Special Meeting, 3 May 1912. The following account draws on the south Wales press, especially *Cambria Daily Leader* and the *South Wales Daily Post*, May–July 1912.

popular culture of the region. The event drew on the organizational network of the Liberal Party in south Wales. The main organizers were Cyrus J. Evans, secretary of the Welsh National Liberal Council, based in Cardiff, and W. J. Cocker, the agent. Evans worked by sending circulars to Liberal and Nonconformist bodies which had been campaigning for disestablishment for some years. One of the main roles of the organizers was to arrange fifty-five special excursion trains from around south Wales to carry demonstrators to Swansea.

Much of the organization was devolved locally since, as the organizers stressed, it was impossible to visit every area. This implies that they visited some. It was hoped that local committees would be formed. Clearly local organization already existed in at least some areas. In Carmarthenshire many meetings were held in favour of the cause in April and leaflets were distributed in both languages on a large scale, and a disestablishment committee was set up which supplied ministers with literature so that they could educate their congregations.[23] One of the methods used to promote the event was by dispatching a 'sandwich van' to south Wales to advertise the event through bill posting. In Lampeter it was attacked by hostile students who threw out some of its stock of leaflets and afterwards pursued it by car towards Llanybydder.[24] Conservative opponents emphasized the effort which was put into this organization, but there was a hint of jealousy in the complaints:

> we believe that after the employment to the point of exhaustion of every organized body connected with Radicalism and militant Nonconformity in Wales to whip up the attendance, and after practically every chapel in the Principality has rung with appeals for a supreme effort, and after all the financial resources of the party have been applied to rouse the lethargic, quicken the interest of the indifferent by the distribution of millions of handbills, and the posting of thousands of placards on every hoarding in Wales, and also to secure railway and other facilities designed to make a trip to Swansea attractive, there is no reason except bad weather, why a considerable body of people should not be brought into the procession, and subsequently around the twelve platforms in Victoria Park.[25]

The Liberal machinery was fully supported by the press, especially the *Cambria Daily Leader*. Founded in 1861, it was the first daily paper in Wales, and by 1912 it was largely the mouthpiece of Alfred Mond, the

[23] NLW, Welsh Political Archive, XJN 1156, Circular Letters from Cyrus J. Evans of the Welsh National Liberal Council, 8, 22 May 1912; *Carmarthen Weekly Reporter*, 26 April 1912.

[24] *Cambrian News* (24 May 1912).

[25] *South Wales Daily Post* (27 May 1912).

local Liberal MP: 'Its policy has been strongly Nationalist. It has been and is still in the front in its advocacy of all the movements that tend to establish Wales as a nation that has to be counted with.'[26] Throughout May it publicized the event and encouraged attendance. Getting a good turnout would be 'a challenge to the south', and the fact that Gaumont planned to film the event to show in local cinemas was an additional incentive. As a result, there was huge demand for the 2000 places at the convention, which could have been filled many times over. 'All Roads lead to Swansea on Whit Tuesday' was a key theme in the publicity. One indication of the air of expectation was a letter sent to William Jones MP by his cousin Rowland. He predicted that 'it will no doubt be a tremendous affair'.[27] Enthusiasm spread widely and caused the postponement for a week of a performance of the drama 'Rhys Lewis' at Felinfoel Public Hall. Even tiny Llanpumsaint was said to be sending 150 people.[28]

Perhaps the publicity was too successful because during the contest with its Tory contemporaries the ghost of Gladstone's visit in 1887 was frequently raised. The Tories effectively claimed that it would be Banquo's ghost since it would show the degree to which Liberalism had lost its grip over the previous twenty-five years. The Liberals countered gamely by claiming that the events of that day would be surpassed and that the biggest political demonstration ever seen in Wales would be the result. In a sense this created a Dutch auction which it was impossible for the Liberals to win. Matching the response of 1887 would be difficult and in many ways the comparison was a false one since it obscured the nature of the demonstration in 1912.

Other newspapers reflected the debate outside Swansea. Inevitably the Cardiff press joined in with strong coverage in the *South Wales Daily News*, while other newspapers carried advertisements and inserted columns which were press releases written by the organizers. The advertisements were not large by modern standards and were usually just a single insertion; in themselves they were not a campaign. But they were clearly part of a campaign which included newspaper opinion, Liberal organizations and the editorial portions of the newspapers. Crucially, Nonconformist organizations were included.

We know of the last of these only from the views of opponents, but there is little reason to doubt their effectiveness. Here is the Socialist opposition in the Rhondda:

[26] J. D. Williams, 'Makers of Welsh Opinion III "Cambria Daily Leader"', *Wales,* 2, no. 1 (January 1912), 21–4.

[27] University of Wales Bangor MS 5466, Rowland Jones to William Jones, 21 May 1912.

[28] *Llanelly Star* (25 May 1912); *Cambria Daily Leader* (18 May 1912).

Who said 'No politics on Sunday'? Every Nonconformist place of worship in the district was turned into an advertising place for Liberalism a fortnight ago. Hung up in the lobbies were posters announcing the disestablishment meeting at Swansea, besides the verbal announcements etc. Still Socialists are regarded as devils incarnate because they 'talk politics' on Sunday.[29]

This underlines the value of Nonconformist organization. In the Rhondda alone it had between 150 and 200 ministers. Socialists criticized the ineffectiveness of such a presence, claiming that Nonconformists were losing members each year or, more cynically, that the main benefit was to the ministers who were drawing salaries of £8 a month. But they could only look with envy at this level of organization which no trade union or political party could match.[30] Clearly in May 1912 this proved to be a vital factor in mobilizing support for the central Nonconformist political cause.

The main attraction at Swansea – apart from the opportunity to promote a central Nonconformist cause – was David Lloyd George. All accounts agree on his role. On the morning of the convention and demonstration he arrived by car from Pembrokeshire, where he had stayed with Lord St David's. People gathered on the roadside at Fynone to catch a glimpse of him and to cheer. One car was showered with flowers in the mistaken belief that it contained the chancellor. The streets were animated from an early hour.

The first event was the convention. The Albert Hall was festooned with a banner proclaiming the motto of the day, 'From Toleration to Equality'. Other banners remembered heroes who had fallen before the victory had been won: Gwilym Hiraethog, Edward Miall, Rees Capel Als, Tom Ellis and Dillwyn, as well as living exemplars like Asquith, McKenna, Ellis Edwards and Lloyd George. The 2000 delegates at the convention were among the few to hear Lloyd George clearly that day. He chaired the meeting and spoke for forty minutes. Most other Welsh Liberal MPs were present. The convention began at eleven with the hymn 'Marchog, Iesu, yn llwyddiannus' to the tune 'Moriah'. Lloyd George's speech followed and then the resolution in favour of disestablishment was put: 'This Convention of Delegates, representing Liberal and Progressive Associations and the Free Churches of Wales, tenders its heartiest thanks to the Government for the Established Church (Wales) Bill, and pledges itself to unremitting support in securing this great and necessary reform.' After further speeches and a vote of thanks the proceedings closed with 'Hen Wlad Fy Nhadau'.

[29] *Rhondda Socialist* (8 June 1912).
[30] *Rhondda Socialist* (25 May 1912).

By the time the convention ended the demonstration was already filing past the Albert Hall. As one journalist noted, describing it was a more difficult task than describing the orderly convention:

> Write up the procession is it? More easily said than done. It can't be done, in fact. You can't boil down the ocean. It was not one procession, or two, but a hundred processions – a cyclone of virile humanity that crowded us out and held up Swansea's ordinary traffic to-day . . . It was a colossal affair, and never has such an imposing moving mass of humanity been witnessed locally engaged in demonstrating for any cause in recent times.[31]

In fact, two processions set off from High St Station and the Guildhall, taking differing routes through the town until they converged on Victoria Park. Banners proclaimed the cause: 'Wales' Reply to the Wail of the Bishops'; 'A Wronged Nation demands Redress'; 'The Unsilenced Voice of Wales'; 'The Bill – The Minimum Demand of the Free Churches'; 'Swansea Solid for Equality'; 'Labour Stands for Religious Equality'; 'Cofiwch Thomas Gee' (Remember Thomas Gee); 'Remember Dillwyn'; 'Religious Equality begets Christian Brotherhood' and 'They ask for Numbers; We give them Numbers'. Rosettes with the theme 'From Toleration to Equality' abounded. Trains arrived every ten to fifteen minutes at High St Station and were met by bands. They were shown their assembly points and then asked to return at 1 p.m. for the march. The northern procession took the contingents from the east and north of Swansea – the arc from Newport to Morriston. It snaked from the station up Walter Road through the Uplands and down to St Helen's Avenue. The southern procession went from Wind Street, along Castle Street, College Road, Gower Street, to St Helen's Road.

Besides the marchers, the town was crowded with people who watched the processions. Both were said to have taken around an hour to pass a fixed point. The problems began in Victoria Park. The two entrances could not handle the volume of people and it took a long time for them to enter, particularly since many people had gone straight to the park in search of a good listening position, but the gates were not opened until the procession arrived. All tried to enter at once. Inside the twelve platforms had been reduced to six. Lloyd George had promised to speak from all of them, but in the event he spoke from only one and gave up shortly after beginning at the second. Many were bitterly disappointed, especially those who had spent some time listening to more minor figures, and the crowd began to melt away. The day ended with a Welsh concert at the Albert Hall. Lloyd

---

[31] *Cambria Daily Leader* (28 May 1912).

George had been due to attend, but was called away because of developments in the London dock strike.

The *Cambria Daily Leader* proclaimed it 'the greatest national gathering in the history of Wales'.[32] Unsurprisingly, the Tory press dissented. The *South Wales Daily Post,* which had organized a census of the marchers, claimed that only 16,324 marchers entered the park. This figure was the subject of controversy for some time afterwards and there were claims that the counting was highly selective. For over a week the *Cambria Daily Leader* mocked the *South Wales Daily Post* with the figure, long after it had ceased to exploit it. Liberals claimed a large attendance of up to 100,000 and double that number in the town. The Tory press countered this with the claim that many of the marchers, especially on the northern march, had been women and children rather than voters. None of this controversy is likely to surprise anyone with an interest in demonstrations, either past or present. Nor is there any easy, or totally objective, way to resolve the controversy.

But certain parameters can be set. The figure of 16,000 marchers is compatible with Liberal estimates of each of the marches taking an hour to pass given points with eight abreast (which seems to have been the case) and assuming a flow of one rank every four seconds past a given point (14,400). Clearly there were far more people in the park than this. Observers who were familiar with football crowds, whether they were Conservative or Liberal, placed the attendance in the park at between 30,000 and 40,000.[33] The agreement is striking and was based on similar assumptions in all respects apart from the political perspective. But how do we assess the people on the streets in Swansea? Conservative sources conceded that there were many thousands and usually explained them away as normal holiday crowds. Liberals were naturally keen to enrol them as demonstrators. Clearly at least some of them were. Not everyone who went to Swansea for a political purpose went on the march; some allegedly went to the sands. But many must have watched the march and made their way to the park. The crush of getting in deterred many and it is obvious that in an age before loudspeakers not many could have hoped to have heard Lloyd George. Hearing him was one of the main attractions of the day and most would have been disappointed to have found themselves out of earshot. Lloyd George has been described as having the appeal of a music hall comedian rather than Gladstone's revivalist preacher style. His comic timing was a great asset, but it was not best employed in the case of

---

[32] *Cambria Daily Leader* (29 May 1912).
[33] *South Wales Daily Post* (28, 29 May); *Carmarthen Weekly Reporter* (31 May 1912).

a huge open-air audience.[34] How did it compare with 1887? The Tories claimed it was a massive failure and that it should have been much bigger given the rise in population since 1887. The deputy chief constable of Swansea, who was present at both events, believed that he had never seen anything as big as the 1912 demonstration. But what exactly did he mean? The march, the park or the general crowd? It was a multiple event (as was that of 1887) and determining exactly what was being compared makes a great deal of difference.

Technology placed limits on the numbers that could be concentrated. Many trains filled up after a few stations on their route to Swansea and left hopeful demonstrators behind on the platform. The crush in the park was another problem. Victoria Park was far smaller (even in 1912) than was Singleton Park, where Gladstone had spoken in 1887. The latter demonstration had been part of a series of activities related to Gladstone's visit. The figure of 60,000 seems to represent the number of people who marched past him in Singleton Park rather than those who listened to his speech. Many works and mines in Swansea had given their workers the day off and all the patronage of the Vivian family was ranged behind the event. It is hard to escape a sense of both civic engagement and a still-Whiggish political culture which was wholly absent in 1912. People wanted to listen to Lloyd George rather than file past him as if he were a monument. His attraction lay in having sprung from the people, something Gladstone, for all his virtues, could not claim to have done. Swansea was en fête for a civic holiday in 1887, but in 1912 the lord mayor declared that it was a party political event rather than an urban holiday. Welsh Liberals liked to blur the distinction between party and people: in 1887 they succeeded, but in 1912 they failed.

Even if we accept the lowest estimates it is hard to describe the day as a failure. Certainly the Tories swiftly abandoned their attempts to write it off. It seems in general to have impressed the English press, which was one of its main functions – some English Tory papers were more disposed to accept attendance figures (up to 50,000) than were the local Tory press. If we assume that there were around 40,000 present in the park, this would render it proportionately twice the size of the Countryside Alliance March upon London in September 2002 and around the same level as the anti-war demonstration in London in February 2003. There is little reason to doubt the view of the *Cambria Daily Leader* that it was a 'great day in the annals of the borough' and also one of the major political demonstrations

---

[34] Peter Clarke, 'Lloyd George and Churchill: What Difference did they Make?', in Ieuan Gwynedd Jones and Glanmor Williams (eds), *Social Policy, Crime and Punishment: Essays in Memory of Jane Morgan* (Cardiff, 1994), pp. 56–7.

in the history of Wales. John Herbert Lewis, enthusing about it in the privacy of his diary when it would have been possible to entertain doubts, reckoned that it had been 'a wonderful display of feeling, fervour and determination'.[35]

This is emphasized when we compare it with the major anti-disestablishment demonstration held in London in July 1912. There were probably 15,000 on this march, but although they were drawn from northern England and the capital as well as from Wales, they did not match the number of demonstrators at Swansea. It was symbolic of Toryism and of the case against disestablishment that the march of July 1912 was held across the border. It was centred on the West End, where prominent north Wales landowners waved from the balconies of their opulent mansions. Actions spoke much louder than words in this display of the political culture associated with the Conservative Party. The bulk of Welsh excursions came from north Wales and there were more from northern England than there were from south Wales.[36] This accords with the success which the defenders of the Church enjoyed at Caernarfon. One aspect of the London demonstration calls for special comment. There were many women present, but since they were not allowed to march they followed up at the rear in coaches. Women were similarly present in large numbers in the Caernarfon meeting with the archbishop and in Swansea. In the latter case, while the Tory press pointed out their significance, it explicitly stopped short of claiming that this made their presence illegitimate – simply that they were not voters. This illustrates John Belchem's view that women were 'active participants in politics in all but Westminster itself', though the symbolic evidence of these demonstrations suggests we might give some attention to their contrasting roles within the various parties.[37]

In order to find a larger political demonstration than that of 1912 it is necessary to move forward to 1935, to the massive protests against the means test which were held across south Wales in that year.[38] These were multiple demonstrations which rolled into a tidal wave on 3 February 1935 when allegedly 300,000 people marched on one day. This was made possible by holding a coordinated cluster of protests in different places. At

[35] NLW, John Herbert Lewis Papers, B26 Diary 1912, entry for 28 May.

[36] Gwynedd Archives Service, M/345/63. 'Official Handbook of the Demonstration against the Welsh Church Bill . . . 12 June 1912'; M/760 'Souvenir in Commemoration of the Great Demonstration'.

[37] John Belchem, *Class, Party and the Political System in Britain, 1867–1914* (Oxford, 1990), p. 14.

[38] Neil Evans, '"South Wales has been Roused as Never Before": Marching Against the Means Test, 1934–1936', in David W. Howell and Kenneth O. Morgan (eds), *Crime, Protest and Police in Modern British Society: Essays in Memory of David J. V. Jones* (Cardiff, 1999), pp. 176–206.

a time when money was very short in south Wales, large-scale travelling to a central point would have been out of the question. The issue concerned the livelihood of whole communities rather than a political principle which some found to be abstract, and there was a distinct civic sense of protest. It was not a case of a party-political creed being advanced, but the values of a society being defended.

The demonstration of 1912 essentially expressed a sense of Welsh nationhood personified in a leader. It was a tribute to the political values which Liberalism had built up since the 1860s and to the enduring capacity of the Liberal Party and of Nonconformity to organize people in Wales. But it was restricted in some ways by the sense of being simply the instrument of a political party in support of one particular measure, however much the progress, honour and pride of Wales was attached to that issue. From the mid-1890s that issue had begun to lose its salience. On the weekend of the Swansea demonstration the national Independent Labour Party conference was held in Merthyr. Keir Hardie, a lukewarm supporter of disestablishment, was otherwise engaged, Ellis Griffith had to be in London because of the dock strike, and Lloyd George had to leave early for the same reason. In the Rhondda on the same day a mass meeting was held to welcome the release of John Hopla and Will John, heroes of Tonypandy, from prison. There were plenty of counter-attractions within the political culture.

The 1912 demonstrations did not of themselves ensure the passage of the Disestablishment Bill in that year, but they played an important part in mobilizing support in Wales for the measure. This contributed to solidifying the Liberal support in Parliament after the first and second readings had been passed by disappointingly small majorities. Apart from putting people onto the streets, they made no innovations in the political culture. Old-fashioned Liberals like John Gibson felt this was unnecessary and that Wales had already spoken over many decades. The attempt to demonstrate popular support was an innovation and one adjusted to the democratic tone of Edwardian political culture. While popular support was demonstrated, it also showed that a form which allowed a mass of people to *hear* a speaker had not been evolved. It was easier to assemble large crowds to *see* sporting events. The Liberal-Nonconformist organization had proved successful at mobilizing its members and cadres for a demonstration, but it had not achieved similar success with its broader support which roamed the streets rather ineffectually and could not be assembled to hear Lloyd George. The emphasis was on numbers of marchers, and the sense of respectability was enhanced by orderly marching and by mixing brass bands among the marchers. There was no attempt to create a spectacle such as that witnessed in the great women's suffrage demonstrations in

Edwardian England. Welsh Liberals had no need of this. No one really doubted their right to take part in public activities; women were challenging the rules of the game much more boldly and needed the softening, indeed feminizing, guise of art to make their innovations acceptable.[39]

Yet national feelings must have been reinforced by such a concentrated public display and by events which were clearly memorable. They were commemorated on postcards as well as in the press accounts, and in the newsreel film shown in Swansea cinemas in the following days. The Welsh nation had been put on public display as much as it had been at Caernarfon for the investiture in the previous year. But little was achieved that was new in Swansea in May 1912. Instead there was a demonstration of what Liberalism stood for, of how it tried to identify with the Welsh nation, and of what had been achieved by that political mobilization over a couple of generations. Less obviously, but unmistakably, there were also signs that it was showing its age.

---

[39] Lisa Tickner, *The Spectacle of Women: Imagery of the Suffrage Campaign 1907–14* (London, 1987), esp. chap. 3.

14

Margaret Wynne Nevinson:
Gender and National Identity in the Early
Twentieth Century

ANGELA V. JOHN

The old lady climbed Parliament Hill with the swift foot of one accustomed to steep ascents. The east wind blew keen and fresh, and she breathed in deep draughts as one half perishing for air . . . The sun was setting red in the west, and the old lady sighed as she thought how the rocks of Cader Idris would glow in the rosy light. A great home-sickness had fallen upon her.[1]

This expression of romantic nostalgia occurs in a short story of 1922 set during the First World War. The old lady is staying in London to look after her pregnant English daughter-in-law. She discovers that her son, Gwilym Jones of the 1st Welsh Fusiliers, has been killed in action. The longing for the Welsh landscape – and the *hiraeth* is couched in words suggestive of a translation from Welsh – is partly assuaged when Mrs Jones is addressed in Welsh by a London omnibus conductor. He is from her native Dolgellau and they chat as she travels to the Welsh chapel.

The author was Margaret Wynne Nevinson (1858–1932). She spent most of her adult life in Hampstead, living close to Parliament Hill. Her biography suggests at first sight a well-travelled, middle-class English woman with little in common with the fictional Mrs Jones. Born in 1858 in Leicester, Margaret Wynne Jones had been educated at home, and in Oxford and Paris. Intelligent and adventurous, she became a pupil-teacher in Cologne, where she gained a diploma in German language and literature.[2] Returning to Britain she spent four years as a classics mistress at South Hampstead High School, a school recently established by the Girls' Public Day School Trust. She left in 1884 on marrying Henry W. Nevinson, whom she had known since childhood. They spent their first

---

[1] Margaret W. Nevinson, 'Killed in Action', in eadem, *Fragments of Life* (London, 1922), p. 161.
[2] For details of her life, see my entry in *The New DNB* (Oxford, forthcoming).

230

year in Germany, where Henry Nevinson was a postgraduate student at the University of Jena. Here Margaret Nevinson gave private tuition in English and her daughter was born.

Returning home the Nevinsons lived for several years in workers' dwellings in east London. They helped with the newly established Toynbee Hall settlement. Margaret Nevinson taught modern language classes there, helped with a girls' club and was, along with Beatrice Potter (later Beatrice Webb), a local rent-collector. She also became a long-serving school manager, working first in the East End under the London School Board, before joining the Haverstock Hill and Fleet Road Group after moving to Hampstead in the late 1880s.[3]

For many years she was also a Poor Law Guardian for the Kilburn ward of the Hampstead Board of Guardians. In June 1920 she became a justice of the peace on the Hampstead Bench, the first woman in London to adjudicate at Criminal Petty Sessions.[4] The following year she was one of three women appointed to the Lord Chancellor's London County Justices' Advisory Committee. In the 1920s she visited the United States to study the American probationary system. She also sat on the Committee of the Society of Women Journalists and published articles, two volumes of short stories and an autobiography. Margaret Nevinson died in 1932. Her son, C. R. W. Nevinson, was especially renowned for his paintings of the First World War and became an official war artist.

Yet despite a life lived largely in London among the intelligentsia of Hampstead and with numerous international links, Margaret Nevinson can be seen as part of the Welsh diaspora. She chose to identify herself as a Welsh woman. She was conscious of her nationality as well as her gender in the shaping of her sense of identity. She surrounded herself with symbols of Welshness, carefully insinuated elements of Welshness into her stories and actions – albeit sometimes more akin to perceived stereotypes than lived experience – and unequivocally defined herself as a feminist.

[3] The headmaster of the flagship Fleet Road School was W. B. Adams. It was known as the best elementary school in London. He and his wife Mary had resigned from teaching at Cyfarthfa, Merthyr Tydfil, because they did not speak Welsh. Mary Adams was head of the junior mixed department at Fleet Road. W. E. Marsden, *Educating the Respectable: A Study of Fleet Road Board School, Hampstead, 1879–1903* (London, 1991), p. 182.

[4] Margaret Lloyd George was one of the first women magistrates. She sat on the Lord Chancellor's Advisory Committee in the wake of the Sex Disqualification (Removal) Act of 1919. This committee recommended women for the commissions of the peace in Wales, Scotland and England. Margaret Nevinson was one of over 200 women in the Lord Chancellor's List of July 1920. This signalled the first sizeable appointment of women as justices of the peace. Lady Rhondda was one of several other Welsh women on this list.

Why was this so and what might her life story suggest about how Welsh history and biography are constructed?

Margaret Nevinson's assumption of both a Welsh and feminist identity can partly be traced to her parents, Mary and Timothy Jones. Her mother was half-Welsh, while her father was a Welsh-speaking Welshman from Lampeter. A High Church Anglican, he was vicar of St Margaret's Church, a poor parish in the centre of Leicester. Margaret Jones was the only girl out of six children. Names such as Meredydd, Mervyn and Lloyd (he became canon of Peterborough) genuflected to Welsh roots. Family holidays were spent in Wales with Welsh-speaking relatives.[5]

Her father firmly believed in the education of his daughter. A classical scholar, he taught her Latin and Greek from the age of 7. Such an enlightened approach was not unknown. The educationalist Emily Davies was one of those who studied classics with a clergyman father. Margaret Nevinson would later use her classical training to argue about contemporary issues, as she did in her pamphlet *Ancient Suffragettes* ([1913]).[6] Her father's early death and her mother's conservatism – she feared that nobody would want to marry a girl who read Greek – helped to shape her determination to resist the traditional destiny of middle-class daughters. The cost of educating four boys meant that hopes of reaching Girton receded. Instead 'marriage was dinned into me from morning till night . . . until I hated the very sound of the word'.[7]

Carving out her own career, she took several posts as a governess and saved money to enable her travel to Germany. Later, when teaching (a profession familiar to many London-Welsh women) she undertook a part-time degree, a form of early distance learning imaginatively provided by the University of St Andrews in Scotland. In 1883 she was one of sixty-three women who gained an LLA (Lady Literate in Arts).[8]

Margaret Nevinson's early years had therefore given her some sense of a Welsh heritage and an awareness of how much gender mattered. Her marriage at the age of twenty-six to the aspiring writer Henry Nevinson helped to cement further her sense of being defined by a dominant culture that was not quite her own and her recognition of the need to assert her own rights and those of other women. The couple shared a love of Greek and German literature and fascination with the work of writers such as

---

[5] In the early years of their marriage the Nevinsons spent seaside holidays in Wales. Margaret Nevinson also went on Welsh walking tours.

[6] Margaret Wynne Nevinson, *Ancient Suffragettes* (London, [1913]).

[7] Margaret Wynne Nevinson, *Life's Fitful Fever: A Volume of Memories* (London, 1926), p. 44.

[8] R. N. Smart, 'Literate Ladies – a Fifty Year Experiment', *Alumnus Chronicle* (University of St Andrews), 59 (June 1968), 20–31.

Thomas Carlyle, but their year abroad immediately after their marriage was not simply due to intellectual tastes. Although neither mentioned it in their writings, she was pregnant. Their marriage produced resentment and regret on both sides.[9]

Henry Nevinson became an eminent war correspondent, a journalist, a writer of essays and fiction as well as a noted campaigner for causes at home and abroad. Although he took some time to establish his reputation, from the end of the nineteenth century until his death in 1941 he was well-known, especially for championing radical causes. Associated with campaigns such as exposing slavery in Portuguese Angola and self-determination in Georgia, he was usually found in the right place at the right time (for a journalist). Thus he was in Ladysmith when the siege began, in Russia in late 1905 and in Gallipoli in 1915. He was even present at the Place-Royal in Mons when the Armistice was declared on 11 November 1918.

Since Henry Nevinson either worked at night as a literary editor at home – their son recalled that he was rarely home before 3 or 4 a.m. – or abroad for months at a time covering wars, the Nevinsons did not enjoy a conventional marriage.[10] He also had several serious relationships. Margaret Nevinson was a deeply committed Anglo-Catholic and they never divorced. Instead they inhabited separate spaces within their house in Downside Crescent, Hampstead, and led independent public lives. They never even achieved a companionate marriage in later life. Seven months after Margaret Nevinson died, Henry Nevinson married the writer, suffragette and pacifist, Evelyn Sharp, with whom he had been involved for thirty years.

Margaret Nevinson had not found motherhood easy. When her son was born in August 1889 she contracted puerperal fever and nearly died. She admitted that the constant demands of small children was both trying and debilitating. Indeed, in her memoirs she baldly stated that 'it is a terrible thing to be a mother'.[11] She was also keen to stress that in comparison 'all other work and vocations are as child's play', yet in the eyes of the law and census, wives and mothers were unoccupied. As she put it, 'Man, carpenter, ten children, wife, no occupation'.[12] Her relationship with her daughter Philippa was never close. She clearly adored 'my boy', but the talented artist C. R. W. Nevinson proved to be obsessed with self and fame and, although he pointed up his mother's European outlook and modernity in

---

[9] This is explored in my forthcoming biography, *Henry W. Nevinson: War, Journalism and Justice.*

[10] C. R. W. Nevinson, *Paint and Prejudice* (London, [1937]), p. 5.

[11] Wynne Nevinson, *Life's Fitful Fever*, p. 113.

[12] Ibid., p. 114.

his autobiography, he never really credited either parent with the support they both provided in their own ways. He told a fellow art student that 'if my mother does happen to be in for a meal she is so engrossed in other things that she hardly hears & certainly never takes in a word I say'.[13]

Clearly, Margaret Nevinson's recourse to her Welsh background and feminism cannot simply be explained in terms of her upbringing and personal disillusionment with marriage. Yet they were important factors. Her published writings do not disguise her bitterness. The first story in her collection, *Fragments of Life,* debated the advantages and disadvantages of divorce. 'An Everyday Tragedy' suggests that a woman remains married because of her son, but can never forgive her husband's betrayals. Two other stories, evincing more polemic than narrative, stress that 'the wives of literary men must get used to being forgotten'.[14] The first few years of married life were the hardest and if a woman survived them without divorce or turning to drink or drugs, she would have learned indifference and have turned to 'philosophy or work or religion as an anodyne to despair'.

It is problematic to read too much into what purports to be fiction, but the title of Margaret Nevinson's autobiography was *Life's Fitful Fever,* a quotation which figures in *Macbeth* at a time when Duncan was in his grave, treason had done its worst and nothing, not even 'Malice domestic', could touch him. Like her husband's triple-decker memoirs, also published in the 1920s, this book refers only sparingly to a spouse and then with detachment.[15] Those who did not know the couple well referred to them as a pair of 'do gooders'. In a novel of 1916 by Gilbert Cannan entitled *Mendel,* the Nevinsons were parodied as the Mitchells who have 'a platform manner of speaking' and 'seemed to have their fingers in innumerable reforms'. But once the government was removed:

> Mr and Mrs Mitchell would raise their fingers and, hey presto! women would have votes, the slums would be pulled down, maternity would be endowed, prostitutes would be saved, prisons would be reformed, capital punishment abolished, the working classes would be properly housed . . .[16]

---

[13] From a letter to the art student Dora Carrington, quoted in Michael J. K. Walsh, *C. R. W. Nevinson: This Cult of Violence* (New Haven and London, 2002), p. 4; Nevinson, *Paint and Prejudice,* chap. 1.

[14] Wynne Nevinson, *Fragments of Life,* p. 119.

[15] Wendell Harris has observed how Evelyn Sharp features much more than Margaret in Henry Nevinson's autobiography. Wendell Harris, 'H. W. Nevinson, Margaret Wynne Nevinson, Evelyn Sharp: Little-Known Writers and Crusaders', *English Literature in Transition,* 45, no. 3 (2002), 291.

[16] Gilbert Cannan, *Mendel: A Story of Youth* (London, 1916), pp. 186–7.

Yet throughout her married life Margaret Nevinson held and articulated views distinct from those of her husband. She marked out her own space through the women's movement and here she gained the comradeship and respect which she lacked at home. This became most evident in the Edwardian years when Henry Nevinson was at the height of his activity. Margaret Nevinson's incipient feminism was now articulated through women's suffrage. She recognized how vital it was for women to extend on to the national stage the influence they could now exert at local government level.[17] She emerged as a witty speaker, but confessed to the 'dizzy sickness of terror' when she first stood up in a cart to address south London gas workers on the subject of suffrage.[18] She was a member of the Women's Franchise Declaration Committee, sat on the committee of the Hampstead branch of Mrs Fawcett's constitutionalist National Union of Women's Suffrage Societies (NUWSS) and joined the Women's Social and Political Union (WSPU) soon after its formation.

When the WSPU split in 1907 Margaret Nevinson became a founder member of the new Women's Freedom League (WFL). In 1909 she participated in a WFL deputation to the House of Commons to protest against the omission of votes for women from the King's Speech. She got caught up in the police charge, narrowly avoiding being trampled upon by horses. Fifty-six women were imprisoned. She gave evidence at one of the subsequent trials, arguing that Emily Duval had been unfairly arrested.[19] The WFL had active branches throughout Britain (including Aberdare, Barry, Cardiff, Carmarthen, Montgomery and Swansea) and it became renowned for its commitment to passive resistance. Margaret Nevinson embraced its tactics. She was a tax resister and was involved in a suffrage vigil outside Parliament in 1909.[20] She became a skilled speaker. At a debate organized by the Belsize Park branch of the Conservative and Unionist Women's Franchise Association, she won a motion 'That the parliamentary vote should be given to qualified women'. The WFL's paper *The Vote* praised her speech for its 'racy vigour and strong good sense, pointed by some admirable arguments and illustrations'.[21] She wrote several WFL pamphlets, including *Five Years' Struggle for Freedom: A History of the Suffrage Movement from 1908–12*. A branch treasurer for the WFL and national treasurer of the Women Writers' Suffrage League for nearly a decade, she was also active in the Hampstead branch of the Church League for Women's Suffrage (which, as

[17] See Patricia Hollis, *Ladies Elect: Women in English Local Government 1865–1914* (Oxford, 1987).
[18] Wynne Nevinson, *Life's Fitful Fever*, p. 212.
[19] PRO, HO144.1033/175.878.
[20] As Margaret Nevinson explained in the journal *Church League for Women's Suffrage* in May 1913, this also led to the founding of the eponymous Anglican suffrage society.
[21] *The Vote*, 5, no. 120 (10 February 1912).

late as 1915, included branches in Bangor, Cardiff, Ebbw Vale, Newport and Swansea).

Margaret Nevinson's gender politics and sense of Welshness coalesced in the Cymric Suffrage Union (CSU). Founded in London, this was the only surviving Welsh suffrage society since early suffrage societies within Wales had been subsumed under titles such as the Bristol and West of England Suffrage National Society. Subsequent societies were branches of, or affiliated to, the WSPU, WFL or, most commonly, the NUWSS.[22] The motto of the CSU was 'O Iesu n'ad Gamwaith' (Oh Jesus do not allow Unfairness) and its badge was a red dragon. Yet it amounted to more than just another special interest suffrage society.[23] It added a public and recreational forum and network for London-Welsh women at a time when they lacked the social and occupational opportunities open to their male counterparts. For Margaret Nevinson, who was outside the well-established chapel culture, this was especially welcome.

That women's suffrage deployed remarkably modern marketing techniques was exemplified in the WSPU's business breakfasts and careful display of suffrage colours. The Suffrage Coronation Procession of 1911, which involved at least 40,000 people, was a superb opportunity for suffrage as a spectacle and it was the one demonstration in which all suffrage societies participated. It included a Welsh contingent of women in home-made national Welsh costume. But in place of red, black and white they wore costumes in the WSPU colours of purple, white and green. This had been orchestrated by a Welsh socialist and suffragette, Edith Mansell Moullin.[24] Encouraged by the Welsh display, she founded the CSU in July 1911, and became a vice-president. Its president was Sybil Haig, wife of the Monmouthshire industrialist and Liberal MP, D. A. Thomas, and mother of the future Viscountess Rhondda, who founded the feminist journal *Time and Tide*.

Margaret Nevinson had been present in the procession, but chose to wear another symbol of significance to women: her graduation gown.[25]

---

[22] See Ryland Wallace, *'Organise! Organise! Organise!': A Study of Reform Agitations in Wales, 1840–86* (Cardiff, 1991), chap. 11.

[23] For these societies, see Elizabeth Crawford, *The Women's Suffrage Movement: A Reference Guide, 1866–1928* (London, 1999).

[24] Born in the late 1850s, her parents were Anne (née Lloyd) and David Collet Thomas, a merchant and shipowner. She was treasurer of the Church Socialist League, joined the WSPU, and was briefly imprisoned in Holloway in 1911. She later became a pacifist, did voluntary work with the blind of St Dunstan's and chaired the Society for Cultural Relations with the USSR. Museum of London, Suffragette Fellowship Collection, Letters from Edith Mansell Moullin to Edith How Martyn 1930–1935, 57.116/76–9.

[25] The Irish feminist, nationalist and teacher, Hanna Sheehy (also a linguist) chose to wear her graduation gown, as did her bridegroom Francis Skeffington, for their marriage in 1903. Margaret Ward, *Hanna Sheehy Skeffington: A Life* (Dublin, 1997), p. 27.

She marched with the contingent of women graduates. But now she joined the CSU.[26] Its headquarters was at the Mansell Moullin home in Wimpole Street, but it also had a few Welsh branches, including Ogmore Vale in the south and Penllyn and Edeyrnion in the north. Charles Mansell Moullin was a surgeon in the London Hospital and a vice-president of the Men's League for Women's Suffrage.

The majority of Welsh women living in London at this time worked in what might be called the 'Three Ds': the dairy trade, drapery (increasingly in the new department stores) and domestic service. It was felt worthwhile to approach the less deferential of these occupational groups. Thus milk-shops were canvassed and Mary E. Davies, the CSU secretary, organized visits to Welsh people living in her area of Fulham. Margaret Nevinson, Rachel Barrett, an Aberystwyth graduate and chief WSPU organizer for Wales, F. M. Thomas, a Pontycymmer headmistress, and Australian-born Muriel Matters, WFL organizer in Cardiff, all spoke for the CSU at the massive Hyde Park demonstration on 14 July 1912. This date was also celebrated as Mrs Pankhurst's birthday. The WSPU leader had actually been born on the previous day but, ever alert to publicity, chose to mark her birthday (13 July) on the following day, Bastille Day.[27] Banners with Welsh slogans were evident. Once again Welshness (of the nineteenth-century manufactured variety) was literally donned as they wore Welsh costume for the occasion.

In her speech Margaret Nevinson claimed that 'Chwarae Teg' (Fair Play) was loved by all in Wales. She even suggested that women's suffrage had not made much headway in Wales because Welsh women were better off than their Saxon sisters. What, for example, would the Welsh farmer do without his wife?[28] Yet, such rhetoric hid as much as it revealed. The hard work of the wives and daughters of many Welsh farmers certainly played a crucial part in the running of farms. But although generalized claims invested with patriotic sentiment may have been well received at the CSU's Platform 18, they avoided the realities of making headway with women's suffrage in Wales and, more fundamentally, the complexities of gender relations.

Margaret Nevinson had echoed similar sentiments at the CSU's first public meeting at the Steinway Hall in mid-March 1912. This event

[26] Angela V. John, '"A Draft of Fresh Air": Women's Suffrage, the Welsh and London', *THSC*, new series, 1 (1995), 81–93; eadem, '"Run like Blazes": the Suffragettes and Welshness', *Llafur*, 6, no. 3 (1994), 28–43.

[27] Paula Bartley, *Emmeline Pankhurst* (London, 2002), p. 15.

[28] *South Wales Daily News* (15 July 1912). See, too, Kay Cook and Neil Evans, '"The Petty Antics of the Bell-Ringing Boisterous Band"? The Women's Suffrage Movement in Wales, 1890–1918', in Angela V. John (ed.), *Our Mothers' Land: Chapters in Welsh Women's History 1830–1939* (Cardiff, 1991), pp. 159–209.

combined belated St David's Day celebrations and the advocacy of women's suffrage. The stewards wore Welsh costume and the secretary's speech was in Welsh. A resolution by the lawyer Walter Roch demanded women's suffrage. This Pembrokeshire Liberal MP was a member of the all-party Conciliation Committee which sought (ultimately in vain) a compromise suffrage bill. Margaret Nevinson seconded the resolution, invoking several stereotypes: 'the Welsh ought to make good suffragists because of the equality of the sexes, their love of democracy, and their power of speech'.[29] The meeting ended to the strains of 'Hen Wlad Fy Nhadau' (Land of my Fathers).

Margaret Nevinson's claims were called into question later that year by the infamous attack on suffragettes at Llanystumdwy in Caernarfonshire. Lloyd George, as chancellor of the exchequer, had already 'torpedoed' the compromise Conciliation Bill in November 1911. His bill would have granted a limited measure of women's suffrage. To add insult to injury, suffrage interrupters of his speech at the National Eisteddfod at Wrexham the following September were not only forcibly ejected and manhandled, but were also described as 'foolish people' by Lloyd George. The subsequent attack on suffragettes by local men during Lloyd George's speech at Llanystumdwy just a few weeks later signalled open season for verbal attacks on English suffragettes by the Welsh press and on Welshness and Liberalism by elements of the English press.

Margaret Nevinson's claims and loyalties were being tested. She wrote in the *Clarion* that 'as a Welshwoman' she had read with 'horror and shame' of the way women had been attacked. It had taken five policemen to extricate from her assailants the suffragette who had interrupted Lloyd George. Others had been kicked, beaten and partially stripped, and narrowly escaped drowning in the River Dwyfor. Until now, Margaret Nevinson warned, she had believed that her countrymen were courteous and chivalrous people.[30]

Internal divisions over tactics in the CSU led to a regrouping. The Forward Cymric Suffrage Union was formed in October 1912, at which time a major split also occurred in the WSPU. Spearheaded by Edith Mansell Moullin, the new Welsh society established closer links with Sylvia Pankhurst and East End suffragettes. They carried on into the war, but there is no evidence that Margaret Nevinson remained active. She had qualified some years earlier as a pioneer masseuse, and now worked for the Almeric-Paget Massage Corps, treating wounded soldiers in Hampstead Military Hospital.

[29] *Votes for Women* (23 March 1912).
[30] *Clarion* (4 October 1912).

Following the war, however, she continued her WFL work and contributed to their paper *The Vote* into the 1920s. In these years she became involved in other feminist campaigns and was a vice-president of the Women's Peace Crusade. She was active in championing the cause of the League of Nations and travelled the country lecturing on subjects such as infant welfare and (before she became a JP) the necessity of appointing women magistrates. Sometimes her talks took her to Wales. In the summer of 1920 she addressed an open-air meeting on the Aberystwyth promenade on both the League of Nations and equal pay for equal work.[31] She also wrote for the Women's True Temperance Committee, arguing not along the familiar teetotaller lines but recognizing that public houses fulfilled a potentially important place in communities and should be welcoming to all in the way that beer gardens and cafes were in Europe. Prohibition, she believed, entailed a dangerous interference with the liberty of the individual. Self-discipline and moderation were better solutions.[32]

Like her husband, Margaret Nevinson was active for many years in a range of causes. Their interests seem at first sight to have complemented each other well, but they held independent views and perspectives. Even when they broadly supported the same causes, they carved out different niches within them.[33] Henry Nevinson was also a key player in women's suffrage. He was a founder member of the Men's League and chaired the more militant Men's Political Union. Between 1907 and 1912 he was much more in sympathy with the Pankhursts than was his wife. He found the WFL dull. Whereas Margaret Nevinson drew upon her Welshness and celebrated it with like-minded London-Welsh suffrage supporters, the Englishman Henry Nevinson aligned himself with Irish cultural nationalism. In the 1890s he had been involved in the Irish cultural revival, reviewing the plays and poetry of Yeats and other Irish literary figures. His friends included a number of Sinn Féiners, he wrote frequently on Irish nationalism and, unlike his wife, stood by Roger Casement in 1916, and campaigned for his reprieve.[34]

On some issues the couple held markedly different views. They disagreed

---

[31] *The Vote* (13 August 1920).

[32] Margaret Wynne Nevinson, 'Self-Control versus Legislation', *The Woman's View* (January 1927), 3–7.

[33] Conversely, their friends Henrietta and Samuel Barnett used marriage as a firm springboard from which to conduct social challenges. Yet, until very recently, Henrietta Barnett has been effectively written out of this political partnership. See Seth Koven, 'Henrietta Barnett 1851–1936: the (Auto)biography of a Late Victorian Marriage', in Susan Pedersen and Peter Mandler (eds), *After the Victorians: Private Conscience and Public Duty In Modern Britain: Essays in Memory of John Clive* (London, 1994), pp. 31–53.

[34] Margaret Nevinson's autobiography displays an unsympathetic and stereotypical picture of both Irish and Jewish communities in the East End of London.

about the South African war, Margaret Nevinson opposing her husband's increasingly pro-Boer stance. Also her religious faith became more prominent as he emphatically rejected organized religion. She lamented the fact that 'the average husband of to-day has degenerated in his knowledge of things spiritual' and contrasted this with the eloquence and devotion of Welsh women during the 1904–5 Revival.[35] In 1905 she heard Evan Roberts preach near Merthyr Tydfil to an overflowing chapel congregation, and later devoted four pages of her autobiography to this Welsh visit.[36]

The Nevinsons did not share party-political beliefs. Margaret Nevinson had flirted with Fabianism in the 1890s. Although alienated by Asquith's opposition to women's suffrage, she became a Liberal. Newly enfranchised in 1918, she went to Scarborough to support the election campaign of the poet Osbert Sitwell, who was standing as a Liberal, as soon as she had recovered from influenza. He found her 'an accomplished and convincing speaker'.[37] In contrast, having briefly aligned himself to the Social Democratic Federation, Henry Nevinson then became a Liberal until, after the First World War, he joined the Labour Party. Both of them turned down several requests to stand for Parliament.

Both were crusading journalists who also wrote fiction. Henry Nevinson's volume of 'slum stories', *Neighbours of Ours,* won critical praise in the mid-1890s.[38] His wife claimed at one stage that she had written this book.[39] Although the style and Henry Nevinson's own notes suggest that he was actually the author, the material for a number of these stories appears to have been based on Margaret Nevinson's experiences as a rent-collector in two large blocks of artisans' dwellings, Lolesworth and Katharine Buildings in Whitechapel. Yet she received no acknowledgement in the publication. She also undertook research at the British Museum for *Celebrities of the Century*, a vast biographical dictionary in seventeen parts. In the preface Henry Nevinson was acknowledged as the editor's 'right-hand man'. Yet there was no reference to a 'right-hand' woman.[40]

As we have seen, Margaret Nevinson also penned short stories, some of which appear to have drawn on personal experience. 'The Story of a Lonely Woman' is about a Welsh high school teacher in London who, in order to avoid a nervous breakdown, escapes to a Caernarfonshire cottage which is haunted by a woman who had committed suicide after discovering

[35] Mrs H. W. Nevinson, 'Juvenal on Latter-Day Problems: an Unscholarly Gossip', *Fortnightly Review*, 87 (1907), 913.

[36] Wynne Nevinson, *Life's Fitful Fever*, pp. 173–7.

[37] Osbert Sitwell, *Laughter in the Next Room* (London, 1950), p. 108.

[38] H. W. Nevinson, *Neighbours of Ours* (London, 1895).

[39] Bodleian Library, Oxford, Nevinson Papers, Journals of Henry Woodd Nevinson, e611/1, 23 January 1901.

[40] Lloyd C. Sanders (ed.), *Celebrities of the Century* (London, 1887), p. vi.

that her husband had been living with another woman.[41] The narrator, like Mrs Jones in 'Killed in Action', prides herself on possessing second sight. So did Margaret Nevinson, attributing it to her Celtic descent. Like her husband, Margaret Nevinson also published stories about working-class people on the margins of society. Indeed, her most influential writing was based on her experiences as a Poor Law Guardian. Whereas Henry Nevinson largely operated on an international basis, Margaret Nevinson dedicated herself to work in the local community. Women had been entitled to stand as Poor Law Guardians since 1875 and Hampstead was one of the first boards in the country to include them. The Hampstead Minute Book reveals Margaret Nevinson's exemplary record of dedication and attendance from her appointment in the autumn of 1904 to the end of December 1921. She attended between fifty and sixty meetings annually, and in some years exceeded this. She chaired subcommittees, attended conferences and was not afraid to ask awkward questions or to champion women's rights.[42]

Such experiences equipped Margaret Nevinson to write about problems facing working-class women. For example, one of her many columns in the WFL newspaper, *The Vote,* argued that prostitution should be seen as an economic rather than a moral problem. Since women were forced into prostitution by low wages, a living wage was much more important than philanthropy. Moreover, she also criticized the allocation of old-age pensions. She also fashioned graphic fictional sketches about workhouse life, which appeared in the *Westminster Gazette*, the *Daily News* and the *Daily Herald.*

In 1918 all twenty-six of her stories appeared in one volume called *Workhouse Characters.* This was highly praised by the American suffrage leader Susan B. Anthony.[43] One, set in a casual ward, was about an old Welsh sailor. Another was turned into a play published by the International Suffrage Shop. It was performed in 1911 at the Kingsway Theatre, London, by a female cast provided by the Pioneer Players (run by Ellen Terry's daughter, Edith Craig). It focused on the fact that a married man still had the legal right to decree that his wife be detained in a workhouse against her will. Its subject matter and politics were deemed offensive and provoked a somewhat dubious coyness from the mainstream press. One critic described the men in the audience as 'suffused with blushes'.[44] The reviewer for *The Times* explained that 'we had walked in so innocently imagining that the

[41] In Nevinson, *Fragments of Life*, pp. 24–43.

[42] Greater London Record Office, Hampstead Minute Book, Hp B.G. vols. 30–40.

[43] Margaret Wynne Nevinson, *Workhouse Characters, and Other Sketches of the Life of the Poor* (London, [1918]); Bodleian Library, Nevinson Journals, e622/3.

[44] Wynne Nevinson, *Life's Fitful Fever*, pp. 224–5.

Pioneering of the Pioneer Players was to be dramatic, not (if it may be pardoned the ugly word) feminist'.[45] But by providing such a strong indictment of the antediluvian state of the law relating to married women, Margaret Nevinson's 'disgusting drama' was instrumental in changing the law two years later.[46]

Yet, despite this and her pioneering work in the 1920s as a woman magistrate, Margaret Nevinson has not been well remembered. She cannot be said to have been airbrushed out of Welsh history for she never entered it. Like many Celtic women and men living in England, her allegiances were complicated and not one-dimensional. A powerful need for identity allied to a sense of being defined by others has recently been explored in a modern setting by Charlotte Williams, the daughter of a black father from Guyana and a white Welsh mother. Growing up in north Wales, then travelling in Africa and the Caribbean, she experienced a need for both roots and wings. This is echoed in Margaret Nevinson's search for what constituted home.[47] And although the category of London-Welsh appeared to provide some sense of belonging, Margaret Nevinson did not qualify as one of the 27,000 or so Welsh-born Londoners living there in 1911.[48]

Apart from fleeting references to her work in London's East End,[49] she has not featured in English historical accounts. This is perhaps not surprising. Unlike her husband, who courted fame, she seemed to shun personal attention. How many other autobiographies can there be where the subject neither mentions when she was born nor includes a picture of herself? Indeed, much of *Life's Fitful Fever* deliberately conceals and confuses.[50] Published in 1926, it needs to be seen as a statement about a woman in her late sixties looking back at lost opportunities. It is best read contrapuntally, providing an unspoken yet distinct challenge to Henry Nevinson's much-praised autobiography. Two of his three volumes had already appeared to great acclaim: *Changes and Chances* in 1923 and *More*

---

[45] Quoted in Lis Whitelaw, *The Life and Rebellious Times of Cicely Hamilton* (London, 1990), p. 125.

[46] Wynne Nevinson, *Workhouse Characters*, pp. 9–10.

[47] Charlotte Williams, *Sugar and Slate* (Aberystwyth, 2002). See also R. F. Foster, *The Irish Story: Telling Tales and Making it up in Ireland* (London, 2002 edn), especially pp. 97–8.

[48] See Emrys Jones (ed.), *The Welsh in London: 1500–2000* (Cardiff, 2001).

[49] See Rosemary O'Day, 'How Families Lived then: Katharine Buildings, East Smithfield, 1885–1890', in Ruth Finnegan and Michael Drake (eds), *From Family Tree to Family History* (Cambridge, 1994), pp. 129–66. See, too, Ellen Ross, *The Lady Explorer in the Slums of London* (Berkeley, forthcoming).

[50] See Foster's assessment of the autobiographical intentions of the Anglo-Irish writer Elizabeth Bowen, whose writings also dealt with the complexities of national identity and belonging: 'Elizabeth Bowen and the Landscape of Childhood', in Foster, *The Irish Story*, pp. 148–63.

Changes: More Chances in 1925.[51] A one-volume abridged version of Henry Nevinson's memoirs, entitled *Fire of Life*, appeared in the mid-1930s after Margaret Nevinson's death. His title genuflected to hers, but asserted a distinctiveness in tone.

Margaret Nevinson's suffrage activities and writings have recently received some attention from historians working in the burgeoning area of modern suffrage studies.[52] Yet she mainly falls into the interstices of historical writing. This can partly be attributed to a lack of personal papers. Henry Nevinson, in contrast, left a very detailed diary covering almost fifty years. His first wife is absent from most of this and, where she does feature, his comments are usually critical and dismissive. Even on the day of her death in 1932 he referred in his diary to their 'dismal marriage' in 1884 and how she was 'little suited to me' and was 'always inclined to contradict me on every point & all occasions'.[53] He did, however, concede that she was 'eloquent in the Welsh manner' and 'humorous & full of observant stories'. Other members of the Nevinson family seem to have believed themselves to be socially superior to the Jones family and had little to do with Margaret Nevinson over the years.[54]

Her life story cautions us about the problems associated with certain sources. Although great care has to be exercised in reading the texts of personal diaries, we do not have a matching source for Margaret Nevinson. There is no parallax view. Knowledge of her opinions is problematically refracted through her husband's perspectives and those of their well-known son, whose own autobiography is notoriously unreliable.[55] Modern biographical studies might now pay more attention to the wives of famous men than used to be the case. However, navigating the divergent interests of Margaret and Henry Nevinson warns us of the dangers of assuming a congruence in purposes and beliefs between couples who at first sight appear to have endorsed similar progressive agendas.

Margaret Nevinson searched for an identity distinct from that of wife and mother. Not surprisingly, contemporaries portrayed her as challenging convention. Ernest Rhys, editor of the Everyman's Library series and a neighbour, described her in his autobiography as 'formidable', gaily

[51] His final volume, *Last Changes: Last Chances,* was published in 1928.
[52] For example, Claire Eustance, 'Daring to be Free: the Evolution of Women's Political Identities in the Women's Freedom League, 1907–1930' (unpubl. University of York D.Phil. thesis, 1993); Sheila Stowell, *A Stage of their Own: Feminist Playwrights of the Suffrage Era* (Manchester, 1992); Maroula Joannou and June Purvis (eds), *The Women's Suffrage Movement: New Feminist Perspectives* (Manchester, 1998).
[53] Bodleian Library, Nevinson Papers, 625/4, Journal of 8 June 1932.
[54] The Society of Antiquaries of London, Nevinson Papers, Diaries of John Lea Nevinson, vol. 3, 15 September 1924.
[55] Walsh, *C. R. W. Nevinson*, p. 1.

regaling his ailing wife Grace 'in a deep voice with some of the mortal horrors' she had recently witnessed in a hospital ward.[56] Nationality and gender mattered to Margaret Nevinson. Living in the shadow of her famous rebel husband and outspoken artistic son, she too rebelled. She eschewed the conventional married life of a woman of her class. Yet she did so when it was difficult for women to be appreciated in their own right. Her Welsh roots formed a vital constituent of the self that she cultivated. Choosing not to be defined by the dominant English culture which surrounded her,[57] she became part of a group of like-minded London-Welsh women. But her rejection of 'otherness' found its most sustained and articulate expression in her claims for citizenship for women and in her interpretation of the legal system in committees, in court work and also in her writing. For example, drawing on her experience as a JP, she published a wide-ranging pamphlet entitled *The Legal Wrongs of Married Women* (1923).[58]

Her canvas was much more modest than that of her husband, but the contribution which she made to society via the local community should not be underestimated. She was a school manager for a quarter of a century, a committed Poor Law Guardian who worked with the dispossessed and fought frequent battles on behalf of her gender within the board for eighteen years, an assiduous justice of the peace, and a member of the Magistrates' Association. This was at a time when women magistrates were a novelty as well as a minority, and she helped to publicize their work in the media by participating in early radio broadcasts on the subject.[59] Women like Margaret Nevinson had to make the most of gendered expectations about what was deemed 'fit work' for them. When she went to enquire at Hampstead Police Court about when she would be sworn in as a magistrate, she was told 'we don't have any ladies here'. Explaining that she was one of the new JPs, the young policeman 'blushed crimson' and replied that it would be very awkward for him: 'We have such dreadful cases here. I shan't know how to say what it is my duty to say, ma'am, with ladies present. Women are always made to leave the Court before these cases are taken, even the women police.'[60] Yet, as Anne Logan has argued, these

---

[56] Ernest Rhys, *Wales England Wed: An Autobiography* (London, 1940), pp. 158–9.

[57] It is worth, however, heeding Kenneth O. Morgan's warning about how Margaret Nevinson's better-known contemporary Lloyd George, another provincial outsider in London, drew upon Welsh life when it suited him. Kenneth O. Morgan, 'Writing Political Biography', in Eric Homberger and John Charmley (eds), *The Troubled Face of Biography* (Basingstoke, 1988), pp. 44–5.

[58] Margaret Wynne Nevinson, *The Legal Wrongs of Married Women* (London, 1923).

[59] For example, BBC Radio, 22 April 1924. I am grateful to Kate Murphy for this reference.

[60] *The Vote* (30 July 1920).

pioneer women helped to change the magistracy and spearheaded new approaches to work on the bench.[61]

Margaret Nevinson's imagined community was a Welsh nation, devout and anxious to dispense justice to men and women (though the events at Llanystumdwy forced some adjustment to this romanticized picture). Her goal was a vote and equality for women. Yet, although in her story of 1922 the north Walian Mrs Jones laughs at what Londoners call a hill, Parliament Hill was a steep climb. And in the mean time the London-Welsh woman Margaret Nevinson (née Jones) continued the unpaid, largely unsung and uphill task of working for a community in north London.

'Exiles' do not always fit easily into accounts of Welsh history. But there is a final irony, one familiar to historians of gender. The opposition of women like Margaret Nevinson to ascribed identities has not infrequently resulted in their actual achievements being sublimated and forgotten precisely because we do not always know how to read and appreciate the identities they constructed.

---

[61] Anne Logan, 'Making Women Magistrates: Feminism, Citizenship and Justice in England and Wales 1918–1950' (unpubl. University of Greenwich Ph.D. thesis, 2002).

15

'Conservative Bloom on Socialism's Compost Heap': Working-Class Home Ownership in South Wales, c.1890–1939

STEVEN THOMPSON

In the late nineteenth and twentieth centuries the industrial valleys of south Wales were characterized by relatively high levels of working-class home ownership. This feature of Welsh industrial society, which set it apart from other coalfields and most other urban areas of Britain, has long been recognized by Welsh, and indeed other, historians.[1] But apart from the recognition of this fact, and some awareness of the building clubs through which many working-class families were able to purchase their own homes, historians have failed to appreciate many of the more intriguing and insightful causes, consequences and implications of this important aspect of modern Welsh society. They have failed to examine the aspirations and motivations which led families to purchase their own homes and the consequences that ownership had for political attitudes and behaviour. An examination of these aspects of working-class life in modern Welsh society allows a fascinating insight into the world-views of working-class people and demonstrates some of the inter-relationships which existed between private and public spheres of working-class life. Such a study allows us to appreciate some of the social bases of Welsh politics in the past.

In common with the Lancashire cotton towns, shipbuilding towns such as Jarrow and, to a lesser extent, the Yorkshire wool districts and some

---

[1] Kenneth O. Morgan, *Rebirth of a Nation: Wales 1880–1980* (Oxford, 1981), p. 72; Martin J. Daunton, 'Miners' Houses: South Wales and the Great Northern Coal Field, 1880–1914', *International Review of Social History*, 25, no. 2 (1980), 143–75; M. J. Fisk, *Housing in the Rhondda 1800–1940* (Cardiff, 1996), pp. 48–56; idem, *Home Truths: Issues for Housing in Wales* (Llandysul, 1996), pp. 10–12; John Benson, *British Coalminers in the Nineteenth Century: A Social History* (Dublin, 1980), pp. 107–8.

isolated suburbs of south-east London, south Wales was an area of relatively high levels of working-class owner-occupation.[2] The precise levels of working-class home ownership, or even home ownership more generally, are difficult to gauge, but some tentative estimates have been made. H. Stanley Jevons estimated in 1914 that the level of owner-occupation in the mining communities in south Wales ranged from about 5 per cent in Merthyr Tydfil to 60 per cent in certain valleys such as the Rhondda Fach.[3] It was claimed in the Edwardian period, for example, that 'the town of Ferndale is largely owned by working men'.[4] Similarly, a housing survey made in the Nant-y-glo and Blaenau Urban District in Monmouthshire in 1920 found that 29 per cent of the houses in the urban district were owner-occupied and this figure had increased to 33 per cent by 1934.[5] The level of owner-occupation was generally higher in the western anthracite district. It was estimated that at least 40 per cent of the workmen residing in the Pontardawe Rural District owned the houses they inhabited, while in the Llanelli Rural District the proportion was in excess of 80 per cent.[6]

The motivations behind such high levels of working-class home ownership require explanation. Martin J. Daunton and Malcolm Fisk have outlined the activities of the building clubs which were used by working-class families to purchase their own houses, but, as Diamaris Rose has commented, such studies do not shed any light on the attitudes of working-class families towards home ownership and the motivations which led them to form building clubs and acquire houses.[7] Historians of other countries have posited a number of different reasons which prompted families to acquire their own homes. They have argued that families viewed home ownership as a sign of social ascendance, as a financial investment, as the only reliable means of acquiring adequate housing accommodation, and as a form of enforced saving. American historians have linked the aspiration

---

[2] Mark Swenarton and Sandra Taylor, 'The Scale and Nature of the Growth of Owner-Occupation in Britain between the Wars', *Economic History Review*, 38, no. 3 (1985), 378.

[3] NLW, H. Stanley Jevons I, 126: Housing in Wales, Prefatory Report, p. 17; NLW, Rhondda Prefatory Memorandum, p. 13.

[4] *Western Mail* (15 November 1907), p. 4.

[5] Gwent Record Office, Nantyglo and Blaina UDC, Sanitary Inspector's Report Book (calculated from the summaries of the Housing Surveys printed at the back of the Report Book).

[6] Ministry of Health, *Report of the South Wales Regional Survey Committee* (London, 1921), pp. 15–16.

[7] Daunton, 'Miners' Houses'; Fisk, *Housing in the Rhondda*; Diamaris Rose, 'Home Ownership, Uneven Development and Industrial Change in Later Nineteenth-Century Britain' (unpubl. University of Sussex Ph.D. thesis, 1984), pp. 259–60.

to home ownership to the 'American Dream' of prosperity, democracy and social status.[8]

The rationale behind working-class house ownership in south Wales has not been explored and yet there is sufficient evidence to reveal many of the motivations of Welsh families. First, building clubs can be viewed as a means of self-help from the housing shortages which afflicted south Wales in the period up to 1914. The supply of houses failed to keep pace with the massive population increases experienced in the mining districts in the late nineteenth and early twentieth centuries. The valleys of south Wales lacked a large middle class which might have invested in housing provision, while other methods of housing provision – by industrialists, speculative builders and local authorities – were insufficient to meet the demand. Consequently, groups of working people came together to provide themselves with houses. Building clubs were viewed as a rational, even admirable, response to housing needs.[9] Mountain Ash, for example, was described as a 'conspicuous example of self-help', where people had 'aroused themselves' and solved 'their own problems in a sensible, business-like manner'.[10] In such accounts, the provision of houses was more important than the question of ownership.

Secondly, many working-class families aspired to own their own houses in order to be free of the exploitation of private landlords and to protect themselves from the insecurity of tenure which characterized rented property. For example, at a meeting of the landlords of Nant-y-moel in the autumn of 1900 it was decided to increase the rents of working-class houses by 10–20 per cent. At a subsequent protest meeting, it was suggested that the workmen in the area should organize on cooperative principles and build their own houses. Job Baker, who was present at that meeting, commented: 'The workmen are cutting their own throats. A fellow workman recently offered my landlord 5s. additional rent if he should occupy my house.'[11] Similarly, an Abertillery councillor, J. E. Rowlands, was in favour of workers owning their own houses because it gave them independence. He

---

[8] Far more work has been carried out on home ownership in a north American context: see Matthew Edel, Elliott D. Sclar and Daniel Luria, *Shaky Palaces: Homeownership and Social Mobility in Boston's Suburbanization* (New York, 1984); Richard Harris and Chris Hamnett, 'The Myth of the Promised Land: the Social Diffusion of Home Ownership in Britain and North America', *Annals of the Association of American Geographers*, 77, no. 2 (1987), 173–90; Richard Harris, 'Working-Class Home Ownership in the American Metropolis', *Journal of Urban History*, 17, no. 1 (1990), 46–69; see also Marc Choko, 'Investment or Family Home? House Ownership in Paris at the Turn of the Twentieth Century', *Journal of Urban History*, 23, no. 5 (1997), 531–68.

[9] *Western Mail* (11 June 1904), p. 4; (15 June 1904), p. 4; (20 June 1904), p. 4.

[10] *Western Mail* (21 June 1904), p. 4.

[11] *Rhondda Leader* (15 September 1900), p. 5.

commented in 1914 that he knew of a tenant who had paid rent faithfully for twenty years but who had received notice to quit from the landlord.[12] Home ownership also entailed independence of a more prosaic kind and it was believed that owners became 'masters of their own particular castles . . . at liberty to alter the interior or add to the premises to suit their individual taste'.[13]

There was also a suggestion that workmen who formed building clubs were able to obtain better and more sanitary housing accommodation than if they rented from private landlords.[14] The houses built by building clubs in the late nineteenth and early twentieth centuries were superior in quality and comfort to the houses intended for workers built in the early nineteenth century.[15] Speculative builders had no incentive to invest in high standards of comfort and, it was argued, merely hoped to extract the highest return from minimal investment. Building clubs and the aspiration to home ownership, therefore, were rational reactions to poor housing standards. On the other hand, 'Matron', the women's columnist in the *Rhondda Socialist*, dismissed building-club houses as being just as insanitary as other houses and claimed that they were unsatisfactory because they were not designed to 'lessen women's labour'.[16]

Lastly, various economic factors underpinned the motivations of many working-class families. Many of them invested in house property as a means of saving for the future and it was commented that miners favoured this form of investment over other methods of saving.[17] Charles Booth suggested that miners in Merthyr invested in cottage property as a strategy to provide for themselves in their old age.[18] This economic rationale for home ownership is further demonstrated by the small number of working-class families who became 'small capitalists' and purchased more than one house.[19] Walter Haydn Davies, for example, remembered how the 'hard working, striving people' of the community joined building clubs in

---

[12] *South Wales Gazette* (15 May 1914), p. 3.

[13] *Pontypridd Chronicle* (3 May 1902), p. 6.

[14] *South Wales Daily News* (17 June 1907), p. 6; *Pontypridd Chronicle* (22 February 1902), p. 4.

[15] See the series of special articles on the housing problem in south Wales published in the *Western Mail* in June and July 1904.

[16] *Rhondda Socialist* (11 May 1912), p. 2.

[17] Commission of Enquiry into the Coal Industry, II, *Reports and Minutes of Evidence* [Cmd. 360], 1919, xii, p. 702.

[18] Charles Booth, *The Aged Poor in England and Wales* (London, 1894), p. 247; similarly, Helen Bosanquet, *The Strength of the People* (London, 1903), p. 238; *Merthyr Express* (9 November 1901), p. 5.

[19] Fisk, *Home Truths,* pp. 10–11; see also Commission of Enquiry into the Coal Industry, II, p. 1081, Q25,550; H. Stanley Jevons, *The British Coal Trade* (London, 1915), p. 647.

order to acquire a second or third property – 'Great faith was put in bricks and mortar', he explained.[20] It is interesting to speculate how workers and 'small landlords' who owned one or two houses acted as landlords. How did they choose their tenants? What rents did they impose? How did they react to arrears of rent? Such questions are extremely difficult to answer with any degree of accuracy, but they could provide fascinating insights into the beliefs and attitudes of working people. It was reported in 1904, for example, that some workers in Merthyr had acquired several houses and even, in some cases, rows of houses, and that they were 'as vigorous in rack-renting as anyone'. 'Complaints against working men landlords are frequent in Merthyr and Dowlais', it was commented.[21]

The thrift required to acquire a house was believed to be an admirable attribute in itself and a sure sign of a man's good character and respectability. At a banquet to celebrate the winding up of the Hillside No. 2 Building Club of Cwm-parc in 1909, for example, the chairman congratulated the members for their thrift and foresight, and proudly noted that there were fewer recipients of parish relief in their district than in other parts of the Rhondda.[22] Moreover, while they focused to a large extent on the economic advantages assumed to derive from home ownership, discussions of the advantages offered by building societies, and the publicity material produced by those building societies, nevertheless gave a great deal of attention to the idea that thrift was an admirable quality in itself, to be encouraged for its own sake as much as for the economic advantages it could bring.[23]

The economic rationale for home ownership assumed a greater significance during the economic depression of the inter-war period. That period witnessed a massive growth in home ownership in Britain as a result of increasing affluence and developments in mortgage provision. In south Wales, however, working-class families were more likely to sell houses than to purchase them, as houses were utilized as a realizable asset that could be liquidated to provide a badly needed source of income. It was noted that in the Nant-y-glo and Blaenau area in the late 1920s a large proportion of the houses formerly owned by miners had either been sold or was heavily

[20] W. H. Davies, *The Right Place – The Right Time: Memories of Boyhood Days in a Welsh Mining Community* (Llandybïe, 1972), pp. 66–7; Davies's parents sold one of the houses they owned to pay for his education.
[21] *Western Mail* (11 June 1904), p. 4.
[22] *Rhondda Leader* (1 May 1909), p. 4.
[23] See the assorted material in Glamorgan Record Office, D/D Vau Box 4; see also the series of articles on the Starr-Bowkett building societies in *Western Mail* (4–23 May 1893).

mortgaged.[24] A respondent to the American sociologist G. H. Armbruster, who conducted research for his doctoral thesis in the Blaenafon–Pontypool area in the late 1930s, noted how house-owners were forced 'to sell the house and eat it' because of the economic difficulties caused by coal strikes and lockouts in the 1920s.[25] This remarkable phrase – 'to sell the house and eat it' – neatly encapsulates the idea of the consumption of housing as an economic commodity to be realized if economic circumstance dictated, an investment to be realized on 'a rainy day'.[26]

This claim, however, needs to be qualified by the difficulties house-owners in the more depressed communities encountered in selling a house or obtaining a mortgage during the inter-war depression. The market in house property ebbed just at the moment when owner-occupiers needed money. Cottage property was said to be almost worthless in Maerdy, where in 1928 one house was sold for a mere £50, while in the Glyncorrwg Urban District many cottages were abandoned and one collier was able to obtain a mortgage of £25 on the house he owned.[27] As was commented at the time, 'houses in these districts are a drug in the market, and both private owners and public authorities find their property almost valueless'.[28] This was in the most depressed areas, however, during the depths of the slump and house-owners were still able to gain some return on their property in other parts of south Wales during the inter-war period.[29]

However, some individuals challenged the alleged economic benefits of home ownership. A correspondent to the *Merthyr Express* in 1908, having pointed out the burdensome costs involved in purchasing his home, claimed that 'it's not all rose-water to become your own landlord' and argued that a family was forced to live in misery in order to repay the mortgage and other costs.[30] Even more critically, a correspondent to the *Glamorgan Gazette* questioned whether or not thrift itself was such a good idea. He claimed that some house-owners 'work and scrape, neglect their bodily needs and mental and moral requirements of themselves and their families'. Such

---

[24] Labour Party Committee of Inquiry, *The Distress in South Wales* (London, 1928), p. 6; see also Hilda Jennings, *Brynmawr: A Study of a Distressed Area* (London, [1934]), pp. 86, 158, 181.

[25] G. H. Armbruster, 'The Social Determination of Ideologies: being a study of a Welsh Mining Community' (unpubl. University of London Ph.D. thesis, 1940), p. 273.

[26] *Rhondda Leader* (1 May 1909), p. 4.

[27] Labour Party Committee of Inquiry, *The Distress in South Wales*, pp. 14, 15; Jennings, *Brynmawr: A Study of a Distressed Area*, p. 92.

[28] Labour Party Committee of Inquiry, *The Distress in South Wales*, p. 16.

[29] The father of George Ewart Evans gradually sold the 'three or four' houses his family owned in the early 1920s as his grocery business suffered; George Ewart Evans, *The Strength of the Hills: An Autobiography* (London, 1983), pp. 26, 27, 31.

[30] *Merthyr Express* (28 November 1908), p. 12; see also *South Wales Gazette* (15 May 1914), p. 3.

people were 'unattractive and even repulsive' because they spent no money on themselves and did not allow their personalities to grow. This was not thrift, he claimed, but suicide.[31] More generally, critics of building clubs argued that the clubs merely enriched middle-class investors who supported the clubs financially.[32]

The high level of owner-occupation in the communities of south Wales inevitably raises questions about the consequences for political attitudes and social behaviour. This has long been a controversial issue. In a series of lectures given in 1872 Friedrich Engels argued that the increased working-class home ownership advocated by some contemporaries would lead to greater control of workers by industrialists and a general deterioration in the living standards of the working class.[33] Unsurprisingly, working-class ownership of housing has formed part of the debate on the conservatism of the 'aristocracy of labour' in the second half of the nineteenth century. It has been claimed that this section of the working class had interests in common with the middle class and stood to gain more by their cooperation with capitalism than by their opposition to it. Home ownership was one of the many aspects of everyday life that set this privileged section of the working class apart from its less wealthy counterparts and contributed to its reformist, cooperative attitude.[34] More generally, some historians have argued that western governments promoted home ownership as part of a more general strategy to secure capitalism and buttress the political status quo.[35] During the 1980s those on the right hoped, and those on the left feared, that the sale of local authority housing to tenants would make the British working class more

---

[31] *Glamorgan Gazette* (26 June 1914), p. 6; see also ibid. (3 July 1914), p. 7. It is notable that property sales occasionally included shares in building clubs, which suggests that families found it difficult to keep up their contributions and were forced to sell their shares; for examples, see *Merthyr Express* (12 February 1910), p. 10; *South Wales Gazette* (8 October 1909), p. 3.

[32] *Western Mail* (15 June 1904), p. 4; ibid. (20 June 1904), p. 4.

[33] Friedrich Engels, *The Housing Question* (London, 1935); for a commentary on these lectures, see Edel, Sclar and Luria, *Shaky Palaces*, pp. 189–94.

[34] Geoffrey Crossick, *An Artisan Elite in Victorian Society: Kentish London 1840–1880* (London, 1978), pp. 146–9; Robert Gray, *The Aristocracy of Labour in Nineteenth-Century Britain, c.1850–1900* (London, 1981), p. 38; Joseph Melling, 'Introduction', in idem, *Housing, Social Policy and the State* (London, 1980), pp. 19, 28.

[35] Edel, Sclar and Luria, *Shaky Palaces*, pp. 171–94; P. Van Den Eeckhout, 'Belgium', in C. G. Pooley (ed.), *Housing Strategies in Europe, 1880–1930* (Leicester, 1992), pp. 199–200; C. G. Pooley, 'Towards a Comparative Perspective', in idem, *Housing Strategies in Europe*, pp. 333–5; Peter Saunders, *Urban Politics: A Sociological Interpretation* (London, 1979), pp. 81–3.

conservative and ensure electoral success for the Conservative Party.[36] Therefore, home ownership has been viewed as an important influence on social beliefs and political attitudes, and it is believed that ownership serves to make individuals more conservative.

It is extremely difficult to correlate forms of housing tenure in the past with political attitudes. It is impossible to identify the forms of housing tenure experienced by individuals who advocated particular political choices or held particular political views. However, there is a great deal of evidence to suggest what contemporaries believed were the consequences of home ownership for political outlooks and attitudes. This impression-istic evidence suggests that individuals who purchased their own houses did indeed become more conservative. The Rhondda writer Ron Berry, for example, described the high level of owner-occupation in the Rhondda as a 'conservative bloom on socialism's compost heap'.[37] More significantly, many individuals advocated that workers should be encouraged and supported in their attempts to own their own houses. Moreover, the arguments they made to further the spread of home ownership are indicative of the benefits which they believed would be obtained by the men and by the community as a whole. For example, at the time of the sale of 175 Bute cottages at Aberdare in January 1916, a writer in the *Aberdare Leader* noted the widespread aspiration among the tenants to purchase their homes:

> This indeed was a natural and laudable ambition. It was not only good for the tenant but good for the district . . . It meant that every such person would have a stake in the parish; it meant better and more thoughtful citizens; more civic pride; greater stability in working men; increased interest in local affairs; and a more jealous survey of the kind of candidates who are put on District Council and Board of Guardians. In short the man who becomes the owner of his own house is often converted from the irresponsible and don't-care-a-hang sort to the stable, serious and reflecting sort. It was to the interest of all who had an interest in the locality to encourage and help the dwellers of the Bute Cottages to purchase their little, modest homes.[38]

When the sale took place it appeared that many tenants were outbid by

[36] D. C. Thorns, 'Owner-Occupation: its Significance for Wealth Transfer and Class Formation', *Sociological Review*, 29, no. 4 (1981), 705–28; Matthew Edel, 'Home Ownership and Working Class Unity', *International Journal of Urban and Regional Research,* 6 (1982), 205–22.

[37] Ron Berry, *History is what you Live* (Llandysul, 1998), p. 14.

[38] *Aberdare Leader* (5 February 1916), p. 2; for another example, see *Pontypridd Chronicle* (2 June 1902), p. 7.

representatives of the Bwllfa Colliery Company, and the correspondent of the *Aberdare Leader* decried the effects this would have on the community.[39]

It is perhaps unsurprising, in view of the effects that home ownership was believed to have on owner-occupiers, that industrialists promoted working-class home ownership. The most active company in this regard was undoubtedly the Ebbw Vale Steel, Iron and Coal Company. It owned a great deal of the building land in the Ebbw Vale district and, from 1896, it embarked on a sustained campaign to promote building clubs to erect houses for its workmen. Providing that all the members of a building club were workmen at its various works, the company advanced money to fund the erection of houses at a rate of interest of 4 per cent and then took responsibility for collecting the repayments from its workers. By 1904 the company was funding sixteen such building clubs, while by 1907 it had advanced £66,000 to its workmen to enable them to own the houses they inhabited, and was promoting and financing three building companies which had built 450 houses by that time.[40] In enabling its workers to purchase their own houses, the Ebbw Vale Company was pursuing a policy that benefited its industrial aims. Not only did it ensure a ready supply of labour but, as was commented, 'a well-housed workman is a good workman'.[41]

There exists even more revealing evidence of the intentions of industrialists who promoted working-class home ownership. Colliery companies in the Pontypridd district promoted building clubs for their workmen despite the fact that there did not seem to be any great desire for home ownership among the workmen.[42] Also, during the inquiries of the commission into the coal industry in 1919, Alfred Tallis, the managing director of the Tredegar Iron and Coal Company, defended his company's record of helping workmen to purchase their own homes by arguing that this made men take a greater interest in the affairs of the town and those of the company, and that the intention was to promote a stabilizing influence over the mining population.[43] The effect of this support from the company was that, of the 1355 houses built on company's freehold estate, workmen and their families owned 1019 (76 per cent) of them, while tradesmen owned 236 houses and other persons ninety houses.[44] Similarly, Sir Henry

---

[39] The *Aberdare Leader* was forced to apologize when it became clear that the colliery company was not involved in the bidding. *Aberdare Leader* (12 February 1916), p. 7.

[40] *Western Mail* (2 July 1907), p. 6; for another example, see *Neath Gazette* (19 March 1910), p. 8.

[41] *Western Mail* (24 June 1904), p. 4.

[42] *Western Mail* (2 July 1904), p. 4; ibid. (9 July 1904), p. 4.

[43] Commission of Enquiry into the Coal Industry, II, *Reports and Minutes of Evidence*, [Cmd. 360], 1919, xii, p. 1081.

[44] Ibid., p. 1079.

Tyler, chairman of the Rhymney Iron Company, claimed in 1906 that workmen who owned their own houses 'become conservatives, and good supporters of general good government, rather than of one or the other political party'.[45]

Large landowners were also prominent in efforts to enable greater levels of working-class home ownership. In 1909 Miss C. M. Talbot of Port Talbot offered to support the efforts of the Margam District Council to ease the housing situation in the district by helping fifty workmen to become the owners of their own houses.[46] Similarly, Edward Davies of Machen House, Newport, was the lessor of the land near Merthyr upon which the Caeracca Building Club built 200 houses in the first few years of the twentieth century. Davies bought a number of shares in the club to 'help forward' the project and provided stone from his quarry free of royalty.[47] Even more remarkably, Lord Treowen, owner of the Llanofer estate, approached the Aber-carn Urban District Council in the early 1920s with the idea of building between 500 and 600 houses for working-class families on part of his estate. Lord Treowen agreed to erect the houses, upon receipt of a subsidy from the council, on condition that tenants wanting to purchase their houses were able to do so on easy terms. With this intention in mind the council and Lord Treowen established an easy payment purchase scheme under which tenants could purchase the house they inhabited for a weekly payment of 10s. 3d., a sum only 9d. more than the weekly rent paid by tenants. The 'creation of a large number of owner-occupiers', it was commented, 'will have a marked effect on the future prosperity and well-being of the district'.[48]

Therefore, advocates of working-class home ownership believed that it would have a stabilizing influence on workers and that this would benefit the community as a whole. Home ownership was viewed as a bulwark against radical, left-wing politics and as an antidote to socialism. Advocates believed that, given a stake in society, workmen behaved in more respectable, acceptable ways and were less susceptible to left-wing ideologies. For their part, many trade unionists and socialists recognized the accuracy of these assertions and opposed home ownership for these and other reasons. Trade unionists and socialists were intensely suspicious of advocates of working-class home ownership and decried the psychological and practical effects of home ownership on workers. This is evident,

---

[45] *South Wales Daily News* (6 June 1906), p. 5.

[46] *Neath Gazette* (18 September 1909), p. 7; part of the motivation in this case seems to have been to pre-empt Labour councillors who favoured municipal provision of houses.

[47] *Merthyr Express* (29 August 1908), p. 9.

[48] *The Welsh Housing and Development Year Book* (Cardiff, 1923), pp. 89–90.

for example, in the comments of one trade unionist from Merthyr in 1901. He wrote:

> The best trade unionist I know is the man who is not up to his neck in his own little individualism. I should again like to point out to you this fact, that the man that owns his own house has in that house his all-in-all, and is quite indifferent to the welfare of others. I have often seen him at public meetings, and, as a rule, you will see him fighting against all local improvements, such as public parks, swimming baths, free libraries, &c. Only once let him understand that by advocating a public improvement the rates will rise a trifle in consequence, and you will find those small capitalists will be loudest in their cry against such improvement.[49]

This observation seems to confirm Richard Harris and Chris Hamnett's description of home-owners as 'militant conservatives' who were active in resisting local change.[50] Home-owners and advocates of working-class owner-occupation were especially opposed to municipal provision of working-class housing on the grounds that it was unfair that thrifty working men had provided for their own houses while 'feckless' workmen who had not provided for their own welfare were rewarded with new houses by the council.[51] Workers, it was claimed, should not expect local authorities to provide them with houses, but should be encouraged to purchase their own houses because this inculcated habits of thrift.[52]

Debates over the provision of houses by local authorities often revealed the attitudes of socialists and others within the labour movement to working-class home ownership. For example, the socialist and prominent housing reformer Edgar Chappell was opposed to home ownership because he believed that it made individuals more selfish and hostile to reform. He preferred municipal provision of housing, as indeed did other trade unionists and socialists. If workers wanted to own their own houses, Chappell argued, they should utilize the Small Dwellings Acquisition Act of 1899 and obtain loans from local authorities rather than 'sell' their independence to private lenders.[53] The Act enabled local authorities to obtain loans from the central government on the security of the rates and to lend up to £200 to people to enable them to purchase the houses they lived in. 'The chief purpose', claimed a local newspaper, 'is to encourage thrift, and a higher sense of citizenship among the working classes, and no

---

[49] *Merthyr Express* (16 November 1901), p. 3.
[50] Harris and Hamnett, 'Myth of the Promised Land', 175.
[51] See, for example, the comments of councillor L. N. Williams, chairman of the Graig Building Club, Aberdare. *Merthyr Express* (16 July 1910), p. 4.
[52] *Pontypridd Chronicle* (2 June 1902), p. 7.
[53] *South Wales Gazette* (10 April 1914), p. 7; (24 July 1914), p. 7.

one will dispute the excellence of this object.'[54] Chappell maintained that socialists were not inconsistent in arguing for municipal housing while also supporting the use of the 1899 Act, but even he felt compelled to add that 'even if there was inconsistency there would be ample justification, for in bringing relief to sufferers from any social evil theoretic considerations must give way to practical proposals'.[55]

However, other socialists opposed the use of the Small Dwellings Acquisition Act. At a meeting of the Abertillery Trades Council in April 1914, for example, several delegates reported that the lodges which they represented had voted in favour of the council adopting the Act and claimed there were large numbers of working men in Abertillery who were anxious to buy their houses. But it was clear that there were differences of opinion within the Trades Council and among the Labour members on the council regarding the advisability of adopting the Act. One member of the Trades Council argued that the Act was 'calculated to place them under a worse form of slavery than they were under at present'.[56]

Many trade unionists were concerned that home ownership would hamper the labour movement during strikes since workers who owned their own houses would be more likely to return to work as a result of the pressure placed upon them by their mortgage repayments and by the fact that they were tied to the area and could not seek work elsewhere. Labour mobility was seen as an important aspect of a worker's independence and as a form of defence against excessive employer exploitation.[57] As Messrs Edwards Bros, housing agents in Dowlais, claimed in 1904: 'we know of people who preach and practice that no working man should own a house or have any fixed stake in any particular district, but, rather, that he should have all his belongings in his bag, box, or bank book, and so be able to pack up and depart at will'.[58] At the time of the dispute between Lord Penrhyn and the quarrymen of north-west Wales at the turn of the nineteenth century, trade unionists in south Wales pointed out the disadvantages which the labour movement in Gwynedd laboured under as a result of the relatively high numbers of workers who owned their own

[54] *Merthyr Times* (24 March 1899), p. 3.
[55] *Llais Llafur* (6 May 1911), p. 7.
[56] *South Wales Gazette* (10 April 1914), p. 6.
[57] Daniel Evans, the first Labour chairman of the Rhondda Urban District, advocated an extensive tramway system in the Rhondda valleys partly to ensure that home owners were not left unemployed by the closure of their place of employment. *Pontypridd Chronicle* (3 May 1902), p. 6.
[58] *Western Mail* (20 June 1904), p. 4.

homes. Many home-owning quarrymen, it was claimed, returned to work before their colleagues who lived in rented accommodation.[59]

Anti-socialists seized upon this antipathy to home ownership as a means of discrediting socialism. In 1907, for example, the Conservative *Western Mail* suggested that socialism stood for the abolition of private property and warned miners in south Wales that they faced losing the houses they had worked so hard to acquire if they supported left-wing political parties and ideologies. In the same vein the editorial column of the Liberal *Pontypridd Observer* commented in 1908 that 'under Socialism every working man in the Graig who by thrift has secured a house for himself will lose it and instead he will get a ticket for so much lodging and so much food the same as the tramps get now'.[60]

Whether or not workers heeded the warnings of socialists is impossible to determine, but it was suggested that the increasing radicalization of the labour movement in south Wales in the late nineteenth and early twentieth centuries, and the greater acceptance of socialist ideas by Welsh workers, affected aspirations to home ownership. While some individuals attributed the decline in the building club movement to the changed economic circumstances of the late Edwardian period and the increasingly unprofitable nature of investment in housing, the South Wales Regional Survey Committee report of 1920 maintained that 'the hostility to individual ownership of houses manifested by certain political and trade union interests had much to do with the breakdown of this form of enterprise'.[61] Similarly, Alfred Tallis complained in 1920 that his workmen were no longer interested in owning houses because they believed that they should be provided by the state. This suggests perhaps that socialist demands for public provision had made an impact on workers in south Wales.[62]

However, it would be misleading to conclude that there was a clear and consistent attitude within the labour movement, and even among socialists, towards home ownership. As has already been shown, individuals within the labour movement differed over the advisability of local authorities adopting the Small Dwellings Acquisition Act. Similarly, John Morgan, a socialist from Pontypridd, argued in favour of working-class home

[59] It was claimed that during the coal strike of 1898 some miners who owned their houses were denied poor relief and were forced to mortgage their houses. *Merthyr Express* (9 November 1901), p. 3; (16 November 1901), p. 3; see also *South Wales Gazette* (15 May 1914), p. 8.

[60] *Western Mail* (15 November 1907), p. 4; *Pontypridd Observer* (28 March 1908), p. 1.

[61] Ministry of Health, *Report of the South Wales Regional Survey Committee* (London, 1921), p. 17.

[62] NLW, E. L. Chappell Papers, South Wales Regional Survey Committee, Briefs and Minutes of Evidence, Summary of Evidence submitted by A. S. Tallis, 13 April 1920; see also Commission of Enquiry into the Coal Industry, II, *Reports and Minutes of Evidence*, [Cmd. 360], 1919, xii, p. 1081, Q25, 546.

ownership. Writing in 1902, Morgan criticized private landlords and urged local authorities to build houses for working-class families under the relevant legislation. Less predictably, he admitted that he himself had recently become an 'embryo house owner' through the 'friendly help' of a building club. Adopting the language employed by building societies, Morgan asserted that the house would be paid for through the weekly payment of 'rent' (that is, mortgage payments) and that after about fifteen years he would own the house 'free of all debt, without having paid a penny for it'. In this way, his earnings were not being used to enrich a landlord, as was the case with those workers paying rent.[63]

These chance remarks of a particular socialist reveal one instance in which the aspiration to home ownership did not lead to political conservatism. More significantly, they demonstrate how home ownership could be viewed as an integral part of working-class, and even anti-capitalist and socialist, consciousness. The example of John Morgan suggests that ownership did not necessarily imply conservatism and that it could be regarded as compatible with socialism. It suggests that home ownership was not something that was merely imposed on passive workers by calculating employers, but that a genuine desire for home ownership emanated from the working class. The popularity and success of the building clubs is evidence enough of this. It would be crude to dismiss individualism and thrift as bourgeois values that were anathema to working-class consciousness, or the aspiration and commitment to home ownership on the part of working-class families as false consciousness.[64] After all, some families in south Wales purchased their homes through the Co-operative movement.

Nevertheless, John Morgan was an exception and, generally, home ownership did lead to political conservatism. Some socialists in south Wales were critical of self-help organizations because they tended to promote a 'selfish', individualistic outlook which militated against collective efforts to further the aims of the labour movement. Thrift and self-help were often considered middle-class values. For many critics of home ownership, there existed a paradox at the heart of self-help methods in that they were collective efforts to improve individual lives.[65]

---

[63] *Pontypridd Chronicle* (22 February 1902), p. 4.

[64] Saunders, *Urban Politics*, pp. 82–3.

[65] On the tension within socialism in its attitudes to self-help associational activity, see Peter Gurney, *Co-operative Culture and the Politics of Consumption in England, 1870–1930* (Manchester, 1996), pp. 178, 182–3; in a German context, see Gunnar Stollberg, '*Hilfskassen* in Nineteenth-Century Germany', in M. van der Linden (ed.), *Social Security Mutualism: The Comparative History of Mutual Benefit Societies* (Berne, 1996), p. 319; on the blurring of the distinction between mutual aid and individual self-help, see Geoffrey B. A. M. Finlayson, *Citizen, State, and Social Welfare in Britain in Britain 1830–1990* (Oxford, 1990), pp. 41–5.

This study of working-class home ownership has a bearing on several arguments made by other historians. Martin J. Daunton, for example, has questioned the extent to which home ownership led to political conservatism. He has noted that the South Wales Coalfield was characterized both by high levels of working-class home ownership and a high degree of labour unrest and trade union militancy in the period leading up to the First World War. Daunton argues that social behaviour and political attitudes cannot be explained with reference to forms of housing tenure alone and that other social and economic factors also influenced political and social attitudes. He further argues that home ownership was an aspect of the solidarity and collectivist ethic of the workers in south Wales rather than a retreat into selfish individualism.[66]

However, Daunton's assertions do not seem to be empirically based and instead seem to derive from more general assumptions of the nature of housing tenure and politics in south Wales. The more detailed study carried out here has offered evidence that, despite exceptions, there were indeed clear political consequences that could be attributed to home ownership and home ownership alone. For example, Daunton's comment that a miner in south Wales was likely to argue that ownership gave him independence from his employer ignores the criticisms made by trade unionists that ownership tied workers to an area and, more importantly, the involvement of employers in promoting home ownership and their avowed reasons for doing so. Moreover, Daunton refers only to the building clubs, which he views as collectivist organizations, and fails to consider the other means by which many working-class families purchased houses. Many workers bought their houses from industrialists, while others arranged mortgages with private lenders or co-operative societies.

Mutualism is not an absolute quality, but comes in many forms. The mutualism of building clubs, for example, differed from that of club practices. In south Wales, members of club practices, the organizations through which workers arranged for access to general practitioner services for themselves and their families, imposed a form of income tax on themselves by contributing 2*d.* or 3*d.* in each pound of their wages to a general fund. The mutualism of these club practices, therefore, possessed an element of redistribution since the greater contributions of better paid workers subsidized poorly paid workers who would otherwise have not

---

[66] M. J. Daunton, *A Property-Owning Democracy? Housing in Britain* (London, 1987), pp. 72–3.

been able to afford general practitioner services.[67] Members of building clubs, on the other hand, only helped each other to the extent that building more than one house at a time was marginally cheaper than building them singly and mortgages were easier to obtain. There was no redistribution of wealth in any form. Building clubs were characterized by a lesser degree of mutual support than other forms of working-class associational self-help. Therefore, building clubs cannot be bracketed with other mutual organizations as expressions of working-class self-sufficiency; nor should they be viewed as merely another aspect of the solidarity and collectivist ethic of Welsh workers. Clearly, building clubs exhibited a greater degree of individualistic self-help than did other working-class mutual organizations.

Furthermore, Daunton treats the coalfield, both in terms of levels of home ownership and political attitudes, as a homogeneous whole and this is clearly unsatisfactory. Apart from the unique case of the Pontypridd socialist John Morgan, we have no idea of the correlation between particular political attitudes and forms of housing tenure. The political militancy of trade unionists, and trade union leaders, in south Wales might have been at odds with the political conservatism of home-owners and it is possible that these two very different political attitudes coexisted within Welsh communities. While home ownership was the cause of social and political conservatism, it did not prevent south Wales from projecting radical, left-wing views and opinions into the British political sphere. The social cleavages produced by different forms of housing tenure help to explain the bitter ideological and political battles which gripped south Wales during the first few decades of the twentieth century. The Edwardian period, in particular, witnessed a struggle between class-conscious members of the labour movement and individuals more committed to the older, Liberal notion of community. This might be partly explained by reference to different forms of housing tenure. However, in defence of Daunton's interpretation, it might be argued that individuals can hold different identities simultaneously. Identities and interests created by different forms of housing tenure were relevant in certain circumstances, but might have had no bearing in other sets of circumstances when class consciousness became the primary determinant of attitudes and action. Expressed in another way, home-owners thought of themselves as home-owners under certain circumstances, but as workers in other situations.

---

[67] See Steven Thompson, 'A Proletarian Public Sphere: Working-Class Self-Provision of Medical Services and Care in South Wales, *c.*1900–1948', in Anne Borsay (ed.), *Medicine in Wales, c.1800–2000: Public Service or Private Commodity?* (Cardiff, 2003), pp. 86–107.

These comments on home ownership and political attitudes not only prompt us to question the historiography of home ownership but also impinge on the historiography of the labour movement in south Wales. In his fascinating comparative study of the Ruhr and South Wales Coalfields, Stefan Berger points out how diverse housing styles in the Ruhr increased the status-consciousness of workers and exacerbated the divisions which existed within the working class. Berger contrasts this differentiation in the Ruhr with south Wales, which was characterized by more monotonous and uniform terraced housing. This, Berger suggests, was one among several factors which produced a much more homogeneous working-class experience and consequently contributed to a more united working class and labour movement.[68] This claim, however, is unsatisfactory and constitutes only a partial consideration of housing and working-class experience. It takes no account of the different forms of housing tenure which existed. While Berger recognizes that many workers purchased their own houses in south Wales and that this partly explains the differences in wage rates between the two coalfields, the significance of working-class home ownership for attitudes and behaviour is not explored. As has been shown, the nature of housing tenure was as important, if not more important, than the physical form of housing in the creation of social divisions. This is not to argue that the working class of south Wales was less homogeneous than that of other industrial areas. Rather, differences in housing style in the Ruhr might have caused divisions in the working class of that coalfield, but differing forms of housing tenure served to create divisions within the Welsh working class.

This study of housing tenure in south Wales, and of the social and political consequences of working-class home ownership, has sought to demonstrate some of the fundamental inter-relationships between public and private aspects of working-class life. It has emphasized the importance of rooting accounts of politics and public affairs in the lived reality of everyday, working-class life.[69] Moreover, the subject itself serves to remind us that generalizations about the 'working class' or 'south Wales', while necessary in certain contexts, often conceal as much as they reveal, and that the reality of working-class life was much more complicated and

---

[68] Stefan Berger, 'Working-Class Culture and the Labour Movement in the South Wales and Ruhr Coalfields, 1850–2000: a Comparison', *Llafur*, 8, no. 2 (2001), 15–16, 23.

[69] For a fascinating exploration of the private bases of working-class political life, see Bruce Scates, 'Gender, Household and Community Politics: the 1890 Maritime Strike in Australia and New Zealand', *Journal of the Australian Labour History Society*, 61 (1991), 70–87.

consequently more interesting than is often appreciated. Similarly, it is simplistic to assume that values such as 'thrift' and 'individualism' are middle-class phenomena and inevitably anathema to working-class consciousness. Nor is it satisfactory to assume that concepts such as 'collectivism' and 'mutualism' adequately sum up working-class values and experiences. The reality was much more complex and far more intriguing.

16

Gardens of Eden: Welsh Missionaries in British India

ALED JONES

Writing in 1891 of the achievements of John Thomas, a fellow Welsh Christian missionary on the southern tip of India, John P. Jones remarked that 'he found the place, in more senses than one, a wilderness, and died leaving it a garden of the Lord'.[1] The image of an Edenic garden of innocence and tranquillity is a powerful and lasting metaphor for the Welsh missionary project in India, seeking as it did to transform through education and conversion the chaos of what it regarded to be a fallen, pagan world into its own vision of what constituted the peace and order of Christ's salvation. On the other side of the subcontinent, however, in Eastern Bengal and Assam, where Welsh Presbyterian missionaries maintained their most significant collective foreign presence anywhere in the world outside Wales, the notion of the 'garden' acquired a far more literal meaning. Here, from the 1850s, the upland wilderness, officially designated by the colonial authorities as 'wasteland', was radically re-shaped on an unprecedented scale into productive and idyllic-looking tea gardens. This chapter will suggest that those industrial gardens, and the broad economic forces that developed them, played a significant role in shaping important aspects of the history of Welsh missionary activity in Eastern Bengal and Assam, if not from the mission's inception in the early 1840s, then certainly from its consolidation in the following decades. The tea-garden economy also provides a valuable point of entry into a broader set of questions about Welsh, or at least some Welsh Nonconformist, attitudes towards British colonial power in the nineteenth and early twentieth centuries.

In recent years the history of foreign missions has deservedly attracted growing international attention, within as well as outside the old colonies

---

[1] *The Cambrian* (June 1891), 163.

of the British Empire.[2] However, few studies of the Welsh Presbyterian mission field in India have indicated how its geographical shape and chronological development might fit into the broader social, economic and political history of the subcontinent. In short, Welsh missionary history lacks a material context. In part, this may be attributed to the legacy of the mission's own historiography, which essentially regarded it as a spiritual engagement, a theological struggle between faiths dominated by a narrative of self-sacrifice and redemption.[3] In addition, there has also been a concern, perhaps a preoccupation, among more secular historians to demonstrate the Welshness of the mission. This perspective has emphasized its cultural distinctiveness as a Welsh, rather than a British imperial, phenomenon, and has drawn attention to the effects which its engagement with India may have had both on the people of north-east India and on the Welsh themselves.[4] While these are all perfectly valid lenses through which to read the meanings of the mission, it is nevertheless reasonable to argue that without a sense of social context they can provide only limited, and in themselves limiting, fields of vision. What is now needed is a far broader sense of how Welsh missionaries operated in the material circumstances that obtained, on the ground, in different contexts. Far more needs to be known, for example, about the ways in which they negotiated with Muslim and Hindu individuals and institutions as well as with the colonial and administrative power, and with the less powerful as well as with the local and regional elites, over such issues as landownership, housing, social customs, personal security, economic and cultural production and access to education and healthcare. Again, the history of tea cultivation allows us to consider the

---

[2] Other Celtic nations have been asking some searching, sometimes uncomfortable, questions about their own imperial and missionary histories. See, for example, Patrick O'Sullivan (ed.), *The Irish World Wide: History, Heritage, Identity,* V, *Religion and Identity* (London, 1990), and John M. Mackenzie, 'Essay and Reflection: on Scotland and the Empire', *International History Review,* 15, no. 4 (November 1993), 714–39.

[3] The most comprehensive of the missionary histories may be found in the three-volume series published by the Mission Board of the Presbyterian Church of Wales: Ednyfed Thomas, *Hanes Cenhadaeth Dramor Eglwys Bresbyteraidd Cymru: Cenhadaeth Casia. Y gyfrol gyntaf, Bryniau'r Glaw* (Caernarfon, 1988); J. Meirion Lloyd, *Hanes Cenhadaeth Dramor Eglwys Bresbyteraidd Cymru: Cenhadaeth Mizoram. Yr ail gyfrol, Y Bannau Pell* (Caernarfon, 1989); D. G. Merfyn Jones, *Hanes Cenhadaeth Dramor Eglwys Bresbyteraidd Cymru, Cenhadaeth Sylhet-Cachar. Y drydedd gyfrol, Y Popty Poeth a'i Gyffiniau* (Caernarfon, 1990). More recent studies include Gwen Rees Roberts, *Memories of Mizoram: Recollections and Reflections* (Cardiff, 2001) and D. Ben Rees (ed.), *Llestri Gras a Gobaith: Cymry a'r Cenhadon yn India* (Lerpwl, 2001).

[4] See Nigel Jenkins, *Gwalia in Khasia: A Visit to the Site, in India, of the Biggest Overseas Venture ever Sustained by the Welsh 1795–1995* (Llandysul, 1995), and Aled Jones, 'Welsh Missionary Journalism in India, 1880–1947', in Julie F. Codell (ed.), *Imperial Co-Histories, National Identities and the British and Colonial Press* (Madison, WI, 2003), 242–72.

history of the mission, and of the work of individual missionaries, from a differently angled and perhaps in a more revealing light.

There is of course another link between the Welsh and their tea. Being dedicated consumers on a large scale since Assamese tea began to flood western markets from the 1860s, Welsh Nonconformists regarded it on religious and moral grounds as a cheap and beneficial alternative to alcohol, and thus a means of turning Wales itself into a garden of social contentment. Some, like the Welsh-American entrepreneur George T. Matthews, made fortunes by importing tea into the United States, often under such reassuring, if slightly bizarre, labels as 'Red Dragon Tea' and 'Eryri Tea',[5] and it was heavily marketed in Wales from the mid-nineteenth century as the natural product of healthy and lovingly tended hill regions. The reality of actual tea production, however, was rather different. Indian tea gardens in the nineteenth and early twentieth centuries were harsh places in which to work, industrial enterprises in which cheap labour was subjected to brutal work disciplines and severe social constraints. While being open-air factories, they were also enclosed human ghettos. Their workers, most of whom were Hindu migrants from distant parts of India, were separated from the surrounding society by their ethnic origins, languages, religions and caste. Indian historians in recent years have tended to regard the tea garden as both an archetype of colonial economic power and as a trope for western cultural dominance. For Kaushik Ghosh, British colonial power sought 'to rid Assam of its wilderness' by 'bringing the wasteland of Assam under colonial culture and productivity' and subjecting it to 'the civilisation of the tea garden'. Furthermore, this 'massive spectacle of order, productivity and enterprise' offered 'a constant picture which provided the self-assurance that was so crucial to the European culture of colonial rule'. Tea, he concluded, 'would give Assam a culture which was worthy of being linked to the . . . Empire'.[6] The tea garden, then, is a potent symbol of the history of the British colonial presence in India, and of the kind of order it sought to impose.

Wild indigenous tea plants were first discovered in Assam in the 1830s, shortly before Thomas Jones set sail for Khasia to establish there the first independent Welsh Presbyterian foreign mission in India. Hitherto, most of the tea consumed in Europe had been cultivated in China, where tea drinking was an ancient practice, and where the tea plant was grown and

[5] Aled Jones and Bill Jones, *Welsh Reflections: Y Drych and America 1851–2001* (Llandysul, 2001), pp. 66–7.

[6] Kaushik Ghosh, 'A Market for Aboriginality: Primitivism and Race Classification in the Indentured Labour Market of Colonial India', in Gautam Bhadra, Gyan Prakash and Susie Tharu (eds), *Subaltern Studies X: Writings on South Asian History and Society* (Oxford, 1999), pp. 14–16.

harvested in essentially pre-industrial forms of farming. The tea gardens of India, in contrast, were to be run on industrial principles. The first commercial tea garden in the Surma Valley, the Malnicherra, was established in Sylhet in 1857, and others were planted in rapid succession from the 1860s. They were fuelled by European investment and by a political imperative to undercut Chinese suppliers, and thereby strengthen European control over China's trade with the West. The success of the Assamese tea industry was thus an essential component in establishing Britain's mid-Victorian trade dominance in the Far East. But it also meant transforming an entire landscape by means of extensive de-forestation and replanting. By 1901 nearly one and a half million acres were under tea cultivation in the districts of Sylhet and Cachar alone, only one-sixtieth of which was owned by native planters.[7] Tea was overwhelmingly a European-owned industry, mainly British and under Scottish management. It was also highly labour intensive, and required the importation of predominantly indentured workers from as far afield as the United and Central Provinces, and even the North West Provinces, of India. The majority were Hindu in religion and Hindi in language.[8] Imported labour was regarded by tea planters as easier to control, and carried less risk of desertion. So-called 'aboriginal' hill tribes people were deemed to be more resistant to malaria and cholera, endemic in many of the forest areas, and thus attracted higher prices for the many unlicensed contractors (*arkathi*) who cajoled or forced them into indentured labour contracts of between three and five years, enforced by threat of imprisonment.[9] Labour shortages caused by the rapid growth of the new sector, exacerbated by the reluctance of local farmers to be reduced to 'coolie' labour, further intensified the efforts of such contractors to attract ever larger numbers of workers during the following half-century. The human cost of this movement of population was high. Of the 52,155 labourers sent to Cachar from the Central Indian Provinces between 1863 and 1868, 2456 died on the journey,[10] while many of the survivors suffered a range of diseases after their arrival in malarial zones which humans had tended in the past to avoid, and where there was little clean drinking

---

[7] Syed Rashidul Hasan and Kazi Shariful Alam, 'Production and Marketing of Tea in Greater Sylhet', in Sharif uddin Ahmed (ed.), *Sylhet: History and Heritage* (Dhaka, 1999), p. 457.

[8] Priyam Goswami, 'Industries and Trade of Surma Valley in the Nineteenth Century', in Ahmed (ed.), *Sylhet*, p. 472.

[9] Ghosh, in Bhadra *et al.* (eds), *Subaltern Studies X*, pp. 38–9, 45.

[10] Manjulika Bhattacharjee, 'Workers' and Peasants' Movements in the Surma-Barak

water or sanitation, let alone appropriate housing and other social amenities.[11]

It was into this rapidly changing world that the Welsh missionaries entered. If they themselves may at times have given the impression to their supporters in Wales of being in an isolated, remote and primitive place, they were in fact caught up in a dramatic process of regional industrial modernization and one of the region's most significant non-urbanizing economic migrations of the modern period, at least until the refugee exodus that followed the Partition of India in August 1947. Moreover, they could hardly have chosen a politically more volatile region to occupy than their missionary field. Not only did it cover a vast and diverse area, in topography and climate as well as in the ethnic, linguistic and religious compositions of the native peoples, but its political boundaries and identities were also subjected to extensive redrawing. When referring to the entire timescale of the mission's history, from 1841 until 1966, it is safer to avoid political designations altogether and refer instead to the more enduring geographical expressions, such as the Hills of Khasia to the north, or the Surma Valley on the plains of the south. The Surma Valley, for example, which extends from Sylhet, the principal urban centre, in the west, eastwards through to Karimganj on the banks of the Chargola river, and Silchar, was divided and reassigned on several occasions within the changing internal political and administrative boundaries of the Empire. Until 1874 Sylhet lay in Bengal, with Bengali and the regional variant, Sylheti, being the main spoken languages. The district was then transferred to Assam, and, following Lord Curzon's partitioning of Bengal in 1905, into the mainly Muslim new province of East Bengal and Assam. In 1911, following widespread Hindu-led protest, including the *swadeshi* (buy Indian) campaign, and the formation in December 1906 of the Muslim League, the partition of Bengal was annulled. Sylhet, however, was again separated from East Bengal and remained part of Assam. Thus, when the Welsh missionary D. G. Merfyn Jones was writing his diary of the Bengal famine at Shaistaganj, near Habiganj, in September 1943, he was positioned close to the state border between Bengal and Assam, a critical frontier across which food and refugees crossed only with difficulty.[12] In the final stages of the British decolonization of India in 1947, Sylhet petitioned to secede from Indian Assam in order to join Pakistan, which

Valley – 19th and 20th Centuries', in Ahmed (ed.), *Sylhet*, p. 247.

[11] Today, tea is the third most valuable agricultural product in Bangladesh after rice and jute, grown mainly in Sylhet district. For the Welsh in jute production, see the history of Aberystwyth-born David Edward Evans, an engineer with Ralli Brothers and superintendent engineer in Bengal, in D. E. Lloyd Jones, 'David Edward Evans: a Welshman in India', *THSC* (1967), 135.

again led to the division of the region. While Sylhet today lies in Bangladesh, Karimganj and Silchar are both in India, the former being adjacent to, though not straddling, the international border between the two countries.

Sylhet and the smaller towns of the plains presented Christian missionaries with particular difficulties and opportunities, and are worthy of closer attention. A hotter, more humid climate, combined with the more pervasive influence of Islam and Hinduism on the social order, created a distinctive environment which the missionary D. G. Merfyn Jones vividly described as 'y popty poeth' (the hot oven). Shaped by the Islamic legacy of Hazrat Shah Jalal's conquest of the region in the fourteenth century,[13] 53 per cent of the population of Sylhet District in the mid-nineteenth century were Muslims, a proportion that rose to 67 per cent in the northern part of the region.[14] The remainder were virtually all Hindus. Sylhet town at the time of the official census in 1872 had a population of 16,846; Karimganj, by comparison, had a population of only 5692 in 1901.[15] But the population of the tea gardens which surrounded them increased exponentially in these decades, and by 1889 it was estimated that some two million workers and their families had migrated into the Assam tea gardens.[16] Unlike in the hills to the north, tea in the Surma Valley was planted on small, low hillocks of ancient alluvial deposits on the flood plains, or, on its southern edge, on the low-lying foothills of the western Assam border. Sylhet town was surrounded by rice fields and tea gardens; some, such as the Khadim garden, were situated only 3 miles from the town centre.

Partly as a consequence of the tea-garden economy, Sylhet was home also to a small but distinctive British population. The European Club, for example, retained an important social function for British planters, engineers and administrators well into the twentieth century. Fifty years after the Welsh missionary Elizabeth Williams had denounced its snobbery,[17] D. G. Merfyn Jones, leaving Sylhet for Shaistaganj in January 1943, described the feeling of relief on being freed from the confines of Sylhet's suffocatingly small and closed European world. 'I never dreamed that such a Victorian society still existed in the 40s', he wrote in his diary:

[12] D. G. Merfyn Jones, *Blwyddyn y Newyn* (Caernarfon, 1981), esp. pp. 82–7.

[13] Abdul Karim, 'Advent of Islam in Sylhet and Hazrat Shah Jalal (R)', in Ahmed (ed.), *Sylhet*, pp. 129–49.
[14] Sharif uddin Ahmed, 'Urban Growth and Development of Sylhet Town: Colonial Period', in Ahmed (ed.), *Sylhet*, p. 738.
[15] It is worth noting here that the vast majority of the 100,000 or so people of Bangladeshi origin resident in the United Kingdom are migrants, or the descendants of migrants, from the Sylhet District.
[16] Jones, *Y Popty Poeth*, p. 55.

the society of the calling cards, and narrow etiquette; a world of imperialist style and thinking, where the 'Sahib' is a demi-god in his own eyes and deceives himself by thinking that he succeeds in conveying the same inflated idea of himself to the native . . . But the society I have been used to in Wales has bidden farewell forever to such ideas.

Wnes i erioed freuddwydio fod y fath gymdeithas Fictoraidd yn dal mewn bod yn y pedwar-degau 'ma; cymdeithas y 'calling-cards' a'r eticet gaeth; byd y steil a'r syniadau Imperialaidd, byd lle mae'r 'Sahib' yn hanner-duw yn ei olwg ei hun ac yn twyllo'i hun wrth feddwl ei fod yn llwyddo i drosglwyddo'r un syniad mawreddog amdano i'r brodor . . . Ond mae'r gymdeithas yr ydw i wedi arfer â hi yng Nghymru wedi ffarwelio am byth â'r fath syniadau.

He also predicted that the Japanese advance from Burma would mean that, even in Sylhet, the days of the old imperial domination 'were numbered'.[18]

William Pryse was the first to extend the Welsh mission to this socially complex, ever shifting region, and it was his forceful personality that dominated its early years until the Calvinistic Methodist connexion finally excommunicated him in July 1867, two years before his death in August 1869.[19] A small, embattled presence remained in the town until 1875, when Griffith Hughes was removed to more fertile ground elsewhere. In 1887, however, John Pengwern Jones, his wife Jane (who died of cholera within a matter of days of their arrival) and Sarah Ann John, reanimated the operation in Sylhet. They were soon followed by Elizabeth Williams in 1890, Thomas John Jones and Ellen Brownlow in 1891, Laura Evans and Elizabeth Roberts in 1892, and Emma and Oswald Osborne Williams, the first qualified doctor, in 1894. Between 1849 and 1966 some sixty-five missionaries from Wales would serve in the Surma Valley, forty-six of whom (72 per cent of the total number) were women. It remained smaller than the mission to the hills. In 1903, for example, thirteen missionaries were serving in the Surma Valley, while there were thirty-six in the Khasi Hills and two in Lushai.[20] But the 1904–5 religious revival in Wales appears to have had a major impact on recruitment to the Surma mission, and significant numbers of young women in particular were drafted into what was widely regarded as the most physically and intellectually demanding area of the mission field in which to proselytize. The largest

[17] NLW, Calvinistic Methodist Archive 7 (B), HZ1/2/102.

[18] Jones, *Blwyddyn y Newyn*, pp. 8–9.

[19] See D. G. Merfyn Jones, *Eryr Sylhet* (Dinbych, 1987) for a fictional account of Pryse's life in Sylhet.

concentration of missionaries in the Surma Valley was to be found between 1906 and 1947, when numbers present at any one time fluctuated between thirteen and eighteen, reaching a maximum of twenty-two at its height in 1925.

Relationships between these missionaries and the colonial authorities changed in important respects during the 117-year timespan of the Welsh mission in the Surma Valley. For much of the seventeenth and eighteenth centuries the East India Company had been wary of advocating or facilitating overt political or cultural forms of westernization in India, especially with regard to such sensitive issues as religion. Nothing was encouraged that might disrupt commerce. That policy had undergone significant change by the early nineteenth century, when a more inter-ventionist policy, for example, legislated against certain Indian social and cultural practices, the most celebrated being the abolition of *suttee* (the immolation of a widow on her husband's funeral pyre). Eighteenth-century 'India men' such as Sir William Jones, a scholar of Sanskrit and founder of the Asiatic Society of Bengal in 1784, as well as a Calcutta jurist, were replaced by British agents who felt little regard for the cultural richness of Indian thought and literature, and, in 1835, English was for the first time enforced as the language of government. The first Welsh missionaries entered the fray precisely at this time, and appear to have shared the company's new value system. William Pryse believed that the suppression of the 1857 Sepoy Mutiny had demonstrated 'the superiority of the European character over the Asian',[21] and the Sylhet in which he lived from 1849 until his death in 1869 was a military base for the suppression of rebellions among the people of the Hills. In the Santal revolt of 1855–6, for example, when 25,000 Santals were alleged to have been killed by company troops,[22] Sylhet was the front-line military base from which sorties to the hills were launched.[23] Yet, only a year later, Pryse believed that the Khasis were more trustworthy than the Sylheti Muslims, whose opposition to British rule was of altogether different and more dangerous order.[24] It was during the 1857–9 crisis, when the missionaries who remained in the Surma Valley daily expected to be slaughtered, that a Welsh Nonconformist foreign policy began to emerge. Put simply, it proposed that the extension of Christianity in India would guarantee its political and social, as well as its spiritual, liberation. The Baptist *Seren Cymru* expressed this view forcefully in August 1857 when it insisted that state legislation should

[20] *The Imperial Gazetteer of India*, XXVI, *Atlas* (Oxford, 1909), p. 55.

[21] *Y Drysorfa* (27 October 1857).
[22] Ghosh in Bhadra *et al.* (eds), *Subaltern Studies X*, p. 23.
[23] National Archives of Bangladesh, Dhaka, Bangladesh (hereafter NAB), Register of Letters Received: Sylhet Collectorate A13.1/250/28, March 1860, p. 255.

enforce religious freedom in India, which would both involve the freedom for Christians to evangelize, and the freedom for the company to repress what were termed 'immoral and cruel social practices', especially among Hindus.[25] Ultimately, it argued, the evangelization of India was as important, if not more so, than the continuation of imperial control.[26] The British government took a more cautious view. Shocked by the events of 1857, Britain abolished the East India Company and imposed direct rule on India the following year. Influential voices within the colonial power were once again circumspect with regard to western cultural interference, largely because British India would henceforth be ruled with the consent and collaboration of the larger Indian landowners, whatever their religion. From 1858, then, missionaries and the colonial state may be said to have pursued two divergent sets of goals, and the one cannot simply be reduced to the other.

Disputes with the state occurred from time to time over several issues. One concerned the legal obstacles to the conversion of Hindus, a matter of some priority since the tea gardens had started to draw in Hindu labour. Pryse lobbied the state government in Calcutta in 1860 for a change in the law that enabled the wife of a convert to Christianity to consider herself a widow, which he argued made conversion unnecessarily difficult and disruptive of family and social life. His pleas were rejected.[27] Others in the same decade demanded that action should be taken against the practice by some Indian Christians of 'substituting for the valid marriage of the law an irregular and invalid ceremony of their own invention'.[28] Again, the state refused to be drawn into what its servants in Fort William regarded as private matters, adding that it would prefer not to take any action that was 'in violation of the rooted habits of the people'.[29] Such government views were regarded by missionaries as being dangerously obstructive to the Christianizing enterprise.

At other times, however, missionaries could act as alternatives to the state, especially in the provision of some services. Writing in 1905 about the Welsh mission in the Surma Valley, B. C. Allen, the official gazetteer of Assam, remarked that 'Sylhet is too civilised to allow of conversion proceeding rapidly, and in the 20 years ending with 1901 the number of native Christians only increased by 130', eighty of whom were members of

---

[24] *Y Drysorfa* (December 1857), 422.

[25] *Seren Cymru* (22 August 1857).
[26] *Seren Cymru* (5 September 1857).
[27] NAB, Register of Letters: Sylhet, William Pryse to G. G. Balfour, 27 April 1860.
[28] NAB, Government of Bengal, Ecclesiastical Proceedings A, list 28, vol. 1, 29 March 1867.
[29] NAB, Government of Bengal, Ecclesiastical Proceedings A, list 28, vol. 1, 16 April

the Welsh Presbyterian Mission.[30] Conversion being a more gradual process in the Surma Valley than it was proving to be in the very different religious environment of the hills, missionaries on the plains were from the beginning obliged to pursue longer term strategies of Christianization. Education played a key role in this respect. William Pryse established two schools for boys in Sylhet during the crisis of 1857, following the closure of the government school which had been opened there in 1840, and which was only reopened on Pryse's death in 1869.[31] His reasoning was characteristically didactic and precise. Writing in 1857, he complained that 'not a tenth of our fellow countrymen, even in India, properly understand Asian society . . . every human relationship, within the entire native society, has been cemented by religion . . . Education and Christianity have combined to loosen this cement from the social fabric'.[32] For Pryse, education was a means of loosening the ties which bound together the 'native' society. Whereas he focused on the formal schooling of the sons of wealthy local Hindus, Elizabeth Williams from the 1890s turned her attention to the education of girls, which in some respects was far more challenging.[33] The Elizabeth Williams Memorial School for Girls opened in 1919, funded by voluntary subscription and a land purchase grant from the government of Assam.[34] By this time state policy and missionary endeavour were beginning once more to work in tandem. In 1914 the state had adopted a policy of 'weaning the Mahommedan community from its addiction to Koran Schools – diverting them from what is educationally a blind alley and bringing them on to the educational high road'[35] of liberal education. Elizabeth Williams's school may be seen as a voluntarist extension of this policy, and was thereby supported. Female missionaries also extended this educational work into the home through their zenana mission, where discussions were held, usually of a non-theological nature on health, childcare and the acquisition of domestic skills, with groups of women when the adult males were out of the home.

Medicine, too, was a longer-term instrument of Christianization, from William Pryse's self-taught homeopathy to the more interventionist medical

1867.

---

[30] B. C. Allen, *Assam District Gazetteers*, X, *The Khasi and Jaintia Hills, the Garo Hills and the Lushai Hills* (Allahabad, 1906), part 1, p. 90.

[31] Ahmed, 'Urban Growth and Development', in Ahmed (ed.), *Sylhet*, p. 735.

[32] *Y Drysorfa* (27 October 1857).

[33] John Hughes Morris, *Ein Cenhadaeth Dramor* (Liverpool, 1930), p. 71.

[34] NAB, Sylhet Proceedings, Sp. 94, list 4, file no. E–524E, F. W. Sudmersen to Second Secretary to the Hon. Chief Commissioner of Assam, Assam Secretariat, n.d.

practices of Oswald Williams.[35] But medical missionaries and nurses also provided important services to colonial administrators and to European planters, engineers, traders and servicemen in their districts, while attending at the same time to their spiritual needs as Protestants. Even Anglo-Indians of mainly Portuguese Catholic descent were included in the Welsh services, as were the Christian Garos who lived in outlying villages. The missionaries themselves lived in secluded compounds, partly for their own security, but partly also in order to remove converts from the often considerable family, financial and social pressures to revert. Missionaries, it could then be argued, were not simply instruments of state colonial policy, but nor were they wholly independent of it. At best, they were semi-autonomous agencies which acted both as irritants to governmental power, and as providers of alternatives or extensions to state provision in education, health and parochial care.[37]

This ambiguous relationship with colonial power may also be seen at work in the Welsh mission's engagement with the expanding tea industry. The new road cut by the East India Company through the hills of Khasia from 1826 to join the Surma and the Bhramaputra Valleys triggered a revolt among the Khasis which was only defeated by the British in 1833. Thereafter, the hills of Khasia and Jaintia, officially designated 'wastelands', were occupied and explored for their economic potential by agents of the company.[38] It was this process that enabled Thomas Jones, along with troops and, later, tea planters, to have relatively free access to this previously impassable region. The establishment of the first outposts of the Welsh mission in Cherrapunji and Shillong at this time appears to have been accomplished in accordance with, if not with the active support of, current East India Company policy, which was to encourage missionaries 'who had had little success with the Hindus of the plains' to enter the new area 'as it was thought that the tribes would be made more civilised by conversion to Christianity'.[39] Half a century later the revival of the mission in the plains, too, may have been stimulated by colonial economic development, in particular the growth of the tea industry, and the new opportunities it provided for work with its large migrant Hindu

[35] NAB, Assam Secretariat, Sylhet B Proceedings, Education Sp. 96, December 1930.

[36] Fuller accounts may be found in B. Pati and M. Harrison (eds), *Health, Medicine and Empire: Perspectives on Colonial India* (New Delhi, 2001), and David Arnold, 'Medicine and Colonialism', in W. F. Bynum and Roy Porter (eds), *Companion Encyclopedia of the History of Medicine*, II (London, 1993), pp. 1393–1416.

[37] For a discussion of missionaries as agents of cultural imperialism, see A. N. Porter, 'Cultural Imperialism and Protestant Missionary Enterprise 1780–1914', *Journal of Imperial and Commonwealth History*, 25, no. 3 (1997), 367–91.

[38] Allen, *Assam District Gazetteers*, X, part 1, pp. 42–53.

[39] Alan Macfarlane and Iris Macfarlane, *Green Gold: The Empire of Tea* (London,

workforce. Considerable energies were devoted to work with the low-caste Namasudra labourers in the Surma Valley, and evidence suggests that Welsh Presbyterian missionaries on occasion came into conflict with Scottish Presbyterian tea-garden managers over the education and conversion of their workers.[40] Christian missionaries from across India also developed a plan to provide employment for children adopted by various missions in the protected environments of the Sylhet tea gardens, under the watchful gaze of John Pengwern Jones.[41] Small chapels still exist on the Khadim and Lakatura gardens outside Sylhet town and, even today, significant numbers of the Sylhet Christian community are tea-garden labourers or their descendants, the majority being converts from Hinduism.

Work with Hindus in the tea gardens, however, was further complicated by the mass politicization of their proletarianized workforce in the years after the First World War, which again coincided with the remarkable growth of the Welsh mission in the Sylhet–Silchar region during these years. In 1920, a Surma Valley Political Conference was held in Sylhet to provide local direction to the anti-imperial non-cooperation and Khilafat movements. This conference, and the industrial unrest into which it tapped, led to the Chargola Exodus which began in May 1921 when up to 20,000 tea workers left the gardens and poured into Karimganj and surrounding bazaars, demanding to be returned to their places of origin.[42] The actions of Gurkha troops, dispatched to contain the ensuing disturbances, led to a general strike (*hartal*) which extended beyond the gardens to the workers on the railways, the river steamers and the British Oil Company in Silchar, which lasted for ten weeks. Four and a half thousand railway workers lost their jobs as a result. But widespread popular support for the tea workers' action eventually compelled the government to arrange transport to their ancestral villages for many of those involved in the exodus. One historian, describing the event as 'the product of an interaction between the Ghandian impact . . . and . . . incipient class militancy',[43] underlines the very modern governing dynamics of the society in which the Welsh missionaries were operating.

The Chargola Exodus, and the resentments which underpinned it, became the subjects of a governmental commission of inquiry. Of the nine commissioners who were appointed (three Europeans, three Indians and three representatives of the government), five were associated with the tea plantations or the Indian Tea Association, while the others, representing

2003), p. 142.

[40] Jones, *Y Popty Poeth*, p. 55.
[41] Ibid., p. 54.
[42] Bhattacharjee, 'Workers' and Peasants' Movements', in Ahmed (ed.), *Sylhet*, p. 251.
[43] A. Guha, *Planter Raj to Swaraj*, quoted in Bhattacharjee, 'Workers' and Peasants'

the government, included the labour minister of the Assam Legislative Council, the deputy commissioner of the Central Provinces, one of the key labour recruiting areas, and a Welsh missionary, Dr Oswald Osborne Williams, of the Welsh Presbyterian Medical Mission at Karimganj. An Aberystwyth graduate, Williams lived and worked in the Surma Valley from 1894 until his death in 1926. The commission's report, published in April 1922, describes a highly politicized workers' rising:

> In January (1921) the sight of thousands of Khilafat volunteers in procession through Silchar town which is practically in the centre of the numerous tea-gardens in that district, showed the strength of the revolutionary movement . . . There was ample proof of attempts on the part of the non-co-operators to interfere with garden bazaars, with a distinctive display of caps, sashes and badges.[44]

Among the most serious of the riots occurred in the Halem tea garden, where most of the workers were native Christians.[45] In Silchar strike leaders 'compared tea garden managers to Satan', and argued that 'the English nation had seized India by foul means'.[46] But if wage reductions and other resentments had fuelled the 'coolie revolt', the trigger, they proposed, was the influenza pandemic of 1919–20, which decimated numbers of workers in the tea gardens.[47] The report concluded that

> the tea garden labourer is often swayed by gusts of unreasoning passion and, in the last year or so, has not infrequently been the tool of the self-seeking political agitator. He has no Trade Union to back his case . . . The tea industry in Assam lives in a world of competition . . . (T)here is a limit to the wage the industry can afford to pay. At the same time there is an awakening among the working classes in India as elsewhere in the world. The tea-garden labourer is not likely to lag behind . . .[48]

To avoid future revolts the commission recommended modest increases in pay, the provision of better healthcare and the relaxation of the illegal practice of imposing penal contracts on labourers. Furthermore, they advocated the introduction into the gardens of more structured forms of

Movements', in Ahmed (ed.), *Sylhet*, p. 254.

[44] *Report of the Assam Labour Enquiry Committee, 1921–22* (Shillong, 1922), p. 4; NLW Calvinistic Methodist Archive 5, 27158 (quoted with the kind permission of the History Department, Presbyterian Church of Wales).

[45] *Assam Labour Enquiry*, p. 5.

[46] Ibid., p. 10.

[47] Ibid., p. 14.

leisure, including football pitches and cinemas, and the extension of tea-garden schools for children. The latter was fiercely contested by Assam's Director of Public Instruction, who informed his government in September 1926 that 'schools are not wanted in tea gardens . . . Cooly children are wage earners and any scheme for their education must take account of that fact'.[49]

What surely is of interest here is why a member of the Welsh Presbyterian Mission was chosen as a government member of the inquiry.[50] Williams consulted the home Church about his appointment only after the commission had completed its work. Writing home to the Executive Committee of the Foreign Mission in April 1922, he explained that 'the tea-committee was hastily assembled in view of public disturbances, strikes, riots etc. on the Tea Gardens'. He then spelled out his own understanding of the thinking behind his appointment, and the reasons why he had agreed to participate in its work.

> As missionaries are the only public persons who could be accepted by the public as friends of coolies, and the poor generally, it appeared to me that I was appointed as their friend and protector and I thought it my duty to join . . . In various ways I hope the influence and position of missionaries and ministers have been the better . . . (for) apart from missionary efforts, these poor low caste indigent labourers, are not led in any way that can permanently uplift them . . . (Yet) the Atmosphere of Tea gardens is not the best Air for Christianity. Occasionally one was glad to meet with sympathetic . . . Christian people among the Europeans, but the number of such is not as great as it ought to be.[51]

Dr Williams thus regarded himself, and the Christian movement which he represented, as an intermediary between the competing demands of workers, international capital and colonial power in India, as the '*only* public persons . . . accepted by the public as friends of coolies'. But he was also, simultaneously, deeply implicated in the historical process which had led to the Chargola Exodus. The mission of which he was part had for the best part of seventy years moved to the rhythms of the expansion of the Assamese tea industry just as surely as it had done to those of the

---

[48] Ibid., p. 106.

[49] NAB, Assam Secretariat, Sylhet B Proceedings. Education. Sl. 96, 'Establishment and Maintenance of Tea Garden Schools'.

[50] Williams was not the only one to be involved in government. Also in the 1920s fellow Welsh missionary Ceredig Evans served as a member of the Provincial Legislative Council of Assam, *Y Cenhadwr* (November 1927), 208.

[51] NLW, Calvinistic Methodist Archive 5, 27287/37, File II, 25 April 1922 (quoted

imperatives of God's calling, and the seismic effects of the 1904–5 Welsh Revival.

The connections between the Welsh mission in India and the home country, which the revival so clearly demonstrates, raises a final, and awkward, question, which is whether the participation of missionaries in the material history of India can, in any meaningful sense, be described as being distinctively Welsh. After all, many missionaries would no doubt have perceived themselves, in the first instance, as Christian evangelists, irrespective of their cultural origin or the language which they spoke among themselves. There exists, however, a real danger of leaching out of their life experiences in India their cultural distinctiveness as Welsh people. While it may be entirely appropriate to see them as evangelical Christians who occupied an often ambiguous role in colonial social and political relations, their Welshness, too, set them apart. In their writings, they constantly refer to Wales and the Welsh language, on occasion in un-ashamedly essentialist ways. The Welsh, they often claimed, were inherently better than the English at learning native languages. They also made explicit connections between their mother and adopted tongues. John P. Jones of the Madura mission in south India, for example, wrote that 'the Tamil language is . . . similar to the Welsh. Its literature is mostly poetic and its poetry unlike any other save the "Gynghanedd Gymraeg" (Welsh Cynghanedd), for it is elaborately alliterative'.[52] In the Surma Valley, John Pengwern Jones and Helen Rowlands drew parallels between the eisteddfod and the Bengali traditions of poetic recitation and song.

Nevertheless, these were subjective responses which reveal little about the ways in which Welsh missionaries were regarded by others. Here the picture is less clear. In 1908 John Pengwern Jones, prevented by the local authority from holding a revival meeting in Habiganj, was told that 'as the English would allow no political meeting *they* would allow no English religious meeting'.[53] Yet this identification of the Welsh with the English-dominated ruling power fluctuated. In October 1921 Pengwern Jones noted that, following enormous changes in the Indian political landscape, 'criticisms of the British' had increased, but that there was 'a greater tolerance of Christians and Christianity'.[54] From William Pryse to Oswald Williams, the Welsh in the Surma Valley had participated in a process of industrial modernization and the extension of colonial control, centred on the expansion of tea gardens, but they had done so, as we have seen, in

with the kind permission of the History Department, Presbyterian Church of Wales).

[52] *The Cambrian* (January 1888), 21.
[53] NLW, Calvinistic Methodist Archive 5, 27287/37, File II, 13 March 1908 (quoted with the kind permission of the History Department, Presbyterian Church of Wales).
[54] NLW, Calvinistic Methodist Archive 5, 27287/37 File II, 17 October 1921 (quoted

ambivalent ways. These missionaries had worked with and alongside the colonial authorities, but they had also challenged them, and could project a detachment both from secular power and from a British identity. But it was their religion, more than their ethnic or cultural identity, that appears to have made the Welsh missionaries distinctive in the eyes of both the British colonial authorities and Indians.

But if their perceived Welshness was of a secondary order of importance, in what sense, then, can their history be seen as a part of the history of Wales? It may be more productive to approach this question from the perspectives, developed by Julie Codell and others, of 'co-history', or the historical study of the dynamic interplay between two or more cultural and geographical spaces connected by global forces.[55] The history of missionaries, or for that matter of migrants, soldiers, traders, prisoners or even of journalists or travel-writers, may provide useful entry points into such conjoined histories. The Revd D. K. Badshah, in his funeral oration at the graveside of Helen Rowlands in Karimganj in 1955, said that she was 'a most beautiful flower from the garden of Wales'. Yet she had lived in India since 1916 and had, shortly before her death, started the process of becoming an Indian citizen.[56] While being an important Welsh-language writer and literary historian, she belonged, like many other Welsh missionaries, also to Indian life and history. E. Rogers elegantly expressed the hybridity of Helen Rowlands's identity in a commemorative verse written shortly after her death:

> Helen Cymru ac Assam,
> Chwaer i bawb ac annwyl fam;
> Câr yr India, câr y byd,
> Karimganj a'i piau i gyd.[57]

Helen of Wales and Assam / Sister to all and dear mother / She loves India, she loves the world / Karimganj owns her entirely.

This sentiment expressed more than a sense of personal loss, or the ritual marking of another corner of a foreign field that was to be forever Wales. Rather, it touched on the intimacy of a historical relationship which had developed across great distance, time, culture and language, and which now deserves further exploration and explanation. It is, of course, debatable whether Eden was ever to be found either in the 'wastelands' of Bengal and

with the kind permission of the History Department, Presbyterian Church of Wales).

[55] See Introduction of Codell (ed.), *Imperial Co-Histories*, *passim*.
[56] *Glad Tidings: Missionary Record of the Presbyterian Church of Wales* (April 1955).

Assam, or in the tea estates that replaced them. But if the tea garden was not after all 'the garden of the Lord', then neither, in any credible sense, was the distantly nostalgic 'garden of Wales' from which the mission had been transplanted. While the histories of these three vivid but imperfect gardens, tended so assiduously by the Welsh of British India, remain inextricably connected, their future relationship may best be conceptualized as the interleaving of the Red Dragon with the tricolour of an independent India and the red and green of a free Bangladesh.

Index

List of Subscribers

The following have associated themselves with the publication of this volume through subscription.

Jane Aaron, University of Glamorgan
Geoffrey G. Allen, The Netherlands
David Barnes, Machynlleth
Geoffrey Barrow, Edinburgh
David Bates, Institute of Historical Research
Ann Benwell, Porthaethwy
John Blair, The Queen's College, Oxford
Peter and Anne Borsay, University of Wales, Lampeter
D. George Boyce, University of Wales Swansea
Rosemary E. A. Broadhurst, Grimsby
David M. Browne, Rhydyfelin
James Callaghan, House of Lords
Proinsias Mac Cana, Dublin Institute for Advanced Studies
Syd and Joan Caplan, Cricieth
Muriel E. Chamberlain, Swansea
Murray Chapman, Welshpool
Fred Cowley, Swansea
Malcolm Crook, Keele University
Aneurin and Betty Davies, Swansea
Ceri Davies, University of Wales Swansea
Clifford S. L. Davies, Wadham College, Oxford
Damian Walford Davies and Francesca Rhydderch, Aberystwyth
Hywel M. Davies, Aberystwyth
Margaret and Jonathan Davies, Caerdydd
Peter V. Davies, University of Glasgow
R. T. Davies, Silver Spring, Maryland, USA
Rees Davies, University of Oxford

Richard G. Davies, University of Manchester
Ron Davies, Caerphilly
Rosina and Tom Davies, Blaendulais
Hugh and Kirstine Dunthorne, Port Eynon
David Wylmer Dykes, Dorchester
Richard Dynevor, Llandeilo
Huw Edwards, Caerfyrddin
Huw Edwards, BBC News, London
Hywel Teifi Edwards, Llanelli
John Elliott, Farnham Common
Bryn Ellis, Welshpool
Tecwyn Ellis, Mynytho
Gareth Elwyn and Kath Jones, Swansea
Arwyn Evans, Gwent
Clive Evans, Donegal
Dylan Foster Evans, Prifysgol Cymru, Caerdydd
Geraint Evans and Helen Fulton, University of Sydney
Mark Evans and Philip Corper, Cwmifor, Llandeilo
Meredydd Evans, Cwmystwyth
Henry Ferguson-Thomas, Llanwrda
Ann Ffrancon a Geraint H. Jenkins, Blaen-plwyf
Hywel Francis, Aberafan
Irene and Michael Freeden, Oxford
Peter Freeman, Swansea
Murney Gerlach, Rutherford B. Hayes Presidential Center, Fremont, Ohio
Rhidian Griffiths, Aberystwyth
W. P. Griffith, Prifysgol Cymru, Bangor
Geraint a Luned Gruffydd, Aberystwyth
Eleri a Robin Gwyndaf, Caerdydd
Tina Hamrin-Dahl, Stockholm University
Sally Harper, University of Wales, Bangor
David and Ceridwen Harris, London, Ontario
Isobel Harvey and Oliver Padel, St Neot, Cornwall
Janet Howarth, University of Oxford
David and Angela Howell, Swansea
John Vivian Hughes, Port Talbot
Rob Humphreys, University of Wales Swansea
Daniel Huws, Penrhyn-coch
David B. James, Llandre
Michael and Sandra James, Ponthenri, Carms.
Kevin Jefferys, Plymouth University
Dafydd Jenkins, Aberystwyth

David Jenkins, National Museums and Galleries of Wales
Gwyn Jenkins, Llyfrgell Genedlaethol Cymru
Barry Jones, Howarden
Bill Jones, Cardiff
Dafydd Morris Jones, Aber-arth
Daniel Gruffydd Jones, Chichester
David Lewis Jones, London
Gwenllian V. Jones, Newport, Gwent
Lenna a Harri Pritchard Jones, Caerdydd
Michael Jones, Nottingham
Peter Meurig Jones, Yr Wyddgrug
Stephanie and R. Brinley Jones, Dyfed
G. E. Kilfoil, Acrefair
Jeremy Knight, Caerphilly
John Easton Law, University of Wales Swansea
Cadoc Leighton, Bilkent University, Ankara
Ceri W. Lewis, Treorci
Richard Lewis, University of Teesside
Judge Humphrey Lloyd QC, London
Terry a Nesta Lloyd, Llanrhidian, Penrhyn Gŵyr
Derec Llwyd Morgan, Aberystwyth
Dorian Llywelyn SJ, Los Angeles
Peter Lowe, University of Manchester
Peredur Lynch, University of Wales, Bangor
David and Judith Marquand, Headington
Ioan Matthews, Caerfyrddin
J. G. Miller, Wrecsam
Louise Miskell, University of Wales Swansea
Katherine Morgan, Finsbury Park, London
David Philpin Morris, Radyr
Bruce K. Murray, University of the Witwatersrand, Johannesburg
John Newman, Sevenoaks
Helen J. Nicholson, Cardiff University
Robert Noel, College of Arms, London
Tony Oldham, Treorchy
Sabhal Mòr Ostaig, Isle of Skye
D. Huw Owen, Aberystwyth
J. G. Owen, Caerphilly
Elaine M. Paintin, Charlbury
David Parry-Jones and Beti George, Radyr, Cardiff
David A. Pretty, Ton-teg
Thomas John Prichard, Llangwnnadl

David and Lilian Pritchard, Swansea
Mark Redknap, National Museum and Gallery, Cardiff
Keith Robbins, Cribyn
Sara Elin Roberts, Prifysgol Cymru Abertawe
William Roberts, Aberystwyth
W. R. B. Robinson, Cheam, Surrey
Emel Rochat, Rhondda and Harrow
Joel T. Rosenthal, New York
Helen Rowlands, Pontypridd
John and Sheila Rowlands, Aberystwyth
Ron ac Ann Saer, Llandaf
John and Janet Shepherd, Anglia Polytechnic University, Cambridge
Michael Simpson, Swansea
David Stephenson, Llanidloes
Catrin Stevens, Casllwchwr
John Stewart, Department of History, Oxford Brookes University
Philip Tait, Little Venice
Elaine A. Thomas, Ferryside
Jenkin Thomas, London
Patrick Thomas, Carmarthen
Roger Thomas, University of Wales Swansea
Clive Towse, University of Wales Swansea
Chris Turner, University of Wales College of Medicine
Roger Turvey, Ammanford
Hywel W. Vaughan, Raglan
A. Geoffrey Veysey, Hawarden
John Vincent, UEA Norwich
Geoffrey Wainwright, March Pres
John and Frances Walsh, University of Oxford
Huw Walters, Llyfrgell Genedlaethol Cymru
Richard G. Waters, Abergele
Thomas Glyn Watkins, Prifysgol Cymru
Maurice Whitehead, University of Wales Swansea
Chris Williams, University of Glamorgan
Elisabeth Williams (née Jones Pierce), Rhiw, Llŷn
Gruffydd Aled Williams, Prifysgol Cymru, Aberystwyth
Huw Williams, Dowlais
J. Dewi Williams, Brentwood
J. G. Williams, Ynysgain, Cricieth
J. Gwynn Williams, Bangor
Lynn Williams, Prifysgol Cymru
Rowland Williams, University of Wales Swansea

Learning Resources
Centre